P9-CMM-909

The Refugee Challenge
in Post–Cold War America

The Refugee
Challenge
in Post–Cold
War America

MARÍA CRISTINA GARCÍA

OXFORD
UNIVERSITY PRESS

OXFORD
UNIVERSITY PRESS

Oxford University Press is a department of the University of Oxford. It furthers
the University's objective of excellence in research, scholarship, and education
by publishing worldwide. Oxford is a registered trade mark of Oxford University
Press in the UK and certain other countries.

Published in the United States of America by Oxford University Press
198 Madison Avenue, New York, NY 10016, United States of America.

© Oxford University Press 2017

All rights reserved. No part of this publication may be reproduced, stored in
a retrieval system, or transmitted, in any form or by any means, without the
prior permission in writing of Oxford University Press, or as expressly permitted
by law, by license, or under terms agreed with the appropriate reproduction
rights organization. Inquiries concerning reproduction outside the scope of the
above should be sent to the Rights Department, Oxford University Press, at the
address above.

You must not circulate this work in any other form
and you must impose this same condition on any acquirer.

CIP data is on file at the Library of Congress
ISBN 978–0–19–065530–3

3 5 7 9 8 6 4 2

Printed by Sheridan Books, Inc., United States of America

For Sherm

Contents

Acknowledgments

I HAVE ALWAYS found the acknowledgments the most daunting section to write in a book. So many people influence the research and writing of a book—sometimes in very subtle ways—that I fear I won't give all of them the proper recognition. I have tried to be conscious of all the assistance I have received, but I will undoubtedly forget to mention some friends and colleagues despite my best intentions. I offer my apologies for any oversight.

I have had the exceptional good fortune to be a faculty member at two excellent universities over the course of my career. My first appointment as a new PhD was at Texas A&M, where my Department of History colleagues modeled what good teachers and scholars looked like. I learned a great deal from them, and their collegiality and support saw me through a successful tenure process. In 1999, I accepted a new appointment at Cornell University, as a faculty member in both the Department of History and the Latino Studies Program. At both universities, I have had the opportunity to teach students who are smart, idealistic, and intellectually curious, and to work with colleagues who inspire me to do my best work. They have all influenced me in some way, and I am grateful.

I want to give special recognition to the history department colleagues at Cornell who generously commented on one or more of my chapters or helped me track down sources: Judith Byfield, Vicki Caron, Holly Case, Derek Chang, Chen Jian, Sherman Cochran, Raymond Craib, Paul Friedland, Durba Ghosh, Larry Glickman, Sandra Greene, Isabel Hull, Mostafa Minawi, Mary Beth Norton, Russell Rickford, Victor Seow, Rachel Weil, and John Weiss. I am also grateful to Ed Baptist, Ernesto Bassi, Julilly Kohler-Hausmann, Fred Logevall, Jon Parmenter, Aaron Sachs, Penny von Eschen, Margaret Washington, and the late Michael Kammen for their many insightful comments and suggestions; and to Barry Strauss, our department chair, for his steadfast support over the years.

Cornell colleagues outside the history department also read chapters or provided feedback that proved extremely helpful to my writing. I offer my thanks to Valerie Bunce, James Cutting, Tim DeVoogd, David Feldshuh, Carol Kammen, Peter Katsenstein, Claudia Lazzaro, Peter McClelland, Vladimir Micic, and Elizabeth Adkins-Regan. During 2010–2013, I was part of the "Immigration" theme project organized by Michael Jones-Correa at Cornell's Institute for Social Sciences. My association with the ISS offered me a reduced teaching load during the second year of the project that gave me time to think about the book, but more importantly, it gave me access to another community of scholars who offered feedback from various disciplinary perspectives. I am grateful for the insights of my "fellow fellows": Amada Armenta, Richard Bensel, Derek Chang, Maria Lorena Cook, Els De Graauw, Kate Griffiths, Doug Gurak, Michael Jones-Correa, Mary Katzenstein, Gerald Kernerman, Vilma Santiago-Irizarry, Sharon Sassler, Leah Vosko, and Steven Yale-Loehr. I also thank the ISS administrative manager, Anneliese Truame, for all the ways she helped us build community at the ISS. My colleagues in the Latino Studies Program are always inspiring and supportive, and I count myself fortunate to know them: Steven Alvarado, Mary Pat Brady, Carol Boyce Davies, Debra Castillo, Maria Lorena Cook, Ray Craib, Ella Díaz, Sergio García-Ríos, Shannon Gleeson, Karen Jaime, Michael Jones-Correa, Oneka LaBennett, Alejandro Madrid, Veronica Martínez-Matsuda, Shawn McDaniel, Ron Mize, Pilar Parra, Vilma Santiago-Irizarry, Hector Vélez, and Sofía Villenas.

The Woodrow Wilson International Center for Scholars in Washington, DC, awarded me a fellowship that allowed me to spend nine wonderful months in residence during the 2013–2014 academic year. My time at the Wilson Center was one of the most productive—and enjoyable—of my scholarly career. I offer special thanks to Cynthia Arnson, Eric Olson, Robert Litwak, and Blair Rubel. The members of the monthly "Law Group" at the Wilson Center, Alison Brysk, Donny Meertens, Douglas Reed, and, most especially, Philippa Strum, provided criticism that proved essential to the chapter on asylum. My graduate research assistant at the Wilson Center, María Fernanda Mata, was the best research assistant I have worked with over the course of my career. Librarians Janet Spikes and Michelle Kamalich tracked down books and other sources for me; and staff members Lindsay Collins, Kimberly Conner, and Arlyn Charles planned social activities that brought the Wilson fellows out of their offices and in contact with each other. I enjoyed and learned so much from my cohort of fellows, especially Sayuri Shimizu, Amal Fadlalla, Jessica Robbins-Ruszkowski,

Donnie Meertens, Alison Brysk, Anne-Marie Brady, and Mae Ngai, who planned dinner parties, long walks around the National Mall, "happy hours" at neighborhood restaurants, and many other opportunities for conversation. Living in Washington, DC, granted me access to exciting lectures and conferences that helped me rethink parts of my project. I am especially grateful to Richard Bush, Elizabeth Ferris, Ted Piccone, and Harold Trikunas at the Brookings Institute for inviting me to participate in events there.

The refugee aid workers I interviewed for this project helped me understand what the refugee resettlement program looks like on the ground level. Judith Bernstein-Baker, the Executive Director of HIAS-Philadelphia, and Sue Chaffee of the Immigrant Services Project at Catholic Charities of Tompkins-Tioga County (NY), in particular, spent hours with me explaining how refugees are selected for specific communities, and the challenges they face upon arrival in the United States.

I was fortunate to be able to access many digitized sources from the comfort of my office (a research technique that was not available to me when I began my scholarly career), but many trips and telephone calls to archives and special collections were still necessary. Many talented librarians and archivists helped me access sources at the John T. Olin Library at Cornell University; the National Archives at College Park, Maryland; the George H. W. Bush Presidential Library, College Station, Texas; the William J. Clinton Presidential Library in Little Rock, Arkansas; the National Security Archive, Washington, DC; and the Library of Congress. While digitization makes research easier and more affordable, it is still immensely rewarding to sift through boxes of letters and memoranda. I am also indebted to the talented researchers of the Congressional Research Service, the Migration Policy Institute, the US Committee for Refugees and Immigrants, the American Immigration Council, Pew Research Center, Human Rights First, and all who preside over important clearinghouses of information on refugees and asylum seekers.

Some of the material in this book was presented at the Massachusetts Historical Society, the University of Pennsylvania Social Science and Policy Forum, the University of Massachusetts–Amherst, the University of Texas at Austin, the University of Southern California, Columbia University, and Canisius College; and at the conferences sponsored by the Society for Historians of American Foreign Relations, the Organization of American Historians, and the Social Science History Association. Questions and comments from copanelists and audiences challenged me to be clearer about my arguments and evidence.

I thank the staff of the Department of History and the Latino Studies Program at Cornell University—Kay Stickane, Marti Dense, Katie Kristof, Barb Donnell, Judy Yonkin, and Maria Montesano—who provide the administrative support that help faculty be better teachers and researchers. We couldn't do what we do without your help. My undergraduate research assistants—Andrew Calvario, Barbara Carrera, Blake Michael, and Andrew White—helped me track down sources, double-checked citations, and drew charts. I hope the assignments gave them a better sense of the historian's craft. Through research stipends, Cornell University offered me the financial resources to conduct my research; and through a "study leave" and a sabbatical, the university offered me time to write. For all this support, I am grateful.

I thank the staff of Oxford University Press and the anonymous readers who made this a better book. Susan Ferber solicited the manuscript, selected the outside readers, and suggested helpful edits and revisions. Editor Alexandra Dauler supervised the production process to ensure that the book was published in a timely fashion. Theo Calderara, the editor-in-chief of the History and Religion lists, kindly answered all my questions. Production editor Paul Tompsett and copyeditor Richard Isomaki reviewed and edited the content to prepare the manuscript for publication. Many others, whose names are unknown to me, assisted with the typesetting, design and marketing of the book.

I have been writing about refugees for many years now, and I struggle not to be discouraged (or numbed) by the ever-growing numbers. I have great admiration for the relief workers who relate to refugees as human beings, not impersonal statistics. Each year they go out, risk their lives and their comfort, and work under impossible conditions, to make life a little easier for the world's displaced populations. They demonstrate that idealism and generosity survive. We should all be grateful for their work.

I thank my family and friends for their love and support. I especially thank my mother, Chary García, who calls me every morning to offer encouragement and perspective; and my husband and partner, Sherm Cochran, who never fails to make me laugh and to look at life more positively.

The Refugee Challenge
in Post–Cold War America

Introduction

REFUGEES HAVE ALWAYS been central to the American national mythology—to the stories Americans tell about themselves as a people, a settler nation, and a haven for the oppressed. In the post–Cold War era, sympathy toward refugees (and immigrants more broadly) has dissipated. Those who seek entry are viewed as economic threats—as people coming to take American jobs or live off welfare—rather than as persecuted people in need of protection. The terrorist attacks of 1993 and 2001 only exacerbated fears that newcomers were taking advantage of American generosity. By the late 1990s, public opinion polls showed that Americans were divided on the issue of accepting more refugees.[1] This was a surprising revelation in a country that had taken pride in, celebrated, and even commercialized its immigrant and refugee heritage. Three decades later, concerns about immigrants and refugees have persisted. Critics of the refugee and asylum system view it as flawed and subject to dangerous manipulations. Human rights activists, in turn, complain that the emphasis on protecting national security has led to the blocking of people in desperate need of refuge.

This book examines refugee and asylum policy in the United States since the end of the Cold War. For over forty years, from the end of World War II to the fall of the Berlin Wall, the Cold War had provided the ideological lens through which the United States had defined who a refugee was. Cold War concerns about the political, economic, and military threat of communism had shaped the contours of immigration policy, particularly refugee and asylum policy. In the post–Cold War era, the war on terrorism has become the new ideological lens through which the US government interprets who is worthy of admission as a refugee, but the emphasis on national security is not the sole determinant of policy. A wide range of geopolitical and domestic interests, and an equally wide range of actors, influence how the United States responds to humanitarian crises abroad, and whom the nation prioritizes for admission as refugees and asylees. This book examines these actors and interests, and the challenges of reconciling international humanitarian obligations with domestic concerns for national security. The case studies in each chapter examine the challenges of the post–Cold War era, and the actions taken by governmental and nongovernmental actors in response to these challenges.

Since 1989, US policymakers have reevaluated refugee and asylum policy against the backdrop of two dominant concerns on the home front: the contractions of the US economy and the possibility of more terrorism on American soil. Americans have questioned the allocation of tax dollars to refugee resettlement projects when citizens were struggling at home. In the aftermath of the terrorist attacks on US cities, Americans also have become increasingly concerned that aspiring terrorists would use the refugee and asylum tracks to establish a foothold in the United States, so they have called for a scaling back of admissions as a protective measure. National security has been framed in political, economic, and cultural terms. Consequently, in the crafting of refugee and asylum policy, policymakers have been responsive to American fears about what a large influx of refugees mean to livelihoods, public safety, cultural identity, and political institutions in the United States.

American legislators have been sensitive to their constituents' fears, but they have also been responsive to advocacy. Humanitarian aid workers, human rights activists, journalists, clergy, scholars, lawyers, and judges have influenced which populations are allowed to resettle in the United States. Through their witness and advocacy, representatives of the humanitarian community (the aid workers who have assisted refugees) and the human rights community (the lawyers, writers, and activists who have framed the discourse on rights)[2] have appealed to international human rights norms, and reminded legislators of American obligations to the world beyond its borders. Consequently, they have helped secure admission for people who have fallen outside the traditional US-identified categories of persecution. Political dissidents, prodemocracy advocates, and victims of torture have continued to receive protection, as was the case during the Cold War; but so, too, have victims of trafficking and criminal violence, as well as those victimized by forced conscription, coercive population control measures, and restrictive gender and sexuality-based rules. Many of those who have been admitted as refugees (or who have received asylum) in the post–Cold War era would never have been considered just a few decades earlier, but their advocates have mobilized political support for them.[3]

In the post–Cold War era, several patterns or developments have become apparent in US refugee policy. First, there is a growing expectation on the part of American policymakers that the international community will address humanitarian crises collectively, as part of burden sharing. Second, the State Department has relied increasingly on the United Nations High Commissioner for Refugees (UNHCR) and other nongovernmental organizations (in addition to its embassy and consular officials) to help identify those who might be potentially eligible for the limited refugee visas. Third, on several occasions, the State Department has resorted to the "in country" processing of refugee visas in order to discourage refugee migrations and minimize the financial burden on countries bordering areas of crisis. This is a surprising development given that international definitions of "refugee" status require people to have crossed an international border. Fourth, when refugee quotas have proved insufficient, Congress, the State Department, and Homeland Security have used a wide range of immigration statuses to accommodate people on humanitarian grounds. Consequently, the data on refugee admissions can obscure populations that enter through other channels, such as parole, asylum, special immigrant visas, the "T" visas (for victims of trafficking), Special Immigrant Juvenile Status, and temporary protected status. Fifth, the refugees and asylum seekers admitted to the United States in the post–Cold War era have originated from a wider range of countries than during the Cold War.

What the case studies in this book ultimately suggest is that the definition of "refugee" in US statute is no longer adequate. In response to the challenges of today, policymakers need to craft policies that take historical precedents into account while addressing the realities of displacement in today's world. The ethical stakes are simply too great.

The Origins of US Refugee and Asylum Policy

The first attempts to craft a distinct and coherent refugee policy occurred in the wake of World War II.[4] Between 1948 and 1956 roughly six hundred thousand refugees, mostly from Southern and Eastern Europe, were admitted to the United States through the Displaced Persons Act and the Refugee Relief Act. This domestic legislation assisted Europe in its postwar recovery by accommodating a share of those left homeless and, in some cases, stateless by the war. Many of these refugees would otherwise not have been granted admission to the United States through established channels because the Immigration Act of 1924 (Johnson-Reed Act) had placed strict national origins quotas on immigration.[5]

Over the next two decades US policies signaled a growing recognition that, as members of an international community, Americans had a responsibility to assist refugees and displaced persons around the world. Drawing on the "parole" authority granted by the 1952 Immigration and Nationality Act (McCarran-Walter Act), the White House authorized the admission of tens of thousands of refugees displaced by the new postwar communist governments in Eastern Europe.[6] In 1962, Congress passed the Migration and Refugee Assistance Act, authorizing the president to provide assistance to refugees whenever it was "in the interest of the United States."[7] Three years later, when Congress passed the 1965 Immigration and Nationality Act (Hart-Celler Act, or INA) to abolish the racist national origins quotas in immigration law, it included in the regional/global allocations a small numerical allotment for refugees. The INA defined refugees as those persecuted on account of race, religion, or political opinion; those uprooted by natural calamity; those fleeing communist or communist-dominated countries; and those fleeing the Middle East.[8] In 1967, when the United States signed the United Nations Protocol Relating to the Status of Refugees (which broadened the definition of refugees in the 1951 United Nations Convention on the Status of Refugees),[9] it officially and symbolically recognized the nation's obligation to the world's persecuted and displaced. As a signatory to the protocol, the United States also recognized that refugees were entitled to certain rights and protections including that of *nonrefoulement* (no forced return to dangerous or repressive conditions); the right not to be expelled; the right to education; the right to have access to the courts; the right to work; and the right to freedom of movement.[10]

US policymakers did not make these decisions based solely on a sense of obligation. They also were greatly influenced by Cold War geopolitics. Escape from a communist country was often sufficient to gain admission to the United States, and the terms "defector," "escapee," "refugee," and "parolee" were used interchangeably by policymakers as well as journalists. Over time, members of Congress became concerned by the overuse of the parole authority in symbolic service of Cold War foreign policy. Parole, they argued, was providing a "back door" to the United States, allowing hundreds of thousands to enter, without congressional input, on the assumption that those fleeing communist countries were more worthy of admission than other immigrants. These concerns eventually led to the passage of the 1980 US Refugee Act, which established a permanent track for refugee admissions that required congressional consultation. Drawing on the United Nation's definition, the 1980 Refugee Act defined a refugee as

> any person who is outside any country of such person's nationality or, in the case of a person having no nationality, is outside any country in which such person last habitually resided, and who is unable or unwilling to return to, or is unable and unwilling to avail himself or herself of the protection of that country because of persecution or a well-founded fear of persecution on account of race, religion, nationality, membership in a particular social group or political opinion.[11]

The law also established guidelines for granting asylum to those already physically present in the United States or at a port of entry.

Since 1980, the White House, in consultation with Congress, has set annual limits on the number of refugees to be admitted from different regions of the world. The president has submitted to the House of Representatives a proposal (known as the consultation document) with the administration's suggested worldwide refugee ceiling and the various regional suballocations. Following congressional discussion, negotiation, and approval, the president then has issued the "presidential determination" establishing the official refugee numbers for the upcoming fiscal year.[12] Both geopolitical and domestic interests have played a role in determining the numerical quota and how it will be allocated. The favoring of particular regions of the world in the overall ceiling has reflected the strategic interests of the State Department, but it also has reflected the growing influence of domestic actors who have appealed for better numerical representation of specific populations they consider at risk.

The 1980 Refugee Act also authorized temporary assistance to refugees to facilitate their cultural integration and economic self-sufficiency in the United States.[13] The Office of Refugee Resettlement has contracted with national, state, and local agencies to assist refugees in finding housing, furnishings, food, and clothing, as well as to provide language instruction and employment training and placement.[14] After one year in refugee status, refugees have become eligible to adjust their status to lawful permanent resident status; and after five years of residence in the United States, they have been able to apply for citizenship, like other immigrant groups.[15]

Even after the Refugee Act adopted the United Nation's ideologically neutral definition of refugee, most refugees continued to come from communist countries. Fleeing a communist country has not guaranteed anyone admission to the United States, but it has maximized an applicant's chances for admission because decision-makers have operated on the premise that communist states are politically and socially repressive. And when refugee quotas have proved insufficient to accommodate the many people who have sought to leave totalitarian states, the attorney general (and since 2002, the Department of Homeland Security) has continued to parole people into the country.

During the Cold War, the majority of refugees came from just three countries: the Soviet Union, Vietnam, and Cuba. Smaller numbers came from Hungary, Poland, Czechoslovakia, East Germany, and other countries of the Eastern bloc, as well as the People's Republic of China, Cambodia, and Laos. Policymakers argued that admitting refugees from these communist countries was important to foreign policy interests because they demonstrated to the rest of the world—especially the nonaligned nations in the developing world—the desirability and triumph of democracy and capitalism over communist totalitarianism. As refugees from communist countries pointed out, they had gone to great lengths to leave their homelands and had experienced great personal and professional losses in making lives for themselves in the West. Thus, for many Americans, refugees from the communist bloc became powerful ideological symbols of an innate human need to live in free societies. The United States also benefitted from these refugee admissions since a good number of those brought in were the highly skilled and educated of their societies, and they sometimes provided important intelligence that informed US military policies overseas.[16]

The end of the Cold War, then, forced US policymakers to reevaluate refugee admissions. Not much changed in the immediate aftermath of the dismantling of the Soviet Union and other communist states.[17] Immigration from the former—and remaining—communist countries continued to dominate refugee, parole, and asylum admissions; but over the course of the 1990s, other geopolitical concerns began to shape refugee policy. Once the Cold War and anticommunism ceased to be the preferred lens through which administrators interpreted refugee status, policymakers considered a wider range of populations as potentially eligible for refuge: victims of war, civil unrest, genocide, trafficking, natural disasters, gender-based discrimination, and religious persecution, and the poverty these conditions created or exacerbated. These conditions were just as coercive as political persecution but had not always secured victims international recognition as refugees, much less resettlement in a country like the United States.[18] People had fled such conditions throughout the twentieth century, of course, but Cold War geopolitics had decisively shaped how the coveted refugee visas were distributed, as well as who was granted parole or asylum.

Post–Cold War Challenges

According to the US State Department, by 1993, more people lived in democracies than at any previous time in history, but the threat of political and economic instability remained. [19] Millions of people were displaced from their homes as nations disappeared, reconstituted themselves, and became politically and economically realigned. The instability in the former Soviet republics, especially Armenia, Azerbaijan, Tajikistan, and Chechnya, created large-scale humanitarian crises. In China, hundreds of thousands of protesters at Tiananmen Square tried to bring about Soviet-style reforms only to see the prodemocracy movement crushed and thousands of Chinese take refuge in the West. The political and economic destabilization of the Yugoslav republics resulted in war and genocide that forced more than two million people to flee by 1992.[20] In the Persian Gulf region, over a million Iraqi and Kurdish civilians crossed borders in the early 1990s.[21] In central Africa, the genocide in Rwanda killed over eight hundred thousand and led to the creation of sprawling refugee camps in Zaire and Tanzania.[22] War, civil unrest, and criminality, as well as environmental catastrophes, poverty, and disease, resulted in the voluntary and involuntary migration of countless peoples around the globe. These migrations—and the political, economic, and humanitarian challenges they presented—forced the United States to repeatedly reevaluate its role in international peacekeeping, its foreign aid programs, and its refugee admissions.

As the twentieth century came to a close, American policymakers could not ignore the complexity and scale of humanitarian emergencies worldwide. Concerns for the long-term impact of refugees and displaced persons on countries and regions elevated refugee policy to a more central place in foreign policy debates than at any time during the Cold War.[23] By the end of the 1990s, there were an estimated fourteen million refugees worldwide, most of them women and children, and the majority were concentrated in the Near East, Asia, and Africa. Tens of millions more were internally displaced within their own countries. Their numbers increased exponentially with each passing decade. By June 20, 2016, World Refugee Day, the number of refugees and displaced persons worldwide had reached 59.5 million.[24]

Refugees posed challenges for the international community because they destabilized countries politically and economically, especially when they fled to the developing nations that bordered areas of crisis. Refugees competed with host populations for land, jobs, housing, and other scarce resources; they exacerbated ethnic, racial, and sectarian tensions; and, as a result, they became scapegoats for local and national problems. They sometimes triggered political conflict that caused more displacement or generated conflict upon repatriation to their home countries.[25] In the post–Cold War era, the United States has tried to mitigate the destabilizing effects of refugee and other humanitarian crises through financial assistance, supporting human rights monitoring and international tribunals that prosecuted war criminals, and supervising free and fair elections.[26] At times, refugee relief efforts, with names such as Operation Open Arms and Operation Sustain Hope, have resembled military operations, with military personnel assisting humanitarian aid workers in efforts to reach the most desperate populations.[27]

The reevaluation of refugee policy has occurred within a broader international conversation on the role and mission of the United Nations High Commissioner for Refugees and other humanitarian organizations. The number of aid organizations and workers has increased exponentially since the end of the Cold War, and international humanitarianism has become increasingly hierarchical and institutionalized.[28] The United States has relied on the UNHCR, the International Organization for Migration, and a handful of other nongovernmental organizations to help identify populations in need of assistance or emergency resettlement. However, the final determination about resettlement in the United States has always been made by domestic actors, namely, the Department of State and, since 2003, the Department of Homeland Security and its Customs and Immigration Services. The select few who are chosen for resettlement in the United States are a tiny fraction of those in need of international protection.[29]

The post–Cold War period has presented yet another challenge to government officials: how to deal with the growing number of people who petition for asylum on US territory, usually at a port of entry such as an airport, a border checkpoint, or on a navy or Coast Guard vessel. Asylum applications were comparatively fewer during the Cold War, and the cases that generated the most media attention were the defections of high-profile individuals—Russian ballet dancers, Cuban baseball players and jazz musicians, Eastern European athletes and coaches, Chinese physicists—whose celebrity or stature made their defections to the West newsworthy. Asylum seekers were generally released on their own recognizance while they waited for an administrative determination or a hearing in an immigration court. By the late 1980s, petitions for asylum had increased primarily because of the political turmoil in Haiti and the civil wars in Central America. Over four hundred thousand people filed for asylum in the United States between 1980 and 1990, and asylum applications increased with each subsequent decade. In response to the growing number of asylum seekers, Congress passed new legislation in 1996 to streamline the adjudication process, but also to discourage the filing of "frivolous" asylum claims that backlogged the system. The government adopted as policies of deterrence such practices as "expedited removal," the denial of work authorization, and indefinite detention. After the terrorist attacks of 1993 and 2001, when Americans demanded that policymakers do more to block the entry routes of terrorists, policymakers became more proactive about curtailing the perceived abuses of the asylum (and immigration) system. These measures had the unintended consequence of deterring bona fide asylum seekers as well.

Navigating the Post–Cold War Bureaucracy

The term "refugee" has always been used freely by journalists, clergy, and advocates to refer to displaced peoples of humanitarian concern, but the term has a more precise definition in American law. In the post–Cold War era, this legal meaning has limited those eligible for resettlement in the United States. Therefore, while the populations potentially eligible for resettlement have expanded, US statutes have imposed certain requirements on those seeking to acquire refugee or asylee status:

- Refugees must have traveled *outside* of their country of origin or of last residence.

- They must prove that they have been persecuted because of race, religion, nationality, membership in a particular social group, or political opinion.
- They must demonstrate that they have a reasonable fear of future persecution.
- They must show that they have failed to receive protection from their state.
- They must confirm that they have not inflicted harm on others (only civilians can be refugees).

This understanding of the refugee condition (drawing on the United Nation's definition) is narrower than other definitions of refugees crafted by governmental and nongovernmental institutions such as the Organization of African Unity, the Organization of American States, and the International Organization for Migration, which have recognized that refugees can result from conditions such as war, civil unrest, and natural disaster (and not just political persecution). Indeed, even the UNHCR has adopted a broader view, recognizing that conducting individual interviews to evaluate refugee status is often not feasible during mass migrations. In such cases, UNHCR officials have argued, conditions warrant that nations recognize migrants as prima facie refugees and grant them assistance.[30] Because of the sheer scale of humanitarian crises in the post–Cold War era, the UNHCR and other international agencies have granted material assistance to many types of displaced populations that have fallen within and outside of their original mandate; but when these organizations have recommended individuals and families for resettlement in the United States, they have taken into account domestic laws and priorities.

The US State Department has categorized refugees according to its "processing priorities." Priority 1 cases are those refugees with "compelling protection needs" who are referred by the UNHCR, a US embassy, or a designated nongovernmental organization. Priority 2 cases have been those of special humanitarian concern to the United States such as persecuted religious minorities, or members of persecuted ethnicities, clans, or nationalities whom the White House has singled out for special protection. Priority 3 cases have been the spouses, parents, and unmarried children (under the age of twenty-one) of persons admitted lawfully to the United States as refugees, asylees, or green card holders.[31] Proving a "compelling protection need" has been the most difficult hurdle for refugees.

Since the terrorist attacks of 2001, refugees must also prove that they do not pose a threat to national security.

A *Historical Approach*

Social scientists and policymakers have produced tens of thousands of articles and book chapters on refugee and asylum policy over the past decade alone. Historical studies are comparatively fewer and have focused largely on analyses of the Cold War period.[32] Historians are sometimes reluctant to write about the recent past, in large part because the sources necessary for a thorough investigation are hard to get at; archival collections have not yet been developed and, in the case of political and diplomatic history, documents are classified. Despite these research obstacles, historians can find ways to scrutinize the recent past and offer perspectives on developments and trends; on context, causes, and particularities; and on the actors who respond to the contingencies of history. In that spirit, this book documents and evaluates the agents of change in the period since 1989, bringing the historical examination of refugee policy more fully into the present. I draw on the sources that are available: presidential, congressional, and administrative records; oral interviews, letters, and email communications with policymakers and refugee advocates; the records of nongovernmental organizations; and various documentary and news media sources.

Although I take a historical approach, the recent international relations scholarship on security and securitization has influenced my understanding of refugee policy.[33] Cold War security studies have focused largely on the military defense of territory and the deterrence of threat. Since the end of the Cold War, the scholarship has expanded its scope to include new forms of insecurity: economic, societal, political, and environmental pressures that contribute to a state of insecurity at the global, national, and individual level.[34] In the traditional security studies that dominated the Cold War, immigrants and refugees were invisible; but in post–Cold War studies, migration is understood as both a product and a cause of insecurity.[35] Cross-border migration was said to pose a threat to the security of the state, and migration had to be carefully managed by pragmatic state policies.[36] Some scholars of security focused on the state's "technologies" of regulating migration such as visas, asylum procedures, surveillance, and incarceration, as well as the physical sites of regulation such as refugee camps and ports of entry such as airports and embassies.[37]

Post–Cold War security studies have also raised important questions about the human security of those displaced from their homes.[38] Indeed, human rights law, refugee law, and humanitarian law all have developed out of concern for the security of the individual.[39] Some scholars have grappled with the discursive politics of security: how and why particular issues are framed as dangerous or threatening.[40] Because refugees and other migrants are "politicized as threatening subjects" or "depoliticized as vulnerable objects," the language employed is critical to understanding the emergence, evolution, and dissolution of particular policies and practices.[41] Scholars of security have addressed the impact of securitization technologies and discursive language on migrants, especially refugees and asylum seekers, who are made vulnerable by such practices. As scholar Ariane Chebel d'Appolonia has written, the security measures adopted by nation-states to minimize the perceived threat of migrants have generated a long list of fears: "of racial profiling, of being a victim of violence, of apprehension and deportation, and ultimately of being perceived as a threat."[42]

These studies have been helpful to my understanding of post–Cold War debates about national security because they have shown how particular discourses have led to the creation of agencies and technologies to regulate refugee flows. Another body of scholarship, on advocacy and legal networks, has informed my understanding of governmental actors. The legislators who crafted policy were responsive to the information and data that they were given by advocacy groups on behalf of refugees and other displaced persons.[43] Advocates called attention to issues, framed them in ways that were comprehensible, urged action, and held political actors accountable.[44] They often transformed the discussion on refugees and helped place them on foreign policy agendas.[45] Lawyers were also instrumental to shaping policy.[46] Activists raised public consciousness about the rights of refugees and other displaced persons, but lawyers "define[d] the realm of the possible, offering advice about the relative efficacy of legal versus political strategies."[47] Whether representing an asylum seeker pro bono, filing a class-action lawsuit on behalf of immigrant detainees, providing testimony before Congress, or drafting reform legislation, lawyers gave refugees agency and helped craft, interpret, and take action in relation to policies. Ultimately, they made refugees and asylum seekers visible, defended their rights, and reminded those who held power of our shared humanity.

Each chapter of this book examines how governmental and nongovernmental actors responded to the humanitarian challenges of the post–Cold war era. In order to illustrate the historical shifts in refugee policy, some of my case studies cover a broader chronology because their roots lay in the Cold War period. This long-term context is necessary to understand the issues at stake and the actors that help set events into motion.

Chapter 1 discusses American responses to refugee flows during the transitional period between the late 1980s and early 1990s. Fleeing a communist state had previously maximized one's chances of admission to the United States, but as early as 1980, policymakers had questioned the logic of assuming that those fleeing communism had more legitimate needs for protection than others. As the Soviet Union and Eastern bloc countries instituted economic and prodemocratic reforms, policymakers also expressed concerns that the United States might be inadvertently poaching the most educated citizenry at the very moment their creative energy was needed in their native countries. In this chapter, the tensions between Congress and the White House, the central actors in refugee policy, become particularly apparent, as each branch of government vied to set the tone and parameters of policy. As government officials struggled to define a coherent refugee policy for the post–Cold War era, a wide range of domestic actors also tried to influence policy, advocating and lobbying on behalf of particular populations whose rights they felt had been ignored. The case studies in this chapter—the Soviet refuseniks, the Chinese university students, the Haitian and Cuban boat people—illustrate the changing political landscape both abroad and at home, as well as the importance of advocacy in eliciting responses from the executive and legislative branches of government.

Chapter 2 considers the importance of leadership and political will in the crafting of refugee policy by examining the uneven responses by government officials to populations displaced by genocide. Despite passage of the Genocide Convention in 1948, the international community failed to prevent the systematic slaughter of millions of people in the post–Cold War era. The end of the Cold War freed the United States to intervene in the affairs of states for reasons other than the containment of communism, but concerns for the safety of American soldiers and fears of another entanglement like Vietnam resulted in policies of intervention that were surprisingly noncommittal even on the issue of genocide. In response to genocide in Iraq, Rwanda, Bosnia, and Kosovo—the case studies in this

chapter—millions crossed international borders in search of safety, destabilizing the countries that reluctantly hosted them. The United States
offered humanitarian assistance but few opportunities for resettlement.
The case studies show how perceptions of the refugees' politics, ethnicity, race, and overall "worthiness" influenced decisions about intervention,
humanitarian aid, and the allocation of refugee visas. Government officials
and refugee advocates had to convince a reluctant American population
that assistance to these populations was in the national interest; when they
failed to do so, the consequences for refugees were significant.

In chapter 3, the immigration bureaucracy is the principal actor. In
response to the terrorist attacks of 1993 and 2001 in the United States,
government officials restructured the immigration bureaucracy to make it
more difficult for anyone to enter—immigrant, tourist, student, or refugee.
Refugees and immigrants were considered potential threats to national
security, regardless of their political ideologies or the areas of the world
they came from, though refugees and immigrants from the Islamic world
were subject to particular scrutiny and exclusion. The chapter outlines the
restructuring of the immigration, refugee, and asylum bureaucracies in
response to the threat of terrorism and evaluates the consequences of that
restructuring for refugees from Afghanistan, Iraq, and Syria.

The fourth chapter examines asylum, the feature of the US immigration system that has been most thoroughly revised and yet remains
most in need of reform. The asylum bureaucracy, with its multiple official
administrative levels, is the central actor, evaluating the merits of each
asylum seeker on a case-by-case basis. Identical cases heard in different
courts have therefore resulted in vastly different outcomes. This chapter
discusses some of the asylum cases heard by courts in the post–Cold
War era to show the complex legal world asylum seekers navigate, often
without the benefit of counsel or even translators. Many asylum seekers
fall outside the defined categories of persecution, and their struggles to
secure asylum raise important ethical and moral questions about who is
deserving of protection.

Refugees will remain a challenge for the United States in the decades to
come, continually testing the country's founding principles and it historical role as a haven for the oppressed. The concluding chapter offers some
reflections on the ideological and structural challenges that lie ahead, as
policymakers continue to reevaluate our humanitarian obligations abroad
and our domestic commitments at home.

I

Now That the Cold War Is Over, Who Is a Refugee?

THE COLD WAR had provided the ideological lens through which Americans defined refugee policy. The majority of all Cold War refugees came from communist countries, especially the Soviet Union, Vietnam, and Cuba. For many Americans, a "refugee" and a defector from a communist state were one and the same. The 1980 Refugee Act had tried to free refugee policy from its symbolic service to US foreign policy by adopting the broader UN definition of refugee and removing all reference to communist states. The law had also tried to make refugee policy more accountable to Congress, requiring the White House to consult legislators in establishing annual numerical limits and regional allotments. In practice, however, Cold War foreign policy interests continued to influence whom the United States paroled into the United States for humanitarian reasons or admitted as refugees.

During the transitional years of 1989–1992, immigration from the former—and remaining—communist countries continued to dominate refugee and asylum admissions. However, by the late 1980s, American policymakers had already begun to question the premise that those fleeing communist countries were more worthy of admission than other immigrants. As the Soviet Union and Eastern bloc countries instituted economic and prodemocratic reforms, policymakers also expressed concerns that the United States might be inadvertently poaching the most educated citizenry at the very moment their creative energy was most needed in their native countries. A wide range of domestic actors—congressional leaders, journalists, scholars, artists, clergy, lawyers, and refugee advocates—tried to influence refugee admissions, advocating and lobbying on behalf of particular populations whose rights they felt were being ignored. Those populations that had influential actors to represent their interests before Congress were more successful in prying open the door to the United States.

Refuseniks and the Soviet Union

In the Soviet Union, one's ethnicity –what the state called "nationality"— largely determined one's opportunities in life. This was certainly true for the estimated 2.5 million Jews in Russia, Ukraine, and the other Soviet republics, who were discriminated against in housing, access to higher education, employment, and professional opportunities. Agents of the state monitored all meetings and gatherings—private and public, secular and religious. After Israel's victory in the 1967 Six-Day War, the government cracked down on any expression of Zionism and Jewish national culture. Hebrew language study and publications were banned, as were Jewish schools and groups for religious study and prayer. Only a handful of synagogues were permitted to stay open, but social harassment discouraged the faithful from attending religious services. Even the baking of matzo was prohibited.

The state also denied Jews the right to create a life for themselves outside of the Soviet Union. During the 1950s and 1960s, only a few hundred Jews were allowed to leave the Soviet Union each year.[1] After the 1967 war, applying for permission to emigrate became particularly dangerous: applicants lost their jobs, and those denied permission to leave often faced charges of "parasitism," "Zionism," and other "anti-Soviet" offenses.[2]

By the early 1960s, the word *refusenik* had entered the American vernacular to refer to Soviet Jews refused the right to emigrate.[3] Over the next three decades, American Jews launched a successful protest movement on behalf of Soviet Jewry; a movement motivated, in part, by a sense of guilt over the failure to rescue European Jews a generation earlier.[4] "Shame created a desperate optimism," wrote journalist Yossi Klein Halevi. "We were not going to lose more millions of Jews."[5] The first public protests against Soviet policies occurred in the early 1960s. In 1964 an estimated one thousand American Jewish students associated with the New York–based Student Struggle for Soviet Jewry (SSSJ)[6] organized a May Day protest outside the offices of the Soviet mission to the United Nations.[7] The following month the SSSJ sponsored an interfaith fast that attracted important civil rights leaders, including Dr. Martin Luther King Jr. Three years later, when

Elie Wiesel published *The Jews of Silence*, a shocking report on the life of Jews in Moscow and other cities behind the Iron Curtain, SSSJ members wore specially made buttons posing the question "Are we the Jews of Silence?" hoping to channel American guilt into direct action.[8]

The SSSJ movement was insistent but nonconfrontational, with members consciously distancing themselves from the strategies of contemporary social protest movements of the era for fear of alienating the conservative Jewish establishment. The highly publicized trial of sixteen refuseniks in Leningrad in 1970 marked a turning point for the organization. Charged with high treason for the attempted hijacking of a plane, the sixteen refuseniks faced the possibility of execution for their crime, but the public outcry helped generate a reduced sentence. Inspired by this success, the SSSJ expanded its advocacy over the next two decades and drew in new allies. Throughout the 1970s and 1980s, they and other human rights activists staged demonstrations outside the Soviet embassy, the UN mission, and other venues of US-Soviet exchange. Under the guise of tourism, American Jews sponsored relief trips to the Soviet Union to deliver books, pamphlets, religious objects, and essential supplies to underground religious communities. The Chicago Action for Soviet Jewry group sponsored an "Adopt-A-Family" program to encourage American Jewish families to offer moral support to individual refusenik families.[9] The National Interreligious Task Force on Soviet Jewry (spearheaded by the American Jewish Committee and the National Catholic Conference) also kept the plight of refuseniks at the forefront of public consciousness through conferences, publications, speeches, and trips to the Soviet Union.[10] Teachers and schoolchildren wrote letters to their congressional representatives asking them to intervene on behalf of particular dissidents. The International Physicians Committee monitored the medical condition of Jewish prisoners of conscience. Journalists from the *New York Times*, the *Los Angeles Times*, and the *Washington Post* traveled to the Soviet Union to interview dissidents. More radical Jews associated with Rabbi Kahane and his Jewish Defense League chose a violent route, bombing Soviet offices in New York and Washington, DC.

The work of American Jewish activists complemented the advocacy of other human rights activists who emerged in the wake of the 1975 Helsinki accords.[11] Together they cataloged abuses in the Soviet Union and Eastern Europe, pressured state leaders, and ultimately made human rights central to Cold War diplomacy.[12] This activism in the United States (and Europe) emboldened the dissident movement in the Soviet Union, which made increasingly greater demands of the state. Refuseniks staged sit-ins, hunger strikes, and demonstrations. Despite the brutal crackdowns by KGB operatives, they smuggled letters out of the Soviet Union to plead their case in newspapers and magazines around the world.[13]

In 1971, in a surprising reversal of policy, the Soviets permitted an unprecedented 25,523 visas—almost all of them to Israel—as a demonstration of goodwill during a temporary thawing in relations with the West.[14] The following year, however, the government of Leonid Brezhnev imposed an exorbitant "diploma tax" on emigrants, which barred all those with higher education or specialized training from leaving. Declassified records would later demonstrate than the majority of refuseniks were not affected by the diploma tax because of their limited education, but in 1972, the announcement elicited immediate anger.[15] Capitalizing on the Soviets' economic dependency on US trade, American Jews lobbied for economic sanctions against the Soviet Union until it allowed Jews to emigrate or abandoned its policies of forced assimilation. The discussions on Capitol Hill so troubled Brezhnev that he called an emergency closed session meeting of the Politburo in March 1973 to discuss the diploma tax. Although the Soviets assured their American critics that the diploma tax would not be enforced—and increased the number of exit permits to thirty-five thousand as a demonstration of good faith—they were unable to dissuade the US Congress from passing the Jackson-Vanik amendment to the Trade Act of 1974, which authorized the president to deny "most-favored nation" trading status to any country that denied its citizens the right or opportunity to emigrate.[16]

Soviet Jews who sought emigration navigated a system that was capricious for anyone except for those the state wanted to expel. The elderly and the infirm were readily allowed to leave, as were the most dogmatic religious nationalists; but scientists (especially those with access to sensitive state records) found it virtually impossible to emigrate. To secure an exit permit, the average Soviet citizen needed an invitation from a first-degree relative living abroad (those seeking emigration to Israel only needed an invitation from a putative relative). The applicant was required to resign his or her job, divest of home and possessions, and settle all financial accounts. Only then was a citizen granted an exit permit and allowed to enter an embassy compound to apply for an immigrant or refugee visa. Vetting usually took several months: during this time the applicant was essentially homeless, forced to rely on friends, family, or neighbors who compromised their own safety by associating with a political pariah. Those who applied for Israeli visas did so at the embassy of the Netherlands (which represented Israeli interests after the Soviet Union severed relations with Israel following the 1967 war). If they secured a visa, they then traveled to Israel via a Western European gateway city, usually Rome or Vienna. By the late 1970s, many Soviet Jews with Israeli visas did not continue on to Israel, but instead stayed in Western Europe and applied for admission to the United States at the nearest US embassy or consulate. Over time, this became the standard exit route for Soviet Jews who sought emigration to the United States but didn't have the required invitations from first-degree relatives.[17] Nearly 110,000 Soviet Jews, most of them from Russia and the Ukraine, emigrated to the United States during the second half of the 1970s before the Soviet Union once again cut back on exit permits.[18]

During the 1980 US electoral campaign, presidential hopeful Ronald Reagan frequently criticized the Soviet Union for its restrictions on emigration and its incarceration of dissidents. In an address before the B'nai B'rith in Washington, DC, Reagan assured his audience that "the long agony of Jews in the Soviet Union . . . [would not] be forgotten in a Reagan administration."[19]

Reagan kept his promise. During his eight years in office, he continually pressed for greater religious and political freedoms in the Soviet Union and for a liberalization of travel and emigration policy. Shortly after he took office, the new president scheduled a highly publicized meeting with Avital Sharansky, the wife of internationally known dissident refusenik Anatoly (Natan) Sharansky, and Yosef Mendelevitch, one of the sixteen Leningrad hijackers, released from the Soviet Union after serving a ten-year prison sentence. Reagan took up Sharansky's cause at the 1985 summit meeting with the newly appointed Soviet general secretary Mikhail Gorbachev. When Sharansky was allowed to emigrate to Israel the following year, one of the first calls he received was from President Reagan.[20]

The Reagan administration pressed for the release of other well-known dissidents and refuseniks, including physicist Dr. Andrei Sakharov and his wife Elena Bonner, who had been banished to Gorki.[21] Secretary of State George Shultz habitually began each meeting with Soviet foreign minister Edvard Shevardnaze by handing him a list of reported human rights abuses in the Soviet Union.[22] On every trip to the Soviet Union, Shultz and other members of the administration met openly with dissidents to communicate American support; and in every meeting with American Jewish leaders, Reagan assured his audience that he was pressing the Soviets for "deeds, not rhetoric."[23] Members of the bipartisan Congressional Human Rights Caucus (CHRC) gave moral support to the administration's efforts. Founded in 1983 by Representatives John Edward Porter and Tom Lantos, the only Holocaust survivor to serve in Congress, the CHRC sponsored resolutions condemning the harassment of Soviet Jews and other minorities and calling for a more liberal Soviet emigration policy.[24] In May 1986, the Senate and House honored Anatoly and Avital Sharansky with a congressional gold medal "in recognition of their supreme dedication and total commitment to human rights and freedoms."[25]

Senator Edward M. Kennedy also took particular interest in the dissident and refusenik cause. His conversations with Brezhnev and other Soviet officials on emigration and other matters during the 1980s served as a back channel, especially when talks between the two countries were at a standstill.[26] Kennedy secured the emigration of several dissidents to Austria; once there he facilitated their visas to the United States, assisted them in securing employment in the Boston area, and even invited some of them to his summer home. But as interested as Kennedy may have been in the plight of Soviet Jews, it was the advocacy of ordinary Americans that pressured public officials like him to intervene. As refusenik Boris Katz noted:

> The final push was, of course, Senator Kennedy's, but if not for the efforts of normal American housewives and working people and others, that never would have happened. There are so many people in the Soviet Union. Why would Senator Kennedy pick this particular case? He did it because the case became known to him, and it became known to him because these people let it be known to him. That was a very unusual—to me at least—way to see how things get done, how all of a sudden if enough people want something, it happens. It doesn't always happen, but as I said, we certainly were lucky that it happened to us.[27]

The Jackson-Vanik amendment offered the president the leverage he needed. During his third summit meeting with Gorbachev in 1987, Reagan warned that Americans had little interest in addressing Soviet economic and trade demands unless they saw improvements in human rights. A rally, attended by a quarter-million Americans in support of Soviet Jewish emigration, held on the National Mall on the eve of this summit meeting, gave credence to the president's warning that Americans wanted more punitive policies toward the Soviet Union. The Soviet state-run newspaper accused the Reagan administration of pandering to "Zionist circles." The president's message had an impact, however. In the wake of the third summit, more churches and synagogues in the Soviet Union reopened, and the government released over three hundred political and religious dissidents from prisons, forced labor camps (*gulags*), and mental hospitals.[28]

The political changes in the Soviet Union were not solely a response to US pressure. Mikhail Gorbachev had his own reformist agenda, independent of any pressure from the Reagan administration. By the late 1980s, Gorbachev's calls for glasnost and perestroika—openness, transparency, and government restructuring—had become increasingly newsworthy. In January 1987, Gorbachev announced a new emigration law designed to shorten the waiting period for an exit permit for all except those who had access to state secrets; by March, ethnic Germans and Armenians, in addition to Jews, were granted permission to emigrate. The change in emigration policy, the new freedoms to speak and communicate openly, and the sudden release of high-profile refuseniks, including Ida Nudel, Vladimir Slepak, and Iosef Begun, signaled a new era.[29] At the fourth summit meeting in May 1988, the president urged Gorbachev to carry his reformist agenda further: to free all political prisoners, lift restrictions on religious worship, permit political and trade union activities independent of the Communist Party, establish an independent judiciary system, and allow elections by secret ballot. Reagan also called anew for the Berlin Wall to be torn down.[30]

As the likelihood of receiving permission to emigrate increased, so did the number of applications for visas to the United States. At first Soviet Armenians were disproportionately represented in the applications for visas, much to the consternation of US officials who argued that, despite the political unrest in Soviet Armenia and Azerbaijan, the Armenians were not bona fide refugees. "Refugee officials have always been troubled by the notion that people leaving the Soviet Union are automatically assumed to be refugees," wrote the Doris Meissner, who in 1993 would become commissioner of the Immigration and Naturalization Service (INS): "There is scant evidence that these Armenians, as a group or individually, are in a more beleaguered position than are other Soviet citizens. They are leaving in search of freedom and a better life. This is not the province of refugee policy."[31] Consequently, the Soviet Armenians who applied for refugee status had a high rejection rate—one source put it at 75 percent in

1989—which INS officials attributed to their failure to substantiate claims of persecution but others attributed to the lack of advocacy in the United States. The Armenian American ethnic lobby had made its presence felt on a number of foreign policy issues over the decades but made comparatively fewer appeals to increase the refugee quota, in part because of concerns that emigration might undermine the Armenian homeland.[32]

By 1989, the majority of Soviet applicants for refugee status were Jews.[33] Israel might have been the destination of choice for Jewish emigrants during the 1960s and 1970s, but by 1989, only 10 to 15 percent of Soviet Jews applied for an Israeli visa.[34] The sanctions against emigration had almost disappeared, said Jewel S. LaFontant, the US refugee coordinator at the Department of State, contributing to an increase in applications and a corresponding burden on US resources. "The militia surrounding our Embassy in Moscow allows normal access to the Embassy. The major constraint, in fact, is the capacity of the Embassy, from physical and security standpoints, to receive all the Soviet citizens now seeking access to our consular section."[35]

A backlog of applicants developed almost immediately, forcing the Reagan and Bush administrations—after emergency consultation with Congress—to raise the Soviet refugee quota from 8,500 to 22,500 in fiscal year 1988, and then to 25,000 for 1989.[36] Those who applied to come to the United States understandably assumed that they would be admitted as refugees, or at the very least paroled into the United States. A 1989 article in The Economist summed up the challenge facing the new Bush administration:

> The United States, which for the past fifteen years has been banging away relentlessly at the Soviet Union to allow its people, specifically the Jews, to leave, faces the awkward corollary of where these people, who are now leaving Russia in ever increasing numbers, should go. More than 90% of the emigrants have no doubts about it. They want to go to America.[37]

But as the Gorbachev government instituted more and more political and social reforms, the INS officials who handled visa applications became increasingly skeptical that Soviet Jews, Armenians, Christian evangelicals, and others who sought exit had legitimate claims to refugee status. At a 1989 congressional hearing, one high-ranking INS official reminded legislators that the 1980 Refugee Act offered guidelines for evaluating eligibility for refugee status:

> INS adjudication ... requires that each case be examined on its individual merit. Decisions are based on a legal analysis which takes into account the statutory definition of refugee, incorporated into US law with the Refugee Act of 1980, US refugee and asylum case law, and international guidance, such as the United Nations High Commissioner Refugees' "Handbook on Procedures and Criteria for Determining Refugee Status." An evaluation is made of the claim of persecution according to a specific legal standard—that the applicant demonstrate a "well-founded fear of persecution," on account of race, religion, nationality, membership in a particular social group, or political opinion.[38]

Economic considerations likely influenced INS perceptions of the Soviet applicants. The US economy had barely recovered from the double-digit inflation of the previous decade and could ill afford an expansion of the social services normally offered to those admitted as refugees. "We're a victim of our own success," said one assistant INS commissioner. "Now we are getting people who we have asked for, for many, many years, and we don't have the money [to process and support them as refugees]."[39] The US embassy in Moscow temporarily ceased processing refugee applications from July 4 to October 1, 1988, to signal to Soviet Jews and their American advocates that the days of granting automatic refugee or parolee status were coming to an end; and in November 1988, Secretary of State George Shultz urged the new attorney general, Richard Thornburgh, to apply a uniform standard for refugee determination and evaluate each applicant on a case-by-case basis.[40]

Navigating the US refugee bureaucracy became a time-consuming and anxiety-ridden process for Soviet applicants and their families. Of the 108,342 residents of the Soviet Union who applied for refugee status at US consulates during the eight-month period from October 1988 through June 1989, only a fraction of qualifying applicants could be accommodated within the FY1989 refugee quota.[41] US embassy officials warned Soviet applicants that admission to the United States was not guaranteed and that they could expect delays of a year or more before their applications were reviewed.[42]

Members of Congress and advocates for Soviet Jewry pressured the Bush administration to expand the Soviet quota. The administration instead chose a number of controversial actions. Keeping the overall refugee quota constant, the administration reallocated part of the Southeast Asian quota to the Soviets. This allowed the administration to raise the Soviet quota to 25,000 in FY1989. When this number proved insufficient, the Bush administration raised the global ceiling by 22,500 (to a total of 116,500) to increase the Soviet quota to 43,500.[43] Attorneys General Edwin Meese and Richard Thornburgh assured Soviet applicants and their advocates that those found ineligible for refugee status were still potentially eligible to be paroled into the United States after presentation of an acceptable affidavit of sponsorship from a relative or friend, a religious congregation, or some other sponsoring organization in the United States. Under the parole program, an additional two thousand persons could be brought to the United States per month. Refugee status was always more desirable than parolee status since, without special congressional legislation, parolees could not acquire permanent residency in the United States, thus making their long-term status in the United States uncertain; they were not entitled to the resettlement benefits extended to refugees, making them entirely dependent on their familial and institutional sponsors.[44]

As the backlog of applicants grew, thousands of Soviet Jews with Israeli visas were stranded in Rome and Vienna hoping to secure permission to come to the United States, and their situation became "unmanageable, extremely costly, and ultimately inhumane."[45] As "temporary visitors" in Italy and Austria, the Soviets emigrants did not qualify for work authorization, schooling, or social services, which made them entirely dependent on voluntary relief agencies for their housing, medical care, and food. To ease the burden on these host societies, the Bush administration announced the phasing out of Soviet refugee processing outside of Moscow. Those requesting admission to the United States after October 1, 1989, would have to apply from within the Soviet Union; and those holding Israeli visas would no longer be considered for refugee or parole status since they had another viable option for refuge.

The centralizing of refugee applications "in-country" challenged the very definition of refugee in international and domestic law, which specified that refugees be situated outside their country of nationality (if stateless, outside of the country of last inhabitance). The centralizing of refugee processing "in-country" (a strategy the State Department would adopt in several other refugee crises in the post–Cold War era) was enacted in this case to ease the pressure on transit countries like Italy and Austria. Administration officials adopted these measures knowing full well that centralizing INS resources in "Embassy Moscow" would result in an increase in applications. Some individuals would have to be prioritized over others, both in the scheduling of interviews and in admissions. As Jewel S. LaFontant testified:

[These new procedures] will not guarantee that we will process everyone who applies or that we will not have backlogs. At current rates of application, and considering the availability of spaces in both refugee and immigration admission to the United States, we simply cannot handle the entire load expeditiously. We do hope, however, that the new procedures will provide us with the ability to identify and process in a timely and orderly fashion family relations cases and others of humanitarian interest to the United States.[46]

In FY1990, more than two hundred thousand Soviet citizens applied for one of the coveted refugee slots, now expanded to fifty thousand.[47] "Embassy Moscow" forwarded refugee applications to the Department of State's Washington Processing Center in Rosslyn, Virginia. The DOS personnel reviewed the applications in Washington and chose which applicants the INS officials would interview in Moscow. The INS interview reports were then forwarded back to the WPC for further scrutiny and final selection. The State Department gave priority to those who had relatives in the United States or who were of "special humanitarian concern," but the rejections increased. In 1989, fewer than 20 percent of Jewish applicants were rejected, and the Justice Department eventually overturned most of these denials;[48] by FY1990, however, over 80 percent of applicants for refugee status were denied.[49]

The policy changes elicited concern—even anger—from a wide range of citizens who felt that the Bush administration was creating obstacles for, or blocking altogether, the very people President Reagan had once championed. Jewish advocacy groups, in particular, argued that Soviet Jews needed to be fast-tracked for admission because they still faced intense persecution in the Soviet Union, especially at the popular and lower bureaucratic levels, where the loosening of controls on free speech had given the Soviet population permission to express deep-seated feelings of anti-Semitism.[50] If the Gorbachev reforms were to fail, they argued, Soviet Jews would face an even more perilous situation. Conversely, if the

Soviet reforms were to continue to succeed, the Bush administration could terminate the refugee/parole program at any time, trapping people in a society that distrusted and marginalized them. Recent developments in Poland and Hungary gave some legitimacy to these concerns: the refugee program for Hungarians and Poles had ended once popular democratic reforms were enacted.[51] Poles and Hungarians could continue to immigrate to the United States, but after November 1989 they could only do so through the more traditional channel of green cards (immigration visas).

In light of these developments, the Hebrew Immigrant Aid Society (HIAS) and other refugee resettlement and advocacy groups lobbied in support of the Lautenberg amendment to the Foreign Operations Appropriations Act (PL 101-167), which called for a relaxed standard of proof for certain categories of people from the Soviet Union, Laos, Cambodia, and Vietnam, especially persecuted religious and ethnic minorities.[52] Jews, evangelical Christians, and Ukrainian Catholics would only be required to demonstrate that they had a credible fear of persecution.[53] "The amendment gives formal recognition to the fact that for Jews there exists an intrinsic relationship between their experience in Russia over the past two centuries and the lives they lead in the Soviet Union today," wrote the president of HIAS:

> Many of the racist beliefs about Jewish people which prompted the pogroms of the late nineteenth and early twentieth centuries that left thousands of Jews dead still exist in Russian society today. The lifting of official sanctions has done little to change the informal, more deeply rooted attitudes and behaviors of ordinary Soviet citizens. In short, Jews in the Soviet Union understand that formal equal treatment does not mean tolerance in practice.[54]

The Lautenberg amendment also served as an "adjustment act," allowing Soviets and Southeast Asians paroled into the United States to adjust their status to legal permanent resident. Congress passed the Lautenberg amendment in 1990 but not without vocal criticism from some congressmen who feared that it would create yet another "backdoor" in the immigration system, privileging those immigrants who had powerful political allies.

Members of the Bush administration disputed the argument that the "window of opportunity" for Jewish emigration would close at any minute. "The reforms in the Soviet Union and the Eastern bloc have already gone farther than any previous attempts," said one official. "The farther they go, the harder it becomes to turn back."[55] Administration officials also disputed accusations that they were biased against Jewish applicants: "We share your concern regarding [the plight of Soviet Jews]," responded one State Department letter to members of an advocacy group on Long Island. "[However,] we must address the consequences of our human rights and foreign policy success with fairness and without distorting or compromising our other [humanitarian] commitments."[56] In letter after letter, administration officials assured concerned citizens that they were taking "extraordinary measures" to guarantee that applicants who failed to secure refugee status would still have opportunities to migrate to the United States either as parolees or through other immigration channels. The White House proposed to Congress a temporary quota of thirty thousand "special immigrants" per year for the next five years for Soviet Jews and others who were of "foreign policy interest." The *New York Times* called the proposal "sensible"; but when members of Congress added twenty-seven national or ethnic groups to the list of potential immigrants who might be considered "special immigrants," one congressional staffer complained, "At this rate, we'll end up with not a refugee program but a buddy system."[57] In the end, the special immigrant visa was not created.

In congressional testimony INS officials frequently discussed the challenges of refugee adjudication in this new era of political reordering. They articulated three principles that they thought should guide the US refugee program in the post–Cold War era. First, the US should no longer accommodate "persons who merely want to leave a generally repressive society for the relative freedom and/or economic opportunities of [the United States] no matter how sympathetically we may view their plight. The United States cannot offer refuge [to] entire groups of oppressed peoples."[58] Second, those in search of refuge should no longer consider European countries of first asylum stepping stones to the United States. Countries that were signatories to international refugee agreements had the moral responsibility to consider the asylum petitions of those who arrived at their borders; and allies should no longer expect the United States to take in a substantial number of their asylum seekers. Third, the United States should strive to keep political reformers in their countries of origin unless they faced life-threatening persecution; otherwise, emigration would undermine the nascent prodemocracy movements in the very countries it hoped to build up.[59] On this last point, the Bush administration was especially sensitive to criticism that their refugee policies

were inadvertently "draining" these emerging democracies of their most
talented labor and their most committed democrats: "It is precisely now,
when positive forces are beginning to work to those ends," said Princeton
Lyman, director of refugee programs, "that we should encourage [dissi-
dents to stay and] to work for change in their own societies."[60]

This rearticulation of refugee policy caught European allies by surprise.
Since the end of World War II, millions of Polish, Hungarian, and other
Eastern bloc refugees had gone to Austria, West Germany, Italy, Spain, and
other Western European countries, and these "first asylum countries" had
counted on the United States and Canada to share the financial and resettlement burden. Austria had served as a country of first asylum to over
two million refugees since 1945, and over four hundred thousand ethnic
Germans from Poland, Romania, the Soviet Union, and East Germany had
fled or emigrated to West Germany in the 1980s alone.[61] Hungary and Italy
had also accommodated large numbers of Romanians, Poles, and other
Eastern Europeans. Governments responded generously to the refugee
crises, but average citizens were often less enthusiastic, as they worried
about increased competition for jobs and housing.[62] A journalist covering
George Bush's 1989 visit to Mainz reflected on the lack of German enthu-
siasm for the president's call to "bring glasnost to East Berlin":

> Somewhere in the back of the room, several people in the audience
> probably shifted in their seats, amid all the cheering, aware that
> West Germany and the rest of "free" Europe would be hard pressed
> to deal with the sudden influx of thousands and thousands of East
> European refugees, should the walls come tumbling down.... The
> problem is this guy Gorbachev. He has a nasty habit, when chal-
> lenged in this fashion, of doing exactly what you dare him to do.[63]

When the Bush administration announced that Hungarians and Poles
would no longer be prioritized in the US refugee program, Austria followed suit, announcing a new "rapid review" policy that would dramatically restrict refugee camp populations to those meeting the strict
UNHCR definition of refugee. Those that did not meet the criteria would
be repatriated. [64]

Americans' prioritizing of Soviet admissions had consequences for
other refugee populations. Rather that expand the overall annual quota,
the administration reshuffled the regional suballocations. The quota for
Southeast Asians continued to be reduced, and the already small refugee

quota for "Eastern Europe" (9,000 in FY1990) was reduced further, to 6,500, and the difference reallocated to the Soviets. Once Hungarians and Poles were excluded from consideration, only those from Czechoslovakia, Bulgaria, Albania, and Romania (of the Eastern bloc countries) were potentially eligible for refugee status. Of these Romania had the worst record of human rights violations.[65] US embassy personnel told applicants not to expect priority processing simply because they came from the communist bloc. "Whatever our practice may have been in the past," testified Princeton Lyman at one congressional hearing, "we should now agree to assess conditions in each country separately. We must differentiate as a matter of fairness. We must ensure that the benefit of US resettlement is available to those in the greatest need. And we must ensure that our refugee policies are not at cross-purposes with our political objectives."[66]

Occasionally, the applications of celebrities were fast-tracked simply for their symbolic value. When Olympic gold medal gymnast Nadia Comăneci of Romania petitioned for refugee resettlement, the State Department designated Comăneci's petition (filed in the Vienna office) a "Category 1" case—an "immediate action case of particular concern to the United States"—and special precautions were taken to ensure her safe passage to the United States. Some in the US news media were dubious about Comăneci's motivations for seeking refuge in the United States, hinting that a romantic entanglement and the potential for higher earnings were drivers of her defection. If Comăneci had defected just a few years earlier, the news media would not have questioned her motivations—indeed, she would have been widely celebrated—as her coaches, Béla and Marta Károlyi, were when they defected in 1981. But by 1989, the American public had become more dubious about refugee admissions. Responding to constituents' concerns that some individuals were fast-tracked over others, Bruce A. Morrison, the chairman of the Subcommittee on Immigration, Refugees, and International Law, requested Justice Department files on certain cases, including Comăneci's, out of "legislative interest." The Justice Department refused, citing confidentiality.[67]

Eastern bloc refugees had their own vocal advocates. Polish immigrants and Americans of Polish ancestry, for example, had created a host of organizations in the 1980s to lend symbolic and financial support to Poland's Solidarity union and other democratic opposition groups. These organizations, concentrated largely in Chicago and New York (the two largest centers of *Polonia* in the United States), engaged in demonstrations, boycotts, and other political action strategies to call attention to the Polish cause, but they also raised funds for humanitarian aid and lobbied Congress to keep the immigration channels open.[68] Some of the most vocal activists were refugees who had fled Poland after 1960 and had prior involvement in Poland's democratic opposition.[69] These organizations now pressured their congressional representatives to support Poland's fragile democracy, but also to facilitate migration for those still at risk of persecution. Representative Dan Rostenkowski, of Polish ancestry and representing a large Polish constituency in Chicago, became a vocal proponent of keeping the channels of migration open (indeed, his assistant for immigrant affairs was a refugee and a former Solidarity union member).[70] Thousands of Poles, Rostenkowski said, had given up jobs, government housing, and higher education in the hopes of finding greater freedoms in the United States, only to find themselves stranded in European refugee camps.[71]

A number of political actors took up the Eastern and Central European cause. Congressmen Richard Gephardt and William Lipinski wrote the White House to complain about the decimation of the Eastern European quota:

Just as the Soviet Union could not extinguish the flame of freedom in their captive peoples' hearts, the United States must not allow the flame of hope, freedom, and opportunity, symbolized by our Statue of Liberty, to be extinguished [in Eastern and Central Europe]. We ask that [the White House] rekindle the flame of hope for hundreds of thousands [of Eastern and Central Europeans] . . . longing to be free.[72]

Congressman Frank Wolf, in turn, spoke out on behalf of Romanian applicants who faced retribution from the Ceauşescu regime for requesting permission to emigrate.[73] In November 1989 the House Subcommittee on Immigration, Refugees and International Law held hearings on the plight of refugees from Eastern and Central European countries. At these hearings Bernard Cardinal Law and representatives from the US Conference of Catholic Bishops pleaded for an expansion of the "Eastern European" quota and the reincorporation of Hungarians and Poles into that quota.[74] Representatives of the Polish American Congress and the Polish American Immigration and Relief Committee also testified, complaining that the government was biased against Eastern bloc applicants.[75] The following year, when the news media brought to light the horrific neglect in Romanian orphanages, Congress once again held hearings, this time to discuss an expansion of quotas to facilitate the adoption of thousands of needy children.[76]

Much of the public debate about refugee policy in the immediate post–Cold War period, then, concerned the expansion and allocation of the annual refugee quota: what groups would be prioritized for admission and in what numbers. But others argued just the opposite: the end of the Cold War had made the refugee program redundant or in need of radical reduction. In the Senate, Alan K. Simpson and Strom Thurmond were the leading spokesmen for retrenchment. Both men had played a key role in the immigration policy debates of the early and mid-1980s that had culminated in the passage of the 1986 Immigration Reform and Control Act (IRCA). They now led the fight against refugee admissions they believed to be spiraling out of control. When President Bush proposed an overall refugee quota of 116,500 for FY1990, they countered with a compromise figure of 75,000. In one of their many letters to the president, the senators wrote: "We must make it clear that the right to emigrate does not carry with it a right to be admitted as an immigrant to any other country":

> We believe it is time to reexamine the "freedom of choice" policy that is now applied toward Soviet refugees. Given the apparent willingness of the present Soviet leadership to liberalize emigration rights, this particular policy—in effect in no other region of the world—could overwhelm our refugee program. In addition, this policy runs contrary to the even-handed, country-neutral application of our refugee laws contemplated by the Refugee Act.[77]

On talk shows and in the media, Simpson argued that the Bush administration was accepting too many people who were not genuine refugees: "We ought to stop this gimmickry of the word 'refugee.' We must distinguish between the right to leave the Soviet Union and the right to enter the United States. They are not the same."[78]

Like Simpson and Thurmond, President Bush personally resisted the idea of granting automatic refugee or parole status to those fleeing countries transitioning from communism. However, he also recognized that the United States had a humanitarian obligation to those populations championed by his predecessor, who had once been at the center of Cold War foreign policy. His administration tried to find a middle way to reconcile the various concerns, but in the end, domestic interests won out. Advocacy on behalf of the Soviets Jews had been vocal, forceful, and persistent for three decades and, not surprisingly, yielded enormous influence in the crafting and apportionment of numerical quotas. While their admission was not automatic, Soviet Jews did find it easier to migrate to the United States during the 1990s than other groups. Their applications were evaluated "in country," and the Lautenberg amendment authorized a relaxed standard of proof, making it easier to secure refugee or parolee status.[79] The 1990 Immigration Act also included a provision that waived the one-year residency requirement for permanent resident status. Those applicants who had to settle for parole status also found it easier to acquire legal permanent residency thanks to the Lautenberg amendment.

After the dismantling of the Soviet Union on December 31, 1991, some scholars and policy analysts predicted that Soviet emigration would decline over the next decade, as the political conditions that had compelled so many to travel slowly disappeared. Others predicted just the opposite. The Heritage Foundation, a conservative think tank in Washington, DC, forecast the "largest peacetime movement of ethnic Russians to the West" since the Bolshevik Revolution.[80] Their forecasts proved to be correct. From 1990 to 1998, 358,445 former Soviets entered the United States as refugees before their numbers dropped dramatically—to 194 and 282 in 1999 and 2000, respectively. See table 1.1.[81] (Thousands more arrived

Table 1.1 Soviet Refugee Arrivals,
1990–2000

Fiscal year	Arrivals
1990	50,716
1991	38,661
1992	61,298
1993	48,627
1994	43,470
1995	35,716
1996	29,536
1997	27,072
1998	23,349
1999	194
2000	282

Source: Department of Homeland Security, Fiscal Year 2000 Statistical Yearbook, http://www.dhs.gov/publication/fiscal-year-2000-statistical-yearbook-refugeesasylees.

as parolees or with immigration visas.) More Jews came from Ukraine than any other region of the former Soviet Union.[82] The Washington Processing Center in Rosslyn continued to review applications through the year 2001 before transferring authority back to staff in the Moscow office. Comparatively fewer refugees were admitted from Eastern and Central Europe: from 1990 to 2000, less than forty thousand refugees were admitted from Albania, Bulgaria, the former Czechoslovakia, Poland, Hungary, and Romania—with Romanians constituting the largest group at 9,932.[83]

During the transitional 1990s, the majority of refugees continued to come from either the former or the current communist bloc countries.[84] However, the changing global political landscape posed a number of challenges to the US Refugee Admissions Program. With the end of the Cold War, what role would ideology and geopolitical interests play in the crafting of refugee and asylum policy?

The Tiananmen Crisis

Heping Shi survived China's Cultural Revolution and came to the United States in 1987 to pursue doctoral studies in sociology at Virginia Tech. His prodemocracy activities in the United States in support of the Tiananmen Square protesters in Beijing drew the attention of Chinese embassy officials in Washington, DC. When efforts to silence him failed, Chinese officials met with his wife, Gan Suxia, who was living in Beijing with the couple's nine-year-old daughter. The conversation was sufficiently threatening that Gan Suxia later tried to kill herself and her daughter. At a 1990 congressional hearing on China's harassment of Chinese citizens living in the United States, Shi tried to explain to congressmen why even the suggestion of his counterrevolutionary behavior would have driven his wife to attempt murder and suicide:

> I wish to explain what it means to have a "counterrevolutionary" in a Chinese family. It means that friends and neighbors will keep away from you for fear; it means it is difficult for you to find a job; it means you will be treated differently in salary and housing—if you are lucky enough to be given a job; it means that the children of the family will be denied a good education; and above all, it means that you are constantly approached and told that your loved one is an "enemy of the people" and that you should "draw a clear line" between you and your loved one.[85]

During 1989–1990, Congress debated how to protect the tens of thousands of Chinese nationals in the United States who feared returning to their homeland after China's violent crackdown at Tiananmen. At these hearings, Chinese nationals—many of them graduate students and researchers at colleges and universities—reported how their government spied on, harassed, and threatened them in order to undermine the prodemocracy movement.

Liang Zhang, who compiled *The Tiananmen Papers*, a selection of Chinese official documents relating to the Tiananmen Square protests of 1989, called Tiananmen "one of the most dramatic and significant episodes in the worldwide pursuit of democracy in the twentieth century."[86] That thousands of Chinese citizens came forward to demand political and social reforms was not unusual; only a few years earlier—in 1985, 1986, and 1987—Chinese students in Beijing had staged protests to call for reforms until their demonstrations were disrupted, and their leaders imprisoned or otherwise silenced.[87] What made Tiananmen unprecedented was the attention and support the protesters received from the West. At the time of the protests an international press corps of twelve hundred journalists had been granted unparalleled access to China to cover the summit meeting with Soviet premier Mikhail Gorbachev, but, much to the embarrassment of Beijing, the student protesters soon became the dominant news. Millions of Americans turned to *CBS Evening News* and the *New York Times* for coverage of the protests. People like Heping Shi played an important role in representing the prodemocracy movement abroad and in interpreting Chinese state actions for a non-Chinese audience. This was sufficient to make them enemies of the state.

The catalyst for the Tiananmen protests was the death of former Communist Party general secretary Hu Yaobang on April 15, 1989. Hu, a veteran of the "Long March," a one-time secretary general of the Communist Party, and a leader beloved by reformers, had been blamed for the 1987 demonstrations and consequently vilified and removed from office.[88] On hearing of his death, students inspired by Hu's reformist agenda gathered spontaneously throughout Beijing to mourn him and to call for his official redemption. Within days the protests assumed a more political character as the students used these gatherings to condemn government corruption and to call for political transparency and democratic reforms. Over the next eight weeks, demonstrations erupted in over two hundred towns and cities, but the protests at Tiananmen Square, at the geographic center of the capital city, became the symbolic heart of what has been called the 1989 prodemocracy movement. Tens of thousands of

students marched or gathered at the square each day singing revolution-
ary songs, chanting antigovernment slogans, and carrying prodemocracy
banners. They boycotted their classes and held sit-ins in front of the Great
Hall of the People and at different locations in the Zhongnanhai compound, insisting on the right to present their list of demands to the party
leadership. They set up tents and encampments, determined to remain
until their demands were met.

The demonstrations grew more boisterous after an April 26 editorial
in the *People's Daily*, the official newspaper of the Chinese Communist
Party, condemned the protests as a "planned conspiracy." These accusations prompted professors, artists and intellectuals, and even ordinary
workers to join the students in solidarity. On the seventieth anniversary of the May Fourth Movement, over one hundred thousand people
marched in Beijing.[89] When the government announced a four-day summit meeting with Mikhail Gorbachev (May 15–19) —the first state visit
by a Soviet premier in thirty-three years—over three thousand students
staged a highly publicized hunger strike on the square to call for Soviet-
style reforms. Officials hastily relocated Gorbachev's welcoming ceremony
from Tiananmen to the airport. On May 17 and 18, over a million people
gathered in and around the square. Workers throughout the country
threatened the government with strikes of their own, promising disruptions in production and transportation if the government did not acqui-
esce to the students' demands. The international news media, congregated
in Beijing to cover the Soviets' apparent reconciliation with China, found
more compelling stories in and around the public square than in the halls
of power.[90] Chinese nationals abroad also held public demonstrations—in
France, West Germany, Canada, and the United States, as well as Taiwan
and Hong Kong—focusing more international attention on Tiananmen.

The Communist Party leadership was initially divided over how to respond to the protesters. Some argued for patience and leniency, hoping that
the protests would die down when the students returned to class. Others
argued for a show of authority. By mid-May, the more lenient voices in the
government had been silenced, and on May 20 the leadership declared
martial law in five districts in Beijing. The People's Liberation Army (PLA)
and the People's Armed Police were called into the city to clear the square,
but the first troops to arrive on the scene were unable—or unwilling—
to disperse the crowds. Students and city residents surrounded the army
convoys, "sometimes to let the air out of tires or to stall engines but more
often to argue with or cajole troops, urging them not to enforce martial law
restrictions and not to turn their guns on their fellow Chinese."[91]

On the night of June 3, more seasoned and well-armed troops converged on Tiananmen Square in tanks and armored personnel carriers and began a violent assault, smashing barricades, tents, and encampments around the city and all those who stood in their path. Over the next twenty-four hours, these troops opened fire on civilians in the square, and in other parts of the city, killing hundreds and wounding thousands. According to witnesses, hospitals were instructed not to treat the civilian casualties, and journalists were detained to prevent them from photographing the violence or interviewing the survivors. Chinese government records state that 241 people died in the crackdown, including twenty-three officers and soldiers of the PLA and the police, and thirty-six students from Beijing universities. Seven thousand were wounded. Nongovernment sources estimated much higher casualties and injuries.[92] By June 21, more than fifteen hundred protesters had been arrested, including six of the twenty-one most visible student leaders of the prodemocracy movement.[93] The total number of executions is unknown.

The year 1989—the fortieth anniversary of the founding of the People's Republic of China—was thus marked by the violent suppression of the prodemocracy movement. Outside of China, Tiananmen entered the international political vocabulary.

President George H. W. Bush, who had once served as chief of the US Liaison Office in Beijing (1974–1975) prior to the establishment of full diplomatic relations with China, was alarmed by Tiananmen and how it might derail his long-term goals for positive diplomatic and commercial relations with China. Only two years earlier, Representative Tom Lantos had strained US-China relations by inviting the Dalai Lama to address the Congressional Human Rights Caucus. Liberal Democrats like Stephen Solarz had been long critical of China on human rights grounds, while conservative Republicans like Jesse Helms were distrustful of—and even hostile to—"Red" China.[94] These and other influential members of Congress now demanded that the administration impose sanctions on China to communicate, in very strong terms, American displeasure. "This is not the time for an emotional response," Bush responded the day after the Tiananmen crackdown at a press conference, "but a reasoned, careful action that takes into account both our long-term interests and recognition of a complex internal situation in China." At another press conference three days later the president expressed his fears for US-China relations: "What I want to do is preserve this relationship [with China] as best I can, and I hope the conditions that lie ahead will permit me to preserve this relationship. I don't want to pass judgment on individual leaders, but I want to make very clear to those leaders and to the rest of the world that the United States denounces the kind of brutality that all of us have seen on our television."[95] Privately, Bush complained about the pressure coming from the congressional leadership. "They don't have any suggestions, but they just want to complicate the [life] of the president."[96]

Bush chose not to impose full economic sanctions on the PRC. Secretary of State James A. Baker later recalled, "It was important not to respond in a way that played into the hands of the [Chinese] hard-liners who were pushing for even more repressive action, which would inevitably lead to more bloodshed."[97] Instead, the administration communicated its disapproval by temporarily suspending all high-level exchanges with PRC officials and temporarily suspending the sale and export of weaponry. Financial institutions were instructed to delay granting any new loans to the PRC. In a four-page letter to Deng Xiaoping, Bush explained his actions: "I have tried very hard not to appear to be dictating in any way to China about how it should manage its internal crisis. I am respectful of the differences in our two societies and in our two systems. . . . But I ask you to well remember the principles on which my young country was founded." Reverence for freedom of speech and freedom of assembly, the president explained, affected the way Americans viewed and reacted to events in China.[98] When Deng communicated an openness to receiving a presidential emissary, Bush authorized a series of "informal meetings" with Chinese officials attended by National Security Advisor Brent Scowcroft, Deputy Secretary of State Lawrence Eagleburger, and Secretary of State Baker. When members of Congress complained about Bush's half-hearted and inconsistent application of sanctions, the administration deflected the criticism, insisting that "informal meetings" were not included in the original ban.[99]

Within months, the Bush administration quietly resumed its normal order of business with the PRC. The White House authorized export licenses for communications satellites and authorized the sale of commercial jets. However, events continually tested both governments' resolve to maintain diplomatic relations. The Chinese leadership took great offense when the US embassy in Beijing granted asylum to astrophysicist and prodemocracy activist Fang Lizhi and his family despite their objections. Bush seemed almost apologetic in his explanation:

We are not violating international law, in the opinion of our attorneys. And it is awful hard for the United States, when a man presents himself—a person who is a dissident—and says that his life is threatened, to turn him back. And that isn't one of the premises upon which the United States was founded. . . . I hope it can be resolved.[100]

It would take a year of negotiations for Fang and his wife, Li Shuxian, to be granted permission to leave the embassy for exile in England. He was eventually allowed to immigrate to the United States.[101]

According to the INS, there were approximately 382,000 Chinese nonimmigrants in the United States by June 1989: 73,000 were students, with 10,000 holding J visas (exchange visitors), and 63,000 holding F or M visas (students in vocational or academic programs). The remaining nonimmigrants held tourist or business visas.[102] Those on student or exchange visas were expected to return to their homeland for two years before they could receive another visa to come to the United States.[103] The mandatory return had been written into US immigration policy—and into bilaterally negotiated educational exchanges—to encourage international students to return to their countries. When news of the arrests and trials of Tiananmen protesters reached the United States, many Chinese students and researchers at American universities understandably feared returning to China, especially if they had engaged in acts of solidarity with protesters while living and studying abroad.

One month after the military assault, the US House Subcommittee on Immigration, Refugees and International Law held the first of several hearings on the plight of Chinese nationals in the United States. "It is imperative that in the wake of these events the United States not only express its dismay to the leaders of China in the international community," said its chair Rep. Bruce A. Morrison, "but that they make every effort to protect the Chinese nationals currently in this country from the risk of harm from this vindictive government."[104]

US immigration policy offered these Chinese nationals few options to stay, but there were historical precedents for making exceptions. During the early Cold War, when racist national origins quotas prevented any significant migration from China, the United States authorized select well-educated Chinese to enter or remain in the United States if they were prodemocracy and had skills necessary to the US economy. Between 1948 and 1955, for example, Congress allowed 3,517 students and 119 scholars afraid to return home in the wake of China's 1949 communist revolution to remain in the United States and to receive funding for living expenses, tuition, and medical care.[105] In addition to these "stranded scholars," Congress allowed an estimated 32,000 Chinese to enter the US during the period 1953–1961, outside of China's tiny immigration quota. And from 1962 to 1965, the Kennedy administration extended humanitarian parole to 15,111 Chinese from Hong Kong.[106] In all these cases, congressional or executive action had been necessary in order to allow people to immigrate or remain in the United States. Such intervention would be necessary in the current crisis.

Justice Department guidelines announced in the immediate aftermath of Tiananmen allowed Chinese students to file for "deferred departure" and stay in the United States for an additional year (until June 5, 1990).[107] "Deferred departure" required applicants to both officially declare unwillingness to return to China and to permanently relinquish the J visa (or other current lawful status), even if that visa had not yet expired.[108] Chinese nationals were understandably afraid to take advantage of this legal recourse for fear of reprisals from the Chinese government once their deferral expired and the United States required them to return home. Should hardliners hold sway over the Chinese government in the post-Tiananmen period and impose a new Cultural Revolution to weed out the ideologically compromised, they would naturally question the loyalty of those who had once sought "deferred departure" status. Seeking asylum was not a realistic option either. Despite the obvious evidence of China's human rights violations, in asylum matters the INS strictly interpreted the "well-founded fear" clause in refugee statute, making it highly unlikely that 40,200 nationals would be able to successfully demonstrate persecution.[109] Members of the congressional subcommittee, then, were determined to come up with a third option, arguing that the United States had a moral obligation to protect those who feared returning home to a communist state resistant to reform.

That option came through HR 2712, the Emergency Chinese Immigration Relief Act of 1989, a bill introduced on June 21 by Rep. Nancy Pelosi, and cosponsored by a remarkable 259 members of Congress, which waived the two-year home country residence requirement for Chinese with expired J visas. As the bill made its way through committee, other features were added: those holding J, F, and M visas were granted work authorization so they would not become public charges in the United States; and the Justice Department was instructed to issue notices of visa expiration to allow visa holders to renew their lawful status in a timely fashion, so that a lapse in status would not put them on the administrative track toward deportation. The most controversial addition to the bill required giving "careful consideration" to applicants who expressed fear of persecution for refusal to adhere to China's "one couple, one child" family-planning policy. A refusal to abort a fetus or to be sterilized was to be considered a "well-founded fear" of political persecution, making one immediately eligible for asylum or some other protected status.[110]

On November 19, HR 2712 passed the House with a vote of 403 to 0 and passed the Senate by voice vote the following day. Fifty-five members of the Senate signed a letter urging the president to place the plight of the Chinese students ahead of Sino-American relations: "Just as you have celebrated the courage of the peoples of Eastern Europe in their recent democratic successes, we ask only that you support the students of China in their continuing struggle."[111] Some very prominent members of Congress and the administration opposed the bill, among them Senator Alan K. Simpson, who had also opposed an expansion of the refugee quota to accommodate the Soviet Jews.[112] Top officials in the State Department and the National Security Council also urged the president to veto the bill, warning that it would affect educational, scholarly, and cultural exchanges and "curtail the flow of Western and American ideas to China."[113] These officials had legitimate reasons for concern: the Chinese had suspended the Fulbright Program in June and were allowing very few of their scholars to travel to the United States as part of the Visitor Exchange Program for fear that they might defect. One East Asian specialist warned the administration that punitive actions against China would encourage "conservative, isolationist, and xenophobic trends."[114]

The US news media, in turn, was generally supportive of congressional measures to protect the Chinese students. Conservative and liberal editorialists were surprisingly in sync on this one issue. "[The Chinese students] represent the best and the brightest minds China has to offer," wrote Carl Shusterman in the *Christian Science Monitor*. "The US recently granted amnesty to over three million illegal aliens [through the 1986 Immigration Act]. Why not do the same for a relative handful of students who one day may be the leaders of a democratic China?"[115] Syndicated columnist Cal Thomas wrote: "Many of these Chinese students in America are converts to democracy from doctrinaire communism. If they admire the ideals of democracy, why should our democratic government put them back in the clutches of a system that would embrace them like Venus flytraps?"[116] Anticipating Bush's veto of 2721, Mary McGrory of the *Washington Post* wrote:

If [Bush] pocket vetoes [2721] ... he will be saying the following: It is okay to use bloody force against peaceful dissidents; it is more important to keep the US-Chinese student exchange program alive than to keep students alive; Geopolitics is more important than human rights; [d]ouble standards and hypocrisy are okay on human rights; [j]ust because we won't tolerate any crackdown by the Soviet Union on peaceful dissidents doesn't mean we won't put up with it from the Chinese.[117]

Thomas Oliphant of the *Boston Globe* was especially critical: "The only thing that has changed since June [in China] is that Bush has become China's puppet, and the ancient totalitarians must smile privately as they pull his strings."[118]

Americans—and Chinese nationals in the United States—wrote the White House to express support for the bill. College and university faculty wrote poignant appeals on behalf of their Chinese graduate students. Seventeen university presidents, including those of Cornell, Yale, and the University of Texas at Austin, signed a letter in support of the bill.[119] The Independent Federation of Chinese Students and Scholars (IFCSS) issued a press release stating, "If President Bush does not sign the bill, he will only be helping Beijing extend its repression tactics to the United States."[120] Perhaps the most poignant letter came from a Chinese national who drew on earlier PRC history to remind the president what happened to idealists who mistakenly believed they could carve out a place for themselves in the communist bureaucracy:

When the Communist Party came to power in China, thousands of scholars returned with the dream of building their motherland into a prosperous and peace-loving nation. You must have heard of some of them, who declined the offer of excellent positions here in the United States and went home. However, it was exactly the same group of people that ended up in prison or labor reform farms. Many of them committed suicide and some even brought their families along when leaving this world. Their only crime was to tell the truth. Today, among the 40,000 Chinese students in the United States, many of us are the children of these victims, but I can assure you, Mr. President, that we still love our country. The tragic experiences of our families have by no means destroyed our sense of duty, because it is the wish of several generations to make the most populous country in the world a democracy, where people live in dignity and abundance, speak without fear and move without restriction, and where the government cares for its own young and patriotism is no longer a crime.[121]

Despite these many appeals, the president considered 2721 a "congressional micromanagement of foreign policy" and chose to take no action on the bill by exercising the pocket veto.[122] From June 1989 to January 1990 the president vetoed four other bills relating to China or had their sanctions portions waived.[123]

An override of Bush's veto became a very real possibility in the early months of 1990. Upon reconvening in January, the Senate held a new round of hearings on the plight of Chinese students.[124] Senators once again expressed concern that the president seemed more preoccupied with smoothing over Sino-American relations than protesting human rights violations. Only a month earlier, as a US delegation feted Chinese leaders at a banquet, Beijing police were beating and arresting students in front of the Ministry of Radio, Film, and Television. The incident elicited no official protest from the White House. Nor did the administration protest the new Chinese ordinances that increased surveillance on university campuses, prohibited demonstrations, restricted the actions of journalists and publishers, and deputized army troops as police officers.[125] Alan K. Simpson chastised his colleagues for wanting to override the presidential veto: "Some seem more interested in using [2172] as a blunt cudgel against the administration than in establishing a rational and sensible foreign policy toward China." It did not serve American interests to alienate the Chinese, he argued, because their cooperation was necessary if the United States was to address important issues such as nuclear proliferation and global warming.[126] There was emerging consensus, however, that an override was necessary if only for symbolism. As Senator Paul Simon remarked: "It is a signal to the administration that we want a stronger, firmer stance in siding with those who stand for freedom in China." In the House, Nancy Pelosi said: "I believe the bill is necessary for us to maintain our own integrity in support of the principles on which our republic was founded."[127]

The White House considered the potential override a challenge to presidential authority on all issues relating to China. While the Senate eventually voted not to follow the House's lead, the White House announced a surprising shift in policy on April 11, 1990—Executive Order 12711—which implemented some of the key features of 2721. In some ways the executive order was even more generous than the Emergency Relief Act: it offered a wider class of Chinese nationals the opportunity to "defer departure" and work in the United States (until January 1, 1994); and it offered qualified applicants the opportunity to apply for permanent residency.[128] Rather than single out China as the sole country engaged in coercive population control measures, the executive order extended protection to foreign nationals fleeing such practices in any country. "My actions today accomplish the laudable objectives of Congress in passing HR 2712 while preserving my ability to manage foreign relations," said President Bush in the official announcement.[129]

The executive order did little to assuage the anxieties of Chinese nationals concerned about their long-term safety. Their fears were validated when a Chinese embassy official in Washington, DC, defected and substantiated his petition for asylum by making public internal government documents on the monitoring and intimidation of Chinese students in the United States.[130] House subcommittees on human rights and on Asian and Pacific affairs met jointly to review the compelling evidence that Chinese officials, or their agents, had systematically threatened students through phone calls, home visits from consular officials, and the videotaping of meetings and gatherings.[131] The evidence showed that the Ministry of State Security recruited loyal, progovernment students to keep tabs on their classmates and to intervene in student activities. Embassy officials also kept detailed reports on those branded "enemies of the Chinese people" and punished them by withholding scholarships, denying passports, and refusing their relatives the opportunity to travel.

In light of these developments, members of Congress considered further penalties against China, citing the Solarz amendment to the Arms Control Export Act as one possibility, which prohibited the sale of arms to any foreign government that harassed people in the United States.[132] At the hearings, one State Department official expressed doubts that Chinese intimidation was sufficiently egregious to warrant invoking the Solarz amendment. Stephen Solarz, the author of the amendment, responded:

I have to tell you that I consider your testimony to be shocking and utterly unrelated to the body of evidence and information we have received in executive session earlier today. Senator McCarthy used to say that if something walks like a duck, talks like a duck, and looks like a duck, it is a duck. This appears to be a duck to everybody but those who seem to be more interested in kowtowing to China than in calling a spade a spade.[133]

Referring back to Heping Shi's testimony that Chinese officials had threatened his wife in Beijing, Solarz responded, "People are not usually driven to commit suicide, let alone kill their children, simply because of a gentle knock on their door or a routine inquiry on the phone."[134] "What I see here is two things," said Solarz, "a systematic effort on [China's] part to intimidate people and a determination on the part of the State Department not to invoke this amendment." Solarz then threatened to further amend the Jackson-Vanik amendment so that China's "most favored nation" trading status would be contingent not only on freedom of immigration but also on the nonintimidation of nationals.[135]

Despite the strong language in congressional testimony, China was never denied "most favored nation" trading status. Over the next two years, dozens of bills were introduced in both houses of Congress to offer more guarantees to Chinese nationals in the United States; the majority were referred to committee, where they promptly died. In 1992, Congress finally passed legislation to normalize the status of those Chinese nationals who had been granted "deferred enforced departure" (DED). Approximately fifty-three thousand Chinese nationals acquired permanent residency as a result of the various policies designed during 1989–1992 to offer them protection.[136]

In 2014, on the twenty-fifth anniversary of the June 4 bloodshed, the subject of Tiananmen remained taboo in China. The discussion of the event—even the mention of the date—was prohibited on the Internet, which was strictly monitored by China's cyber police. Only in Hong Kong did students stage an annual demonstration at Victoria Park in memory of the violent crackdown. The memory also remains alive in the United States. The Congressional Human Rights Commission has routinely acknowledged the anniversary of the massacre; and survivors of Tiananmen spoke before the commission—and a televised American audience—on both the twentieth and twenty-fifth anniversaries. "The Chinese leadership hoped that the world would soon forget the Tiananmen Square massacre," said Rep. Tom Lantos in 2006. "Our job in Congress is to ensure that we never forget those who lost their lives in Tiananmen Square that day or the pro-democracy cause for which they fought."[137]

In the years following Tiananmen, refugee admissions from China remained low. From 1990 to 1997, only five Chinese applicants received refugee status.[138] A decade later refugee admissions had increased only slightly: 423 refugees entered during the period 2004 to 2013. However, the PRC was the top source country for all asylum petitions in the United States.[139] Several of the best-known student leaders of the Tiananmen generation eventually found refuge in the United States. Wei Jingsheng, China's best-known dissident, spent eight years in prison before the Clinton administration negotiated to have him released and brought to the United States in 1997.[140] Wang Dan spent nine years in prison before the state released him for medical reasons and exiled him to the United States; he earned his doctorate at Harvard and now teaches in Taiwan.[141] Liu Gang sought asylum in the United States in 1995, after serving six years in prison for "counterrevolutionary activities"; he now works on Wall Street. Xiong Yan sought asylum in 1992, after serving nineteen months in prison; he converted to Christianity, became an army chaplain, and served a tour in Iraq. Zhou Fengsuo also fled China in 1995; he, too, converted to Christianity, pursued a career in finance, and became the cofounder of Humanitarian China, a group that promotes civil society in China and raises money for Chinese political prisoners. Chai Ling escaped to France after hiding for ten months following the crackdown; she eventually made her way to the United States, earned a degree from Harvard Business School, founded an Internet company, and created All Girls Allowed, an advocacy group that campaigns against restrictive family-planning policies in China.[142]

"Is One Kind of Refugee from Communist Dictatorship, or Any Dictatorship for That Matter, More Worthy Than Another?"

In 1991, President George H. W. Bush proclaimed October 30 as "Refugee Day" to encourage Americans to reflect on the nation's immigrant heritage and on American responsibilities to the displaced of the world. "Because the refugee crisis is primarily the result of systematic government repressions and bitter civil strife in some regions of the world," said the presidential proclamation, "the United States will continue to promote respect for human rights and the rule of law, as well as the peaceful resolution of conflicts."[143] To achieve these ends, the Bush, and later the Clinton, administration focused on economic development—especially through the negotiation of free trade agreements—which the White House hoped would foster the economic growth and geopolitical stability necessary to prevent internal displacement and cross-border migration. Policymakers believed that economic development was a realistic strategy for stemming migration over the long term, even if it stimulated migration in the short term by raising expectations and enhancing the ability to travel.

During the final years of the Cold War, the number of refugees worldwide doubled from 7,300,000 to 16 million. Eleven million of these refugees were women and children, and most were concentrated in the Near East, Asia, and Africa.[144] As early as 1989, the US Refugee Program resources spent "about twice as much on the ninety-nine percent of refugees who remain[ed] overseas as we [spent] to resettle the refugees admitted each year to the United States."[145] During the 1990s, the United States committed hundreds of millions of dollars to the UNHCR, the World Food Program, the International Committee of the Red Cross, the International Organization for Migration (IOM), and other nongovernmental organizations to assist in the housing, medical care, and material support of refugees and displaced persons around the world.

The Bush and Clinton administrations often clashed with the UNHCR over the US refugee resettlement program, specifically American commitment to the UN principle of *nonrefoulement* (no forced return to dangerous or repressive conditions). The UNHCR, the Organization of African Unity, the Organization of American States, and various nongovernmental organizations generally favored a lenient response to the so-called nonconvention refugees: those who did not meet the strict definition of the term "refugee" outlined by the UN Convention and Protocol but who had fled their homes, had crossed an international border, and were living in refugee-like conditions. The Organization of African Unity, for example, defined a refugee as "every person who, owing to external aggression, occupation, foreign domination, or events seriously disturbing the public order or nationality, is compelled to leave his place of habitual residence in order to seek refuge in another place outside his country of origin or nationality."[146] The 1984 Cartagena Declaration on Refugees, crafted in response to the wars in Central America, also expanded the definition of refugee to include persons who flee their country "because their lives, security or freedom have been threatened by generalized violence, foreign aggression, internal conflicts, massive violations of human rights or other circumstances which have seriously disturbed public order."[147] And the Intergovernmental Committee for Migration (now International Organization for Migration) acknowledged two types of refugees: "political refugees"—persons subjected to persecution and violence—and "displaced refugees"—indirect victims obliged to emigrate because of the destruction of their means of subsistence.[148] In the United States, refugee status was interpreted more narrowly. The Departments of State and Justice regularly rejected the refugee and asylum petitions of individuals who could not meet the "well-founded fear" standard of refugee statute. In the post–Cold War era, the US government increasingly contended that most of those who crossed borders were economic migrants rather than bona fide victims of persecution.

During the first half of 1990s, the overall quota for refugees was never higher than 123,500 (in FY1992), and foreign policy interests continued to influence how the refugee quota was distributed. The reallocation of part of the Southeast Asian quota to the Soviet refugees in 1989 was one early example of the new challenges of interpreting who should be prioritized for admission. An editorial in the *Philadelphia Inquirer* remarked, "It is unsettling to see refugees from one region pitted against those from another vying for the right to live here. . . . This raises an ugly moral question: Is one kind of refugee from communist dictatorship, or any dictatorship for that matter, more worthy than another? Are the Vietnamese, many of whom may have once had links to the United States, somehow less deserving?"[149]

During the 1970s and 1980s, those advocating on behalf of refugees from right-wing dictatorships in Chile, Argentina, El Salvador, and Guatemala had posed similar questions.[150] Nationals from these countries were generally allowed to immigrate through traditional channels if they met the criteria of the US immigration bureaucracy and could financially afford its assorted fees; but refugee or parole status, or asylum, was much more difficult to secure. During the 1980s, for example, Salvadorans and Guatemalans were rarely successful in securing asylum, in spite of the documented human rights abuses in their homelands, and the UNHCR's urging of a more generous response to Salvadorans and other nonconvention refugees.[151] It was the vocal advocacy of concerned Americans—first through protests and civil disobedience, then lobbying, and ultimately through lawsuits—that forced a change in policy toward the Central American asylum seekers of the 1980s.

American responses to the Haitian and Cuban "boat people" of the early 1990s offer compelling examples of the lingering shadow of the Cold War; the difficulties of disentangling political from economic motivations for migration; and the importance of advocacy networks in securing a humanitarian response. Cubans and Haitian both fled political repression, human rights abuses, and economic hardship, but Cuba was an ideological enemy, while Haiti was a longtime ally. The legitimacy of the Haitians' rights to asylum was always contested, while the Cubans' was not. These two case studies demonstrate the importance of advocacy groups in the crafting of refugee and asylum policy, especially when the government is reluctant to offer refuge.

The Haitian and Cuban Boat People

The migration of Haitians in the early 1990s was part of a longer migratory tradition. The political regimes of François "Papa Doc" Duvalier (1956–1971) and his son, Jean-Claude "Baby Doc" Duvalier (1971–1986), had cast into exile tens of thousands of people who sought to escape the intense poverty, political repression, torture, and murder that was a fact of life under the Duvaliers. Unlike other groups fleeing repression, the Haitians were never prioritized for entrance to the United States during the Cold War, either as refugees or as immigrants. Despite the substantially documented record of human rights abuses, the Duvaliers' anticommunist and probusiness orientation made them important US allies in the Caribbean, and few demands were made until ever-escalating migration from Haiti created a crisis for the United States. Because they were fleeing one of the most impoverished nations in the Caribbean, Haitians—like Central Americans—were perceived to be economic immigrants rather than political refugees. Neither refugee status nor parole nor asylum was offered to the Haitians, and only those with financial resources, or with powerful allies, were able to successfully navigate the US immigration bureaucracy. The first documented boatload of Haitian asylum seekers arrived on US shores in September 1963. All twenty-three were denied asylum and deported.[152] The Haitian American population, numbering roughly five thousand in 1960, was not large enough to successfully advocate on their behalf.[153]

Despite the unlikelihood of asylum, Haitians continued to flee the Duvalier regime throughout the 1970s and 1980s. Most of them fled on crudely made crafts, hoping to reach safety in the United States or some nearby country. Many did not survive the crossing. Bodies routinely washed up on Florida's beaches.[154] Those who reached the United States alive were detained in prisons, often waiting months for their asylum hearings. Occasionally, when prisons filled to capacity, the INS released some detainees on bond but offered them no work authorization, thereby forcing them to depend on charity or to work illegally in the service economy (which undermined their case for asylum). Because of the growing backlog of asylum cases, judges ruled quickly to ease the burden on the overcrowded detention system. Asylum applicants were given little time to secure pro bono legal representation or to put together a compelling and substantiated case for asylum. INS records offer an incomplete picture of the number of Haitians who requested asylum in the 1970s. According to one source, between thirty thousand and fifty thousand Haitians fled to the United States during the period 1972 to 1980, but it is unclear how many officially requested asylum. The records only show that less than fifty Haitians received asylum during this period. In FY1981 only five Haitians received asylum.[155]

"Race is undoubtedly a factor in the treatment of the Haitians," said one spokesman for the American Civil Liberties Union. "Why else are Haitians the only nationality being detained by the United States as a matter of policy while their political asylum claims are being determined?"[156] Justice Department officials denied that the Haitians were singled out for detention and exclusion because of their race and poverty. Indeed, as the number of asylum seekers grew in the 1980s, the policy of interdiction, detention, and deportation was extended to several other groups, including those fleeing the civil wars in El Salvador and Guatemala.

Refugee advocates criticized the US government for denying Haitians the right to a fair asylum hearing and deporting them to a society that persecuted them upon return. By 1975, advocates had filed twenty-one lawsuits in federal court to have the courts define the Haitians' rights.[157] Many more cases were filed during the 1980s, including *Haitian Refugee Center v. Civiletti* (1980), which challenged the policy of mass deportation, and *National Council of Churches v. Egan* (1980), which challenged the US government's practice of revoking work authorization while applicants were released on bond. In the most significant ruling, handed down in *Haitian Refugee Center v. Civiletti*, Judge James Lawrence King refuted the government's claim that Haitians were economic immigrants: "The Haitians' economic situation is a political condition," he stated.[158] Judge King chastised the Justice Department for not granting asylum seekers sufficient time to secure legal counsel or to prepare for their hearings:

Those Haitians who came to the United States seeking freedom and justice did not find it. Instead, they were confronted with an

Immigration and Naturalization Service determined to deport them. The decision was made among high INS officials to expel Haitians, despite whatever claims to asylum individual Haitians might have. A Program was set up to accomplish this goal. The Program resulted in wholesale violations of due process and only Haitians were affected.[159]

The experience of Haitian asylum seekers contrasted sharply with that of the Cubans. The 125,000 Cubans expelled by the Castro dictatorship during the six-month Mariel boatlift of 1980 were theoretically eligible, with some exceptions, to remain in the United States and become permanent residents as a result of a series of Cold War legal precedents established over the previous two decades. The Haitians' advocates argued that Haitians should have expanded opportunities to make a case for asylum in the interest of overall fairness. Members of the Carter administration found it difficult to justify the two very different policy responses. Carter, who had made respect for human rights one of the pillars of his foreign policy agenda, was understandably sensitive to domestic and international criticism that, by deporting asylum seekers, the United States was complicit in the human rights abuses of Haitians. In response to criticism, on June 20, 1980, President Carter announced a compromise—a special category called "Cuban-Haitian entrant (status pending)"—that granted a temporary reprieve to the ten thousand Haitians who had arrived during the same period as the Mariel Cubans. This placed the groups on equal legal footing, while the administration evaluated their asylum claims. After four years of limbo, the Justice Department ruled that both the Haitians and Cubans who arrived during 1980 would be allowed to establish permanent residency.[160]

This temporary policy allowed a select number of Haitians—those who had arrived before January 1, 1981—to normalize their status and remain in the United States. It was the first time the US government had granted any large group of Haitians that opportunity. After Ronald Reagan assumed office, however, the policy of proactive interdiction, detention, and removal resumed. In 1981, Reagan signed an accord with Haiti to permit the Coast Guard to interdict Haitians on the high seas and return them to their country. Over the next decade, the Coast Guard intercepted 433 boats and returned 23,551 Haitians to their country; only 28 were allowed to apply for asylum.[161] A lawsuit challenging interdiction, *Haitian Refugee Center v. Garcey* (1986), failed to offer relief because, as the judge ruled, "The interdiction program . . . occurs outside the jurisdiction of the United States."[162]

The Haitian Refugee Center in south Florida once again brought a class action suit against the government, *Louis v. Nelson*, to challenge the discriminatory detention of those Haitian asylum seekers who managed to reach the United States.[163] The attorneys argued that Haitians were more likely to be detained—and for longer periods of time—than other asylum seekers, pending the review and appeal of their cases. A federal district court ruled in favor of the plaintiffs, but the court failed to find that the plaintiffs were incarcerated because of their race or national origin: "The mere fact that more Haitians were detained and kept in detention for longer periods of time than aliens of other nationalities [did] not render the policy discriminatory," said the court. "Regardless of its ultimate impact, the policy was intended to be applied and was in fact applied equally to all similarly situated aliens regardless of their race and/or national origin."[164] As a result of this ruling, 1,771 Haitians were released from detention, but when the Justice Department won its appeal a year later, the court ruled that those apprehended at a border could be detained indefinitely.

These were the policies in place for Haitians as the United States moved into the post–Cold War era. Thousands of refugees from the former Soviet Union and East-Central Europe were accommodated, but Haitians were routinely interdicted, detained, and removed from the United States. As the US Committee for Refugees reported, Haitians faced a presumption of ineligibility that led to politicized practices that made it "next to impossible for even the most deserving of asylum seekers to wend their way through the asylum process successfully."[165]

In December 1990, Jean-Bertrand Aristide, a Roman Catholic priest, became the first popularly elected president in Haiti in the twentieth century, elected with an overwhelming majority of the vote. Aristide instituted a program of modest social and political reform that targeted the institutions most responsible for the repression and exploitation of his countrymen. Perhaps as a sign of the renewed hope of the Haitian people, the boat exodus tapered off for the first time in decades.

Aristide's term in office proved short-lived. In September 1991, a military junta supported by wealthy interests in Haiti removed Aristide from office, forcing him to flee to the United States. A violent repression of the civilian populace began as the junta tried to weed out Aristide supporters. Four hundred Marines were deployed to the US naval base at Guantánamo, Cuba, in case the estimated seven thousand Americans in Haiti needed to be quickly evacuated and relocated.

Haitians again fled their homeland in large numbers, some crossing the border into the Dominican Republic, but many more hoping to reach safe haven in the Haitian American community, which by 1990 stood at 225,000.[166] Within months of the coup, the Coast Guard had rescued thirty-four thousand people at sea.[167] Instead of bringing these Haitians to the United States for proper asylum interviews, the Coast Guard took the refugees to Guantánamo, where they were detained in camps surrounded by barbed wire. After their screening, 10,747 were allowed to pursue asylum claims in the United States.[168]

The George H. W. Bush administration tried to discourage the dangerous sea journeys through broadcasts in Creole on the Voice of America. As it had with the Soviet refuseniks, the administration established an "in-country" refugee registration center, this time at the US embassy in Port-au-Prince, to try to control the migration and facilitate a safer and more orderly departure for a select number of carefully chosen refugees. The Bush administration also tried, through diplomatic channels, to find refuge for the Haitians in other countries in the Caribbean and Central America. When these various efforts failed, Bush issued an executive order on May 24, 1992, known as the Kennebunkport order, calling on the US Coast Guard to resume interdiction.[169] Sadako Ogata, the UN high commissioner for refugees, criticized the administration for failing to offer the Haitians the opportunity to petition for asylum. Bush dismissed such criticisms, once again insisting that most Haitians were economic immigrants rather than political refugees: "Yes, the Statue of Liberty still stands, and we still open our arms under our law to people that are politically oppressed. I will not, because I have sworn to uphold the Constitution, open the doors to economic refugees all over the world. We can't do that."[170] Bush had popular support for this decision: public opinion polls conducted throughout the early 1990s revealed that over half of Americans supported blocking the entrance of Haitians.[171]

Members of Congress had long criticized the interdiction, detention, and deportation policies of the US government as applied to the Haitian and Central American asylum seekers, but in 1990s, the Congressional Black Caucus—forty members by 1994—became especially vocal and influential advocates on Capitol Hill. Months before the Kennebunkport order, Representative Charles Rangel questioned why the Haitians were disproportionately represented among America's deportees. "We ought not to be in a position to be accused of detaining refugees from violence, or worse, returning them to an impending cataclysm from which we have warned our own nationals to flee."[172] Rangel wrote the president to remind him that there were legal options other than asylum to ensure the safety of the Haitian refugees. Temporary protected status, a feature made possible by the recently passed Immigration Act of 1990, for example, would have offered the Haitians the security they sought, allowing them the opportunity to live and work in the United States until conditions in their home country allowed their return.

> I am aware of the argument that relaxation of our historically restrictive policies toward Haitian refugees would invite a flood of boat people. The experience of the seven months of the Aristide government, when few if any Haitian refugees appeared on our shores, is convincing evidence that the overwhelming majority of the population is content to remain in their homeland as long as their lives are not in danger.... But even the appearance of a flood of refugees on our shores should not prevent us from taking humanitarian action. In the interest of liberty, fairness, and compassion, America has made far greater sacrifices in the past.[173]

In public Rangel took a less measured tone, calling US policy "racist and vicious ... anything but humane." He argued that the Haitians would not have been deported if they were European.[174]

> What does it take to convince the administration that a sane person doesn't take a 50-50 chance of dying at sea, as the Haitians have, if his life is not endangered in the place he left behind? The administration's policy has been a failure up to now. It has been mean-spirited and racist. Is the president picking up the phone to help these poor people? This is an emergency.[175]

Likewise, Representative John Conyers called the administration's policy of interdiction "homicide."[176]

Congressmen from South Florida, speaking on behalf of their Haitian Americans constituents, also complained to the president about the disparity in treatment:

> While the policy [of alien interdiction at sea] has existed for some time, [the disparity] was brought forcefully home when a boatload of Haitians and two Cubans was interdicted by the Coast Guard. The

Cubans were taken to the United States, and the Haitians, with the exception of six requiring medical attention, were forced to return to their country. Furthermore, when Haitians do manage to reach this country they are detained for far longer periods than any other nationality before a determination is made on their legal status. This kind of disparity is outrageous and destructive to our South Florida community.... we believe the time has come for a thorough review of this policy with a view toward once and for all eliminating even the perception of discrimination or unequal treatment. The present situation is simply not fair and cannot be allowed to continue.[177]

Administration officials continued to deny the charges of bias and insisted that they were simply enforcing the laws enacted by Congress: "The differing treatment of Haitians and Cubans that you [the south Florida congressmen] allude to in your letter is a reflection of this collection of laws, enacted decades apart, to address different types of problems facing the United States."[178] In response to one of the many letters from Charles Rangel—this one cosigned by thirty-five of his congressional colleagues— the White House told the congressmen that most of the Haitians were not true political refugees. Only a quarter of those interviewed had been found to have claims sufficiently plausible to qualify for full asylum interviews. The administration was working with the UNHCR and the IOM to find temporary safe havens for the Haitians in different countries around the region, but many Haitians, upon hearing that they would be sent to Venezuela or Honduras instead of the United States, opted to return to their homeland, suggesting that their motivations were indeed economic.[179]

Noticeably absent as a signatory in the letter of the south Florida congressmen was Cuban American representative Ileana Ros-Lehtinen, a tireless advocate for the Cuban American community. Though sympathetic to the plight of Haitian immigrants, Ros-Lehtinen and her Cuban American constituents worried that continued comparisons with the Haitians might lead to a change in policy toward the Cubans who fled a communist homeland. In her own letter to the president, Ros-Lehtinen wrote:

I do not think that it is appropriate to compare the thirty-two year reign of communism of Castro's Cuba with the situation in Haiti which celebrated a democratic election. To differentiate between communism and democracy is not discrimination but rather it is a political distinction of great ramifications. There are no liberties whatsoever in Cuba: no freedom of expression, of assembly, of practicing one's religion, of the press. Every aspect of a person's life is closely monitored by the Cuban communist regime: where one studies, works, lives.[180]

Instead she proposed that the administration adopt "a more humane immigration policy" that would give Haitians sufficient time "under more normal conditions to fully explain why they are victims of political persecutions and why they should, therefore, not be returned to Haiti."

The Bush administration agreed with her distinction between the two groups but not her recommendation. A Justice Department official responded: "I appreciate your concern over the oftentimes superficial comparison of the handling of Cubans and Haitians without reference to differences provided under the law and factual differences in our relationships with the two countries."[181] However, he assured Ros-Lehtinen that no revisions of immigration policy were necessary; the officers who interviewed Haitians were well trained and used a revised—and lengthier—series of questions to ascertain whether there was a "credible fear" that warranted a full asylum hearing. The INS had instituted in 1990 a new corps of professionally trained asylum officers, who were versed in international relations and law, and who had access to a special documentation center with continually updated information on country conditions and human rights. These officers were capable of making informed assessments on asylum matters, he said.[182]

The officers interviewing Haitians interdicted at sea presumably had this more specialized training, but refugee advocates wondered if those traumatized by political violence had the emotional wherewithal to competently answer the questions posed to them by uniformed agents, few of whom were native speakers of Creole. As Charles Rangel put it:

It's too much to expect a terrified and sick refugee who does not speak English to explain to the satisfaction of a Coast Guard officer why he should be considered a political rather than economic refugee, or why he should be allowed to come to the United States to press his case. We are not talking about the law. We are talking about compassion. We are talking about what should be our proper response to people who undertake to escape from their homeland knowing that fifty percent of them will die in the attempt.[183]

The Haitian American population in the United States did not have as organized or effective an ethnic lobby as the Cubans, the Soviet Jews, and other Cold War immigrant groups, in part because so many in this community were first-generation, non-English-speaking immigrants, were poor, or lacked permanent immigration status. The Haitians also faced considerable antipathy from an American public that viewed them as a burden on society because of their poverty, unskilled labor, and lack of English. Some Americans even viewed them as carriers of the AIDS virus.[184] Despite these obstacles, Haitians and their advocates did create a number of vital organizations that provided opportunities for networking, support, and social services. Many of these organizations became vocal and persistent critics of US policy. The Haitian-American Democratic Club of Miami, for example, wrote the White House to complain of the "great double standard" with regards to Haitian applicants who must "face rules that change continually."[185] On the eve of the 1992 New York presidential primary, a Brooklyn-based group, Haitian Enforcement Against Racism, organized a demonstration in Times Square, attended by thousands, to remind the presidential candidates about the plight of Haiti and its refugees.[186] Criticism of the Bush administration intensified.[187] On September 9, 1992, NAACP executive director Benjamin L. Hooks, TransAfrica executive director Randall Robinson, and tennis star Arthur Ashe led protesters down Pennsylvania Avenue in a highly publicized march; among the 650 protesters were District mayor Sharon Pratt Kelly, several members of the Congressional Black Caucus, Hyman Bookbinder, the retired president of the American Jewish Committee, and eighty-two-year-old dancer-choreographer Katherine Dunham, who had staged a forty-five-day hunger strike to protest the forced repatriation of Haitian refugees.[188] Ninety-five of the protesters, including Ashe, were arrested. Throughout the early 1990s *Washington Post* columnist William Raspberry also used his syndicated column to discuss Haiti and its refugees.

Officials of the Departments of State and Justice continued to dispute the charges made against them. At press conferences and in interviews, officials assured concerned Americans that the "repatriation" of Haitians was intended to save lives; that the returnees were safe once they arrived home; and that opportunities for an orderly departure from Haiti and a legal entrance to the United States were still available. In one letter to the Maryknoll religious order, Brunson McKinley, a Refugee Program official, assured his Catholic critics that Haitians could easily—and safely—approach the refugee processing center at the US embassy in Port-au-Prince, noting that even members of President Aristide's personal staff had applied for refugee status without interference from the Haitian authorities.[189]

> In our contacts with over 2,000 returnees since early February, we have encountered no evidence of mistreatment connected with repatriation. . . . There has been some criticism that our policy is racist. This is not true. . . . some 140,000 Haitians have been given legal status here in the past ten years. Only four countries sent more of their citizens here in that period. More Haitians than Cubans came in, despite Cuba's much larger population. . . . In sum, we believe that a fair and comprehensive process is in place.[190]

Contrary to these assurances, there was reason for Haitians to fear a forced return to their homeland. When returnees arrived in Port-au-Prince, US officials turned over the ships' manifests with the names, ages, and hometowns of each returnee, who were then fingerprinted, questioned, and photographed by uniformed officers of Haitian armed forces.[191] Human rights groups compiled lists of Haitians who upon return to their country were arrested, abducted, raped, tortured, mutilated, and murdered.[192]

The lawsuits continued. In July 1992, refugee advocates secured a partial victory when a federal appeals court put a temporary halt on the forced repatriations: "The plain language of section 243(h)(1) of the Immigration and Nationality Act clearly states that the United States may not return aliens to their persecutors, no matter where in the world those actions are taken."[193] A year later, however, in *Sale vs. Haitian Centers Council*, the US Supreme Court overturned the ruling, stating that neither §243(h)(1) of the Immigration and Nationality Act of 1952 nor Article 33 of the United Nations Convention Relating to the Status of Refugees limited the president's power to repatriate undocumented aliens intercepted on the high seas:

> It is perfectly clear that 8 USC section 1182(f) grants the President ample power to establish a naval blockade that would simply deny illegal Haitian migrants the ability to disembark on our shores. Whether the President's chosen method of preventing the "attempted mass migration" of thousands of Haitians . . . poses a

greater risk of harm to Haitians who might otherwise face a long
and dangerous return voyage, is irrelevant to the scope of his authority to take action that neither the Convention nor the statute
clearly prohibits.[194]

As the courts deliberated on the legality of interdiction, detention,
and deportation, the human rights situation in Haiti further deteriorated.
Congressional hearings addressed the ongoing state-sponsored brutality
against Aristide supporters. The Haitian advocacy network tried to influence the policies of the newly elected president, William Jefferson Clinton,
who had called Bush's policy callous and immoral while he was on the
campaign trail. The UNHCR, the Carnegie Endowment for Peace, and
the Inter-American Commission on Human Rights (of the OAS), among
other institutions, urged the new president to honor the principle of *nonrefoulement*, and presented him with their recommendations for dealing
with the refugee crisis.[195] Shortly after Clinton took office, the Reverend
Jesse Jackson led over five thousand people in a peaceful march through
Miami's Little Haiti to remind Clinton of his campaign pledge to give
temporary protection to Haitian refugees.[196] A year later, when little had
changed, the protests escalated. Dozens of politicians and advocates
were arrested for civil disobedience, including Neil Abercrombie, Alcee
Hastings, Kweisi Mfume, and Maxine Waters. Randall Robinson staged
a twenty-three-day hunger strike to protest the treatment of Haitian refugees.[197] When the courts failed to halt discriminatory practices, members
of the Congressional Black Caucus cosponsored bills to stop the interdiction of Haitians, to grant temporary protected status, and to impose economic sanctions on Haiti.[198]

Once in the White House, Clinton bought into the rumors that a
"huge, uncontrollable invasion of economic refugees" loomed on the horizon,[199] and ordered Coast Guard cutters and navy vessels to intercept
and return any Haitian craft destined for the United States. It was Clinton
administration officials who appeared before the Supreme Court to argue
in favor of interdiction in *Sales v. Haitian Centers Council*.[200] Thousands of
Haitians were detained in Guantánamo and at the Krome Detention facility in south Florida, including 158 Haitians whose asylum was revoked
when they were found to have AIDS.[201] In many cases, the detainees had
families and friends willing to assist them financially while they waited
for their asylum hearings, but the bail bonds were set unreasonably

high, presumably to prevent the detainees from disappearing into the service economy. A number of status adjustments or accommodations might have been explored by the Clinton administration including temporary protected status (TPS)—or even UNHCR safe-haven sites within Haiti—but the administration focused, instead, on restoring Aristide to office, hoping that political stability might curb migration and the need for asylum.[202]

Asylum approvals rates did increase temporarily in FY1994—from 5 percent to 30 percent—in part because of a temporary suspension in the policy of interdiction. Under pressure from the UNHCR, the Clinton administration agreed to give Haitians more opportunities to petition for asylum. Clinton assured Sadako Ogata, the UN high commissioner for refugees, that his administration would establish an "internationally credible system of refugee treatment."[203] The hospital ship USNS *Comfort*, moored off the coast Kingston, Jamaica, became a screening center for Haitian refugees. The administration also negotiated temporary safe havens in Suriname, Belize, and several other countries. According to one State Department official, the relocation to other countries forced Haitians to decide "whether the need for protection or the desire to immigrate [to the United States was] the primary motivation [for migration]."[204] The offshore screening of Haitians did not last long, however. According to Ogata, "The numbers awaiting interviews grew too rapidly, and many wound up being taken to Guantánamo. Because of the continuing political instability in Haiti and the proximity of affluent America across the sea, the mixed Haitian migration and asylum-seeking issue persisted through the decade and even beyond."[205]

On October 14, 1994, Jean-Bertrand Aristide was finally able to return to his country to complete the rest of his presidential term. The 4,198 Haitians still held in Guantánamo voluntarily returned to their homeland. With Aristide back in office, the Clinton administration reinstated the policy of interdiction. Over 67,000 Haitians had been interdicted at sea from 1991 to 1994; over the next two decades, the number of interdictions decreased, ranging from a low of 288 (1997) to a high of 3,229 (2004).[206]

Between 1990 and 2000, only 6,065 Haitians received asylum in the United States (see table 1.2), and 6,866 were admitted as refugees (see table 1.3).[207] The Congressional Black Caucus tried to facilitate other possibilities for permanent residency. When the 1997 Nicaraguan

**Table 1.2 Haitians Granted Asylum
by Asylum Officers, 1990–2000**

Fiscal year	Arrivals
1990	3
1991	1
1992	116
1993	626
1994	1,054
1995	746
1996	1,485
1997	699
1998	394
1999	187
2000	754

Source: Department of Homeland Security,
Fiscal Year 2000 Statistical Yearbook,
http://www.dhs.gov/publication/fiscal-year-
2000-statistical-yearbook-refugeesasylees.

Adjustment and Central American Relief Act excluded Haitians from the normalization of status offered to undocumented Central Americans, the CBC introduced—and Congress passed—the 1998 Haitian Refugee Immigration Fairness Act, which allowed Haitian nationals (and their spouses and minor-age children) to become permanent residents if they had requested asylum or had been paroled into the United States before December 31, 1995.[208]

The Haitian refugee experience in the early 1990s contrasted sharply with that of the Cuban *balseros* (those who traveled on *balsas* or rafts) of the same period. Cubans had long been beneficiaries of a parole, refugee, and asylum policy that privileged those who fled communist states. The Cuban Adjustment Act, passed by Congress in 1966, allowed Cubans paroled into the United States to acquire permanent residency after living in the United States for one year. Over the next few decades, a liberal interpretation of this adjustment act allowed even those who arrived in the United States without authorization to normalize their status relatively quickly. The controversy surrounding the Mariel boatlift of 1980 marked the first time the Cubans' claims to refugee status were challenged.[209] A decade later, when

Table 1.3 Haitian Refugee Arrivals
by Fiscal Year, 1990–2000

Fiscal year	Total arrivals
1990	—
1991	—
1992	54
1993	1,307
1994	3,766
1995	1,485
1996	39
1997	75
1998	—
1999	91
2000	49

Source: Department of Homeland Security, Fiscal Year 2000 Statistical Yearbook, http://www.dhs.gov/publication/fiscal-year-2000-statistical-yearbook-refugeesasylees.

Cuban *balseros* once again took to the seas in large numbers, Americans again questioned whether politics and not economics were the true drivers of Cuban migration.

Cuba experienced the worst economic crisis of the Castro era in the wake of the ideological, economic, and political restructuring of the Soviet Union. The decentralization in economic decision-making in the Soviet Union led to disruptions in the production and delivery of goods, and ultimately led to critical shortages in oil, food, and other basic necessities in client states like Cuba.[210] Living conditions on the island became desperate. One expert at the Council on Foreign Relations, writing about the "breathtaking pace" of Cuba's "economic disintegration," predicted that it was only a matter of time before Cuban communism collapsed.[211] Dissident groups on the island called for economic and democratic reforms, which in turn led to a violent government crackdown that fueled the popular disaffection. In 1992, Congress, responding to an influential Cuban American lobby that wished to hasten the Castro government's collapse, passed the Cuban Democracy Act to increase the economic pressure on the island.[212]

The clandestine migration of Cubans across the Florida Straits had been a small but regular feature of life for three decades, but the numbers increased dramatically as a result of these political and economic developments. In one eight-month period—January 1 to August 15, 1994—the US Coast Guard rescued more than 6,200 *balseros* (up from 467 in 1990).[213] After a series of antigovernment demonstrations in Havana turned violent, an angry Fidel Castro announced on August 13 that his government would no longer put obstacles in the way of people who wished to leave the island. Following Castro's announcement, thousands of Cubans set off on homemade rafts from Cuba's beaches and ports trying to reach the United States. As the Castro government had done so many times in the past, it used emigration as a means of exporting dissent.

Anticipating another Mariel boatlift, the Clinton administration instructed the US Coast Guard to transport any *balseros* to the Guantánamo naval base in Cuba, where they would have to remain until they requested repatriation to Cuba or sought immigration to a third country. This constituted a stunning reversal in policy. Over the previous three decades, Cubans who had arrived on US shores without authorization had been released to family, friends, or sponsors while their paperwork was processed, and most were able to normalize their immigration status quickly. Attorney General Janet Reno explained Clinton's new policy at a press conference: "The most important point right now is not to play into Castro's game, not let him dupe us as he did in 1980, but address the issue through legal immigration and right now ensure safety and protection for those who would try to cross the Straits."[214] The announcement had popular support: a Gallup / CNN / *USA Today* poll revealed that an overwhelming 91 percent of Americans believed that the United States should not treat Cuban refugees more favorably than citizens of other countries.[215] The Guantánamo naval base was quickly refitted to house up to forty thousand Cubans in addition to the thousands of Haitians already waiting for asylum hearings.

When the announcement failed to discourage the boat traffic from Cuba, the Clinton administration increased its economic pressure on the Castro government, prohibiting Cuban Americans from sending remittances to their relatives on the island, so as to sever one of the Castro government's remaining economic lifelines. The boat traffic continued, however. The Coast Guard intercepted thirty-six thousand *balseros* during one four-week period in 1994.[216]

In order to resolve the crisis, representatives from both countries began meeting in New York, Washington, and Havana beginning in September

1994. The meetings culminated in the immigration accord of 1995. Under the terms of the new accords, the Cuban government agreed to actively discourage boat traffic to the United States, and gave assurances that there would be no retaliation against those *balseros* who opted to return to Cuba. The United States, in turn, agreed to admit up to twenty thousand Cuban immigrants per year (in addition to a special visa lottery of five thousand per year). When the accords were announced, over one thousand Cuban detainees at Guantánamo agreed to return to their homeland.

Arguing that the Clinton administration was coercing the Cubans to "voluntarily" repatriate, Cuban Americans in south Florida brought a class action suit against the federal government, *Cuban American Bar Association v. Warren Christopher.* Like the lawsuit *Haitian Refugee Center v. Christopher* (1995) the plaintiffs argued that the United States violated the Cuban detainees' right to due process including a meaningful access to counsel. The US Court of Appeals for the Eleventh Circuit expressed sympathy for the detainees but ultimately ruled that they "did not hold cognizable legal rights under the US Constitution, domestic statutory law, or international law, since they were not within, or at the borders of, the United States."[217]

The Clinton administration did allow a select few to enter the United States: minors (and their parents), the elderly, the infirm, and the pregnant. The rest were told that they would remain in Guantánamo until they agreed to repatriate to Cuba, which most refused to do. Over the next eighteen months, the administration tried to negotiate the Cubans' migration to a third country, with limited success. When the indefinite detention of the Cubans proved to be financially and ethically untenable, the administration quietly paroled the remaining twenty-one thousand Cuban detainees into the United States, counting their numbers against the agreed-upon twenty-thousand quota over the next three years. Only the mentally ill and those with criminal histories were repatriated.

In the wake of the 1994 US-Cuba immigration accords, US policy toward unauthorized Cuban migration became known as the "wet foot / dry foot" policy: Cubans interdicted at sea were said to have "wet feet" and were returned to Cuba unless interviews aboard the Coast Guard cutters demonstrated a credible asylum claim that warranted a full asylum hearing in the United States. Those who made it to US territory were said to have "dry feet" and were offered a one-year extendable parole, after which they could apply for permanent residency. Hoping to take advantage of this policy, Cubans traveling to Mexico to cross the US-Mexico border increased in number over the next two decades; but unlike their Mexican and Central American counterparts who were detained and deported, Cubans were generally allowed to enter the United States and become permanent residents. Their countrymen traveling through more traditional channels— namely, the visa program negotiated in the 1995 accord—also found their admission expedited. Yet more programs were created to facilitate Cuban migration: in 2006, the Department of Homeland Security established the Cuban Medical Professional Parole Program to allow Cubans doctors and other healthcare professionals working in third countries to apply for parole at a US embassy or consulate; and in 2007, the DHS created the Cuban Family Reunification Parole Program to allow US citizens and permanent residents to apply for parole for their family members living in Cuba.[218]

Critics of the anachronistic "wet foot / dry foot" policy frequently called for its repeal in the interest of fairness and consistency. No other immigrant or refugee group had benefited from such generosity, they argued, despite the numerous compelling humanitarian crises worldwide. The Cuban government had also long criticized the policy for enticing Cubans to risk their lives to reach the United States. Following the normalization of diplomatic relations in 2016, the termination of the program seemed inevitable. Tens of thousands of Cubans quickly traveled to Central and South American countries, hoping to undertake the overland journey to the United States before the Obama administration closed the door to unauthorized Cuban migration once and for all.

In January 2017, a week before leaving office, President Obama announced the termination of the "wet foot / dry foot" policy and the special parole program for Cuban doctors and healthcare professionals. Unauthorized Cuban nationals were now subject to expedited removal, like other unauthorized immigrants, and by mid-February, 680 Cubans had been deported to their homeland. While the Cuban Family Reunification Parole Program remained in effect, applications would be henceforth evaluated on a case-by-case basis. Cubans' privileged status in US immigration policy had ended, and along with it the last vestiges of Cold War refugee policy. The fact that this privileged status had lasted for so many decades demonstrated the reach of the politically influential Cuban American community, with its high voter participation rate and vocal representation in Congress.

Back in October 1994, a Gallup/CCFR survey had revealed that 72 percent of Americans interviewed considered the "large numbers of immigrants and refugees coming to the United States" as one of the most critical issues facing the country.[219] The case studies in this chapter illustrate the type of advocacy and governmental action that would be necessary to carve out a space for refugees and asylum seekers in a society increasingly unsympathetic toward immigrants. The US Committee for Refugees offered perhaps the most eloquent rationale for advocacy:

> Refugees and asylum seekers lack a natural constituency in the United States. They cannot vote, and their numbers are small; they are often poor and not well educated. And the American people are not well informed about refugees, the conditions that produce them, and how they differ from other immigrants.[220]

In the decades to come, the executive and legislative branches of government would become increasingly concerned with immigration enforcement, and it would fall on refugee advocates to suggest alternative possibilities.

2

US Refugee Policy in the Age of Genocide

IN DECEMBER 1948, in response to one of the worst mass murders of the twentieth century, the United Nations General Assembly passed the Convention on the Prevention and Punishment of the Crime of Genocide.[1] Raphael Lemkin, a lawyer of Polish-Jewish ancestry, had coined the term *genocide* in 1944, to describe the Nazi government's systematic slaughter of the Jews during World War II. Prior to 1944 there was no word for such actions in any language.[2] Lemkin sought to distinguish genocide from classic war crimes that occurred on the battlefield and during military occupation—and to codify them in international law—to hold states accountable for atrocities committed during war and peace.[3] The International Military Tribunal at Nuremberg in 1945 charged the Nazis with "crimes against humanity," but lawyers at the hearings also used the term "genocide," reflecting the uneasy conflation of the two terms that would persist over the next few decades. The term *genocide* would not have a specific legal meaning until the UN Convention of 1948.

Article II of the UN convention defined genocide as

> any of the following acts committed with intent to destroy, in whole or in part, a national, ethnical, racial or religious group, as such: killing members of the group; causing serious bodily or mental harm to members of the group; deliberately inflicting on the groups conditions of life, calculated to bring about its physical destruction in whole or in part; imposing measures intended to prevent births within the group; [and] forcibly transferring children of the group to another group.[4]

Despite the attempt to standardize a definition, the nations that criminalized genocide questioned, interpreted, and adjusted the legal language according to their own priorities, often resulting in tepid and inconsistent responses to genocide from the international community.[5]

The United States was one of the forty-one original signatories to the convention. Constitutional law required the advice and consent of two-thirds of the Senate, and members of the Senate were less enthusiastic about the convention. Opponents of ratification on Capitol Hill, influenced largely by the American Bar Association, expressed concern about the document's legal language. What actions constituted "intent to destroy," they asked? What numbers constituted a "partial" destruction of a group? And what types of events or actions might trigger a preventive or punitive response from the international community? Opponents also expressed concern that ratification might encourage international adversaries to make charges against the United States; or even leave the United States vulnerable to claims from American Indians or racial minority groups. President Truman urged his colleagues to work past these concerns and ratify the treaty because the United States had "long been a symbol of freedom and democratic progress to peoples less favored."[6] Despite significant popular support for ratification, the Senate failed to ratify the treaty in 1949.

Calling the Senate's failure to ratify the convention a "national shame," William Proxmire became a tireless champion of ratification. For nineteen of his twenty-two years in the Senate, Proxmire began every morning with a speech on the floor of the Senate chambers—3,211 original speeches in all (oftentimes before an empty gallery)—in support of ratification.[7] In February 1986, a few years before Proxmire officially retired, his Senate colleagues finally ratified the treaty with a vote of eighty-three to eleven, making the United States the ninety-eighth nation to support the international agreement. (Ironically, Cambodia, Guatemala, and Rwanda, countries that enacted their own genocidal campaigns in the final decades of the twentieth century, acceded long before the United States.) Senate ratification listed several "reservations" that imposed limitations on the enforcement of the treaty: the Senate affirmed the supremacy of the US Constitution over the treaty's provisions and required US consent "before any dispute to which the United States is a party may be submitted to the jurisdiction of the International Court of Justice." The Senate also listed several "understandings" that further limited the scope and definition of terms such as "intent," "mental harm," "armed conflict," and "extradition," thus undermining the enforcement of the treaty.[8]

Ratification required implementing legislation on the domestic front, so the following year, the bill popularly known as the "Proxmire Act"—the Genocide Convention Implementation Act of 1987 (PL 100-606)—brought US law in line with the international treaty by imposing the penalty of death or up to life in prison (and a fine of not more than one million dollars) on individuals who committed or attempted to commit genocide.[9] At the congressional hearings, opponents once again complained that the law would make the United States vulnerable to charges from domestic groups and from the international community. Representing the conservative Liberty Lobby, Trisha Katson argued:

The United States has no business charging other nations with genocide since it has been guilty of sanctioning by law the killing of millions of unborn children; committing genocide against the American Indians; funding genocidal communist regimes; building up Israel's powerful war machine against the Palestinians, and aiding in other genocidal activities through its meddling internationalistic foreign policy. Implementing legislation will set in motion the machinery to try Americans before a world court, in our view, without their constitutional rights of due process. This bill means a great bonanza for lawyers and increased litigation which will tie up the court system at the expense of the American people.[10]

By 1986, this was a minority position, however. Testimony at the hearings generally affirmed the belief that genocide was not likely to take place within the borders of the United States but that action was necessary nonetheless, as a "symbolic act," underscoring "our role of leadership in the free world on behalf of the cause of human rights."[11] Proxmire explained why it was important for the United States to take "definitive action" on this issue:

Some members of Congress say: forget it. It's unnecessary. They argue [genocide] cannot happen here. Well, maybe it will never happen here. But xenophobia, the hatred of those who are different, along with the extreme and brutal racism and ultimately the terrible crime of genocide, have come to countries inhabited by good people in Europe, in Asia, in Africa, and elsewhere.[12]

On November 4, 1988, President Ronald Reagan signed the Proxmire Act into law at a brief ceremony at O'Hare Airport in Chicago. "We finally close the circle," said President Reagan. "I am delighted to fulfill the promise made by Harry Truman to all the peoples of the world—and especially the Jewish people."[13]

Despite the commitment of the United States and other nations to fight genocide wherever it might occur, the international community failed to prevent the systematic slaughter of millions of people in the post–Cold War era, people who were targeted for elimination because they posed a perceived threat to the social, political, or economic order. As scholar Samantha Power noted, the phrase "never again," which came to symbolize international resolve to prevent another Holocaust, became "the world's most unfulfilled promise."[14] Determining what constituted genocide was always disputed in the international community, and sometimes even the most compelling evidence of the need for military and humanitarian intervention was ignored because of geopolitical or domestic interests. The end of the Cold War potentially freed the United States to intervene in the affairs of states for reasons other than the containment of communism, but concerns for the safety of American soldiers—which affected all foreign policy discussions after the Vietnam War—inhibited military and economic intervention even for the most noble of reasons.[15] Consequently, many found US foreign policy in the "age of genocide" surprisingly noncommittal and even isolationist.[16]

In response to genocide, millions crossed international borders in search of safety, creating humanitarian crises for the societies that received them, politically destabilizing fragile emerging democracies, and putting enormous pressure on refugee and asylum programs worldwide. This chapter examines US responses to the genocide-driven refugee crises in Iraq, the former Yugoslavia, and Rwanda. Sadly, many more case studies could have been included in this chapter, for there have been far too many cases of genocidal purges of populations since 1989. These case studies were chosen for what they illustrate about humanitarian crises in the post–Cold War era in general, as well as what they illustrate about US refugee policy in particular.

Policy analysts have noted that refugee crises have developed more rapidly in the post–Cold War era, increasing the financial and human costs of humanitarian assistance. One million Rwandans fled into Zaire over the course of five days, for example, and two million Kurds fled their homes in a two-week period.[17] The challenges of assisting refugee and displaced populations are many. As one congressional report outlined:

> The needy are often difficult to reach, either because of the remoteness of their location or continuing conflict. Security must be provided for refugees, aid workers, and even the aid itself. All this has greatly increased the cost of response operations. The need for speed, increased manpower, and security has led to growing involvement of military forces in responding to humanitarian crises.[18]

By 1996 the United Nations reported that the proportion of UN aid spent on addressing humanitarian emergencies had jumped, from 25 percent (in 1988) to 45 percent. Similarly, more and more of US aid overseas was spent on disaster relief than on economic development projects.

UN peacekeeping missions—and the manner in which the United States participated in them—also changed during this period.[19] When President Clinton came to office, the United Nations was deploying more peacekeepers around the world than ever before: seventy-eight thousand peacekeepers were in the field by 1993 in places such as Mozambique, the former Yugoslavia, and Somalia. By the end of his presidency, the UN Security Council had become more reticent in approving missions, in large part because of policy failures in Bosnia and Somalia. Only twelve thousand peacekeepers were deployed by 1999.[20] The Clinton administration played a prominent role in the movement to reform UN peacekeeping efforts, advocating in their place responses from regional "coalitions of the willing."[21] The reforms in UN peacekeeping efforts would have consequences for the UNHCR, the IOM, and other agencies entrusted to safeguard the rights and well-being of refugees and displaced persons.

These developments would also have consequences for US refugee policy. The number of refugees admitted to the United States from these devastating humanitarian crises was surprisingly small, especially compared to the numbers admitted during the Cold War. The following three case studies demonstrate how American perceptions of refugees' politics, ethnicity, religion, and race influenced humanitarian responses and ultimately who was prioritized for admission to the United States as a refugee or parolee.

The First Gulf War and the Kurdish Refugees

On August 2, 1990, Iraq invaded and annexed its neighbor, Kuwait. In the months leading up to the invasion, the Iraqi government, heavily in debt from the Iran-Iraq war, had accused Kuwait of slant-drilling to siphon crude oil from the Ar-Rumaylah oil fields located along their common and historically disputed border and of overproducing oil beyond OPEC quotas to keep prices down on the world market. Iraq also accused Kuwait of denying it full access to the Persian Gulf. Arab nations tried to negotiate a satisfactory resolution to the conflict, but, when talks failed, one hundred thousand Iraqi troops crossed the Kuwaiti border with tanks, helicopters, and other materiel of war. Within an hour Iraqi troops reached Kuwait City and began their assault of the emirate. Six days later, having installed a provisional government, Iraq officially annexed Kuwait, a territory many Iraqis believed had always been—and should be—a province of Iraq.

Iraq's invasion of Kuwait was widely condemned by the international community, including two-thirds of the twenty-one-member Arab League. Within days of the annexation, US fighter planes, accompanied by NATO and other allied troops, arrived in Saudi Arabia as part of a military buildup to counteract a possible Iraqi invasion of Saudi Arabia. When Iraqi leader Saddam Hussein failed to comply with the UN Security Council's January 15, 1991, deadline for withdrawal from Kuwait, coalition forces began a massive air offensive against Iraqi targets known as Operation Desert Storm, which destroyed the Iraqi air force within days. This was the first UN authorization of force since the Korean War. On February 24, a ground offensive moved into Kuwait and southern Iraq; and over the next four days, coalition forces quickly drove Iraqi forces out of Kuwait. On February 28, President George H. W. Bush, who had committed half million US troops to the war effort, agreed to a cease-fire. Coalition forces declared victory. According to the terms of the peace, Iraq accepted Kuwait's sovereignty. It also agreed to destroy its arsenal of biological and chemical weapons and be inspected by the United Nations for years to come. Saddam Hussein's refusal to comply with the terms of this treaty led to another war a decade later during the administration of President George W. Bush.[22]

Coalition casualties in this Gulf War were comparatively small (three hundred). An estimated ten thousand Iraqi forces and one hundred thousand Iraqi civilians were killed in the conflict. Many more were displaced from their homes and forced to seek safety elsewhere, including three hundred thousand Palestinians living in Iraq who

resettled in Jordan, and more than five hundred thousand foreign workers (Egyptians, Pakistanis, Bangladeshis, Sri Lankans, Filipinos, and
Indians) who lost their livelihoods and were forced to move elsewhere.
An estimated one hundred thousand Iraqis fled to Jordan, and thirty-
seven thousand Iraqis, mostly Shiites (also known as Shia), settled in
Saudi Arabia. Even Iran claimed to have given refuge to 530,000 Iraqi
(mostly Shiite) refugees.[23]

The Kuwaiti invasion and the Gulf War of 1991 exacerbated sectarian
tensions rekindled during the Iran-Iraq war (1980–1988).[24] Long excluded
from political governance, the Shiites, who comprised 55 percent of Iraq's
population, rebelled against the ruling Sunni Arabs. Shiite forces quickly
controlled Basra, Iraq's second-largest city, where their numbers were
larger. However, by March 1991, Saddam Hussein's forces had regained
control, and Hussein's cousin, Ali Hassan Majid, began a brutal reprisal against the Shiite population, destroying homes, businesses, and
mosques. By September 1991 an estimated two hundred thousand people
had been publicly executed or otherwise killed.[25]

Although the Bush administration had encouraged Iraqis to rebel
against the government of Saddam Hussein, the administration did
little to support the insurgents.[26] In March 1991, the Kurdish minority
also staged uprisings—this time in northern Iraq—hoping to finally win
their independence; they, too, were brutally suppressed by Hussein's
forces. In a matter of weeks an estimated two million Kurds, Shiites,
Assyrians, Palestinians, and other minorities were forced to flee as a result
of the crackdown: one million settled in Iran, and between 360,000 and
760,000 concentrated in the Turkish-Iraqi border region.[27] UN officials
reported that "at no time in their memory had such a large concentration
of refugees amassed so quickly."[28]

The delivery of humanitarian relief (potable water, food, tents, blankets, and medicine) was hampered by the rugged mountainous terrain,
harsh weather, and the lack of suitable navigation equipment. Local road
networks were poor and some refugee encampments were accessible only
by foot. Physicians estimated that between four hundred and one thousand refugees died each day from starvation, exposure to the elements,
and intestinal and respiratory infections. Neither Turkey nor Iran forcibly repatriated the refugees, but border guards and custom authorities
often impeded the delivery of humanitarian aid.[29] Voluntary relief agencies encountered numerous bureaucratic obstacles, and American staff
workers, in particular, encountered a hostile response from the Iranian

government, which even barred a US congressional delegation from visiting the refugee camps.[30]

The refugee crisis was not just the product of the Gulf War, however. For decades, Hussein's Ba'ath regime had forcibly relocated—or eradicated—minority groups they considered oppositional. Kurds were particularly suspect since they had sought independence or political autonomy on and off since World War I. During the period 1974–1987, for example, roughly 46 percent of the Kurdish population was expelled from northern Iraq as part of a calculated campaign to suppress the Kurdish insurgency and populate the area with Arabs.[31] Iraqi forces destroyed hundreds of Kurdish villages, and tens of thousands of Kurds (and perhaps as many as half a million, according to Kurdish sources) were murdered or relocated to army-controlled settlements in southern Iraq, far from their ancestral homes in Iraqi Kurdistan.[32]

In 1987, Saddam Hussein began a more proactive genocidal campaign against the Kurds on the grounds that they had aligned with Iran during Iraq-Iran war. The eradication campaign, called al-Anfal, was carried out by Hussein's cousin, Ali Hassan al-Majid (nicknamed "Chemical Ali" by Americans), the chief of Iraq's northern administrative bureau, who ordered Iraqi forces to drop mustard gas, sarin, and other deadly chemical agents on civilian populations. Iraq had previously used chemical weapons against Iran, but this was the first time it had attacked its own citizens with chemical weapons.[33] The worst attack came on March 16, 1988, at the end of the Iran-Iraq war, in the city of Halabja in southern Kurdistan, where Iraqi forces killed up to five thousand men, women, and children, and injured ten thousand more. Over one hundred thousand Kurds (roughly 28 percent of the population) were gassed or executed during the Anfal, and over four thousand villages destroyed.[34] In the south and central regions of Iraq, between three hundred thousand to four hundred thousand Marsh Arabs and Shia were also forced to flee their homes.[35]

Despite early evidence that Iraq was using chemical weapons against civilians,[36] and despite the calls from the international human rights community to censure and impose sanctions on the Hussein government,[37] the Reagan administration took limited action against Iraq because it was an important ally that helped check the regional influence of the Iranian Islamic state of Ayatollah Khomeini and helped protect Persian Gulf oil production. The United States and Iraq had only recently restored diplomatic relations in 1984, and geopolitical and economic interests outweighed concerns for human rights.[38] State Department officials readily agreed that Iraq was one of the world's worst violators of human rights, but feared that sanctions—or even public criticism—might undermine the still-fragile US-Iraqi relations.[39] In 1983 State Department officials recommended that the administration discuss Iraq's use of chemical weapons with high-ranking Iraqi officials in order to "avoid unpleasantly surprising Iraq through public positions we [might] have to take on this issue."[40] However, the White House did not push Iraq too hard on this issue. The fact that Kurdish insurgents had sided with Iran during the Iran-Iraq war made them "implicated victims" whom the United States found easy to ignore in 1983—and later in 1988—despite recent ratification of the UN genocide convention.[41] As Samantha Power wrote in *A Problem from Hell*: "Kurds were in fact doubly implicated.... As 'guerrillas,' the Kurds thus appeared to be inviting repression. And as temporary allies of Iran, they were easily lumped with the very forces responsible for [American] hostage-taking and 'Great Satan' berating."[42]

During the period 1983–1988, when Western banks found Iraq to be too great a financial risk, the United States provided $2.8 billion in credits and guarantees through the Commodity Credit Corporation (CCC) so that Iraq could purchase US agricultural products. An embargo prohibited the sale of military equipment to Iraq, but the Reagan administration approved the sale of forty-five Bell helicopters to the Iraqi government that were used by the Iraqi military in its patrols of (and perhaps attacks on) northern Kurdish territory, despite assurances that these would be used only for civilian transport. US companies were authorized to assist Iraq to develop missile production capability.[43] The United States chose not to condemn Iraq at the January 1989 Paris Conference on Chemical Weapons, nor did it press for sanctions at either the 1988 or 1989 sessions of the UN Human Rights Commission.[44]

The Kurds did not have a visible immigrant presence in the United States and consequently had no advocacy group that could plead their case in Washington or in the news media. They did have important advocates in Senators William Proxmire, Claiborne Pell, George Mitchell, and Daniel Patrick Moynihan and Representative Howard Berman, all of whom passionately argued for sanctions against Iraq. Pell's bill, the Prevention Against Genocide Act, was drafted by the congressional staffer, Peter Galbraith, who was instrumental in uncovering the evidence of chemical warfare against the Kurds. The bill banned the sale of military equipment of any kind to Iraq; banned all credits, loans, and guarantees; barred the sale or transfer of any item subject to export controls; and banned the import of Iraqi petroleum products. Despite significant support in the Senate, the bill died in committee because of the intense opposition from the Reagan administration and the US farm lobby, which did not want to sabotage its commercial interests in Iraq.[45] A similar but watered-down bill barring the sale of arms, goods, technology, or chemicals passed the House but was shelved when Congress adjourned.

Pell also proposed an amendment to the 1961 Foreign Assistance Act that would have made aid contingent on a presidential determination on Iraq's human rights record. Since such a determination would have required the White House to acknowledge Iraq's human rights abuses, the administration opposed the amendment, arguing that Iraq was "impervious to leverage." One State Department official complained: "Congress is not very protective of our relationship with Iraq."[46] Senator Daniel Inouye, in turn, proposed a rider on the 1980 Foreign Assistance Appropriations Act that banned the US Export-Import Bank from carrying out transactions with Iraq. Inouye's proposal became law, but only after it was watered down to allow the president to override the ban if deemed in the national interest. Thus, when President Bush signed National Security Directive 26 to offer Iraq one billion dollars in agricultural loan guarantees, he argued that "normal relations" between the United States and Iraq served American interests and promoted stability in the Gulf and the Middle East. Not until Iraq invaded Kuwait did Bush finally call for a total embargo on Iraq and freeze its economic assets in the United States. By then the credits and loan guarantees had allowed Saddam Hussein to "fortify and modernize his more cherished military assets, including his stockpile of deadly chemicals," and "American grain [had kept] the Iraqi army fed during its occupation of Kuwait."[47]

When the Kurds and the Iraqi Shiites began their respective rebellions in early 1991, they underestimated the capabilities of the besieged Iraqi military—and they overestimated the support they might receive from the UN coalition, and more specifically, from the United States. Kurdish towns such as Dahuk, Zakho, and others were quickly encircled by Iraqi troops. Fearing another genocidal campaign, Kurdish civilians panicked and fled on foot into the mountainous borderlands with Iran and Turkey.[48] The trip to Turkey took one to two weeks in good conditions, but the refugees' travel coincided with some of the worst winter weather of the year. Thousands of refugees—especially children and the elderly—died from exposure.

A permanent resettlement of Kurdish refugees in Turkey was impossible because of long-standing tensions with Turkish Kurdistan.[49] Instead, the international aid workers who arrived on the scene encouraged the refugees to settle in camps in the lowland areas in northern Iraq, just inside the Iraqi-Turkish border, until the international community could negotiate the refugees' safe return to their homes. However, the Kurds would not leave their mountain refuges without credible assurances that they would be protected. Iraqi secret police continued to operate in the area, threatening their lives; and Kurds who had foolishly believed Hussein's promise of amnesty had been imprisoned and/or executed upon returning home.[50] Consequently, the air-dropping of emergency food and medical supplies to the refugees in the mountains became the first order of business, to prevent death from starvation and exposure while a long-term solution was negotiated. When the full scale of the humanitarian crisis became evident, coalition forces, backed by UN Security Council Resolution 688 (April 5, 1991), secured a portion of lower ground in northern Iraq as a refugee "safe zone," which became "no fly" zones patrolled by US and British aircraft.[51]

The relief program, known as Operation Provide Comfort, became the largest humanitarian relief effort of the late twentieth century. The United States spent $133 million for emergency supplies during the first nineteen days alone.[52] According to one congressional report, the relief operation in northern Iraq, together with a smaller operation in Kuwait and southern Iraq, resembled a military campaign more than a traditional relief operation: "The command and control structure, including a dozen full star generals from several nations, along with logistics, supplies, and military precise objectives, were all the hallmarks of a military operation."[53] Twelve thousand US soldiers helped patrol the region as part of a twenty-one-thousand-troop allied ground effort, and more than fifty humanitarian organizations participated in the relief efforts.[54] According to Sadako Ogata, the UN high commissioner, the operation "broke new grounds in civil and military collaboration."[55] The ratio of international relief workers to refugees was one to one hundred—one of the lowest ratios for any humanitarian crisis—and consequently, the mortality rate of Kurdish refugees dropped to less than ten per day in a matter of weeks.[56] The Bush administration "directed that no effort be spared to help the refugees" but also insisted that the international community assume their share of the costs of refugee relief and work with the United States to oversee a peaceful resolution to the crisis.[57] The goals were to protect the refugees and offer immediate humanitarian assistance. Responsibility for Kurdish security was then transferred to the United Nations in June 1991, and humanitarian aid workers remained in the region, offering assistance.[58]

Tragically, protection could not be completely guaranteed. In 1992 and in 1995, Turkish forces attacked the Kurdish sanctuaries in northern Iraq, hoping to weed out Kurdish guerrillas they claimed had hidden among the refugees.[59] In 1996, Saddam Hussein's forces also penetrated the safe haven in northern Iraq, kidnapping and killing many. By 1996, the borders to Turkey and Iran were completely blocked, trapping refugees and relief workers in Iraq. The Pentagon eventually ordered the evacuation of those Kurds who had worked with American agencies in the north, and their family members, to protect them from reprisals. More than sixty-six hundred Kurds were transported first to Turkey and eventually to Guam, where they were screened and processed for admission to the United States as part of Operation Pacific Haven.[60]

Public opinion polls in the United States showed that there was little support for American involvement in refugee relief efforts. A 1991 Gallup poll revealed that 66 percent of those surveyed opposed US military personnel playing any role in the construction and operation of Iraqi/Kurdish refugee camps.[61] The White House did not call for a large-scale resettlement program in the United States.[62] Instead, the administration announced that it would only accept up to three thousand people for possible resettlement in the United States in FY1991, prioritizing those with families in the United States (in line with US immigration policy as a whole, which favors family reunification) and those at risk of retaliation because of their cooperation with coalition forces as interpreters, guides, and supply clerks. Most of this small quota went unfilled, however.[63] The numbers increased modestly in subsequent years, with the majority of the refugees being Iraqi Christians or Kurds with relatives in the United States.[64] Refugee numbers peaked in 1994 (see table 2.1).

By the end of the 1990s, there were an estimated 20,000 Kurds living in the United States: a small fraction of the 1.1 million in the Kurdish diaspora (650,000 in Germany alone).[65] Nashville, Tennessee emerged as an important center of Kurdish resettlement. An estimated 13,000 Kurds have settled in Nashville since Saddam Hussein's first crackdown in 1976, but the majority have settled there after the genocidal campaign of 1991, assisted by the relief agency Catholic Charities. The southern part of the city has become known as "Little Kurdistan," home to a mosque as well as bakeries, food markets, and other commercial establishments.

Table 2.1 Iraqi Refugee Admissions, 1991–1998

Fiscal year	Total admissions
1991	842
1992	3,442
1993	4,605
1994	4,984
1995	3,482
1996	2,528
1997	2,679
1998	1,407

Source: Department of Homeland Security, Fiscal Year 2000 Statistical Yearbook, http://www.dhs.gov/publication/fiscal-year-2000-statistical-yearbook-refugeesasylees.

Compared to the tens of thousands of refugees admitted from Southeast Asia and other war-torn areas during the Cold War, these war refugees were surprisingly small in number. The Kurds did not have a forceful advocacy network cultivating political will on their behalf in the 1990s. A decade later, Iraqis, Afghans, and Syrians would encounter similar resistance from an American public that found them too culturally different and too potentially threatening to resettle in the United States.

Refugees from the Wars in Bosnia and Kosovo

The Balkan wars of the 1990s have often been depicted as the consequence of ancestral ethnic hatreds that erupted after the death of Yugoslav president Josip Broz Tito. According to this interpretation, Tito had successfully subsumed class, ethnic, and national distinctions within a supranational socialist framework, but upon his death the communist bureaucracy unraveled, allowing self-serving politicians to mobilize their constituencies to exact violence for particular ends.[66] This interpretation overemphasizes ethnic conflict and nationalism as the dominant rationale for the wars in the region. According to political scientist V. P. Gagnon, the violence that occurred in Bosnia and Kosovo was indeed planned and executed in strategic ways by conservative ruling elites in Belgrade and Zagreb, working with allies in the war zones, but the violence was not the consequence of mass mobilization, nor was it a response to popular pressure to remove ethnic populations from particular territories:

[In] the places where the wars were actually fought—places with the highest pre-war levels of positive coexistence—the violence almost without exception was imported into those communities as the result of strategic decisions on the part of the leaderships in Belgrade and Zagreb. [The wars] ... did not draw on or appeal to the lived experiences or the processes of identification of people in the communities most affected.[67]

The strategies pursued by the conservative ruling elites, Gagnon argued, were designed to demobilize those populations that were actively organizing against them to reform the political and economic power structure. These elites successfully shifted discourse away from issues of political and economic change and toward the "grave injustices purportedly being inflicted on [Serbian] innocents" in areas where Serbs were the minority. The fact that most people were not mobilized toward violence suggests that this discourse did not appeal to their identity or their lived experience; and the areas that saw that greatest violence often had the highest levels of interethnic families.[68] As author Slavenka Drakulić wrote:

The whole world was surprised by this war. We, the citizens of Yugoslavia, were even more surprised. ... Why didn't we see it coming? Why didn't we do something to prevent it? Why were we so arrogant that we thought it could not happen to us? ... But one day we discovered that it was not necessary to have an outside enemy to start a war. The enemy could be inside—and indeed it was. ... it was easy to manipulate [Yugoslav history] in order to antagonize one another.[69]

Unfortunately, many in the West bought into the discourse of an "ethnic war" in the former Yugoslavia, with significant consequences for peace-keeping, for refugee assistance, and eventually for historical representation.

The existence of a post–World War II Yugoslavia depended on the co-operation and interdependence of multiethnic populations living within the territorial boundaries of six republics: Serbia, Croatia, Slovenia,

Bosnia-Hercegovina, Macedonia, and Montenegro (in 1974, Kosovo and Vojvodina were granted "autonomous" provincial status within Serbia). During the 1960s and 1970s, reformers within the League of Communists of Yugoslavia (LCY), mostly from the rising technocratic and educated middle class, called for a decentralization of political power from Belgrade to the individual republics. These changes were strongly resisted by conservatives in the Communist Party, who tried to prevent change by portraying Yugoslavia as a society teetering on the brink of nationalist violence and in need of a strong central authority to keep these impulses in check. This discourse facilitated the purging of key reformers from top government positions, but the decentralization of power continued regardless, and each republic and province developed a fair amount of political and economic autonomy. By the end of the 1970s, as comparative politics scholar Valerie Bunce has noted:

> Yugoslavia had ceased to be either a regime or a state. Instead, it had become an international system composed of six, relatively autonomous dictatorial entities of varying political and economic, not to mention national, persuasions. Indeed, the number, six, may be too small, if we include the two autonomous provinces attached to Serbia and the growing political independence of Kosovo in particular, beginning at the end of the 1970s; the Yugoslav National Army as an increasingly autonomous political actor; and the growing isolation of the Yugoslav central government.[70]

During the 1980s, Yugoslavia's economic situation spiraled downward, exacerbated by the global economic recession and the eight inefficient economies run by eight different Communist Party bureaucracies.[71] The federation had one of the highest per capita foreign debts in the world. Double-digit inflation, shortages of basic consumer staples, and workers' strikes became increasingly common. By 1984, over one million people— mostly the young and educated—were unemployed.[72]

After the death of President Tito in 1980, the Communist Party leadership in Belgrade resisted the calls for economic privatization and entrepreneurship, insisting instead on ideological orthodoxy. Belgrade (and Serbs, in general) had a strong stake in a united Yugoslavia—Serbs were overrepresented in the key institutions of Yugoslav society, especially the military—and Belgrade oversaw economic decision-making concerning production and distribution. Further decentralization of this very artificial state would result in its complete destruction, at great economic and political cost to Serbia.[73] Communist Party members in Belgrade, working with leftist intellectuals and sympathetic journalists, launched a nationalist campaign to portray the reformist agenda as a deliberate attack on the Serbian people.[74] Belgrade orchestrated mass demonstrations in the major Serb-populated areas to protest what they claimed was a planned genocide of Serb minorities in Kosovo and the other republics and provinces. Reformist leaders were accused of indifference and corruption. Belgrade's goal was to mobilize support for the overthrow of reformist party leaders at the local, republic, and federal level.[75] Ethno-religious conflict was strategically stoked to undercut the reformist agenda.

The elections of 1990 resulted in the disintegration of the old Yugoslavia as Croats, Slovenes, and other nationalities voted for the establishment of their own independent states. Slovenia and Croatia, the wealthiest republics, were the first to declare their independence in June 1991. Without its traditional allies in the federation, Bosnia-Hercegovina followed suit in April 1992. By 1992, the Federal Republic of Yugoslavia consisted solely of Serbia and Montenegro. Slobodan Milošević, the president of the Serbian League of Communists, and his allies plotted to create a larger Serbian republic reconfigured through the annexation of Serbian-populated areas of the old Yugoslav federation; to do that, territorial space needed to be reconfigured in ethno-religious terms, which was ultimately accomplished through ethnic cleansing—the killing or mass expulsion of particular ethnic populations. Such a strategy would allow them to maintain control over the economic resources in these territories.[76]

War erupted in Slovenia, Croatia, and Bosnia. Slovenia's war lasted only ten days.[77] In Croatia, the war between Serb insurgents and Croatian security forces lasted seven months and left ten thousand people dead and seven hundred thousand displaced from their homes.[78]

The war in Bosnia was especially brutal, lasting over three years. Though 63 percent of Bosnian voters had endorsed independence, the Serb minority boycotted the referendum. Led by Radovan Karadžić and aided by Slobodan Milošević, Bosnian Serbs proclaimed the independent state of Republika Srpska and plotted to link territory in Bosnia with Serbia and Montenegro to create a "Greater Serbia." A two-year siege of Sarajevo followed. By the summer of 1992, Bosnian Serbs (second in population size to the Bosnian Muslims) had gained control of much of Bosnia-Hercegovina, and through detentions, deportations, and executions they began "cleansing" the territory of non-Serbs to make it ethnically homogenous. They were assisted by Yugoslav military forces, who supplied the insurgents with the military stockpiles still housed in Bosnia. Communities were shelled with mortars and then looted; agricultural fields were burned, livestock killed, and water sources poisoned to drive non-Serbs away from their homes and into neighboring republics. The Serb leadership created over six hundred concentration camps: the most infamous was Omarska, where over five thousand were starved, beaten, and tortured. Paramilitary groups humiliated and terrorized civilians, castrating young boys, raping tens of thousands of Muslim girls and women as a deliberate strategy to "impregnate them with Serbs," and shooting anyone who tried to rescue or otherwise intervene. Edicts controlled the gathering, movement, communication, commerce, and day-to-day life activities of the populations. To erase Muslim history and culture, Serbs systematically destroyed mosques, libraries, cultural institutions, and even graveyards to remove any record of their presence. When the United Nations imposed an arms embargo in 1991 to try to quell the escalation of violence, they prevented the Muslim population from effectively defending itself against the more heavily militarized Serb forces. When Serbian civilians opposed the violence against their neighbors, they too were targeted. Tens of thousands of Serbs in Bosnia and Croatia were among the refugees and displaced persons.

The wars in Croatia and Bosnia (and eventually Kosovo) generated one of the largest movements of persons in Europe since World War II. By 1992, the UNHCR estimated over 1.3 million refugees and displaced persons, and by 1995, over 3.5 million.[79] Hundreds of thousands more were trapped in the Bosnian capital of Sarajevo, the city of Gorazde, and other population enclaves, surrounded by hostile forces and assailed by constant bombardment.

The United Nations tried to provide humanitarian assistance and to broker and enforce a peace plan. The UN Security Council imposed economic sanctions, deployed peacekeepers, funded the longest-running humanitarian airlift since the Berlin airlift, and eventually set up a war crimes tribunal to punish the perpetrators. Despite more than ample evidence of human rights abuses by different parties, member states refused to intervene militarily to stop the war crimes or the genocide.[80]

As in Iraq, the White House avoided the use of the term "genocide" because, as Samantha Power has argued, "a genocide finding would create a moral imperative."[81] Instead, policymakers referred to the situation in Bosnia as a civil war that gave expression to ancient tribal hatreds that could not be easily addressed. Occasionally, policymakers used the term "ethnic cleansing" or the adjective "genocidal" in their references to Serb actions, but they always stopped short of calling it genocide. Bosnia, they argued, was a "European problem" that did not threaten US interests in the same way as the Iraqi invasion of Kuwait. The White House did not press for a lifting of the UN arms embargo nor for a coalition military response: responses that might exacerbate and prolong the conflict, officials argued, and endanger the delivery of humanitarian aid.[82] Instead, the Bush administration deferred to the newly reconceptualized European Community (EC) and assumed a supportive role in humanitarian relief. From 1991 to 1995, the United States contributed over one billion dollars to the UNHCR, the International Red Cross, and other nongovernmental organizations for relief efforts; participated in emergency airlifts of food and other relief assistance to the war victims; and provided military protection for UN humanitarian convoys. "There is no easy solution to the Bosnian conflict, let alone the larger Balkan crisis," said one Bush administration official, "so we will persist in our strategy of containing and reducing the violence, making the aggressors pay, and relieving the suffering of victims, all while lending our full support to the quest for a settlement."[83] Endangering the lives of American soldiers was not an option, even for the most humanitarian of reasons. Some key advisers in the Bush administration, most notably General Colin Powell, took an even harsher position, opposing any US participation in the delivery of humanitarian aid or in the enforcement of a no-fly zone over Bosnia.[84] For these advisers, the recently reconstituted states of the former Soviet Union were of greater geopolitical interest.

This policy of limited engagement had its critics in the news media, most notably Anthony Lewis of the *New York Times*, who used his syndicated column to criticize the Bush administration's perceived apathy:

> The excuse for [Bush's] inaction has been that the Serbian war on the other peoples of what was Yugoslavia has not aroused the American public. But Americans were not greatly exercised about Iraq's occupation of Kuwait either—until George Bush skillfully used all his powers as president to bring the country into the Persian Gulf war. But there was oil in Kuwait, the Bush people say, and there is no such American interest in Yugoslavia. No, nothing except the European stability that has been at the heart of our international policy for decades.[85]

Lewis's criticisms of US policy continued during the next administration: "President Clinton [has] failed to take the bold action that would have made a difference.... [he] will join George Bush as the American presidents who did not stand up against genocide."[86]

On Capitol Hill, Senator Robert Dole and Congressman Frank McCloskey became vocal critics of Serb actions—and of US policy—after their own dangerous fact-finding trip to the Balkans. McCloskey, in particular, became known for his insistent pressuring in congressional hearings, in public speeches and op-eds, and in private meetings with administration officials. He criticized the Clinton administration for refusing to use the term genocide (even calling for Secretary of State Warren Christopher's resignation). His urging for more forceful intervention in the Balkans was surprising given his past opposition to the Vietnam War and his vote against the 1991 Persian Gulf War.[87] Neither the Clinton administration nor McCloskey's own constituents were convinced of the wisdom of military intervention. After serving six terms in the House of Representatives, McCloskey lost reelection in 1994 because, as the *Indianapolis Star* noted, "Hoosiers were much more interested in local events than the problems of a region half a world away."[88] Despite vocal support for intervention from some members of Congress, Clinton favored the use of force only when required to guarantee the delivery of humanitarian aid.

When no country seemed ready or willing to accept refugees, even on a provisional basis, the United Nations established six "safe areas" in Bosnian cities and towns such as Srebrenica and Mostar as a form of "preventive protection." The goal was to concentrate displaced persons in specific locales to facilitate humanitarian assistance and to offer military protection. These "safe areas" were anything but safe. Only a fraction of the forces needed to protect the populations arrived, making the civilians and relief workers easy targets. In one particularly tragic example, in July 1995, Serbian forces of the Republika Srpska seized control of Srebrenica from an outnumbered Dutch battalion and over a nine-day period rounded up and killed over eight thousand Muslim men and boys.[89]

Some were killed at close quarters by firing squads, others by machine guns and grenades fired into pits of imprisoned people, others by knives, yet others gunned down on hills and fields as they tried to flee—at a series of diverse locations across northeast Bosnia. Those who were murdered at a killing site were then buried in mass graves dug by heavy earthmoving equipment. These mass graves, however were soon deemed inadequate to cover up the crime of genocide they represented. So, they were dug up a few months later, as negotiators prepared for the Dayton talks, and the decaying remains transported to smaller secondary graves. In a number of cases, these secondary graves were dug up and the body parts removed again and relocated on dump trucks to tertiary graves. The remains of one young victim, Kadrija Music, 23 at the time of his murder, were found in five locations up to 20 miles apart.... The Srebrenica genocide was a massive enterprise. It required not [just] an army of perpetrators but also an army of disposers driving buses, diggers and trucks, and coordinators scheduling the buses, diggers, trucks and cleanup crews, telling those involved where to bury the body parts. The total number of Srebrenica-related sites where human remains have been recovered is 407.[90]

UN peacekeeping forces were criticized for their failure to evacuate populations at Srebrenica, Zepa, and other locations, but their numbers were insufficient to address the realities on the ground.[91] Peacekeepers were often taken hostage or killed in the line of duty; 207 UN personnel lost their lives in the Bosnian mission.[92] When NATO finally launched air strikes against Serb targets in 1995—conducted without UN Security Council approval—the actions were applauded by many in the humanitarian relief community as the only way to protect the population and to "deter further crimes against humanity."[93]

More than two hundred thousand people were killed in the Bosnian war. Half of the people lost their homes and were either internally displaced within their country or forced to cross borders in search of refuge.[94] The war made obvious the inadequacy of the UN's definition of refugee and the challenges of crafting a humanitarian response. Under such conditions it was impossible to evaluate individual claims of persecution, and the UNHCR eventually designated some populations as prima facie refugees.[95] But were former soldiers and draft evaders entitled to protection? aid workers asked. How did one distinguish between the victims and the perpetrators? Were the internally displaced entitled to assistance, or was the crossing of a political border a necessary criterion for the granting and receiving of aid? With the breakup of Yugoslavia into different states and the contesting of boundaries, the distinction between the internally and the externally displaced was difficult to maintain, complicating the debate on international obligations and taxing already-stretched resources.[96]

The Yugoslav republics that bordered the areas of conflict initially kept their borders open even though some were ill prepared to accommodate a mass migration. Croatia was both an exporter and importer of refugees, driving tens of thousands of its citizens into other countries, but also accepting over four hundred thousand Bosnian refugees. By 1992, Slovenia had given refuge to roughly twenty-five thousand refugees. Several European nations agreed to accommodate refugees. Many of them were already home to thousands of Yugoslav workers, since unlike other communist countries, Yugoslavia had adopted an open borders policy beginning in the 1960s and thousands of Yugoslavs had sought economic opportunities elsewhere.[97] Hungary, which only a few years earlier had blocked its own citizens from emigrating, accepted forty-five thousand refugees.[98] Austria, Germany, Sweden, Denmark, Italy, and the United Kingdom agreed to either defer the deportation of the Yugoslav arrivals, or to offer them some type of temporary protected status until the UNHCR could oversee their safe return to their homelands.

As the refugee population grew larger, without any foreseeable ebbing in numbers, several countries imposed visas, quotas, and other legal barriers, effectively barring refugees from entry or from staying very long. Visas were difficult to secure because the supporting documents required for administrative processing, such as birth certificates and identification cards, had usually been destroyed along with homes and municipal buildings. Consulates in the former Yugoslav republics were poorly staffed or closed altogether because of the wars. The bureaucratic hurdles were many. The United Kingdom, for example, did not have a consulate in Bosnia in the early 1990s, so asylum seekers who wished to settle there had to travel to a British consulate in a third country to apply for a visa. However, once refugees transited though a third country to reach the consulate, they became ineligible if the transit country was considered a "safe third country" that offered another option for asylum.[99] After the US-brokered Dayton agreement of November 1995 brought a tentative peace plan to Bosnia, Croatia, and Serbia, many countries of "first asylum" asked Bosnian refugees to repatriate, forcing the issue by removing legal status and welfare benefits. In 1996, when Germany tried to forcibly repatriate Bosnians before US officials considered it safe to return, the Clinton administration offered the repatriates the option of resettlement in the United States.

According to Bill Frelick of the US Committee for Refugees, the UNHCR advocated keeping refugees close to their homelands "either to ease their integration into similar cultures or to make it easier for their eventual return [to their homes]."[100] The realities of life in the former Yugoslavia often made this impossible. The UNHCR's first appeal for resettlement assistance came in September 1992 when the horrors of the Serbian concentration camps were first revealed. For the surviving detainees, only an offer of resettlement could secure their release from camps. The United States responded slowly to the UNHCR appeal, allegedly because of concerns that resettlement might further contribute to the ethnic cleansing of these territories. The Bush administration eventually agreed to take in one thousand of the Bosnians detainees (three hundred detainees and seven hundred of their family members); however, by the end of 1992, no detainees had been resettled in the United States because of the difficulties of vetting the refugees.[101]

During the Clinton administration, the Bosnian refugee quota increased: from three thousand in FY1993 to seven thousand in 1994, and ten thousand in 1995. The UNHCR identified, screened, and referred refugees to the United States for possible resettlement. They prioritized women at risk of violence; families of interethnic marriages; the physically or mentally disabled; victims of torture; persons in need of medical treatment; conscientious objectors; and those who wished to be reunited with relatives living in the United States.[102] The slow pace of vetting the refugees meant that some years the "Bosnian quota" went unfilled: only 1,887 Bosnian refugees were admitted to the United States by the end of FY1993, for example, and only a third of them were UNHCR referrals.[103]

Responding to public pressure, the US Immigration and Naturalization Service (INS) began sending its own representatives to war-torn areas to assess conditions and to screen refugees. By 1995, eleven INS officers had made seven trips to Belgrade and 234 trips to various sites in Croatia and Slovenia. The majority of the refugees accepted by the United States—85 percent—were Bosnian Muslim, who Americans felt bore the heaviest burden of the war. "It is the Muslim population which has no other place to go," said one State Department official in congressional testimony:

> If you are a Serb and you got chased out of your home, you can go to Serbia. That is what the Serbs in Krajina did. If you are a Croat, you can go to Croatia. And a number of Bosnian-Croats are there. But if you are a Bosnian Muslim and you have been chased out of your home, you really do not have a country of refuge nearby.[104]

In congressional testimony, refugees tried to convey the desperation of their countrymen:

> It is essential that you realize that refugees do not come here because they just feel like a change or because they are up to some "country shopping." They decide to come here because they have no other place to go, because elsewhere they would be physically eradicated.[105]

"When you have a war in which even many decent people become hateful and malicious," said one Bosnian refugee from Mostar, "it will take a long time for the victims to have enough trust to go back and face the same neighbors again."[106]

While the United States did not bar Serbian refugees from resettlement in the United States, the State Department's Bureau for Population, Refugees, and Migration (PRM) did not prioritize refugees in Serbia and Montenegro for any type of humanitarian assistance in part because they were the perceived aggressors. The US Committee for Refugees criticized this policy, calling it an apparent move "to coerce the political leadership in Serbia and Montenegro into acceptable behavior" with the unfortunate consequence of "turning food and medicine into political weapons."[107]

More than 125,000 Bosnian refugees settled in the United States between 1993 and 2000 through refugee [and other] status (see table 2.2). St. Louis, Missouri, became home to the largest population—an estimated thirty-five thousand—because of the many offers of sponsorship in this area.[108] An additional twelve thousand settled in New York state (five thousand in the town of Utica alone).[109] The United States also granted temporary protected status (TPS) to four hundred Bosnians already in the country at the time of the war to allow them to legally stay and work until it was safe for them to return home. Their TPS status was routinely extended—until February 10, 2001—when the State Department determined that these Bosnians were no longer in need of temporary refuge.

Immigration officials later brought charges against several hundred Bosnian immigrants who concealed their involvement in wartime atrocities in order to secure entry. Over half of those under investigation were alleged to have participated in the genocide at Srebrenica. While most were Serb, immigration officials also identified Bosnian Muslims and Croats who participated in attacks against Serbs and thus became

Table 2.2 Bosnian Refugee Arrivals,
1991–2000

Fiscal year	Total admissions
1990	—
1991	—
1992	—
1993	1,887
1994	7,088
1995	9,870
1996	12,030
1997	21,357
1998	30,906
1999	22,699
2000	19,033

Source: Department of Homeland Security, Fiscal Year 2000 Statistical Yearbook, http:// www.dhs.gov/publication/fiscal-year-2000-statistical-yearbook-refugeesasylees.

ineligible for permanent residency. By February 2015, 150 were scheduled for deportation to face charges of war crimes in their home countries, but immigration officials estimated that as many as 600 might be deported.[110]

The "shuttle diplomacy" of Assistant Secretary of State Richard Holbrooke played a critical role in negotiating the Dayton peace agreement of November 1995 that ended the conflict between Bosnia-Herzegovina, Croatia, and the Republic of Yugoslavia (Serbia). The Dayton agreement outlined the terms of the cease-fire and military withdrawal, as well as the terms of political sovereignty and territorial boundaries. The three warring countries agreed to respect human rights, prosecute war crimes, and assist the International Committee of the Red Cross (ICRC) to locate missing persons. Annex 7 of the peace agreement dealt specifically with the rights of refugees and displaced persons in the region, which granted them the right to safely return home; to regain lost property or just compensation; to move freely throughout the country without harassment or discrimination; and to participate in the electoral process.[111]

Once peace was secured, the UNHCR focused on the repatriation of refugees and displaced persons, especially those from Bosnia, who constituted the largest numbers. The Clinton administration granted the UNHCR a "quick impact [funding] package" of $85.6 million to assist with "economic and infrastructure reconstruction" and humanitarian aid.[112] Many found it difficult to return to their homelands, however. The sporadic paramilitary violence, the presence of landmines that made travel precarious, and the repeated violations of the Dayton accords threatened the successful reintegration of all those displaced by the war, but most especially the Bosnian Muslims. By 1998 less than half a million refugees and displaced persons had returned to their communities.[113]

The Dayton agreement was unable to stop genocide in the Yugoslav territory of Kosovo. The purge of the Muslim Kosovar Albanians—who constituted 85 percent of Kosovo's population—began in 1988 "as an accompaniment to political moves aimed at altering the status of Kosovo from than of an 'independent' province with its own constitution and special status within the Yugoslav federation . . . to that of a wholly subordinate province within the republic of Serbia."[114] The region of Kosovo was important to the Serbs because it is regarded as the birthplace of the Serbian Orthodox Church and thus the location of the church's most important shrines, monasteries, and seminaries. The area is also rich in mineral and energy resources. For a combination of reasons—the poverty of the region, Tito-era policies designed to curtail Serb influence, and the high ethnic Albanian birthrate that led to increased competition for jobs and land—Serbs had migrated out of Kosovo in large numbers so that by the 1980s they constituted roughly 10 percent of the population. After Kosovo became autonomous, the Serbs who remained in the state lost political and economic influence. Inspired by Belgrade's charged rhetoric, Serb nationalists plotted to reestablish cultural, political, and economic control.

As a result of Belgrade's political maneuverings, the Kosovo party leadership (handpicked by Belgrade) and the Kosovo assembly abolished Kosovo's autonomy and recentralized political authority in Serbia. The Serbian authority imposed a series of restrictions on the ethnic Albanian population to prevent Kosovo's secession and perhaps its eventual absorption into neighboring Albania. The government violently suppressed any public gatherings and even placed quotas on the number of Albanian children who could attend school.[115] International human rights activists monitoring conditions in Kosovo were intimidated, harassed, imprisoned, and expelled.

Since the Dayton accords failed to address Kosovo's status, ethnic Albanians escalated their confrontations with political authorities. The Kosovo Liberation Army (KLA) attacked Serbian police, civilians, and those ethnic Albanians who cooperated with the Serbian state.[116] Serbian police, military, and paramilitary groups, in turn, began a full-fledged campaign of ethnic cleansing: fathers and sons were removed from their families and imprisoned, starved, tortured, and/or executed; women were brutally raped and their children slaughtered in front of them.[117] Security forces especially targeted leaders in the community who might organize against them—doctors, intellectuals, lawyers, and prominent businessmen. As in Bosnia, Serb forces surrounded communities, subjected civilians to shelling and sniper attacks, and cut them off from food and medical supplies. In some areas, paramilitaries carried out a "scorched-earth campaign": burning crops and food stores, killing livestock, and contaminating water wells with the carcasses of dead livestock. When farmers dared go into the fields to harvest crops, they were shot and killed by snipers.

By the end of the decade, over one hundred thousand people were missing and presumed dead. An estimated eight hundred thousand people were living outside of Kosovo, especially in neighboring Albania, Montenegro, and Macedonia (which won its independence in 1991). The Albanian government distributed food and blankets at "collective centers" near the border, but Albania, like Macedonia and Montenegro, were ill equipped to deal with thousands of people crossing their borders each week. From 60 to 80 percent of the refugees (whom the Serbs called "deportees") were taken in by strangers, at great sacrifice to their own families and well-being. Thousands more were forced to live in the overcrowded border camps hastily built by NATO and poorly staffed by members of international relief agencies. The camp at Brazda, the largest of the nine camps in Macedonia, for example, was designed to hold a maximum of twelve thousand people, but held twenty-six thousand. One report detailed the difficult conditions:

Overcrowding has forced as many as ten people to occupy tents designed to accommodate four. In most tents there is no room for cots, so residents must sleep on the cold ground. When it rains, the beaten dirt turns to a sea of mud. On sunny days, people flee the hot, fetid air of their tents to seek what little shade they can find. Even outside, there is little relief, as the air is laden with the stench of overflowing portable latrines.... "It would have been better if

Milošević had murdered us in Kosovo!" exclaimed a woman as she hauled two large jugs of water to her tent. "We have a very hard life here." Adult refugees spend much of the day standing in lines for bread, canned fish, soap, water and other necessities. Women wash clothes—often the same ones they have worn since they were expelled from their homes—at a single, outdoor laundry area consisting of a hose and a few plastic tubs. Only young children attend the camp's school. When they are not standing in line, older children and teenagers hang out around two basketball hoops and a ping-pong table.[118]

An additional four hundred thousand to six hundred thousand ethnic Albanians were internally displaced—over half of them under the age of eighteen. After hearing the heartbreaking testimony at a 1999 Senate congressional hearing on Kosovo, Senator Patrick Leahy, a longtime advocate for refugees, remarked:

As a child I heard stories of those coming back from World War II who had gone to refugee camps and talked about the terror, and wondering why people didn't move quicker, why more things weren't done. And you have to think . . . that we wouldn't see this today, but we are, just as we have in other parts of the world.[119]

Unlike in Bosnia, however, the international community became more proactively involved in stopping the violence. In February 1999, at a conference in Rambouillet, France, the United States and its allies presented Belgrade with an ultimatum demanding the immediate withdrawal of Serbian forces from Kosovo, and the granting of political autonomy to the region. When Belgrade refused, NATO forces under the command of American general Wesley Clark began a military operation, Operation Allied Force (March–May 1999), which ultimately secured the Serbian retreat. In a videotaped message to the Serbian people, President Clinton explained NATO's actions:

The [nineteen] NATO nations have tried to avert this conflict through every means we knew to be available. Each of us has ties to Serbia. Each respects the dignity and the courage of the Serb people. In the end, we decided that the dangers of acting are outweighed by the dangers of allowing this conflict to continue, to worsen, to claim the lives of more innocent civilians—including children—to result in tens of thousands of more homeless refugees.[120]

Following the military operation, Kosovo was placed under a transitional UN administration, and fifty thousand peacekeepers protected the fragile peace.

NATO's seventy-eight-day air campaign was the first time in the post–Cold War era that the United States and its European allies had intervened to stop genocide. Although the Department of Defense had initially opposed intervention in Kosovo, by early 1999, the Joint Chiefs of Staff agreed that a military campaign "was the best available option to show aggressive action, to keep NATO's word, to keep our NATO allies together, and to give us a chance to preserve [US] objectives."[121] In a joint press conference with Secretary of Defense William Cohen, President Clinton remarked:

> We have seen this kind of evil conduct before in this century, but rarely has the world stood up to it as rapidly, and with such unity and resolve as we see today with NATO's coalition of nineteen democracies, each with its own domestic pressures and procedures, but all united in our outrage, and in our determination to see this mission through.[122]

Critics charged that NATO's actions had established a dangerous precedent,[123] but members of the Clinton administration assured Americans that intervention was in the national interest because the warfare could easily spread throughout the Balkans, drawing Albania, Greece, and Turkey into the conflict and threatening US geopolitical interests.[124] Congress remained unconvinced. On May 4 the Senate voted seventy-eight to twenty-two to table a bill that would have authorized Clinton to use "all necessary force" to prevail in the war over Kosovo. The House passed a bill requiring congressional authorization for the use of ground troops in Kosovo.

The most brutal actions of the war occurred during NATO's intervention, however.[125] During the air strikes of March–June 1999, Serbian authorities expelled 1.3 million ethnic Albanians, Roma and Hashkalija "Gypsies," Slavic Muslims, and other ethnic/religious minorities. UNHCR officials working on the frontlines described Kosovar refugees streaming in all directions "as reminiscent of the last days of World War II when

Europe was awash with refugees."[126] Refugees encountered landmines en route to the border, or died from starvation and exposure to the elements. Humanitarian relief personnel were also forced to evacuate.

International human rights observers criticized NATO for carrying out the strikes "with virtually no thought about how to contain the humanitarian disaster that would follow" and without consulting with international relief agencies that would have to assist the refugees.[127] NATO forces mistakenly bombed hospitals, trains, and caravans of displaced persons.[128] On March 5, 1999, as the final Serbian offensive was underway, the Clinton administration announced Operation Sustain Hope to coordinate refugee relief efforts in Albania, Macedonia, and Kosovo. Thirty-six thousand metric tons of food—enough to feed half a million people for three months—and other life-saving supplies were placed at strategic locations along Kosovo's borders with Albania and Macedonia. In the weeks that followed, tents, medical supplies, and the equivalent of 1.1 million daily rations were sent to assist the refugees in Albania. By April 1999, the United States had committed over $150 million in financial and material assistance to address the humanitarian crisis in the region.

The Clinton administration would come to regard the intervention in Kosovo as one of its greatest successes: the strikes had ended the ethnic cleansing in Kosovo, eventually permitted the return of eight hundred thousand refugees, and prevented a wider conflict from engulfing the region.[129] As in Bosnia, the administration resisted calling the events in Kosovo genocide, which they considered a moral straitjacket. UN officials also resisted using the term "genocide." At a March 31, 1999, news conference, a UN spokesman said:

> You've noticed we have not yet used the term genocide, because we don't feel we have firm enough evidence. We don't know what's going on. . . . We'll have to see whether [the high commissioner for refugees] gets, from those interviews [with the refugees], a basis to make a determination. Under the Convention, you know, it's governments who are parties who then agree to take actions once they've established that genocide is taking place.[130]

Throughout the 1990s, polls revealed how conflicted Americans were about the possibility of a long, drawn-out war in the Balkans. Many Americans had never heard of Kosovo, so in his speeches the president used maps to try to convey the area's strategic importance to US interests. In his March 24 address, the president said:

> Take a look at this map. Kosovo is a small place, but it sits on a major fault line between Europe, Asia, and the Middle East, at the meeting place of Islam and both the Western and Orthodox branches of Christianity.... All the ingredients for a major war are there: ancient grievances, struggling democracies, and in the center of it all a dictator in Serbia who has done nothing since the cold war ended but start new wars and pour gasoline on the flames of ethnic and religious division.[131]

Gallup polls conducted in early April 1999, after weeks of NATO strikes, revealed that over half of Americans (57 percent) believed that the United States should participate in international peacekeeping forces; however, only 36 percent believed that the murder of "large numbers" of ethnic Albanians was critical to US interests and justified the use of US troops.[132] President Clinton continued to try to convince Americans about the legitimacy of US and NATO actions:

> I would far rather be standing here answering these questions [about NATO actions] ... than I would to be standing here having you ask me why we are permitting wholesale ethnic slaughter and ethnic cleansing and the creation of hundreds of thousands of refugees and not lifting a finger to do anything about it.[133]

Americans may have been conflicted about US military participation in Kosovo, but they were less equivocal about humanitarian relief. As the news media carried more and more stories about the devastation in Balkans, letters to the White House urged the president to do more to ease the pain and suffering of the population. The White House established a special phone line (1-800-USAID-RELIEF) where Americans could call in to donate to the humanitarian relief efforts. Through their churches, schools, and civic organizations, Americans raised millions of dollars for refugee relief or volunteered to sponsor refugee families.[134] US companies also provided much-needed supplies. The Gerber Baby Products Company, for example, donated close to twenty-two thousand cases of baby food products for infants in the refugee camps.

In order to ease the pressure on Albania and Macedonia, the Clinton administration announced that the United States would admit up to twenty thousand Kosovar refugees as part of Operation Open Arms and Provide Refuge. As with the Bosnians, select populations were prioritized for resettlement.[135] Despite the public's concerns for the Kosovar Albanians, the initial beneficiaries of the US resettlement program were the refugees from Krajina (a region within Croatia) who had been relocated to Kosovo by Serbian authorities as part of a campaign to alter the province's ethnic composition. When the violence in Kosovo escalated, these Krajina refugees feared retaliation and were forced to flee. A second group of beneficiaries consisted of ethnic Serbs from the predominantly Muslim sectors of the Bosnian Federation, who were members of ethnically mixed marriages, victims of torture, formers detainees, or the surviving spouses of persons killed in the concentration camps.[136] However, by November 1999, the 15,825 Kosovar Albanians refugees resettled in the United States had become a more representative sample of Kosovo's population.

President Clinton and First Lady Hillary Clinton met with refugees in camps in Germany, Macedonia, and Fort Dix (New Jersey). During the May 6 visit to Ingelheim, President Clinton remarked:

> Most people in the world would have a hard time believing what has happened to you. . . . But it is very important that your stories be told. . . . In places where people who have different religions and different ethnic groups, different racial groups, where they get along together, where they work together, where they help each other, people find what has happened to you to be literally almost unbelievable. And so the world needs to know the truth of Kosovo. And we need to make sure that we are all strong enough to stay with you and to support you until you can go home.[137]

Once resettled in the United States, however, the State Department offered to pay the transportation costs of all those who wished to return to their homeland and to cancel any existing travel loans from the United States, as long as the refugees left before May 1, 2000. Whether this effort was strategically designed to be part of the UNHCR's repatriation campaign is unclear. Of those resettled in the United States, 2,748 accepted the State Department's offer to return to Kosovo.[138]

In December 1999, the US State Department released two studies of Kosovo, which were distributed widely to assist in the prosecution of war crimes, crimes against humanity, and genocide by the International Criminal Tribunal for the former Yugoslavia (ICTY).[139] The State Department also interviewed refugees at Fort Dix and funded an American Bar Association war crimes documentation project to help the ICTY accumulate evidence on human rights violations. By 2011, 161 men (and a few women)—Croats, Serbs, Bosnians, and Albanians—faced prosecution for war crimes before the international tribunal, including Goran Hadžíc, responsible for the destruction of the Croatian town of Vukovar, where ten thousand lost their lives. Many more were tried in district and cantonal courts, trials that proceeded at an even slower pace.[140]

In September 2000, the Yugoslav people finally voted Slobodan Milošević out of office.[141] The following month, when he still refused to submit to the people's will, citizens staged a peaceful revolt that ultimately forced him out of power. The United States, which had financially invested in the democratic opposition, then resumed diplomatic relations and lifted sanctions on the new Yugoslavia. Milošević became the first sitting head of state to be indicted for war crimes, and the new Federal Republic of Yugoslavia eventually extradited him to stand trial, but he died in prison in The Hague in 2006 before he could be sentenced.

According to international relations scholar Kathryn Sikkink, international criminal tribunals like the one created for Yugoslavia were part of the "justice cascade," a "dramatic new trend in world politics toward holding individual state officials, including heads of state, criminally accountable for human rights violations."[142] Establishing genocide proved to be more difficult. In 2007, the International Court of Justice finally heard—and rejected—the charges of genocide filed by Bosnia-Herzegovina against Serbia in 1993. A majority of the court's fifteen judges ruled that there was insufficient evidence that Serbia had an "intent to destroy, in whole or in part, a national, ethnical, racial or religious group," as genocide is defined by the 1948 Convention. While the judges acknowledged that genocide had occurred in Srebrenica and that Serbia had supplied the Bosnian Serb army and thus failed to prevent the genocide, they stopped short of stating that Serbia had control over the slaughter. Eight years later, the International Court of Justice also rejected Serbian and Croatian claims of genocide during the Croatian war. However, the UN's International Criminal Tribunal for the former Yugoslavia (ICTY) had convicted dozens for war crimes. As late as 2016, Kosovo, which declared its independence in 2008, was threatening to file suit against Serbia for genocide committed during the 1998–1999 war.

Over the past decade, the remains of almost seven thousand of the victims of Srebrenica have been excavated and identified through DNA evidence. Without giving a name to the horrific events that occurred during the war and recognizing the complicity of many in these events, the emotional wounds will be impossible to heal. On July 11, 2015, the twentieth anniversary of the massacre at Srebrenica, an angry crowd of Bosnian Muslims attacked the Serbian prime minister, Alexander Vucic, when he came to Srebrenica to lay a wreath in memory of the dead. Many of the Bosnians in the crowd had lost brothers, fathers, and sons in the massacre and demanded that the guilty admit to their crimes. "Only on truth we can build a future," said one woman.[143]

American Responses to the Rwandan Genocide

The civil war that erupted in Rwanda in the wake of decolonization led to one of the most shocking cases of genocide in the second half of the twentieth century. During a four-month period, April to July 1994, an estimated eight hundred thousand people were slaughtered, and over one million people were internally displaced or forced to take refuge in neighboring Uganda, Zaire, Tanzania, and Burundi. The scale and rapidity of the genocide and the refugee crisis astounded even veteran humanitarian aid workers. On a single day, April 28, more than two hundred thousand Rwandans crossed into Tanzania through one border post;[144] and one million Rwandans fled into Zaire during a five-day period.[145]

The civil war in Rwanda was over thirty years in the making, the legacy of German-Belgian colonial policies that deliberately privileged one minority population group (the Tutsi) over the majority (the Hutu). The two populations essentially shared the same language, culture, and religion, but colonial policies had allowed international and local actors to manipulate identities and pit communities against each other for their own political and economic ends.[146] Rigid social and occupational distinctions emerged as a result, privileging the numerically smaller Tutsi (roughly 14 percent of the population), especially the Tutsi's Nyinginya clan. This fanned resentment in this poor, densely populated country, where the population already competed for limited fertile land and resources.

The Hutu uprising of 1959–1961 ended Tutsi control and forced over a hundred thousand Tutsi into neighboring Burundi. Between 1962 (the year of Belgian withdrawal) and 1967, Tutsi refugees tried to reclaim their place in society and staged ten attacks on the Hutu government, each leading to retaliatory killings and the flight of even more refugees into Uganda, Tanzania, Zaire, and Burundi. When Major General Juvenal Habyarimana, a Hutu, became president following the 1973 coup, discrimination against the Tutsi was further institutionalized. Arguing that population pressures were already too great, the government blocked the repatriation of Tutsi refugees and relied on identity cards to block their movement. According to the UNHCR, the failure to address the problems of the Rwandan refugees in the 1960s and 1970s contributed substantially to the genocide of 1994.[147]

By 1965, there were an estimated 850,000 refugees of different nationalities throughout Africa, most of them displaced by postindependence political conflicts like Rwanda's. The number grew to over a million by the end of the decade.[148] The 1951 UN Refugee Convention had imposed temporal and geographic constraints on the definition of refugee: refugees were those displaced before January 1, 1951, and most signatories interpreted the geographic scope as Europe. By the mid-1960s the majority of refugees assisted by the UNHCR had become refugees after 1951 and were located outside of Europe. These realities led to the drafting of the 1967 UN Protocol on the Status of Refugees, which broadened the definition of refugee and expanded the scope of international obligations.

The nations that comprised the Organization of African Unity, however, determined that a separate regionally based legal instrument was necessary to address the realities of the refugee situation on the African continent. The OAU's definition of "refugee" expanded the list of conditions that might generate a "well-founded fear of persecution" to include external aggression, foreign occupation or domination, and events disturbing public order. Under the OAU convention, individuals were entitled to protection as refugees even if they could not establish a "well-founded fear." Since the large numbers of refugees in Africa made individual screening impossible, the UNHCR also granted prima facie group determination of refugee status in certain cases.[149]

By 1990, the Tutsi refugee population had grown to almost seven hundred thousand. This population, especially those concentrated in Uganda, demanded the right to return to their homeland.[150] In October 1990, the Tutsi-dominated Rwandan Patriotic Front (RPF) launched an invasion of Rwanda, and civil war ensued for the next three and a half years, killing thousands and displacing close to a million people. In August 1993, representatives of the Habyarimana government and the RPF forces finally signed a peace agreement—the Arusha (Tanzania) Accords—that established a transitional government until elections could be held. A UN peacekeeping mission—the United Nations Assistance Mission for Rwanda (UNAMIR)—was brought in to monitor the cease-fire and ensure the enforcement of the accord, which also allowed for the repatriation of refugees and the creation of a unified military force comprised of soldiers from all sides. The program to repatriate and reintegrate refugees was never enacted, however. Over the next year, UN officials and Western diplomats became increasingly concerned about the millions of refugees and internally displaced persons in the Great Lakes region from many different countries, who had little chance of returning to their homelands or finding permanent homes elsewhere. Such conditions incubated resentment and raised the likelihood of ongoing warfare, they said, which would undermine any chance for long-term economic and political stability.[151]

Rwanda's fragile peace ended on April 6, 1994, when a plane crash just outside the capital city of Kigali killed Rwandan president Juvénal Habyarimana and Burundi president Cyprien Ntaryamira and their entourages as they returned from Arusha. The Tutsi-dominated RPF was blamed for the crash. Almost immediately, members of the presidential guard began killing Tutsi civilians in a residential area near the airport; within hours, the violence had spread throughout Kigali, killing Tutsi of all walks of life, as well as politically moderate Hutus like Prime Minister Agathe Uwilingiyimana, and the ten Belgian peacekeepers assigned to protect her. Journalists, aid workers, religious clergy and nuns, the elderly, women, children, and even infants were brutally raped, tortured, and killed. Government and military leaders deliberately incited the violence, using the radio and news media to warn the Hutu population that the Tutsis wanted to take their lands, reclaim their positions of relative privilege, and cast the Hutus once again into the second-class status of the colonial era. They called the Tutsis "cockroaches" that required extermination and distributed the machetes and other armaments that were used to kill over a million people.[152]

France, Belgium, Italy, and the United States sent planes and soldiers to evacuate their nationals, fully aware that the 2,519 UNAMIR forces in Rwanda would be unable to guarantee their safety. UNAMIR had neither the mandate nor the equipment to protect the population from the massacres that occurred right before their eyes.[153] After the brutal murder of the ten Belgian peacekeepers by the Rwandan Armed Forces (RAF), Belgium withdrew its troops. The UN Security Council eventually reduced the overall size of UNAMIR first to 550 peacekeepers and in time to an anemic 270.[154] Most humanitarian agencies, with the exception of the International Committee of the Red Cross and Médecins Sans Frontieres, withdrew their workers.

The lack of an international peacekeeping presence facilitated the genocide. The military and the Interahamwe paramilitary troops—and even ordinary civilians—lashed out, an action Gérard Prunier has argued was "partly classical genocide with the systematic massacre of an allegedly racially alien population, and partly political with the systematic killing of political opponents":

> *Interahamwe* manning the roadblocks asked people for their identity cards. To be identified on one's card as a Tutsi or to pretend to have lost one's papers meant certain death. Yet to have a Hutu ethnic card was not automatically a ticket to safety.... southern Hutu suspected of supporting opposition parties were also killed. And people were often accused of having a false card, especially if they were tall and with a straight nose and thin lips. Frequent intermarriage had produced many Hutu-looking Tutsi and Tutsi-looking Hutu. In towns or along the highways, Hutu who looked like Tutsi were very often killed, their denials and proffered cards with the "right" ethnic mention being seen as a typical Tutsi deception.[155]

Victims were frequently hacked to death by machetes and left to rot where they had fallen; at some massacre sites, corpses were dismembered and body parts stacked in piles. The Interahamwe paramilitaries called their massacres "bush clearing." Prunier recounted the "catalogue of horrors" so "one should never forget how great were the horrors which the survivors experienced":

> The killings were not in any way clean or surgical. The use of machetes often resulted in a long and painful agony and many people, when they had some money, paid their killers to be finished off with a bullet rather than being slowly hacked to death with a *panga*. Sexual abuse of women was common and they were often brutally killed after being raped. If some children joining the *Interahamwe* became killers, others were victims, babies were often smashed against a rock or thrown alive into pit latrines. Mutilations were common, with breasts and penises often being chopped off.... On the campus of Butare University, a Hutu teacher whose Tutsi wife

was in an advanced state of pregnancy saw her disemboweled under his eyes and had the foetus of his unborn child pushed in the face while killer shouted "Here! Eat your bastard!" In some cases, militiamen tried to force women to kill their children in order to save their own lives. Some people were burnt alive as their relations were forced to watch before being killed themselves. In other cases the *Interahamwe* told families that if they would kill a certain relation the rest of the family would be spared.[156]

Those who survived the genocide often reported having to hide under the blood-soaked corpses.

Some civilians refused orders to kill, and hid neighbors or helped them escape.[157] Olive Mukankusi, for example, harbored one woman and two teenage girls in a pit behind her home: "I knew these girls. I saw how much pain they were in," she said. "I was ready to die with them, whatever would happen to me or my family." When a neighbor tipped off the Interahamwe, Mukankusi and the three women were taken to a killing site by the river. Mukankusi had sewn all her cash from the recent harvest in the hem of her dress—the equivalent of $140, a significant amount in that poor country—and offered it as a bribe for their freedom. The militiamen accepted the bribe and allowed them to escape.[158] Silas Ntamfurigirishyari also refused to be complicit in the violence. Returning to his military camp one day, he encountered a truck full of soldiers transporting a group of Tutsi, including an old woman and a child. "They were going to kill them, so I stopped the militias and told them not to waste their time on the old woman, that I would kill her myself," said Ntamfurigirishyari. The soldiers assigned him the task of killing the old woman and the child. "We went in the bushes and . . . [I] told her . . . to wait for me. That night I went back and took her to Burundi, with the child she was carrying on her back. I safely returned to the camp without any incident."[159] Paul Rusesagagina, a manager at a Belgian-owned hotel in Kigali, is perhaps the best known of the rescuers due to the 2004 Hollywood film *Hotel Rwanda*, which dramatized his hiding of over twelve hundred Hutus and Tutsis.[160]

Forty-eight hours after the plane crash that killed Habyarimana and Ntaryamira, the RPF resumed their military operations against the Hutu government. Hutu officials eventually recognized that political and military defeat was inevitable and ordered the evacuation of the Hutu population. Entire communities of Hutu fled together on foot, either out of fear of Tutsi retaliation, or because they were coerced to leave by their government officials. As the Hutu left Rwanda, an estimated 700,000 Tutsi refugees—many of whom had been born abroad—returned from exile.[161] In turn, an estimated 1.3 to 2 million Hutu took refuge in camps in Tanzania, Uganda, and Burundi, but especially Zaire (Democratic Republic of the Congo), which became home to thirty-five refugee camps. The five largest camps—Katale, Kahindo, Mugunga, Lac Vert, and Sake—emerged around Goma, the administrative capital of North Kivu province in Zaire, and collectively housed roughly 850,000 people; the other thirty camps, south of Lake Kivu, together housed an estimated 650,000 refugees.[162] Despite the 1969 OAU Convention (Article II.6) that established that refugee camps be located at a "reasonable distance" from an international border, the majority of the refugee camps were located within a few miles of Rwandan borders, facilitating cross-border raids by military units. Over time, the largest refugee camps came to function as cities in their own right, with restaurants, hostels, bars, cinemas, pharmacies, stores, hairdressers, and mechanics.[163]

Overcrowding, violence, disease, and starvation were common in the refugee camps, killing as many as six hundred people a day.[164] Over two hundred aid agencies sent personnel to Goma, and over the next few years, these humanitarian aid workers struggled to provide material assistance and security to the civilian refugees but ultimately lost influence in the camps as Hutu army officers of the Rwandan Armed Forces (FAR), as well as criminal elements, controlled the distribution of food and medical supplies, sold humanitarian aid for personal gain or to finance military operations, and used the refugee camps as strategic bases from which they launched their war against the new Tutsi government of Rwanda. Practically all the Hutu politicians and military men responsible for the genocide settled in Zaire, where President Mobutu Sese Seko offered them freedom of movement.[165] Zairean officers, in turn, demanded payments from humanitarian agencies to let the planes carrying refugee relief land in Zaire. Aid workers were repeatedly harassed and threatened, forcing some organizations, including Médecins Sans Frontières, to withdraw altogether from the camps. The UNHCR was forced to cancel its repatriation efforts when refugees and aid workers were threatened with violence. Approximately 140,000 Hutu managed to repatriate on their own by 1994, but rumors of political killings in Rwanda and Zaire slowed the repatriation to a trickle by 1995.[166] Fighting continued for many years after between forces of the now Tutsi-led Rwandan government and the former *genocidaires*, the ex-FAR and the Interahamwe, reigniting hatreds, contributing to the deaths of many more civilians, and leaving humanitarian aid workers alone to deal with the "living hell."[167]

Aid continued to flow into the refugee camps, however, despite international criticism that it was inadvertently contributing to the continuation of war and criminal violence. Asked why the UNHCR did not withdraw from the camps, UNHCR commissioner Sadako Ogata responded, "There were also innocent refugees in the camps; more than half were women and children. Should we have said: you are related to murderers, so you are guilty, too? My mandate—unlike those of private aid agencies—obliges me to help."[168] Screening the refugee population to separate the innocent from those responsible for war crimes proved almost impossible. From 1994 to 1996, more funding was spent on the camps than on humanitarian aid to Rwanda: $2,036 billion versus $897 million.[169] The international aid community explored a variety of options to encourage refugees to return to their homes, but the camps became a permanent feature of the Rwandan borderlands.

The scale of the genocide, the ongoing refugee migration, and the seemingly permanent camp populations destabilized the governments of the African Great Lakes region and the Congo basin for the next two decades. In 1996, the Tutsi-led Rwandan government went to war against Mobutu's government, the First Congo War, which resulted in his ousting and the creation of the Democratic Republic of the Congo under the leadership of Laurent-Désiré Kabila. The Congolese civil wars ultimately involved nine nations and resulted in the deaths of over five million people.

Distracted by the humanitarian crises in Haiti, Iraq, and the Balkans, Rwanda was an inconvenience for the Clinton administration. President Clinton publicly condemned the mass murder of civilians, as did many heads of state, but he knew that it would be hard to mobilize public opinion in support of US intervention. The Clinton foreign policy doctrine, as articulated by Secretary of State Warren Christopher and General Colin Powell of the Joint Chiefs of Staff, called for the use of American forces only when American interests were at stake, and only when a clear exit plan was in place. The 1993 killings of eighteen US soldiers who were part of a UN peacekeeping force in Mogadishu, the Somali capital—and the shocking scenes on television of cheering mobs dragging the bodies of dead American soldiers through the streets of the capital—had intensified domestic pressure for a US withdrawal from Somalia and led to a reevaluation of American participation in UN peacekeeping efforts around the world. Sensitive to public opinion, Clinton knew that it would be impossible to justify American casualties in Rwanda, a country most Americans could not locate on a map. Although Clinton would later call his Rwanda policy one of his greatest regrets, in 1994 his administration refused to call the events that transpired genocide, which would have morally mandated intervention.[170] Instead, senior officials carefully chose their words, opting to say that acts of genocide may have occurred. "As a responsible Government, you don't go around hollering 'genocide,'" the US ambassador to Rwanda stated. "You say that acts of genocide may have occurred and they need to be investigated."[171] Some administration officials preferred to call it a civil war rather than a genocide targeting an ethnic minority, since the Hutu were also killed in large numbers. Human rights activists working on the ground viewed this as a false equivalency. Allison Des Forges of Human Rights Watch recounted the organization's attempts to influence US and UN policy in Rwanda:

In a war, you can also have war crimes, and either side can be guilty of war crimes. In this particular war, both sides were guilty of war crimes. One side was guilty of genocide. So it must be clear that you don't confuse these things; you don't make any equivalence between them. The government of Rwanda, at that time, some of its military forces, its militias, were used to carry out a genocide against Tutsi and to eliminate political opponents and people who opposed the genocide. They also engaged in some war crimes and crimes against humanity in their attacks on civilian targets during war and so on.[172]

Many in the human rights community condemned the Clinton administration for failing to intervene, but also for failing to use its influence before the UN Security Council, as it had done with Kuwait and Iraq.[173] The Clinton administration ignored a January 11, 1994, telegram sent to the UN leadership and the US ambassador from a high-ranking informant, detailing the militia's plans to kill the Tutsi; it ignored a February 24 telex from the Belgian minister of foreign affairs warning of a genocide; and it ignored a CIA study of January 1994 warning that if combat were to begin Rwanda, up to half a million civilians would be killed.[174] Consequently, when Canadian major general Roméo Dallaire requested additional troops to supplement the twenty-five hundred UN forces already in Rwanda, the UN Security Council denied his request. The Clinton administration, which supplied one-third of the UN's budget, feared that the United States would have to carry the entire peacekeeping operation if the international community did not provide enough troops. On May 3, 1994, as the carnage was underway, Clinton signed Presidential Decision Directive 25 to specifically define the limited role the United States would play in peacekeeping operations in the post–Cold War era. During his administration, the scope and the size of UN peacekeeping missions would remain modest—and some argued, ineffectual.[175]

In a June 1994 op-ed in the *Washington Post*, Herman "Hank" Cohen, a former assistant secretary of state for Africa, criticized the Clinton administration for viewing Rwanda as a traditional peacekeeping operation:

> Traditional peacekeeping calls for a negotiated cease-fire followed by the arrival of lightly armed multilateral forces who monitor and observe. Rwanda, on the other hand, is a case of planned, systematic murder of men, women and children who happen to belong to a particular group—the Tutsi. Both the self-proclaimed government of Rwanda, which has armed the death squads who are doing the ethnic killing, and the rebel Rwanda Patriotic Front fighters, do not want to stop fighting until they can finish the genocide or dominate militarily. Waiting to intervene until there is "progress toward a cease-fire," in [Secretary of State] Albright's words, is like a doctor telling a heart attack victim, "Take two aspirins, and call me in the morning." . . . If anything is going to destroy the credibility of the international community in the area of conflict resolution, the American policy is going to do it. . . . It may be too late to save the Tutsi of Rwanda. . . . Another Holocaust may have just slipped by, hardly noticed.[176]

In the popular press, syndicated columnist Anthony Lewis criticized the cautiousness of the Clinton administration: "Those of us who came to oppose the Vietnam war naturally applaud the cautiousness of military leaders. But like any doctrine, this one can be overdone. . . . The United States is the one remaining superpower. If it cannot use force to prevent disasters, then the world is truly condemned to chaos."[177] During 1994, only one editorial on the genocide appeared in the *New York Times* and only one appeared in the *Washington Post*; but neither editorial urged US intervention to stop it. Both the House of Representatives and the Senate passed resolutions condemning the massacre in Rwanda, but the congressmen urged the participation of the US troops only to assist in the delivery of humanitarian aid.

Many years later, in his powerful *Eyewitness to a Genocide*, Michael Barnett called the behavior of the United States "simply unconscionable" and called the UN's lack of concern for the Rwandans "arrestingly callous." "Diversionary tropes such as the 'UN' and the 'international community,'" wrote Barnett, "must not be allowed to conceal the simple fact that individuals were aware of the crimes being committed and were in positions of responsibility—but chose not to act."[178] Samantha Power also blamed the failure to intervene on the failure of leadership:

But imagine if the president had taken his profound political capital and charisma, and if it had been him going to African countries, urging them to send troops, saying, "Hey, look, there's a division of labor on this earth. The United States is involved in Haiti now. We were involved in Somalia. This is one we're not going to be involved. We're not going to be boots on the grounds. . . . But the fact that we're not going to put boots on the ground doesn't disqualify us from exerting leadership." The really profound mistake was to think that if US troops are taken off the table, or if they never even go near the table . . . then that somehow disqualifies the United States from playing a prominent leadership role.[179]

Mark Doyle of the BBC World Service, in turn, attributed American and international indifference to the fact that the victims were Africans: "I don't think there can be any doubt that if hundreds of thousands of Europeans or Americans were being killed in the way that Rwandans were being killed—do you think the world would not have intervened? I think it was because they were Africans."[180] General Roméo Dallaire would later agree with this assessment. On the tenth anniversary of the genocide, Dallaire called the failure to intervene in the Rwandan genocide an example of "self-interested racism":

Not all humans are human in the international context. Some countries are seen as important, but we have coldly created a tier of orphan nations. . . . Ten years ago, Bosnians counted much more because they were Europeans, and the Balkans represented a strategic interest worthy of international military intervention. . . . I'm sure there would have been much more reaction [from the international community] if someone had tried to exterminate Rwanda's three hundred mountain gorillas.[181]

A modest force of five thousand men could have made a significant difference, said Dallaire. Instead, he and his remaining 270 troops barely escaped with their lives and watched helplessly as people were butchered or starved to death.

US intervention in and around Rwanda was limited to humanitarian relief, as mandated by the July 1994 defense appropriations bill. Congress authorized $170 million in emergency aid to Rwanda (with an additional $50 million a month later). The United States provided 40 percent of the supplies offered as aid.[182] US forces provided air traffic control assistance at airfields, to allow the cargo planes carrying humanitarian assistance to land, and they provided surveillance aircraft to help track refugees.[183] Two hundred troops helped with relief efforts at the Kigali airport, and four thousand troops assisted at refugee sites outside of Rwanda.[184] US forces were required to withdraw by October 1, 1994, but over the next few years, they remained in the region in a range of capacities. In 1996, for example, four thousand US troops assisted in a multinational humanitarian aid mission in Zaire to deliver supplies to the more than one million refugees in camps along the Rwandan border.

In the wake of the genocide, the Clinton administration created or expanded economic development programs in the region, hoping such programs would nurture political stability. Congress passed the African Growth and Opportunity Act, targeting sub-Saharan Africa, which offered economic incentives (such as the duty-free import of certain products into the United States) to develop a market economy. The administration also facilitated a restructuring of debt by the World Bank and the International Monetary Fund through the Heavily Indebted Poor Countries (HIPC) program.[185] Finally, the administration doubled humanitarian aid to assist in the treatment and prevention of HIV/AIDS, especially in South Africa and Botswana, where as many as a third of all adults were HIV positive.[186]

During the 1990s, the number of immigrants and refugees coming to the United States from African nations more than doubled (especially from countries in West and East Africa), making them one of the fastest-growing populations in the United States. In 1990 Africa received only 3,500 of the 110,000 slots for refugee admissions, but by the year 2000, they received 18,000 of the 90,000 spaces, second only to Europe's 44,500.[187] By 2009, more than half of the Africa-born people living in the United States had arrived between 1990 and 2000. Immigrants and

Table 2.3 Rwandan Refugee Arrivals, 1990–2000

Fiscal year	Total arrivals
1990	—
1991	2
1992	3
1993	7
1994	31
1995	88
1996	118
1997	100
1998	86
1999	153
2000	345

Source: Department of Homeland Security, Fiscal Year 2000 Statistical Yearbook, http://www.dhs.gov/publication/fiscal-year-2000-statistical-yearbook-refugeesasylees.

refugees from Rwanda comprised only a tiny fraction of this population, however. Nigeria, Egypt, and Ethiopia provided the largest number of immigrants; and Somalia and Sudan accounted for the largest number of refugees.[188] Only 933 refugees were admitted from Rwanda (as compared to 35,308 from Somalia and 15,593 from Sudan), in large part because of the impossibility of distinguishing who among the refugees were war criminals (see table 2.3).[189] An additional 648 received asylum from FY1994 to FY2000.[190] Citizens of Rwanda visiting the United States at the time of the genocide qualified for temporary protected status (TPS) from June 7, 1994, to December 6, 1997.[191]

Despite the intensive screening, over the next two decades, several war criminals were identified among the Rwandan refugee and asylee population in the United States and were subsequently deported. Jean-Marie Vianney Mudahinyuka, for example, came in 2000 and settled in Chicago, where members of the Rwandan exile community eventually identified him. In 2005 he was convicted of immigration fraud and assault of a federal officer, and sentenced to fifty-one months in prison, after which he was transferred to the custody of Immigration and

Customs Enforcement (ICE) to await deportation. Having exhausted all avenues for appeal, he was finally deported to face charges of genocide and war crimes.[192] In 2013, Rwanda exiles also identified war criminal Beatrice Munyenyezi, who was living in New Hampshire. Munyenyezi was convicted of immigration fraud and sentenced to ten years in prison. Her sister, Prudence Kantengwa, was also convicted of lying under oath during immigration proceedings. Munyenyezi's husband, Arsene Shalom Ntahobali, and mother-in-law, Pauline Nyiramasuhuko, were later brought up for war crimes before the UN-backed International Criminal Tribunal for Rwanda. The tribunal, based in Arusha, Tanzania, had, by 2013, convicted and sentenced a mere sixty-five people, and dozens of cases remained pending. Communal courts in Rwanda known as "Gacaca" also played a role in the prosecution of war criminals.[193] But the vast majority of those who committed violence remained unidentified and unpunished, making national reconciliation difficult if not impossible.[194] In the two decades since the genocide, various institutions have tried to document this painful history. The stories of perpetrators, survivors, and rescuers have been collected to educate the new generation, half of whom were born after the genocide.

Rwandan genocide survivors living in the United States also have been proactive in collecting stories; in testifying against war criminals; in raising funds for fellow survivors back in the homeland; and in raising international awareness about the events that unfolded in the 1990s. Clemantine Wamariya, for example, now travels throughout the country to raise awareness about genocide. Wamariya and her sister lived in seven different refugee camps until the IOM identified her for resettlement in the United States. In 2006, her high school essay on Elie Wiesel's *Night* won a national competition and an appearance on *The Oprah Winfrey Show*, where Winfrey surprised Wamariya with a reunion with her parents, who she had thought were dead. "If people saw me on the street," she said, "they would never recognize the things I have gone through and the pain others are still going through. . . . I really want to do all I can to be a human rights activist educating people about genocide, war, and crimes against humanity."[195]

Pregnant Eugenie Mukeshimana survived the genocide thanks to the generosity of the strangers who hid her. For years she was ashamed to say that she was from Rwanda, but a turning point came one day when sitting in a college class: "The professor couldn't pronounce my last name, and I had to state it for him. Then the professor asked me where I was from, and when I said Rwanda there was no response." Soon after she founded the Genocide Survivors Support Network to help genocide survivors rebuild their lives.[196]

At age nine, Jacqueline Murekatete lost her parents, her six siblings, and her extended family to the violence. She became a lawyer, human rights activist, and motivational speaker before founding the Genocide Survivors Foundation, a nonprofit foundation in New York City, that raises awareness about genocide prevention, and supports victims of mass atrocities.[197]

Perhaps the best known of the Rwandan refugees in the United States is Imaculée Ilibagiza, a motivational speaker and author of seven books about the genocide, including the memoir *Left to Tell: Discovering God amidst the Rwandan Holocaust*, in which she recounts how she survived the genocide because a Hutu pastor hid her—and seven other women—for ninety-one days in a tiny three- by four-foot bathroom. She sought asylum in the United States in 1998 and worked at the United Nations before dedicating herself full-time to public speaking and writing about the genocide. Her Left to Tell Charitable Fund supports Rwandan orphans.[198]

In 1998, a Senate subcommittee hearing on Rwanda discussed whether a larger, well-armed, and strategically positioned peacekeeping force, with a strong mandate to intervene, might have prevented the "machete-wielding" *genocidaires* from carrying out their destruction. "Have we really learned any valuable lessons from the horrors of 1994?" asked subcommittee chairman, Christopher Smith:

> Somehow the international community, as it likes to call itself, has failed to learn the most important lesson of all. When we have information that suggests innocent people are about to be massacred, we must act on that information, rather than ignoring it and hoping it will go away.[199]

Yet, as the congressman duly noted, less than a year after the Rwandan genocide, UN peacekeepers in Bosnia ignored the warning signs and "let the massacre at Srebrenica happen."

On the tenth anniversary of the Rwandan genocide, Roméo Dallaire, the Canadian major general who headed the peacekeeping forces, had harsher words for the United States and the international community. Had the big powers reacted to the genocide, he said, "We would have saved millions from this calamity. But I'm afraid we haven't learned, and the same thing could happen again. How do you live with that?"[200]

Two decades after the genocides of the 1990s, millions more were at risk—this time in Syria, Burundi, Somalia, the Central African Republic, Myanmar, and Nigeria. What the Iraqi, Balkan, and Rwandan case studies have demonstrated, however, is that widespread and horrific violence does not guarantee that victims will receive refuge in the United States. As troubling as the news of genocide might be to American readers, their unfamiliarity with certain regions of the world (and perhaps their suspicion of racial and cultural difference), makes them unlikely to call for the admission of large numbers of refugees. If refugee populations have few coethnics living in the United States, or other advocates of goodwill, their chances of admission further diminish. In such cases, legislators must be especially proactive in creating opportunities for refuge, not because their constituents demand it, but because it's the moral thing to do.

3

Refuge in the National Security State

BY 2014, THE number of refugees in the Near East was staggering. The three million Syrian refugees in the region were the largest refugee population under the UNHCR's mandate, followed by Afghans, at 2.7 million, who had held the top position for more than three decades.[1] The burden of accommodating these refugees was borne by neighboring countries, namely, Pakistan, Iran, Jordan, Turkey, and Lebanon. "In 2014, we have seen the number of people under our care grow to unprecedented levels," said UN high commissioner for refugees António Guterres. "As long as the international community continues to fail to find political solutions to existing conflicts and to prevent new ones from starting, we will continue to have to deal with the dramatic humanitarian consequences."[2]

US assistance focused on humanitarian aid packages to facilitate the UNHCR's work on the ground. In 2007, for example, the United States supplied one-third of the UNHCR's $60 million appeal for humanitarian assistance to Iraqi refugees. The sum paled in comparison to the estimated $2 billion a week the United States spent to wage the war that "directly or indirectly . . . caused four million Iraqis to be forced from their homes."[3]

The number of Iraqi (and other Near Eastern) refugees resettled in the United States were also "a drop in the ocean."[4] Refugees encountered a hostile immigration bureaucracy that viewed them as potential threats, and sometimes not even the UNHCR's endorsement could help secure a coveted visa. After the terrorist attacks of 1993 and 2001, the US government restructured the immigration bureaucracy to make it more difficult for all travelers to enter in order to convey to Americans a greater sense of safety. Terrorism on US soil was not a new phenomenon, but the terrorists' targeting of important and highly symbolic landmarks—and the high number of casualties—had elicited a fear unknown since the early

Cold War. The George W. Bush administration, often with the cooperation of Congress, reconfigured government agencies to address the vulnerabilities in the immigration system that had allowed the terrorists to enter the United States and remain undetected. In the wake of 1993 and 2001, immigrants were viewed as potential threats to national security, regardless of their political ideologies or the areas of the world they might come from. Those from the Islamic world were subject to particular scrutiny; but over time, all immigrants bore the burden of increasingly draconian securitization policies. Not surprisingly, the number of refugees admitted to the United States decreased significantly in the immediate aftermath of these events. Refugee quotas remained unfilled during the first decade of the twenty-first century in large part because of fears of granting terrorists access to the United States.

The First World Trade Center Bombing

At 12:17 p.m., on February 26, 1993, a bomb exploded beneath the twin towers of the World Trade Center (WTC) carving a one-hundred-foot crater several stories deep and several more high. Six people died in the explosion, and more than one thousand were injured. The casualties could have been significantly higher. The bomb-makers had planned for the explosion to topple the towers, knocking one into the other like falling dominoes, to kill a quarter-million people in New York City.[5]

The principal architect of the attack was Ramzi Yousef (an alias for Abdul Basit), an engineer of Pakistani origin, who arrived at John F. Kennedy International Airport on September 1, 1992, from Pakistan. A coconspirator, Ahmad Ajaj, traveling on the same flight, was detained and interrogated by US authorities because his forged Swedish passport attracted suspicion. When police searched Ajaj's suitcase they found bombmaking manuals and videotapes of suicide bombers. Yousef's Iraqi passport also aroused suspicion, but he deflected further scrutiny by requesting asylum, which immediately referred him to immigration authorities, who then sent Yousef to an INS detention facility in New Jersey. The facility was overcrowded at the time of his arrival, so authorities released Yousef on his own recognizance and told him to return for his asylum hearing. He never showed up.

Yousef was not a "lone-wolf terrorist" but part of a loosely affiliated group of men of different nationalities who came together in New York City to plot an attack.[6] These men did not act on behalf of any nation, nor were they part of an organization with an identifiable structure, base of operations, or well-established means of fund-raising. The only immediate link between them was that several of the coconspirators were followers of Sheikh Omar Abdel-Rahman, a blind, fifty-two-year-old Egyptian-born cleric who preached at the Al-Farouq mosque on Atlantic Avenue in Brooklyn, known for his anti-American, anticapitalist teachings. Yousef and his fellow conspirators stockpiled the chemical ingredients they needed for their bomb making in a rented storage locker in New Jersey, and tested the explosives at different locations. Once satisfied with their plan, they chose a date, loaded their homemade bomb, which weighed an estimated twelve hundred to fifteen hundred pounds, into a rented van, parked the van on a ramp beneath the WTC, lit the twenty-foot fuses, and sped off in another car. The explosion on February 26 knocked out the WTC sprinklers, generators, elevators, public address system, emergency command center, and more than half of the high-voltage lines that fed electricity to the complex.[7] As rescuers worked late into the night to rescue or evacuate the survivors, Yousef was on a plane to Pakistan. During the two years it took to capture him he conspired in several other acts of terrorism around the world.

The FBI eventually traced the van back to one of the conspirators, Mohammed Salameh, and through him the other conspirators were identified. In March 1994, a federal jury convicted Salameh, Ahmad Aja, Nidal Ayyad, and Mahmoud Abouhaima of carrying out the bombing and sentenced them to life in prison. The following year, a jury found Sheik Abdul-Rahman and nine others guilty of various terrorism-related charges, including a plot to blow up the George Washington Bridge, the United Nations, the Holland and Lincoln Tunnels, and other New York City landmarks and offices. In 1995, Yousef and Eyad Ismoil, the driver of the van, were finally arrested in Pakistan and Jordan, respectively, and extradited to the United States. Calling him "a virus that must be locked away," a US district judge sentenced Yousef to life in prison plus 240 years. Today he remains in solitary confinement in a seven- by eleven-foot cell in a super-max prison in Florence, Colorado.[8] The last conspirator, Abdul Yasin, fled to Iraq after being questioned and released by the FBI; two decades later, he remains at large. Yousef's maternal uncle Khalid Sheikh Mohammed would later play a role in the terrorist attacks of September 11, 2001.

As the complex details of the 1993 conspiracy came to light, journalists and media personalities, elected officials, and even the president himself expressed incredulity that a man who had arrived with problematic travel documents, on a flight transporting a suspected terrorist, could be released so readily into US society by immigration authorities. Subsequent investigations revealed other irregularities. Many of those associated with the WTC and NYC landmarks conspiracies had manipulated the immigration bureaucracy in order to stay in the United States: three had received amnesty under the Special Agricultural Workers Program; six had secured permanent residency by marrying US citizens; and others had remained in the US illegally past the expiration of their tourist visas.[9] Sheikh Abdel-Rahman, who had given ideological and financial support to Yousef and his fellow conspirators, entered and exited the United States several times during the early 1990s despite his presence on an FBI "look-out" list. Abdel-Rahman was implicated in the assassinations of Egyptian president Anwar Sadat and Israeli rabbi and extreme right-wing politician Meir Kahane, but he nevertheless received a "green card" in 1991 to establish permanent residency in the United States. (The New York Times had located Abdel-Rahman in Brooklyn four months before he received his visa and had alerted readers to his presence.)[10] When State Department authorities finally arrested him in August 1992 and revoked his residency, Abdel-Rahman requested asylum and was allowed to remain in the US to await his hearing.[11] In an interview on Good Morning America, New York governor Mario Cuomo expressed what was becoming the prevailing American sentiment in the post–Cold War period:

> All the asylum laws are a joke. We all know that. It's not just the sheikh, that just made it dramatic. You come in, you say asylum, they say "OK." It'll take us a year to figure out whether or not you're telling us the truth. Meanwhile, go down . . . and get yourself a job. They disappear. It is a joke. That has to be changed.[12]

The terrorist attack of 1993 set into motion a radical restructuring of the US immigration bureaucracy that would have lasting effects into the twenty-first century. Strengthening US national security meant restricting the entrance of all state and nonstate actors that might potentially harm the United States, be they terrorists, drug smugglers, or other criminals;[13] but immigrants, refugees, and asylum seekers became the real casualties of this restructuring since they, too, were increasingly identified as threats to the state and to the safety and well-being of Americans. Threat was defined not only in political and military terms but also in social, cultural, and economic terms. By competing with Americans for jobs, or refusing to culturally assimilate, immigrants were threats to the American way of life, some argued, and thus had to be barred from entering the United States. Landed ports of entry—vulnerabilities readily exploited by migrants and other nonstate actors—required increased vigilance and even militarization. Immigrants already on US soil, regardless of status, were also viewed as potential internal enemies and subject to increased surveillance.

In the aftermath of the 1993 WTC bombing, the FBI watch lists expanded, and more and more individuals were apprehended at US airports or at the US-Canada border;[14] but for many Americans, the US-Mexico border—and not these other ports of entry—became the symbol of the country's vulnerability simply because of the sheer number of Mexicans and Central Americans who crossed that political borderline day in and day out, to work in *el norte*, often without legal authorization. In a July 1993 press conference discussing his proposed immigration reform package, President Bill Clinton complained that US borders "leak[ed] like a sieve" and that the Border Patrol was "breathtakingly understaffed."[15] Two months later, the president proclaimed illegal immigration the major threat to the security of the United States: "The simple fact is that we must not and cannot surrender our borders to those who wish to exploit our history of compassion and justice.... We must say no to illegal immigration."[16] The term "illegal immigration" was associated with migration from Latin America, not the Middle East, so the president's words refocused attention on the US-Mexico border and away from other permeable points of entry. Keeping the United States safe from terrorists might have been the initial impulse driving immigration, refugee, and asylum reform after 1993, but controlling the movement of undocumented laborers from the Americas ultimately became its major focus. If the ideologically driven lone-wolf terrorist could not be stopped completely from accessing the United States, stopping the immigrant worker at the border at least demonstrated accountability to one's electoral constituents. Refugees, asylum seekers, and even labor migrants became the casualties of the new reform policies.

Making the Border Less Permeable

A CNN / *USA Today* poll taken months after the 1993 World Trade Center bombing found that 76 percent of Americans believed that immigration should be stopped or greatly reduced. "If you can picture the image of the Statue of Liberty dissolving, and being replaced by the image of the World

Trade Center after it was bombed," said Arthur C. Helton, then director of the Refugee Project of the Lawyer's Committee for Human Rights, "you have the sense of the negative trends in the current [immigration] debate." A spokesman for the Federation for American Immigration Reform (FAIR) put it more bluntly: "The American people want a sense that there are limits and that immigration policy isn't set by a poem [on the base of the Statue of Liberty]—a lovely poem but one never voted on."[17]

The attack on the World Trade Center occurred a month after President Clinton assumed office, and the president's experience, as governor of Arkansas, had taught him how an immigration-related crisis could undermine a political administration. The intense negative publicity surrounding the 1980 Mariel boatlift from Cuba, and the internment and subsequent rioting of the Cuban refugees sent to Fort Chaffee, Arkansas, derailed Clinton's chances of reelection in the fall of 1980—the first time an Arkansas gubernatorial incumbent had been defeated in a quarter-century.[18] The expanding news coverage on undocumented immigration in 1993 only heightened the president's concerns that immigration would once again be his albatross. Thousands of undocumented immigrants were intercepted each week. During the first five months of 1993, the Coast Guard interdicted over sixteen hundred men, women, and children from China alone. Perhaps the most dramatic case involved the *Golden Venture*, a cargo ship smuggling 286 workers from China's Fujian province, which ran aground on a sandbar two hundred yards from Jacob Riis Park in Queens.[19] Six weeks after the *Golden Venture* incident, President Clinton announced the administration's proposals for immediate and long-term immigration reform.[20]

Members of Congress also rushed to propose their own immigration reform bills. Over eighty immigration-related bills were introduced during the 103rd Congress, most of them focused on the policing of immigrants.[21] Hoping to influence the debate, the US Commission on Immigration Reform—a commission authorized by the 1990 Immigration Act—released its first interim report, *US Immigration Policy: Restoring Credibility*, in September 1994. Many of the commission's conclusions were hardly surprising. "Enforcement efforts have not been effective in deterring unlawful immigration," lamented its authors, which included chair and former congressional representative Barbara Jordan. "This failure to develop effective strategies to control unlawful immigration has blurred the public perception of the distinction between legal and illegal immigrants." However, rather than stress immigrants' threat to public safety, the report addressed the economic drivers of unauthorized entry, including the role of US employers played in luring and exploiting unauthorized workers. To counter unauthorized immigration, the report urged the "vigorous" enforcement of labor standards; the targeted investigation of industries that had a history of hiring unauthorized workers; increased sanctions on those employers who knowingly hired and exploited the undocumented; and increased penalties on those who produced counterfeit identification documents. To produce a long-term reduction in unauthorized migration, the commission urged the government to reassess the country's diplomatic and economic policies.[22]

From 1993 to 1996, as the Clinton administration addressed humanitarian crises in Haiti, the Balkans, and Rwanda, and another boatlift from Cuba, Congress heatedly debated the specifics of a new immigration policy. In September 1996, Congress passed the Illegal Immigration Reform and Immigrant Responsibility Act (PL 104-208), a comprehensive immigration act whose 750 pages covered topics as diverse as "mail-order brides," foreign physicians, employment eligibility, and visa processing.[23] However, the principal focus of the law was controlling unauthorized immigration, which, though not specifically referenced, was associated with Mexico, Central America, and the Caribbean, not the Middle East.

To deter unauthorized immigration, this new legislation strengthened patrols along the US-Mexico border and made punishment for violators more severe. IIRAIRA expanded the US Border Patrol by five thousand agents over the next five years; authorized the purchase of state-of-the-art equipment including aircraft, helicopters, night-vision goggles, and sensors to assist in the patrolling of the US-Mexico border; imposed harsher penalties on those who smuggled immigrants under the guidelines of the Racketeer Influenced and Corrupt Organizations Act (RICO); and imposed harsher penalties on those apprehended in the United States without authorization, or who stayed past the expiration of a visa. On this last point, those unlawfully present in the United States for more than 180 days, but less than a year, were barred from reentering the country for a period of three years; those unlawfully present for more than a year were barred from future admission for ten years.[24] To facilitate the incarceration and deportation of immigrants, IIRAIRA reclassified several misdemeanor crimes as aggravated felonies if committed by an undocumented immigrant. In sum, IIRAIRA was the most punitive immigration legislation since the Johnson Reed Act of 1924. Passed almost in tandem was the

1996 Welfare Reform Act, which eliminated food stamps to 730,000 disabled or otherwise needy legal immigrants, including children.[25]

Several of IIRAIRA's provisions dealt specifically with refugees and asylum seekers. First, as a nod to evangelical Christian advocacy groups, Congress allowed the entrance of up to one thousand persons per year from countries that imposed population control measures such as abortion and sterilization, institutionalizing a policy first adopted by the George H. W. Bush administration. Second, in order to discourage the filing of frivolous asylum claims to delay deportation, immigrants were required to apply for asylum within one year of entering the United States, and they were barred from work authorization for 180 days pending the resolution of their asylum cases. Third, those with criminal records, or who engaged in the persecution of others, were barred admission to the United States. And, fourth, those who traveled through a "safe third country" on their way to the United States could be required to return to that country to file their asylum claim.

Refugee advocates objected to many of these provisions. The bar on those with criminal records, for example, raised the possibility that legitimate asylum seekers might be barred from entrance for political acts criminalized in their home countries but not criminalized in the United States. The one-year filing deadline penalized the severely traumatized, who often delayed requesting asylum for fear that they might not be believed and then deported to face their persecutors. The IIRAIRA provision that elicited the loudest objections from refugee advocates, however, was the provision requiring the "expedited removal" of those apprehended without proper documentation. Individuals who fled persecution often lost or were denied official identification papers; or they secured counterfeit documents with new identities to avoid detection by their own state police. The "expedited removal" of such individuals, without a chance to prove their identities and legitimate claims to asylum in an immigration court, constituted a violation of the UN principle of *nonrefoulement*, argued many refugee advocates.

The expanded militarization of the US-Mexico border mandated by the 1996 law came just as the Clinton administration was establishing "the world's largest free trade area" through the North American Free Trade Alliance (NAFTA).[26] The administration regarded the unhindered movement of trade desirable, but not the free movement of laborers. The INS budget grew from $1.5 billion in FY1993 to $4.8 billion in FY2001, and INS personnel expanded from seventeen thousand to thirty thousand, including 6,700 new Border Patrol agents and immigration inspectors.[27] By the end of FY2000, the Border Patrol had over nine thousand agents. To restore public faith in the government's ability to control the country's borders and keep Americans safe from threat, the INS staged highly publicized policing operations along the "busiest illegal border-crossing corridors in the nation"—operations with provocative names such as Hold the Line (El Paso), Gatekeeper (San Diego), and Safeguard (southern Arizona). The administration heralded its success by releasing statistics on the apprehension, detention, and "removal" of aliens. From FY1993 to 2000, the average daily population of INS detainees increased from 5,877 to approximately 19,000; and more than 181,000 "criminal and other undocumented aliens" were "removed," quadruple the number removed in FY1993.[28]

The crackdown came at a human cost. The militarization of the border strained long-established family and commercial relations in the US-Mexico borderlands, making it difficult for Americans and Mexicans alike to freely shop, attend school, and visit family on the other side of the political border, as residents of the borderlands had done since the mid-nineteenth century. Over time, the militarization of high-traffic areas of the US-Mexico border redirected the flow of unauthorized migration across more dangerous stretches, especially across the Sonora/Arizona desert, leading to more immigrant deaths and an expansion of the smuggling enterprises the administration had tried so hard to curtail.[29]

September 11

In a letter to the *New York Times*, Nidal Ayyad, one of the conspirators of the 1993 bombing, told readers that Americans would continue to be targets of violence because they were complicit in their government's actions in the Middle East. An earlier draft of the letter, deleted by Ayyad on his computer but later recovered by FBI forensic specialists, included this prophetic statement: "Unfortunately, our calculations were not very accurate this time; however, we promise you that next time, it will be very precise and WTC will continue to be one of our targets."[30]

Eight years later, on September 11, 2001, nineteen militants claiming affiliation with the terrorist group al-Qaeda hijacked four planes and crashed two of them into the towers of the World Trade Center, and one into the Pentagon in Washington, DC. A fourth plane crashed into a field in rural Pennsylvania, its original destination unknown but presumed to have been the White House or Capitol building. Over three thousand people died in the September 11 attacks, and thousands more were injured. For the next three days, civilian air travel over the United States and Canada was suspended as the federal government tightened security and assessed how to respond to the tragedy.

On September 20, President George W. Bush, in an address to a joint session of Congress, formally announced a "War on Terror" that would be fought on many fronts, domestic and international: "Our war on terror begins with al-Qaida, but it does not end there," said the president. "It will not end until every terrorist group of global reach has been found, stopped, and defeated."[31]

The Bush administration outlined the four cornerstones of its new counterterrorism strategy: (1) "make no concessions to terrorists and strike no deals"; (2) "bring terrorists to justice for their crimes"; (3) "isolate and apply pressure on states that sponsor terrorism to force them to change their behavior"; and (4) "bolster the counterterrorism capabilities of those countries that work with the United States and require assistance."[32] On the diplomatic front, fifty nations agreed to cooperate with these efforts through the sharing of information on the financial assets of various groups.[33] The UN Security Council adopted Resolution 1373, mandating member states "prevent and suppress the financing of terrorist acts ... improve border security, clamp down on the recruitment of terrorists, intensify information sharing and law enforcement cooperation ... and deny terrorists and their supporters any support or safe haven." The resolution complemented the agenda set forth in twelve previous UN conventions on terrorism.[34]

Over the next decade, the Bush administration and its coalition allies increased economic and political pressure on those governments that financed or gave safe haven to terrorists. They also intervened militarily. Within a month of the 9/11 attacks, US-led forces launched Operation Enduring Freedom to topple the Taliban government in Afghanistan for serving as "the incubator for al Qaeda and for the 9/11 attacks."[35] By mid-decade, the Bush administration had deployed more than ten thousand American soldiers to Afghanistan, who were joined by soldiers from NATO and other allied countries in the region. Tens of thousands more would follow in the years to come. In 2003, coalition forces launched the controversial Operation Iraqi Freedom, a war against the government of Saddam Hussein for allegedly supporting al-Qaeda and stockpiling weapons of mass destruction.[36] Claiming extraordinary wartime powers, the

Bush administration used the naval base at Guantánamo and CIA facilities around the world for the indefinite detention and "enhanced interrogation" of men the administration called enemy combatants.[37] The administration also authorized military trials for these combatants to circumvent constitutional due process guarantees and the habeas corpus requirements of the US legal system, a course of action the government claimed was necessary to protect classified sources essential to counterterrorism.[38] The use of detention facilities and military trials outside US legal jurisdiction and the use of "extraordinary rendition" (the rendering of some detainees to intelligence services of third countries for "enhanced interrogation") violated international law. As the Migration Policy Institute noted, although "international human rights law [has become] increasingly important to US jurisprudence and public discourse ... the position of the Executive Branch has been clearly on the side of 'American exceptionalism' as the Bush administration has violated and withdrawn from a number of human rights treaties and other international agreements."[39]

Some of the Bush administration's antiterrorism policies were challenged in court. In 2004, in *Hamdi v. Rumsfeld*, for example, the US Supreme Court ruled unconstitutional the indefinite detention of suspects the administration claimed were "enemy combatants." In 2006 and 2008, the Supreme Court further challenged the administration's policy on detainees, upholding their rights to habeas corpus. However, as the War on Terror entered its second decade, the federal government legally extended or continued to exercise many emergency powers,[40] dividing Americans at home and undermining the United States' moral authority in the international community. As Daniel Prieto of the Council on Foreign Relations noted in 2009:

> The United States is, in effect, engaged in war *about* terror. There is fundamental disagreement on the most basic questions—how to address the threat posed by al Qaeda, the lengths that the United States will go to combat terrorism, and the potentially corrosive effect of national security efforts on America's commitment to longstanding moral values and individual liberties.[41]

According to Prieto and other critics, international skepticism of US surveillance and detention policies undermined the United States' ability to achieve its foreign policy goals, hampered counterterrorism and cooperation with other nations, contributed to the radicalization and recruitment of terrorists, and undermined US credibility in promoting democracy and human rights. If, as during the Cold War, the War on Terror was fought to win the hearts and minds of individuals around the world, the war would be won only if the United States adhered to its fundamental values and guiding principles.[42]

Policies on the domestic front were equally controversial. Forty-five days after the attacks, Congress passed the USA Patriot Act. Many senators and representatives later admitted to not having read the 131-page bill,[43] which authorized emergency surveillance powers to investigate and prosecute terrorists at home.[44] The National Security Agency's Terrorist Surveillance Program (TSP), authorized by the president in 2001 (but not disclosed to the public until 2005), allowed the surveillance, without court order, of communications between persons in the United States and persons abroad believed to be connected to terrorist organizations.[45] Law enforcement agencies detained and interrogated citizens and aliens alike on suspicion of providing material assistance to groups labeled terrorist by the administration, even if they did so unknowingly through donations to charitable subsidiaries of these organizations.[46] Political and faith-based activists, academics, students, and local organizers came under surveillance by local authorities who viewed their activism as "threats to the state."[47]

Immigration reform became critical to the War on Terror. Shortly after taking office, President Bush had made immigration reform one of his top priorities, but for reasons other than national security. The economic growth of the Clinton era had increased industry demands for skilled and unskilled labor, but the post-1996 immigration restrictions had reduced the immigrant labor pool.[48] At the time of the 9/11 attacks, the Bush administration was working on an expansion of special visa programs such as the H1 and H2 visas, to increase the pool of professional, skilled, and agricultural labor available to corporate America. After 9/11, these plans were indefinitely shelved to allow the administration to address the vulnerabilities in the immigration system that had allowed the terrorists to enter the United States and remain undetected.

None of the 9/11 hijackers were immigrant "green card" holders, refugees, or asylum seekers. The US National Commission on Terrorist Attacks Upon the United States ("the 9/11 Commission") revealed that the perpetrators had entered the country a total of thirty-three times using either tourist or student visas and had been on the radar of US intelligence agencies for years. Fifteen of the nineteen men might have been intercepted by the INS had the FBI, CIA, and NSA shared the information in their separate databases with immigration and customs officials. Instead, the men entered the United States with relative ease despite their political histories, visa violations, and fraudulent documents.[49] (Even as late as July 2003, Khalid Sheikh Mohammed, the principal architect of the 9/11 attacks, indicted in other terrorist plots, obtained a visa to come to the United States using an alias and an intermediary.)[50] The 9/11 Commission also concluded that immigration reform was necessary for national security. "The challenge for national security in an age of terrorism," it reported, "is to prevent the very few people who may pose overwhelming risks from entering or remaining in the United States undetected."[51]

Apprehending the "very few" was a daunting task: more than five hundred million people crossed US borders at legal entry points each year—330 million of them noncitizens pursuing educational, tourism, and commercial opportunities—and half a million more entered without authorization or remained past the expiration of their visas. Reform was critical, the commission argued, because inhibiting travel and mobility was as powerful a weapon against terrorism as the targeting of its sources of funding. As the commission report noted:

> For terrorists, travel documents are as important as weapons. Terrorists must travel clandestinely to meet, train, plan, case targets, and gain access to attack. To them, international travel presents great danger because they must surface to pass through regulated channels, present themselves to border security officials, or attempt to circumvent inspection points.[52]

According to the 9/11 Commission, no government agency had systematically analyzed the travel strategies of terrorists. Had they done so, the commission argued, "they could have discovered the ways in which the terrorist predecessors to al Qaeda had been systematically but detectably exploiting weaknesses in our border security since the early 1990s." One study of 212 suspected and convicted terrorists in North America and Western Europe from 1993 to 2003 found that these individuals had used every available immigration visa category to enter their country of target. Of those who came to the United States, 25 percent entered the country holding tourist visas; 12 percent held student visas; and 3 percent had permanent residency (green card) visas. Sixteen percent had filed for asylum.[53]

The post-9/11 immigration reforms, therefore, had two immediate goals: first, to track down any persons who might have slipped through permeable borders and checkpoints with the goal of executing an attack; and second, to structurally revamp the immigration bureaucracy to provide more effective screening. As political scientist Robert S. Leiken described it:

> We can view our immigration system as a sequence of gates: consulate, [point of entry], interior enforcement, culminating in the naturalization process. There are also side gates such as asylum and visa waivers and there are gateless stretches (poorly staffed border zones). We want these gates to keep out unwanted entrants but to swing open easily for those we wish to admit. We want 21st century gates that an authorized traveler can open with the swipe of a fast pass but that will lock stubbornly on the unauthorized.[54]

To achieve the first goal—track down alleged terrorists who had already entered the United States—the Department of Justice used the administrative proceedings of the immigration system to detain and interrogate persons because these proceedings denied suspects the due process rights and protections generally available through the criminal court system.[55] Hundreds of noncitizens—mostly Arab or Muslim—were arrested for immigration violations and, while in detention, interrogated about their possible ties to terrorist groups. These "special interest detainees" remained in prison with no chance of posting bond and were denied consular, family, or attorney access until authorities were convinced that they did not have connections to terrorist groups. Material witnesses were also subjected to "preventive detention." Neither the names of the detainees nor the locations of their detention were released by the Justice Department, which shrouded proceedings in secrecy. According to Human Rights Watch:

> Detainees were not informed of their right to counsel or were discouraged from exercising that right. The Immigration and Naturalization Service (INS) ... failed to inform attorneys where their clients were confined or when hearings were scheduled. Detainees in some facilities were permitted one weekly phone call, even to find or speak to an attorney; a call that did not go through nonetheless counted as the one permissible call. Not having prompt access to lawyers, these "special interest" detainees were unable to

protest violations of immigration rules to which they were subjected, including being held for weeks without charges (some detainees were held for months before charges were filed). The government never revealed the alleged links to terrorism that prompted their arrest, leaving them unable to prove their innocence.[56]

As the Migration Policy Institute noted "rather than relying on individualized suspicion or intelligence –driven criteria, [the government used] national origin as a proxy for evidence of dangerousness" and ultimately "deepened the perception abroad that America is anti-Muslim and that its principles are hypocritical."[57] The ACLU compared the arrests to the "disappearances" of the "dirty wars" of Latin America in the 1970s.[58] The Office of Inspector General (OIG) later confirmed the mistreatment of hundreds of detainees in US custody.[59] According to the OIG report, detainees at the Metropolitan Detention Center in New York and the Passaic County jail in New Jersey were especially ill-treated: "insulted, threatened, and beaten by guards on a routine basis ... deprived of natural light, exercise, medical care, and housed with ordinary criminal detainees."[60] By November 2001, the Department of Justice's Office of Public Affairs reported the detention of more than twelve hundred men from Middle Eastern and South Asian countries, plus an additional seventy material witnesses; but over the next few months, as public criticism of these actions increased, the government ceased to release any more data, and the total number of detainees was never officially disclosed. Some of these men were arrested simply because ordinary citizens expressed suspicions to police, perhaps motivated more by racism and xenophobia than actual credible evidence of wrongdoing[61]; 752 were subsequently charged with immigration violations and deported. Immigration hearings involving these "special interest detainees" were closed to the press; they were not even listed on the public calendar in immigration courts.[62] In removal proceedings, immigration judges were allowed to consider confidential evidence that was not made available to the detainees or their lawyers for examination or rebuttal. By 2006, only one of these special interest detainees had been charged with a terrorism-related crime.[63] Several class action lawsuits were filed on behalf of the detainees with limited results.

In order to better monitor those who entered the United States, the Justice Department in 2002 implemented the National Security Entry-Exit Registration System (NSEERS), which required men (sixteen years of age and older, from twenty-five countries, and on certain types of visitor visas) to register with the federal government and be interviewed, photographed, and fingerprinted. Over eighty-five thousand men registered, against whom thirteen thousand the government later initiated removal proceedings for immigration violations. DHS authorized a number of coordinated operations between federal agencies and local and state law enforcement officials (e.g. Operation Flytrap, Operation Tarmac, Operation Community Shield, and Operation Wagon Train) to raid workplaces that might be targeted for terrorism, such as airports and train stations, public utility companies, and manufacturing plants. These operations resulted in the arrest of thousands of undocumented assembly-line workers, janitors, members of cleaning crews, and food service workers (the majority of whom were Mexican, Central American, or South American) who had used false identification to secure employment.[64] Rights groups questioned the logic of these domestic counterterrorism strategies:

> These tactics . . . risk alienating and driving underground members of communities who themselves fled terror and who would otherwise be more than willing to cooperate with law enforcement. . . . Immigrants will not come forward if this might lead to their arrest, detention, or deportation. Identifying terrorists can be likened to finding a "needle in a haystack." Absent community support, this becomes virtually impossible.[65]

Others argued that this increased state authority disproportionately affected Latino/a workers whose only crime was to seek a better livelihood for their families.[66] The Justice Department generally dismissed such criticism. The department's director of public affairs offered "no apologies for finding every legal way possible to protect the American public from further terrorist attacks. The consequence of not doing so could mean life or death."[67]

To achieve the second goal—the structural overhaul of the immigration bureaucracy to screen immigrants more effectively—Congress passed the Homeland Security Act in 2002, which brought together twenty-two federal departments and agencies, including those responsible for border security, into a new cabinet-level agency, the Department of Homeland Security (DHS).[68] Since the immigration system had provided opportunities for the 9/11 terrorists to enter and remain in the United States, the INS was folded into the new Department of Homeland Security and its responsibilities coordinated among various departments: the United States

Customs and Border Protection (USCBP), which included the Border Patrol, now oversaw immigration inspections at all ports of entry and made decisions about expedited removal; the United States Citizenship and Immigration Services (USCIS) oversaw all matters relating to immigration visas and naturalization, including asylum and refugee adjudications; and the Bureau of Immigration and Customs Enforcement (ICE) oversaw the detention and removal of those detained for immigration violations, including asylum seekers awaiting resolution of their cases. After 2002, asylum seekers and other immigrants would have contact with two or more of these departments in their quest for permanent residency, making the immigration bureaucracy daunting to navigate.

President Bush's hopes for an expanded temporary worker program—and for a more free movement of labor, in general—never materialized during his eight-year administration. Instead, the post-9/11 reforms made it more difficult for foreign-born students, scholars, merchants, tourists, and immigrants to travel to the United States. In 2002 Congress passed the Enhanced Border Security and Visa Entry Reform Act (EBSVERA), which added three thousand new immigration inspectors; required heightened scrutiny of visa applications from countries believed to be harboring terrorists; and required university administrators to keep better track of the international students admitted to their schools. Consular officials evaluated the eligibility of visa applicants under new federal guidelines to promote national security. Between 2001 and 2004, the number of nonimmigrant visas issued by US consular officials dropped by one-third; but visas to citizens of countries with large Muslim populations dropped between 50 and 83 percent.[69] To better record the entry and departure of visitors, in 2004, DHS replaced NSEERS with the US Visitor and Immigration Status Indication Technology (US-VISIT), which collected biometric data at a port of entry/exit and ran this data through the new consolidated criminal and security databases. Congress funded new detention facilities and enforcement capabilities through the Intelligence Reform and Terrorism Prevention Act (IRTPA) of 2004; and mandated the construction of over seven hundred miles of double fencing and improved electronic surveillance along the US-Mexico border through the Secure Fence Act of 2006.

By mid-decade, the borders of the United States had become harder to cross than Checkpoint Charlie.[70] A new post–Cold War national security state was in place, and many human rights activists doubted that a refugee and asylum system located in a Department of Homeland Security—an agency whose primary mission was to prevent terrorist and other criminal

attacks –would enable the United States to meet its humanitarian obligations. The immediate drop in refugee and asylum admissions was one
indication of the challenges that lay ahead.

Refugees and Asylum Seekers in
the New National Security State

Refugees and asylum seekers became casualties of the new security
measures. After 9/11 the federal government imposed a freeze on refugee admissions. Hundreds of people who had received clearance to
come to the United States, but had not yet traveled, were left stranded
pending the Bush administration's overhaul of the immigration and refugee system. Admissions resumed in 2002 once the new policies were
in place: mandatory checks of applicants against the new consolidated
intelligence databases; verification of identities before boarding flights
to the United States; and the fingerprinting of all approved applicants
before and after they arrived in the United States.[71] The refugee ceiling was set at seventy thousand each year for most of the next decade,
but actual refugee admissions never reached this number. Admissions
dropped to fewer than twenty-nine thousand in 2002 and 2003 —the
lowest number in over a quarter-century—before improving somewhat
in FY2004 (see table 3.1).

Elements of the pre-9/11 refugee adjudication system remained in
place but with enhanced participation on the part of the Departments of
State and Homeland Security. The State Department ranked applications
according to one of three "priorities." Priority 1 cases were those candidates referred to the US refugee program by the UNHCR, a US embassy,
or other designated NGO because they had "compelling protection needs,
and [were] in danger of attack or of being returned to the country they
fled." Priority 2 cases were groups of special humanitarian concern to the
United States such as religious minorities, members of particular ethnicities, clans, or nationalities. Priority 3 cases were the spouses, parents, and
unmarried children (under the age of twenty-one) of persons admitted
lawfully to the United States as refugees, asylees, or green card holders.[72]
The Department of Homeland Security, and more specifically, USCIS and
USCBP, evaluated whether these priority cases were admissible: interviewing and interrogating applicants; conducting biographic, biometric,
and other security checks; and scheduling medical and psychological

Table 3.1 Refugee Arrivals to the United States,
FY2002–FY2010

Year	Refugee quota	Actual admissions
2002	70,000	26,785
2003	70,000	28,286
2004	70,000	52,840
2005	70,000	53,738
2006	70,000	41,094
2007	70,000	48,218
2008	80,000	60,107
2009	80,000	74,602
2010	80,000	73,293

Source: Department of Homeland Security, Refugee Arrivals
by Region and Country of Nationality: Fiscal Years 2001 to
2010, Yearbook of Immigration Statistics: 2010 Refugees
and Asylees, http://www.dhs.gov/xlibrary/assets/statistics/
yearbook/2010/ois_yb_2010.pdf.

screenings. Only a small percentage of those referred and screened were admitted.

Those who requested asylum on US territory found the asylum bureaucracy especially difficult to navigate. The 2001 USA Patriot Act, the 2005 Real ID Act, and other security-related legislation expanded the grounds on which asylum seekers might be excluded from the United States.[73] For example, those who secured fraudulent documents in order to escape their countries—as many asylum seekers were forced to do—could be barred for document fraud.[74] Under the new sweeping definitions of "terrorist organization" and "material support" to terrorist organizations, those who unlawfully used armed force or who assisted any group that used armed force, either voluntarily or through coercion, were barred admission. A 2009 *Human Rights First* report found that over eighteen thousand refugees and asylum seekers and their spouses and children were in some way affected by these expanded definitions of terrorism. These cases included one man from Bangladesh whose application for permanent residence was placed on indefinite hold because he took part in his country's successful struggle for independence in 1971, and a Sri Lankan who was detained for two and a half years for having paid a ransom (considered "material support") to his kidnappers.[75] According to the report, "the result [of these policy changes] has been to label as "terrorist" an ever-expanding range of individuals and groups who pose no threat to the United States and have not engaged in any conduct that would be considered criminal under international law." Ironically, included under the "tier III" definition of terrorist organization were some of the Afghan and Iraqi groups that were encouraged by the United States to rise up against the Soviets and Saddam Hussein, respectively, during the 1980s and 1990s, and some seeking entry were flagged for having participated in those armed resistance movements.[76]

In the post-9/11 period, detection, detention, and removal became cornerstones of immigration policy, particularly asylum policy. As part of Operation Liberty Shield —a "comprehensive national plan to protect the Homeland" announced by DHS secretary Tom Ridge on the eve of the Iraq war[77]—the Department of Homeland Security announced the automatic detention of asylum seekers from thirty-three countries and two territories where al-Qaeda and/or other terrorist groups operated.[78] Haitian boat people (but not Cubans) were also subsumed into this category.[79] Asylum seekers were detained for longer periods of time while their cases were reviewed and adjudicated and their identities checked against FBI, State Department, and CIA databases.

The United States negotiated "smart border" agreements with Canada and Mexico to harmonize border enforcement policies that would facilitate the flow of commercial goods, tourists, and other authorized travelers while barring the migration of undesirables. The Bush administration found cooperative partners in the administrations of President Vicente Fox and Prime Minister Paul Martin. Cooperation on border security was especially important to Canadian officials because of the growing perception in the Bush administration that "indulgent asylum and other immigration policies in Canada" had attracted jihadists to Canada for the sole purpose of carrying out attacks on the United States.[80] As a consequence of these smart border agreements, however, asylum seekers found it much more difficult to find protection anywhere in North America as all three countries cooperated in the detention and rapid removal of those who crossed their borders without authorization. The US-Canada "safe third country" agreement (first proposed in the 1996 IIRAIRA and finalized in 2004) also limited chances for asylum: the agreement mandated that asylum seekers apply for asylum in whatever country they reached first, which almost always meant filing in the United States, where their chances for securing asylum were lower than in Canada. The agreement drew vocal criticism from Canadian refugee advocates. The impact of the agreement was immediately noticeable: asylum claims in Canada dropped to 17,300 in 2005 from an average of 29,683 during the period 1989 to 2004.[81]

As happened in the wake of the 1993 World Trade Center bombing, policies were increasingly crafted to control the movement of labor migrants across the US-Mexico border in the name of national security. The massive restructuring of the immigration bureaucracy, designed to instill greater confidence in the general public, did just that, as Americans felt more assured that their security agencies were tracking down terrorists. This allowed their elected officials to once again focus on undocumented migration from the Americas, which many perceived as a more immediate threat to their day-to-day lives. When the news media addressed immigration matters, coverage once again focused on undocumented immigrants from Mexico and other parts of the Americas, vulnerable populations historically and racially constructed as outsiders, who were physically marginalized and excluded from political life and thus vulnerable to restrictive state policies.[82] The "expedited removal" policy established by the 1996 IIRAIRA was expanded to include not only those arriving at landed ports of entry or interdicted at sea, but also all undocumented persons caught within one hundred miles of the US-Mexico border who had been in the country fourteen days or less. In 2005, Representative James L. Sensenbrenner, the sponsor of the Patriot Act, introduced a new bill, this time to increase penalties on unauthorized immigrants and their smugglers: the Border Protection, Anti-Terrorism, and Illegal Immigration Control Act of 2005 (HR 4437).[83] Though the bill catalyzed the mass protests of millions of immigrant workers across the country in 2006 and was subsequently shelved, it served as another reminder of how labor migration had been subsumed into conversations about national security. Through the new "Secure Communities" program,[84] ICE enlisted the assistance of local police forces across the country to identify, detain, and remove undocumented immigrants. The number—and privatization—of detention facilities increased, as did deportations, especially during the administration of President Barack Obama, when 369,000 people were deported in 2013 alone.[85]

By 2014, the US Border Patrol had increased to more than twenty-one thousand agents, and its web page listed as its "primary missions" two goals: "preventing terrorists and terrorist weapons, including weapons of mass destruction, from entering the United States" and "prevent[ing] the illegal entry of aliens into the United States."[86] The Department of Homeland Security regarded these "missions" as complementary. This linkage prompted the editors at *The Economist* to remark:

> A mass murder committed by mostly Saudi terrorists [has] resulted in an almost limitless amount of money being made available for the deportation of Mexican house-painters. America now spends more money on immigration enforcement than on all the other federal law enforcement agencies.[87]

Similarly, the news network *Al Jazeera America* asked:

> How have these missions come to be viewed as overlapping? Do migrants—economic refugees displaced from their livelihoods by US-sponsored free trade agreements—require the same serious level of attention as terrorists?[88]

Human rights activists, in turn, questioned the nation's commitment to refugees and displaced persons. As a consequence of these stricter deterrents, which made it difficult for asylum seekers to even access the bureaucracy to file a petition for protection, the number of asylum petitions dropped steadily after 2002. Over the next decade, the number of foreign-born granted asylum also decreased: from 36,923 in 2002 to 21,113 in 2010 (see table 3.2).[89] Country of origin affected one's chances of securing asylum, but not always in predictable ways. Asylum seekers from countries with large Muslim populations were automatically suspect in the post-9/11 period and more often than not barred from accessing the asylum bureaucracy altogether; however, if allowed to access the asylum bureaucracy, they had a better chance of securing asylum in the United States than individuals fleeing other parts of the world. Iraqis and Eritreans, for example, had a 13 percent denial rate from FY2004 to FY2010, while those from the Americas had a 75 percent denial rate (with the exception of Venezuela and Colombia at 56 and 60 percent, respectively).[90] One study found a positive correlation between a country's status as an ally or enemy of the United States in the War on Terror and the asylum grant rate for that country, suggesting

Table 3.2 Asylum Petitions Granted,
United States, FY2002–FY2010

Year	Asylum petitions granted
2002	36,923
2003	28,733
2004	27,347
2005	25,228
2006	26,242
2007	25,179
2008	22,832
2009	22,090
2010	21,113

Source: Department of Homeland Security, Individuals Granted Asylum Affirmatively or Defensively: Fiscal Years 1990–2010, Yearbook of Immigration Statistics: 2010 Refugees and Asylees, http://www.dhs.gov/publication/yearbook-immigration-statistics-2010-refugees-and-asylees.

that "foreign policy is operative in the asylum adjudication system [in the post-9/11 period] although in a much more subtle way than it was during the Cold War."[91]

The following case studies demonstrate the numerous hurdles Afghans, Iraqis, and Syrians—three of the populations most affected by the War on Terror—have faced when seeking refuge in the United States. It also highlights the challenges facing the United States in meeting humanitarian obligations while addressing security concerns.

Afghanistan

On September 11, 2001, Sadiq Mir, his wife Najia, and their six children were packed and waiting to go to the Islamabad airport to fly to the United States. The Mir family, converts to Christianity, had fled to Pakistan in the 1980s from their native Afghanistan and were now under the protection of the UNHCR. Their paperwork was in order, their airline tickets purchased, and they awaited their ride to the airport; but as the hour of their trip approached, they learned that planes had crashed into important buildings in the country that had offered them refuge, and American airspace was closed to all international air traffic. Although American airports would reopen within a few days, it would take the Mir family another two and a half years to immigrate to the United States.[92]

The Mir family's predicament was not unique. The US Department of Justice froze thousands of visas in the weeks that followed the terrorist attacks of September 11, as they began an overhaul of the immigration bureaucracy. Even applicants such as the Mir family, Christians who had the protection and support of the UNHCR, found it difficult to overcome the red tape. Eventually they were among the more fortunate ones given permanent resettlement in a third country. Others in similar situations never found the refuge they sought.

Since the Soviet invasion of 1979, Afghanistan had experienced one of the world's largest and ongoing migrations. Millions had crossed borders because of war, civil unrest, and environmental disasters, ultimately resettling in sixty-nine different countries.[93] Neighboring Pakistan and Iran accommodated the largest number, even though poverty and political turmoil challenge their generosity. The percentage of migrants that met international definitions of "refugee" was difficult to determine. Afghan males had a long tradition of migrating for social and economic networking that made it difficult to distinguish those displaced by violence from those who crossed borders as part of a larger migratory tradition.[94] It was also common for those who crossed borders to return to their country during relatively stable periods, only to migrate again in response to economic and political pressures. Consequently, the limitations of the legal term "refugee" become evident in the Afghan case: migration is cyclical and most likely influenced by a variety of factors, making it difficult to disentangle political motivations from economic ones.

Afghan migration increased exponentially after the Soviet invasion of December 1979, the subsequent insurgency mounted by the mujahideen, and the rise of the Taliban state, suggesting that much of the post-1979 migration was generated by war and violence rather than pure economic decision-making. By 1981, the UN estimated that 3.7 million Afghans had fled to neighboring Iran and Pakistan; and by the late 1980s, the UNHCR estimated over six million Afghan refugees worldwide.[95] By 2001, one in four Afghans was living outside their homeland.[96] Many Afghans disappeared into towns and cities, where they hoped to have better chances of finding employment and housing. If they had the financial resources to do so, they settled in the West.[97] The violence generated by Operation Enduring Freedom (October 2001–August 2003), and by the missions undertaken by NATO's International Security Assistance Force (August 2003–June 2013) produced yet another generation of refugees and internally displaced peoples.

When Operation Enduring Freedom began in October 2001, UN agencies predicted that as many as two million people would join the ranks of those Afghans outside their country. Those displaced by the escalation of the violence faced a number of new hurdles, however. Tired of accommodating a disproportionate share of Afghans, Pakistan had closed its border with Afghanistan in 2000; and the border remained closed after the start of the US-led war in part because of pressure from the United States, which sought to block al-Qaeda operatives from disappearing into Pakistan. Afghans were turned away at border checkpoints either by Pakistani guards or by members of the Taliban, who were in search of men they could conscript into their forces. If Afghans had the financial resources to do so, they enlisted smugglers to transport them across more isolated and treacherous mountain terrain, but the estimated 250,000 landmines left over from the Soviet occupation made such travel risky.[98] Over the next few years, Pakistan occasionally opened its borders to a limited number of refugees, but these openings were never publicized for fear that they would draw thousands more to the border zone. In 2002, a year after the launch of Operation Enduring Freedom, two hundred thousand people were believed to have successfully crossed the border into Pakistan; but two million more were redirected to isolated settlements around the country. Disease, violence, and starvation became facts of life for the internally displaced persons (IDPs) in these settlements, and yet they attracted virtually no international media attention.[99]

In 2002, after the defeat of the Taliban, the UNHCR worked with the governments of Pakistan and Iran, and the Afghan Ministry of Refugees and Repatriation (MORR), to create a legal framework for the voluntary repatriation of Afghan refugees. From 2002 to 2007, more than 5.5 million Afghans repatriated, making it the largest assisted-return operation in UNHCR history. An additional 1.5 million refugees returned to Afghanistan without NGO assistance. The high number of repatriates caught UNHCR officials by surprise because it suggested that they had vastly underestimated the refugee diaspora over the past thirty years. In

2007 the UNHCR and other NGOs again revised their estimates and stated that perhaps as many as eight million Afghans still remained outside Afghanistan.[100]

US policy toward the Afghan refugees was subsumed into the larger reconstruction project for Afghanistan. According to US Department of State records, from 2001 to 2008, the US government provided more than $500 million in humanitarian assistance to Afghan refugees, returnees, and other victims of conflict through US government agencies, the UNHCR, and other international NGOs.[101] Historically, the United States has often accepted refugees as a way of fostering political stability in postconflict societies; resettlement helps ease the demands on fragile governments and facilitates remittances to communities back home. Despite strategic interests in the region, however, the United States accepted only a token share of Afghan refugees, even in the wake of Operation Enduring Freedom. (See table 3.3.) Instead, the United States encouraged Afghans to remain in the region until they could be reintegrated into their native country. Repatriation was important because it served as a gauge of American success in the region. While Afghans played an important economic role when they sent much-needed remittances to their families and communities back home, they

Table 3.3 Afghan Refugee Arrivals, United States, FY2002–FY2007

Year	Arrivals
2002	1,683
2003	1,453
2004	959
2005	902
2006	651
2007	441

Source: Department of Homeland Security, Refugee Arrivals by Region and Country of Nationality, 2001–2010, Yearbook of Immigration Statistics, 2010, http://www.dhs.gov/publication/yearbook-immigration-statistics-2010-refugees-and-asylees.

served an even more valuable function once repatriated, validating US intervention and signaling to the region the emergence of a stable new post-Taliban society. Afghan president Hamid Karzai, elected in June 2002, was doubtful about this plan; over the next decade he appealed to countrymen living abroad to invest in their homeland and to send remittances, but he also warned Americans that large numbers of repatriates would place enormous stress on a fragile society affected by three decades of political conflict.[102]

Encouraging repatriation was important for geopolitical reasons, however. The Bush administration was cognizant of the fact that Afghan refugees were a destabilizing force in Pakistan. The government of Pervez Musharraf repeatedly complained that Pakistan had borne the weight of the Afghan refugee crisis for far too long. The refugees, he argued, contributed to smuggling and other criminal enterprises, displaced Pakistanis from their jobs, and ultimately undermined their national security. Consequently, in 2007, when Pakistan authorized the construction of fences and the planting of landmines along its border with Afghanistan, the Bush administration did not protest, nor did it object when Pakistani officials took more forceful measures to speed up the process of repatriation.[103] Pakistan was not a signatory to the 1951 UN Convention on Refugees, nor the 1967 Protocol, and was not bound to accept refugees nor protect them from *refoulement*. Pakistan was a tenuous ally in the global War on Terror, so the Bush administration muted its criticism of these policies.

Resettling large numbers of Afghan refugees in the United States was not an option. When pressed, Bush administration officials attributed the low number of refugee admissions to the violence in the region, which prevented DHS officials from traveling to the region to interview applicants.[104] But there was also no popular mandate for accommodating large numbers of refugees from this area of the world. The trauma of 9/11 and Americans' association of Islam with extremism made many Americans wary of assisting Muslim populations. The US news media carried few stories and photographic images of the refugees that might have sensitized Americans to their predicament, in part because journalists were barred access to refugee camps and settlements.[105] Instead, as Joanne Van Selm of the Migration Policy Institute has written, the common perception Americans had of Afghan refugees was that of "burkha clad figures and dusty desert fighters to whom they found it difficult to relate."[106] The government fulfilled its humanitarian obligations through foreign aid rather than through resettlement programs, especially since there was little public mandate for the latter. Even faith-based nongovernmental organizations known for their advocacy of refugees and internally displaced people were comparatively silent on the sponsorship of Afghans and others from the Central Asia during this period. American emotions in the wake of 9/11 were still too raw.

Consequently, the number of Afghan refugees admitted to the United States decreased with each passing year. In the fiscal year preceding the terrorist attacks of September 11 (October 1, 2000, through September 30, 2001) 2,930 Afghan refugees were admitted to the United States; but by FY2009—despite an overall refugee quota of eighty thousand, with thirty-seven thousand slots reserved specifically for people from the Near East / South Asia—only 349 Afghans were admitted as refugees.[107] The only Afghans prioritized for admission—albeit in very small numbers— were the interpreters and translators who assisted US armed forces during Operation Enduring Freedom and were now in danger because Taliban sympathizers and other insurgents viewed them as ideologically compromised.

Over 8,000 Afghan interpreters worked for the United States from 2001 to 2009, at great risk to their lives and the lives of their families. At least 264 interpreters serving troops in Afghanistan and Iraq were killed from 2003 to 2008, and 403 wounded.[108] Section 1059 of the 2006 National Defense Authorization Act (PL 109-163) authorized fifty "special immigrant visas (SIVs)" for Afghan and Iraqi nationals—and their spouses and children—if they had worked for the US armed forces or the US embassies in Kabul and Baghdad for one year or more and had provided valuable service that subsequently rendered them vulnerable to retaliation. The following year PL 110-36 increased the number of visas to five hundred for both FY2007 and FY2008 before reverting back to fifty in FY2009. Afghans and Iraqis who entered with one of these US visas did so as priority immigrants, not as refugees, which made them ineligible for the resettlement assistance offered refugees. As the plight of the Afghan and Iraqi interpreters grew more dire and American public sentiment seemed to shift in their favor, Congress passed other legislation to facilitate Afghan (and Iraqi) resettlement. The Consolidated Appropriations Act of 2008 (PL 110-161) made Afghan and Iraqi SIV holders eligible for the same resettlement assistance and benefits granted refugees admitted under the US Refugee Admissions Program for up to six months. The period of eligibility was later extended to eight months.[109]

In 2009, when the special immigrant visa program was set to expire, Congress passed the Afghan Allies Protection Act (as part of an omnibus appropriations act), which authorized the admission of up to fifteen hundred SIV holders annually through FY2013, together with their spouses and dependent children. However, by 2011, the US embassy in Kabul had not processed a single SIV; and by November 2013, only 1,648 SIVs of the allocated 7,500 visas had been issued. After waiting for years, some Afghan applicants received perfunctory rejections, with no explanations or chance for appeal. Others were told that they had failed to convincingly demonstrate that there was a significant threat to their lives as a consequence of their employment with a US agency. "They have trusted us with their weapons and their missions. We have worked with them on their bases," said one Afghan applicant who worked with US troops for almost nine years. "And now, after they have decided to leave us, they find out that we are bad guys."[110] In 2014, the year before US forces were scheduled to withdraw completely from Afghanistan, Congress authorized three thousand SIVs through 2015. The pace of issuing visas increased, and when the quota of three thousand was met in August, Congress authorized an additional one thousand visas, and then an additional three thousand in November 2015.[111] The Afghan SIV program was scheduled to terminate once all seven thousand visas were allocated. Thousands of applicants remained in the backlog, however, holding demonstrations in front of the US embassy in Kabul and resorting to social media to draw attention to their plight. The Facebook page of the Afghan SIV Applicants Association appealed to their American allies: "Our lives are in danger; we supported you, now it is your turn to support us! SIV is our last hope!"

Despite their two and a half years of uncertainty, the Mir family were among the privileged few Afghans who secured entry to the United States in the wake of 9/11. It is unclear how their lives have unfolded in the years since their admission, and whether they have found the religious tolerance and safety they sought. Perhaps they have continued to encounter resistance, suspicion, and perhaps even persecution because of race, ancestry, or religion. Whatever their circumstances, thousands of their countrymen sought but were denied the opportunity to follow them into exile.

Iraq

In February 2003, on the heels of Operation Enduring Freedom in Afghanistan, the Bush administration accused the government of Saddam Hussein of developing and harboring weapons of mass destruction. A month later, when Hussein had not acquiesced to US demands to step down from power, the United States and its coalition allies launched military strikes against Iraq. The Bush administration assured the American public that Operation Iraqi Freedom would be quick and decisive with comparatively little financial or human cost to the American people. The Iraqi people, eager for democracy, administration officials argued, would support the US invasion and assist in their own liberation. They would then assist in the reconstruction of their country, allowing Americans to withdraw. On May 1, in a speech to troops aboard the aircraft carrier USS *Abraham Lincoln*, President Bush declared combat operations ended under a banner that read "Mission Accomplished."

Despite Bush's pronouncement, fighting in Iraq continued as US and Iraqi forces battled various insurgent groups who challenged the authority of the provisional and, later, the elected Iraqi government. Most of the insurgents were ethnic Sunnis or other minorities long excluded from political decision-making by the predominantly Shiite government. The UN Security Council never endorsed military action in Iraq but subsequently recognized the occupation government, which some felt compromised its position in Iraq and left its staff members vulnerable to attack. On August 19, 2003, three months after Bush's speech aboard the *Abraham Lincoln*, a suicide bomber detonated his explosives at the UN Headquarters in Baghdad, killing internationally known refugee advocate Arthur Helton, as well as UN envoy Sergio Viera de Mello and twenty of his staff. Over a hundred people were wounded in the blast, including Helton's colleague and fellow refugee advocate Gil Loescher, who lost both his legs.[112] A subsequent bomb on September 22 killed a UN security guard and two Iraqi police officers.

Over the next nine years, Saddam Hussein and his top officials were caught, tried, and executed; Iraqis participated in the first open parliamentary elections in decades; and US troops gradually increased to more than 150,000 to compensate for the withdrawal of coalition forces from Iraq. In August 2010, Iraqi forces finally assumed full responsibility for security operations, and US troops officially withdrew in December 2011. The Iraqi war had cost the United States $800 billion by 2013, twice as much as the war in Afghanistan and far more than the $50–$60 billion the Bush administration had forecast in 2003.[113] No weapons of mass destruction were ever discovered, undermining the credibility and legacy of the Bush administration. American moral authority was also challenged by reports of the torture of prisoners by US military and CIA personnel at the Abu Ghraib prison and the shooting of Iraqi civilians by the Blackwater military contractors in Baghdad.[114] After thirty years of war, sanctions, occupation, and ethnic and sectarian violence, Iraq remained in a fragile state after US forces withdrew. By August 2014, Prime Minister Nouri al-Maliki had resigned, and his successor, Haider al-Abad, faced continued threats from insurgents. The Iraqi army that the United States had built with billions of dollars was near collapse, under continued assault from ISIS (also known as ISIL or the more pejorative term Daesh),[115] a splinter group of al-Qaeda, whose goal was to create an Islamic caliphate across Sunni areas of Iraq and Syria. By January 2015, ISIS controlled key areas of the region, forcing the United States to once again intervene, launching airstrikes against ISIS targets.

The war in Iraq caused over forty-eight hundred US and coalition casualties between 2003 and 2014. The US Army placed Iraqi casualties at roughly one hundred thousand by 2010.[116] However, one 2013 study conducted by US public health experts, in cooperation with the Iraqi Ministry of Health, provided a more comprehensive portrait. The researchers included in their tallies the day-to-day casualties caused by the war-related social breakdown in Iraqi society. According to this study roughly half a million Iraqi civilians died between 2003 and 2011 as a direct or indirect consequence of the war, the insurgencies, and the sectarian strife.[117]

By 2008, the UNHCR estimated that nearly 4.7 million Iraqis were displaced from their homes: 2.7 million were internally displaced within Iraq, and 2 million had fled the country.[118] António Guterres, the United Nations high commissioner for refugees, declared the Iraqi exodus the largest population shift in the Middle East since the displacement of the Palestinians in 1948.[119] Only a decade earlier, hundreds of thousands had fled Iraq because of the 1991 Gulf War and Hussein's brutal repression of the Kurds and the Shiites. The removal of the Saddam Hussein regime had presented these exiles with the opportunity to return to their country once again, but that hope proved short-lived. The sectarian violence that erupted in the wake of the 2003 invasion—and the failure of coalition forces to address it—once again uprooted those who had returned home.[120] According to the UNHCR and other NGOs working in the region, the first to flee Iraq were the affluent and skilled classes, who could pay for their transportation and travel documents, bribe border guards, and hire smugglers. With each passing year, those who fled were poorer and traveled on foot. Ethnic and religious minorities were also among the more likely to flee abroad: almost 40 percent of UNHCR-registered refugees were Christians.[121] Those internally displaced moved in with family members around the country or stayed in abandoned buildings or in the makeshift camps set up by the Iraqi Red Crescent Society. Internal displacement contributed to the sectarian tensions by creating populations of poor, desperate people who competed for limited resources. Overwhelmed by the refugee crises in Afghanistan and other parts of the world, the UNHCR convened an international conference in Geneva in 2007 to try to rally financial support from the international community. Despite pledges of support, international aid was slow in coming in large part because of the perception that Iraq was an American problem.[122]

As in other refugee crises, neighboring countries bore the burden of accommodating the refugees. Syria, Jordan, and Lebanon were reluctant hosts to the Iraqi refugees even though they were not signatories to the 1951 UN Convention or 1967 Protocol on Refugees, had no domestic refugee legislation, and could not guarantee any legal protections or financial assistance. Fearing that the Iraqis would become a permanent population like the Palestinians, all three countries militarized their borders and changed their visa requirements to make it more difficult for the refugees to establish authorized residence. Unauthorized migration continued, however.[123] By 2007 an estimated 750,000 Iraqis were living in Jordan; and up to 1.7 million had crossed the border into Syria.[124] Tens of thousands more had taken refuge in Egypt, Iran, and Turkey. Many disappeared into the populations of large urban areas, making it difficult for international aid agencies to identify and assist them. In cities like Amman and Damascus, the refugees encountered discrimination in housing, education, medical care, and social services. Because of their lack of legal status, they were forced to work in the underground economy, where they were easily exploited and threatened with deportation if they complained. Trafficking, sexual exploitation, prostitution, and domestic violence became an increasingly normal part of life in some refugee communities.[125]

By 2008, the UNHCR had over three hundred staff working in the field trying to identify the most vulnerable, and refer them to third countries like the United States. On the UNHCR's list of "most vulnerable" were victims of severe trauma or torture; women and older persons at risk of trafficking, neglect, or violence; those with medical conditions and disabilities who could not access treatment; unaccompanied or separated children; stateless persons; and members of ethnic or religious minority groups.[126] The UNHCR was especially helpful in screening applicants from Syria, where the Assad government had barred American officials from entering.[127] In addition to these vulnerable populations, the United States prioritized for potential admission the embassy personnel, translators, and technicians who had assisted the United States during the war.[128] Iraqis who were members of a persecuted religious (especially Christian) or ethnic minority group and who had close family members in the United States also received priority screening.

Despite these efforts, Iraqi refugee admissions were shockingly low. Sixty-six Iraqis were admitted in FY2004 and 198 in FY2005. By May 2007, only 701 Iraqi refugees had been admitted to the United States despite the thousands of applications and referrals. (See table 3.4.) Christian minorities filed 62 percent of the applications.[129] The Bush administration attributed the low numbers to the enhanced security screening. John Bolton, US ambassador to the United Nations, was more blunt in his explanation, raising questions about the administration's

Table 3.4 Iraqi Refugee Arrivals, United States, FY2004–FY2007

Year	Arrivals
2004	66
2005	198
2006	202
2007	1608

Source: Department of Homeland Security, Refugee Arrivals by Region and Country of Nationality, 2001–2010, Yearbook of Immigration Statistics, 2010, http://www.dhs.gov/publication/yearbook-immigration-statistics-2010-refugees-and-asylees.

commitment to refugee resettlement. The refugees had "absolutely nothing to do with our overthrow of Saddam," he said. "Our obligation was to give them new institutions and provide security. We have fulfilled that obligation. I don't think we have an obligation to compensate for the hardships of war."[130]

Refugee advocates, area specialists, journalists, and members of Congress were vocal in their criticism of the Bush administration's refugee and humanitarian policies. Other nations, with no immediate responsibilities to Iraq, far outpaced US resettlement efforts. Sweden, for example, which opposed the invasion and did not participate in the coalition forces, took in over eighteen thousand Iraqi refugees by 2007. "The US policy towards the exodus from Iraq was, until 2006, simplistic: pretend it is not there," wrote Middle East expert Joseph Sassoon:

> After the media started focusing, the Bush administration still would not focus on [the refugee crisis] because to do so was to admit the failure of US policy towards Iraq. . . . The fact remains that while the USA has spent hundreds of billions between 2003 and 2008 on its war effort, at most half a billion dollars, a trifling amount in comparison, were spent to aid Iraqi refugees.[131]

In December 2006, the Iraq Study Group, chaired by James Baker III and Lee Hamilton (former vice-chair of the 9/11 Commission), warned that the number of Iraqi refugees and internally displaced persons posed a threat to the administration's long-term goals in the region: "If this situation is not addressed," the ISG report stated, "Iraq and the region could be further destabilized, and humanitarian suffering could be severe. Funding for international relief efforts is insufficient, and should be increased."[132]

In January 2007, the Senate Judiciary Committee held hearings on the plight of the Iraqi refugees. As he had done so many times in the past, Senator Edward Kennedy, the chair of the committee, became a voice for refugees on Capitol Hill, reminding his colleagues of their obligation to those uprooted by this US-led war:

> The answer, of course, is not to bring every Iraqi refugee to the United States, but we do have a special obligation to keep faith with the Iraqis who have bravely worked for us and often paid a

terrible price for it, by providing them with safe refuge in the United States.... We should work urgently with Iraqis' neighbors, especially Jordan, Syria and Lebanon, who are bearing the greatest refugee burden. Prompt action is essential to prevent destabilization of the region, and to relieve suffering and save lives.[133]

The Senate hearing put a human face on the Iraqi refugee crisis, especially those who were targeted for violence because of their assistance to US forces. One witness, who identified himself under the pseudonym "John," a truck driver of Chaldean Catholic ancestry, had delivered water to American servicemen in the camps. As members of a religious minority, John, his wife, and their six children were already socially and politically compromised in Iraqi society, but his service to the Americans drew the attention of extremists:

> On two occasions I was beaten by Islamic terrorist groups that knew my name and threatened that if I did not leave the country, I would be killed. On the day of the first attack, I went to work delivering water to the Americans along with my son. At about 9:00 in the morning, we saw that—what appeared to be a road blockade ahead. Before we could realize what was happening, my son and I were dragged out of the cab of our truck. We were positioned face down on the side of the road by a group of terrorists.... They kept saying to me, "Don't work with the Americans." And one of them struck me in the face with the butt of his gun, permanently damaging my jaw. Another man twisted my son's arm so severely that he broke it. They knew my name and instructed me that this was a warning, and that I would be killed if I continued assisting the Americans. After they made their threat, they departed, leaving us bloodied on the side of the road. It was at this point that everything began to change for my family. My wife feared for our children's lives so much that she refused to let them go to school, and I stayed up most of the nights watching out for any signs of trouble near our house.

John continued delivering water to the American camps because it was his only source of income, so the threats continued. After another brutal beating, John was left alone and unconscious in the desert. When he woke, he made his way home and told his family that they were leaving their country:

> We had family in America, and since my assistance to American soldiers was partly responsible for my family's persecution, we decided to flee Iraq for the United States. Two years ago, after traveling through five countries within four continents, we took a taxi cab from Mexico to the United States, to its border. Just one week later, asylum was granted.[134]

Sami al-Obiedy (a pseudonym) also testified before the Senate Judiciary Committee. Sami, a twenty-seven-year old Sunni Arab, volunteered to work as a translator for the US and coalition forces because he believed they had come to liberate the Iraqi people. In his work as translator, he tried to negotiate a working relationship between the military forces and local civic and religious leaders:

> I accompanied US soldiers on hundreds of convoys through hostile territory. Often the military vehicles in which we traveled were targeted by anti-Iraqi insurgents and terrorists with roadside bombs, rocket-propelled grenades, and ambush and sniper fire. During the time I served as translator, I honestly believed that I would be killed.

In his testimony, Sami recounted the fate of others who had worked for the coalition forces. Soon he, too, was targeted for assassination:

> My name was listed on the doors of several mosques calling for my death. Supposed friends of mine saw my name on the list and turned on me because they believed I was a traitor. Encouraged by many US soldiers, I decided that I would leave Iraq on November 9th of 2005 . . . [but] I was seriously injured in a targeted car bombing. . . . I am fortunate to be alive.

Shortly thereafter, Sami fled Iraq for the United States. He became the first recipient of the new "special immigrant visa" for Iraqi and Afghan translators under the 2006 National Defense Authorization Act. Translators, he said, were special targets because they opened the path for a free and democratic Iraq:

Without the ability to communicate with Iraqi people in their own language, democracy and freedom will be at risk. Terrorists understand this concept all too well, and that is why they have and will continue to especially target Iraqi translators and kill those who have dared to give freedom and democracy a voice in Iraq.[135]

This was no exaggeration. In 2006, when British forces withdrew from the city of Basra, the interpreters who had assisted the coalition forces were rounded up and killed.[136]

The White House remained curiously silent on the issue of Iraqi refugee resettlement. In February 2007, Secretary of State Condoleezza Rice announced the establishment of the Iraqi Refugee and Internally Displaced Persons Task Force to coordinate the organizations involved in assisting refugees and IDPs; by the end of the year, however, the task force had met only occasionally, and the lack of interagency cooperation continued to prevent Iraqis from gaining access to the US Refugee Admissions Program.[137] Subsequent congressional hearings discovered that the administration "was doing next to nothing to assist those Iraqis who put their lives in jeopardy to assist the United States in our efforts in Iraq":

> Not only wasn't the administration helping them, they didn't even know how many Iraqis actually worked for us, so they naturally had no idea how many people needed our help.... [The] administration was woefully unprepared to process refugees referred to us by the United Nations High Commissioner for Refugees ... [and] had the capacity to process merely a few hundred refugees a month, but wasn't working anywhere near even that limited capacity.[138]

Whatever steps the US government took during this period to facilitate the entry of Iraqi refugees were initiated by Congress. The bipartisan Refugee Crisis in Iraq Act, spearheaded by Senators Edward Kennedy and Gordon Smith, became law on January 28, 2008, and had four major provisions: (1) it established "in country" refugee in facilities within Iraq; (2) it gave "P-2" resettlement priority to Iraqis suffering persecution for their work with a US government agency, contractor, media organization, or NGO; (3) it created five thousand special immigrant visas (SIVs) each year for five years for Iraqis who had worked for the US government in Iraq for a year or more, and who experienced ongoing threat because of that service; and (4), it authorized the reopening of certain asylum cases concerning Iraqi refugees who had been denied asylum.[139] Once SIV holders arrived in the United States, they received their green card (lawful permanent resident status) and were authorized to work. Their spouses and children were also allowed to immigrate.

As American opposition to the Iraqi war grew, public and congressional criticism of Bush's handling of the refugee crisis also increased. Representatives of twenty-one refugee advocacy groups signed a letter castigating the president for his lack of leadership.[140] A widely publicized report from the Migration Policy Institute called US responses to the humanitarian crisis "wholly inadequate."[141] New advocacy groups emerged, such as the List Project and the Iraqi Refugee Assistance Project, which worked to secure pro bono legal representation for the Iraqi allies.[142] "All of us understand that 9/11 changed a lot of things," said Representative Gary L. Ackerman at a March 2008 congressional hearing on Iraqi refugees, "and one of those things is that the United States needed to be much more careful about who gets into our country . . . [but] the only person in the executive branch who can make all the agencies march in the same direction is the President, yet I can't remember President Bush speaking about the refugee crisis or the need of the United States to respond aggressively to it, except in passing."[143]

In April 2008, the Senate published its own fact-finding report on the humanitarian crisis in Iraq, giving a detailed account of the poverty, harassment, and exploitation of Iraqi refugees, and the "excruciating delays" for those in the application pipeline. In response to the report, eighty-nine members of Congress signed a letter urging the president to take a more proactive role in humanitarian assistance:

> Rarely does confronting a crisis align our moral and national security interests as closely as does providing assistance to the Iraqis displaced by violence. There are few more important tests of our foreign policy than our leadership in response to the growing crisis confronting the displaced population of Iraq.[144]

Senators Edward Kennedy and Joe Biden were harsher in their criticism:

> [The] findings suggest a startling lack of American leadership in a crisis that much of the international community considers a result of our intervention in Iraq. Acknowledging that the war in Iraq has resulted in one of the greatest humanitarian crises of the post–Cold

War era is a bitter pill to swallow. Ensuring that this refugee population receives the humanitarian treatment and dignity that it deserves
requires American leadership of a kind not seen to this point.[145]

Over the next few years, the number of Iraqis who entered the United
States as refugees increased steadily. In FY2007, only 1,608 of the 12,000
Iraqi refugee referrals had gained entry, but by 2009, the number had
jumped to 18,838.[146] By 2013, 84,902 of the 203,321 Iraqi referrals had been
admitted. (See table 3.5.)[147]

SIV processing, evaluated separately, occurred much more slowly.
George Packer, reporting in the *New Yorker*, wrote that over thirty thousand
SIV applications were filed with the US government by July 2011 but only
four thousand had been processed, and a third of these had been denied:

> The [processing of applications] remains excruciatingly slow, and
> the rate of rejections is strangely high. Consider that, in order to
> work in the Green Zone and on military bases, these Iraqis already
> passed background checks that many of the people reading this post
> would probably fail. They are, in the words of Kirk Johnson, founder
> of [the Iraqi refugee advocacy group] The List Project, "the most
> heavily documented refugees on the planet."[148]

Table 3.5 Iraqi Refugees Referred to the USRAP
and Admissions, FY2007–FY2013

Year	Referrals to the USRAP	Admitted
2007	12,098	1,608
2008	28,769	13,823
2009	49,276	18,838
2010	46,472	18,016
2011	39,878	9,388
2012	15,878	12,163
2013[a]	10,950	11,066
Total	203,321	84,902

[a] By April 30, 2013.

Source: United States Citizenship and Immigration
Services, "Iraqi Refugee Processing Fact Sheet," http://
www.uscis.gov/humanitarian/refugees-asylum/
refugees/iraqi-refugee-processing-fact-sheet.

Drawing on stories collected by the Iraqi Refugee Assistance Project (IRAP),[149] Packer discussed the months and sometimes years applicants had to wait for updates on their status. "Multiply these brief stories by the thousands," he wrote, "and you have one of the most disgraceful legacies of the decade since September 11—a scandal that has only grown worse during the Obama years."

Even notable Iraqi human rights activists, with family in the United States who could sponsor them, found it difficult to convince Washington bureaucrats of the worthiness of their case for refuge. In a letter to the *Washington Post*, Becca Heller, cofounder and director of the IRAP, reported one tragic but all too common story:

> Consider the plight of one client, a woman who worked for many years as a human rights organizer in Iraq and whose organization received funding from the US Agency for International Development. Forced into hiding by militants, she applied to come to the United States, where her parents are citizens. For three years, she waited for an answer from the Department of Homeland Security, only to be denied. The reason? She was convicted under the regime of Saddam Hussein for the crime of being raped. A man she rejected kidnapped her, drugged her, forced her to sign a marriage certificate and beat and raped her for weeks. After she escaped, he sued her for alimony, and she was found guilty and sentenced to prison. Thankfully, her conviction was soon vacated. But sixteen years later, DHS officials interviewing her for refugee status determined that she was a criminal and denied her application.[150]

"Our failures in the area will have national implications," wrote Heller. "If the world watches the United States abandon its friends, we will hemorrhage credibility in regions where we need it most and struggle to find people to help us in the future."[151]

The delays in visas persisted in large part because of the ever-intensifying security checks.[152] Citing the United States' "moral obligation" to the Iraqis, the Center for American Progress submitted an "action plan" to the Obama administration proposing that the administration airlift US-affiliated Iraqis to Guam or some other location for expedited vetting and resettlement processing.[153] No airlift was established. The US government has never released official statistics on the number of interpreters who worked for the US armed forces translating their communications, acting as intermediaries, and interpreting the cultural world around them to soldiers largely ignorant of Iraq and the Middle East. The Iraqi Refugee Assistance Project estimates that fifty thousand Iraqis and Afghans worked as military interpreters. Another source estimates that one hundred thousand Iraqis were employed by US contractors to provide a wide range of services from janitorial work to office management.[154] Most of these workers were not—and will never be—resettled in the United States. From October 2006 through April 2016, 14,383 Iraqi applicants and their dependents were granted admission under the SIV program.[155]

The escalating war between Iraqi forces and ISIS forced the US embassy in Baghdad to evacuate "nonessential personnel" and temporarily suspend the refugee and SIV interviews and processing of applications. The State Department assured Iraqis that the SIV program (reauthorized in January 2014) would continue until all twenty-five hundred visas had been issued, or all qualified applicants (if less than the number of visas allocated) had received visas. Acknowledging the unpredictability of the process, however, the State Department web page warned hopeful applicants: "You should NOT make any travel arrangements, sell property, or give up employment until and unless you are issued a US visa."[156]

Syria and the Regional Aftermath

On May 27, 2014, President Barack Obama announced a gradual withdrawal of US troops from Afghanistan. At its peak in June 2011, the surge against Taliban forces had drawn in one hundred thousand US soldiers.[157] NATO's International Security Assistance Force (ISAF) transferred authority to the Afghan National Security Forces (ANSF) at the end of 2014. NATO troops numbering 140,000, representing forty different countries, withdrew from Afghanistan, but NATO assured the Afghans of their commitment to "train, advise and assist the ANSF [and] contribute to the long-term sustainment of [ANSF] forces."[158]

On the eve of American and NATO withdrawal, the State Department reported economic and social gains in Afghanistan: the gross domestic product had grown an average of 9.4% per year from 2003 to 2012; life expectancy at birth had increased by twenty years to over sixty-two years; girls now had more opportunities for education and over a third of the eight million school children were female; and 28 percent of the population had reliable access to electricity.[159] In the April 2014 presidential elections, over seven million of the eligible twelve million Afghan voters defied threats from Taliban insurgents and voted for one of two candidates; 38 percent of the voters were women.[160] Many challenges remained ahead, however, and area specialists worried that, with the withdrawal of coalition forces, the Taliban insurgency would draw the country back into war.

The UNHCR oversaw the largest voluntary repatriation program in its history—5.8 million Afghan refugees (20 percent of Afghanistan's population) returned to their homeland after 2002 (4.7 million with UNHCR assistance); but hundreds of thousands more remained in Pakistan and Iran.[161] Any resurgence of war would add to those numbers.

After withdrawing from Iraq, US warplanes were called into action once again in late 2014, this time to prevent ISIS from advancing further into Kurdish territory (which was a hub for US oil and gas companies), and to protect religious minorities from certain genocide. By the fall of 2014, ISIS controlled hundreds of square miles of territory, from Syria's Mediterranean coast to just south of Baghdad. Rejected as too extreme even by Osama bin Laden's successors, ISIS ruled according to an especially harsh interpretation of Islamic sharia law, beheading and crucifying non-Muslims and even Shiite Muslims, who were regarded as infidels. According to Amnesty International, ISIS carried out summary executions, child abductions, sexual assaults, forced religious conversions, and "ethnic cleansing on a historic scale."[162] Hundreds of thousands of people fled as ISIS fighters advanced on their communities. By August 2014, the UNHCR had declared a "Level 3 Emergency" in Iraq—its highest designation for a humanitarian crisis that identified the country as a top priority for funding and personnel. An estimated 1.2 million internally displaced people were in dire need of humanitarian assistance, including an estimated seven hundred thousand in the Kurdish region.[163] President Obama, who fulfilled his campaign promise to bring US troops home from Iraq, refused to commit US ground troops for fear that it would draw the United States into another war.[164] US actions were limited to strategic bombings of ISIS targets, advising Iraqi and Syrian opposition forces, and dropping food, water, and other humanitarian supplies by aircraft to refugees and IDPs.

Neighboring Syria was also a Level 3 emergency. The Assad government's brutal crackdown on antigovernment protests in 2011 had led to civil war. Fatigued by over a decade of war in Afghanistan and Iraq, the international community was initially noncommittal, offering little more than verbal condemnation of the Assad regime, even after news that Assad had used chemical weapons against his citizens. By 2016, the fifth anniversary of the civil war, the death toll stood at 470,000.[165] Some 4.8 million Syrian refugees had crossed international borders in search of safety, half of them children. An additional six million people—or one third of Syria's population—were internally displaced.[166] UN officials called the decimation of eastern Aleppo by Syrian forces and their Russian allies a probable war crime.[167]

Once again, the countries that bordered areas of crisis carried the disproportionate burden of accommodating refugees. Lebanon, Jordan, Turkey, and Iraq became the reluctant hosts to three-quarters of all Syrian refugees. Over 1.3 million Syrians fled to Lebanon, where they comprised a quarter of Lebanon's resident population and placed enormous burdens on the country's resources and infrastructure.[168] As a result Lebanon had the highest per capita concentration of refugees worldwide. Over 900,000 Syrians settled in Jordan, with 20 percent living in the refugee camps of Za'atari and Asraq.[169] An estimated 1.7 million Syrians settled in Turkey and 400,000 in Iraq.[170] Of these countries, Turkey was the only signatory to the United Nations Convention and Protocol on Refugees, but this did not prevent the nonsignatories from providing assistance.

Europe attracted a comparatively smaller share of the Syrian refugees, but it commanded the lion's share of the media attention in the West. The Greek island of Lesvos, a popular tourist destination on the Aegean Sea, became the front line of the refugee crisis because thousands of new refugees arrived there each day en route to the continent.[171] Over 970,000 Syrian refugees requested asylum in European countries between April 2011 and February 2016, 61 percent in Germany and Serbia, and 27 percent in Sweden, Hungary, Austria, Netherlands, and Denmark.[172] (Hundreds of thousands more came from Eritrea, Libya, Somalia, Nigeria, and other countries, creating what news media called "the migrant crisis" in the European Union.) Of these countries, Germany adopted the most generous policy, agreeing to accept up to eight hundred thousand refugees from Syria and other parts of the world, but taking in 890,000 by the end of 2015.[173]

Syrians traveled dangerous stretches of land and sea to reach Europe, making themselves vulnerable to criminal gangs, smugglers, traffickers, and corrupt police forces, in the hopes of eventually reaching safety. According to the International Organization for Migration (IOM), in 2015 alone, more than thirty-six hundred Syrian and other migrants died trying to reach safety in Europe. Nearly 100,000 of the 1.3 million people who sought asylum in Europe in 2015 were unaccompanied minors.[174] Because of the European Union's Dublin agreement, which requires the country of first arrival to process asylum claims, refugees tried to move quickly across borders to reach a country where friends or relatives awaited them. Neither asylum nor temporary protected status was guaranteed, however. While the EU tried to implement uniform standards and procedures for assessing asylum claims across its twenty-eight member states, asylum practices varied across EU (and non-EU) nations. The immigration courts became backlogged, and asylum applicants waited months, if not years, for their applications to be evaluated and their personal histories vetted. Asylum approval rates varied, often dramatically, from one quarter to the next.[175]

As signatories to the UN Protocol on Refugees, European states recognized—at least theoretically—that refugees had the right to work, to receive an education, and to have access to the courts, but its citizens were much more reluctant to acknowledge those rights. In Great Britain, anger over the migrant crisis encouraged voters to support a referendum calling for "Brexit," the withdrawal of Britain from the European Union. Public pressure forced some European governments to adopt deterrent policies toward the Syrians (and other refugees and migrants). Sweden and Finland, generally known for their generous policies toward immigrants, now threatened to expel tens of thousands of asylum seekers; and Denmark introduced legislation authorizing police to confiscate refugees' cash and valuables.[176] Even Chancellor Angela Merkel of Germany announced that Syrians were expected to return to their country once the conflict ended.[177]

These policies and pronouncements did not deter Syrians from fleeing their homeland. They had little choice. The delivery of humanitarian aid had been blocked by bureaucratic red tape, by theft and extortion, and by shelling and aerial bombardment.[178] UN commissioner António Guterres repeatedly tried to call international attention to the magnitude of the Syrian refugee crisis: "Syria as a civilization is unraveling," he said in June 2013; and a week later, on World Refugee Day, he called Syria the "worst humanitarian disaster since the end of the Cold War."[179] The international agency launched an appeal for $6.5 billion in donations, the largest humanitarian appeal in UNHCR history.[180] In testimony before the Senate Foreign Relations Committee, Jan Egeland, the secretary general of the Norwegian Refugee Council, likened the situation to the "horrors of Bosnia and Rwanda" and warned Americans that they—and the rest of the international community—had "a moral obligation not to prevent a return to those dark days": "If we do not act now to protect the region's future," he said, "the fallout from this conflict will be felt for generations."[181]

The Syrian refugee population was several times the population of Washington, DC, and yet, by April 2014, the United States had admitted a total of 121 refugees.[182] In September 2015, President Obama announced that the refugee quota for FY2016 would be increased to 85,000 (and 110,000 in FY2017) to accommodate a minimum of 10,000 Syrian refugees each year. Experts predicted that the new quotas would go unfilled, since the rigorous security screening took, on average, eighteen to twenty-four months, but the Obama administration met its goals the first year: 12,486 Syrians were admitted to the United States in FY2016.[183] Indeed, 2016 was the first year since 9/11 that the United States had filled its refugee quota. (Canada, by comparison, admitted 38,713 in 2016.)[184] Obama's announcement proved to be unpopular, however, and thirty governors tried to block the resettlement of Syrian refugees in their states. Republican presidential candidates successfully manipulated American fears about Muslim refugees during the 2016 electoral campaign, resulting in the election of Donald Trump, who campaigned on the promise of a moratorium on further admissions. Trump kept his promise. One of his first executive orders reduced the FY2017 refugee quota to 50,000, imposed a 120-day moratorium on refugee admissions, and barred Syrian refugees altogether.[185]

"As the world's richest country, and one that justifiably prides itself on protecting refugees," wrote Eleanor Acer of Human Rights First, "it needs to be doing much more."[186] However, in the post-9/11 period, the United States relied almost exclusively on aid to address the humanitarian challenges of warring and postconflict societies.[187] Of the various "durable solutions" advocated by the UNHCR (voluntary repatriation, local integration, and resettlement in third countries), the resettlement of refugees in the United States was the least attractive option to American policymakers. Refugee resettlement had been an important ideological and geopolitical tool during the Cold War, but in the post-9/11 national security state it posed a threat.

4

The New Asylum Seekers

Uwe and Hannelore Romeike, evangelical Christians in Germany, sought asylum in the United States because homeschooling is illegal in their country. The Romeikes claimed that they had a "fundamental right" to decide how they wanted to teach their children.[1]

Twelve-year-old Santos Maldonado-Canales traveled alone to the United States from his native El Salvador because he had been beaten and threatened since the age of ten by members of the M-13 gang, the same group that had shot and killed his sixteen-year-old brother, José Ever, for refusing to join the gang. Santos made his way across Central America and Mexico but was apprehended by the US Border Patrol in Texas and placed in a detention facility to await deportation.[2]

José Alarcón, a twenty-seven-year-old police officer from Ciudad Juárez, Mexico, fled to the United States with his family and asked for asylum in a Dallas courtroom. He argued that he was a member of a persecuted social group—police officers—and that the Mexican government offered them little protection from the widespread violence in Juárez, a city with one of the highest homicide rates in the world.[3]

These individuals are just a few of the hundreds of thousands of men, women, and children who have sought asylum in the United States since the end of the Cold War. Unlike refugees, who are identified abroad for resettlement in the United States, asylum seekers petition for refuge on US territory, usually at a port of entry like an international airport, or along the US-Canada or US-Mexico borders.

The policymakers who crafted the 1980 Refugee Act probably never imagined that, within a generation, the United States would have a vast asylum bureaucracy, comprised of multiple official administrative levels, and numerous nonofficial participants who also shape the decision-making process. Asylum applications were comparatively few during the Cold War. From 1973 to 1979, for example, the United States received 22,722 applications for asylum, ranging from a low of 896 in 1976 to a high of 5,801 in 1979.[4] Asylum seekers generally did not make the evening news. The cases that generated the most media attention were the defections of high-profile individuals whose celebrity or stature made their defections to the West newsworthy. Asylum seekers were usually released on their own recognizance to await their hearing in an immigration court. Some disappeared, never to be heard from again, but the numbers were small enough that they did not generate concern.

By the late 1980s, the United States faced a very different situation. Petitions for asylum increased in large part because of the political turmoil in Haiti and the wars in Central America. Over four hundred thousand people filed for asylum in the United States from 1980 to 1990, with Central Americans filing roughly half of all applications. (See table 4.1.)[5] Many refugees bypassed the asylum bureaucracy altogether and remained

Table 4.1 Asylum Cases Filed,
1980–1990

Year	Cases
1980	26,512
1981	61,568
1982	33,296
1984	26,295
1985	16,622
1986	18,889
1987	26,107
1988	60,736
1989	101,679
1990	73,637

Source: Department of Homeland Security, "Asylum Cases Filed with INS District Directors and Asylum Officers," http://www.dhs.gov/publication/fiscal-year-2000-statistical-yearbook-refugeesasylees.

undocumented in the informal economy. With a less than 5 percent chance of securing asylum in the 1980s,[6] many Salvadorans and Guatemalans who came to the United States chose to carry out their lives as anonymously as possible until conditions in their countries of origin improved and they could safely return home.

The growing undocumented migration from Central America and Haiti—as well as Mexico, China, and other parts of the world—signaled to many Americans that the United States had lost the ability to control its borders. Concern over the permeability of US borders resulted in the passage of two important immigration acts: the 1986 Immigration Reform and Control Act and the 1996 Illegal Immigration Reform and Immigrant Responsibility Act (IIRIRA). The 1996 law, in particular, addressed some of the problems in the asylum bureaucracy that the Ramzi Yousef case had dramatically highlighted.

In the post–Cold War era, the asylum office, entrusted with fulfilling the country's humanitarian commitment to safe haven, has been subsumed into the Department of Homeland Security. The asylum seekers who petition for protection on US territory thus have navigated a complex and impersonal bureaucracy that has competing and often contradictory missions. Over 80 percent of all asylum seekers request asylum at one of the DHS service centers and immigration officials call these petitions "affirmative applications."[7] If they are denied asylum, they are immediately subject to removal from the United States unless they have filed for—and have been granted—Withholding of Removal, which protects them from deportation and offers work authorization, but does not offer a green card or a pathway to citizenship.[8] Those apprehended for unlawful entry by law enforcement before they have a chance to file for asylum must deal directly with the immigration courts of the Department of Justice, and these cases are known as "defensive applications."[9] In all these cases, the burden of proof is always on the individual asylum seeker who, like a refugee, must offer compelling evidence that she or he (1) has been singled out for persecution because of race, religion, nationality, membership in a particular social group, or political opinion; (2) could not receive protection from his government; (3) could not have avoided persecution by resettling in another part of his country; (4) faces imminent danger should he return to his country of nationality or last residence; (5) did not persecute or inflict harm on others, or commit certain types of crimes; and (6) is not a national security risk.

Many asylum seekers are denied access to a meaningful judicial review of their cases. Since the passage of the IIRIRA, immigration officers remove from the United States those who at the initial interview do not seem to have a credible fear of persecution; and those who do demonstrate a credible fear are often detained in prisons for months and even years while their cases make their way through the bureaucracy. In order to deal with the backlog of cases, asylum officers and judges must work through their caseloads as quickly as possible, raising doubts about the system's ability to offer careful review. As a result, the likelihood that a bona fide asylum seeker will be returned to dangerous conditions is great. As legal scholars Andrew Schoenholtz, Philip Schrag, and Jaya Ramji-Nogales have noted, the stakes are high in asylum decisions:

> All asylum applicants claim that they reasonably fear persecution if sent back to the country from which they fled. If the agency makes a mistake by wrongly excluding an applicant, the person could face detention, torture, and even death upon return to the home country. . . . On the other hand, an erroneous grant of asylum can allow fraudulent applicants to remain in the United States, using the asylum process to obtain immigration benefits for which they might not otherwise be eligible for many years, if at all. Mistakes in favor of people who should not be granted asylum also harm genuine asylum applicants. . . . False but successful claims threaten the accuracy of the asylum adjudication process, and reports of fraud can spur political attacks that weaken America's legal commitment to protecting refugees.[10]

If the executive and legislative branches of government are responsible for crafting refugee policy, the judiciary plays a more central role in the crafting of asylum policy. However, only a small percentage of asylum cases ever make it to the US circuit courts of appeal and fewer still to the US Supreme Court. The vast majority of "defensive" cases are determined by immigration judges and the Board of Immigration Appeals (BIA), both of which are part of the Executive Office for Immigration Review (EOIR) within the Department of Justice. What Americans regard as due process is often absent in immigration courts. The majority of asylum seekers navigate the bureaucracy without legal representation, or even competent interpreters. Unlike criminal courts, where there is a presumption of innocence until guilt is proven, in immigration hearings there is often a presumption of deception until merit or "worthiness" of asylum is demonstrated. The burden of proof is always on the individual asylum seeker. The decision to grant asylum is determined on a case-by-case basis.

Over the years, the circuit courts have remanded cases back to the BIA, requiring them to expand the range of considerations in their decision-making. The courts have recognized, for example, that a pattern of persecution of persons similarly situated to the petitioner may, indeed, constitute a "well-founded fear" of persecution. In response to class action suits, the courts have also helped to define the rights of asylum seekers in and out of detention and at various stages of the adjudication process. However, the many lawsuits filed by advocates on behalf of asylum seekers demonstrate that rights continue to be violated.

Critics of US asylum system argue that the categories of "refugee" and "asylee" have become meaningless in the post–Cold war period. Asylum, they say, has become a "back door" for undocumented immigrants who manipulate the system in order to remain in the United States. Advocates agree that the asylum system is in need of reform, but for entirely different reasons; the ad hoc nature of asylum decisions, they argue, creates a system that is inconsistent, unfair, and often inhumane. In 1989, as the communist bloc began to unravel, the US Committee for Refugees warned American policymakers that the humanitarian tradition of granting refuge to the persecuted was in serious jeopardy. If the United States, "with its historic adherence to due process and its wealth, [cannot] see fit to offer minimal levels of protection to refugees who throw themselves on our mercy, the whole system of refugee protection throughout the world [ran] the risk of unraveling."[11] Three decades and several reforms later, this humanitarian tradition continues to face serious challenges.

Navigating the Asylum Bureaucracy

The 1948 UN Declaration on Human Rights recognized the right of individuals "to seek and to enjoy" asylum.[12] International law recognizes a state's right to grant asylum. An individual, however, has no internationally recognized right to receive asylum.[13] While the United States does not have a statutory obligation to grant asylum, it does recognize the principle of *nonrefoulement*, which is articulated in the Immigration and Nationality Act (INA) as well as in the international conventions the United States has supported since the end of World War II.

The 1980 Refugee Act allowed for five thousand asylum seekers and their family members to acquire legal permanent residence (LPR) each year as long as they were physically present in the United States for one year after receiving asylum and continued to meet the definition of a refugee. The small quota was appropriate for the early Cold War period when comparatively fewer requested asylum, but by the late 1980s the quota proved to be a major obstacle. Petitions for asylum had increased dramatically: 101,679 petitioned for asylum in 1989 alone.[14] Those who received asylum soon found themselves in a second backlog: those waiting for legal permanent residence. With an annual limit of five thousand, those who were approved for asylum in the 1980s had to wait as long as a decade to adjust their status to LPR.[15] The 1990 Immigration Act tried to address this problem when it increased LPR adjustments from five thousand to ten thousand per year. It also temporarily cleared the backlog by allowing those who had filed for adjustment before June 1, 1990, to acquire LPR status outside of the new numerical limits. Given the high number of asylum applications, however—over a million people over the next fifteen years[16]—the long wait for LPR continued until the REAL ID Act of 2005 (PL 109-13) eliminated the numerical limit on LPR adjustments altogether.

Since backlogs in the asylum bureaucracy were the new reality, the 1990 act established a corps of professional asylum officers with targeted training in international human rights law, country conditions, and national and international refugee law, to facilitate the quick review of asylum cases. By 1994, there were eight asylum offices throughout the country: Los Angeles (Anaheim), San Francisco, Newark (Lyndhurst), Houston, Miami, Chicago, Arlington, and Rosedale, New York. The 1990 act also authorized the creation of a Resource Information Center (RIC), a library and documentation center modeled in part after Canada's Immigration and Refugee Board (IRB) libraries, to respond to inquiries on specific issues and "to collect and disseminate to asylum officers information on country conditions needed to make quality asylum adjudications."[17] Despite these improvements, by 1992, the backlog of asylum cases had grown to 291,000, forcing two of the busiest INS offices—Los Angeles and Miami—to stop working on tens of thousands of old asylum cases to devote themselves to the new cases.[18] Two years later, the backlog had increased to 425,000 cases.[19] Critics of the US asylum system blamed the ever-growing backlog on undocumented immigrants who requested asylum, often on the advice of their lawyers, in order to acquire immediate work authorization, and as a defensive strategy to delay deportation for as long as possible. "[Asylum] has obviously lost all credibility," said Dave Simcox, then-director at the Center for Immigration Studies. "It's just a terrible system that has allowed asylum to become an alternate route of immigration." A Department of Justice report agreed with this assessment, calling the asylum system a "magnet for abuse."[20]

From 1993 to 1995, the Clinton administration authorized preliminary reforms in the asylum bureaucracy in anticipation of a more comprehensive immigration reform package from Congress. After 1995, asylum seekers received a work permit only after asylum was granted, or 150 days past the date of filing, if a decision was still pending. The number of asylum officers increased from 150 to 325, and the number of immigration judges expanded from 112 to 179. The backlog continued, however, and asylum seekers spent months, and often years, waiting for resolution to their cases.

By the mid-1990s, the debates about immigration and asylum reform had been absorbed into the larger debate about national security. Undocumented immigrants, who had always been a vital part of the immigrant labor force in the United States,[21] were increasingly portrayed as menaces to public safety, another set of nonstate actors who posed a threat to the security of the United States. The rhetoric of immigration reform drew on the language of environmental disaster: immigrants were said to come in "floods," "swarms," "tidal waves," and "hordes." They were coming to "mooch," to "overwhelm," to "abuse." The proverbial American melting pot was said to be "boiling" and "overflowing." The terrorist attacks of 1993 only compounded such rhetoric.[22] In this climate, passage of the 1996 Illegal Immigration Reform and Immigrant Responsibility Act (IIRIRA, PL 104-208) was inevitable.

Included in IIRIRA were three controversial measures that affected asylum seekers: the one-year filing deadline; expedited removal; and mandatory detention.[23] These three measures were kept in the post-9/11 reforms of the immigration bureaucracy.

IIRIRA required foreign nationals physically present in the United States to file applications for asylum (the I-589) within one year of arrival, either in person or by delivering the application to a DHS service center. The one-year deadline drew vocal criticism from refugee advocates, who argued that it penalized the severely traumatized, who were often too afraid to come forward for fear that they would not be believed and then deported to face their persecutors. In such cases, an asylum seeker preferred to remain undocumented and only file a "defensive" claim for asylum when apprehended by authorities, to prevent deportation.

Those without authorized entry who were apprehended by law enforcement before filing for asylum ran the risk of immediate removal. Prior to IIRIRA, only immigration judges had the authority to order persons removed from the United States. The 1996 law authorized the "expedited removal" of any foreign national apprehended at a port of entry, without proper documentation. (In 2004 the Department of Homeland Security authorized expedited removal for those encountered within one hundred miles of the border and within fourteen days of unauthorized entry.) However, an immigration officer at a port of entry was required to ask a series of "protection questions" to determine which individuals might have a fear of persecution if returned to their homeland, thereby distinguishing the bona fide asylum seekers from ordinary migrants. If foreign nationals expressed fear of returning to their homelands, they were to be detained and more thoroughly interviewed by asylum officers.

For many asylum seekers who arrived without proper legal documents, then, the first point of contact with the US asylum bureaucracy was the immigration officer they met at the airport or the border checkpoint, or when they were apprehended at sea. The immigration officer assessed the answers to the "protection questions," but the screening was a subjective evaluation with virtually no oversight. US law did not require that an interpreter be present. The immigration officer, who served as a "gatekeeper," had the authority to order a foreign national removed from the United States without further hearing or review. To mitigate the chances that a true asylum seeker might be removed, immigration officers were given specialized training in country conditions and cultural sensitivity. However, since the system offered little oversight and no real chance for appeal, mistakes were bound to occur. In the presence of uniformed officers, traumatized individuals often exhibited a particular affect during an interview (e.g., appeared nervous, failed to make eye contact, etc.) because in their countries of origin uniformed officers are complicit in inflicting trauma. Without proper training, immigration officers could misinterpret such affect as an attempt to deceive, with devastating consequences for the asylum seeker who was then returned to his homeland to face his persecutors. In 2005, for example, the US Commission on International Religious Freedom reported that one-sixth of those observed at US ports of entry who expressed a fear of return were still denied the opportunity to apply for asylum.[24] Those removed from the United States were also barred re-entry for a period of five years.

If asylum seekers at a port of entry passed the preliminary screening, they were referred to an asylum officer, the second point of contact with the asylum bureaucracy. As they waited for their interview with the asylum officer, they were subject to mandatory detention and still considered in "expedited removal" proceedings. The request for asylum was regarded as "defensive asylum processing," and the decision to detain could not be appealed to an independent authority. The interview with the asylum officer was supposed to be nonadversarial. If the asylum seekers did not speak English, however, they had to arrange for their own interpreter. Once an asylum officer established that asylum seekers had a "credible fear of persecution" (a significant possibility that they could establish eligibility for asylum under the "well-founded fear" standard of proof), the asylum officer referred the applicants to an immigration judge. This hearing with the immigration judge was designed to be adversarial, and only now were the asylum seekers offered an interpreter.[25] If the asylum officer did not find a credible fear of persecution, the asylum applicants were ordered removed from the United States unless they appealed the decision and asked for a hearing with an immigration judge. Many were not informed that this was an option, however.

The asylum seekers who established a credible fear might be "paroled" (in this context, meaning that they are released on their own recognizance) while they waited for their court date, but only if they met certain conditions: they had to establish proof of identity; they had family in the US or other community ties; they posed no danger to the community; and they were not otherwise barred from asylum.[26] These conditions were difficult to meet. Since 9/11, the decision to hold anyone in prison has been left to the discretion of the Department of Homeland Security. Individuals who did not meet these conditions—to the satisfaction of DHS—were left in detention. The Lawyer's Committee for Human Rights (now Human Rights First) noted in 2003:

> These efforts to detain asylum seekers—even if they demonstrate in their individual cases, that they present no security risk and otherwise satisfy the criteria for parole—reflect[ed] a fundamental lack of understanding of US obligations to asylum seekers and a perception that asylum seekers should be treated as threats to US security.[27]

If asylum seekers were fortunate to be paroled, they were still barred from seeking employment for 150 days after first filing an application for asylum—plus an additional 30 days to process the employment application. In the interim, they were unable to support themselves (or to receive social services and medical benefits) and had to depend on the generosity of friends, faith communities, or advocacy groups for months (or sometimes years, if the EOIR "stopped the clock" for whatever reason).[28] By 2011, delays in the adjudication process ran three years in some immigration courts.[29] While they waited for their cases to be adjudicated, asylum seekers often learned that their 180-day "asylum clock" for work authorization had been extended for reasons that seemed unclear and sometimes capricious. In response to a 2013 class action lawsuit settlement filed on behalf of asylum seekers around the country (including one man from China who had been waiting ten years for his case to be resolved), several changes were mandated to make this process clearer and more uniform.[30] Despite greater procedural accountability, the waiting period for work authorization persists.

Either party—the asylum seeker or the INS/USCIS—could appeal the ruling of the EOIR immigration judge to the Board of Immigration Appeals (BIA) and, in the case of another unsatisfactory ruling, the circuit court of appeals. These administrative or judicial bodies are the asylum seeker's fourth and fifth points of contact, respectively, with the asylum bureaucracy. However, most asylum seekers never made it this far.[31] The success of navigating the bureaucracy to these higher levels (and securing release from a detention facility in the interim) depended on the availability of legal counsel. Unlike in criminal cases, the federal government is not required to provide asylum seekers with legal representation, since immigration matters are considered civil, not criminal, cases. Many attorneys, translators, law school clinics, expert witnesses, and immigrant advocates assist asylum seekers pro bono with their petitions, but the demand for assistance far exceeds the supply. These unofficial actors, when available, are enormously influential in securing a successful outcome. During FY2010, for example, only 11 percent of those without legal representation were granted asylum; with legal representation the success rates rose to 54 percent.[32] The judges of the circuit courts of appeal—assisted by their judicial clerks—evaluate which cases they consider for review. In the best of outcomes, the appeals court remands the case back to the BIA for further review.

All these procedural gauntlets have deterred asylum seekers from pursuing a petition, which critics argued was the intended goal. By the late 1990s there was a significant reduction in the number of asylum cases received, from 147,430 in 1995 to 37,938 in 1999. Asylum claims rose slightly again in 2001–2002 before dropping in 2003 to 46,272 in response to the post-9/11 changes in the immigration bureaucracy. Over the next decade, asylum claims were inconsistently reported by the USCIS. Approval rates increased only slightly from 29 percent in 2003 (in the immediate post-9/11 period) to 30 percent in FY2014. The overall numbers admitted were low: in FY2014, for example, 23,533 individuals were granted asylum either affirmatively or in defensive proceedings (an additional 8,325 individuals received admission to the US as "follow to join" spouses and minor children of asylees). The People's Republic of China was the top source country of both affirmative and defensive petitions for asylum for over a decade. In FY2014, the source countries with the highest approval rates were China (33.5 percent), Egypt (12.2 percent), and Syria (4 percent). Nationals of these three countries accounted for roughly half of all persons granted asylum in 2014.[33]

These figures obscured the fact that since 1996 hundreds of thousands were denied the opportunity to even establish a foothold in the asylum bureaucracy because of the expedited removal process. In 2013 alone, 44 percent of the 438,421 individuals deported were removed through expedited removal and "did not have a hearing, never saw an immigration judge, and were deported through cursory administrative processes where the same presiding immigration officer acted as the prosecutor, judge, and jailor."[34] An ACLU study drawing on a small sample of eighty-nine individuals suggested that government safeguards failed to protect asylum seekers:

Fifty-five percent said they were never asked about their fear of persecution or that they were not asked anything in a language they understood. Only twenty-eight percent said they were asked about their fear of returning to their country of origin by a border officer or agent; forty percent of those asked about fear said they told the agent they were afraid of returning to their country but were nevertheless not referred to an asylum officer before being summarily deported.[35]

Establishing Persecution

Asylum officers and judges assess the risk of future harm to an asylum applicant. Past persecution establishes a presumption of future prosecution, but the government can challenge that presumption. There is no statute that defines a "well-founded fear of persecution." The Supreme Court observed that a " 'well-founded fear'... can only be given concrete meaning through a process of case-by-case adjudication."[36]

The standard of proof for a "well-founded fear" has changed over the years largely in response to administrative and judicial decisions in deportation cases. Those who do not qualify for—or are denied—asylum may request a "withholding of removal" to prevent deportation.[37] To qualify for "withholding of removal," the applicant must establish a "clear probability" of persecution as opposed to a "well-founded fear" of persecution. In the legal decision *Matter of Acosta* (1985), the Board of Immigration Appeals (BIA) held that the "clear probability" standard and the "well-founded fear" standard were not meaningfully different "and, in practical application, converge."[38] Two years later, in *Matter of Mogharrabi* (1987),[39] the BIA held that an asylum applicant established a well-founded fear if a reasonable person in his circumstances would fear persecution "even where its likelihood is significantly less than clearly probable." An asylum seeker's testimony in an asylum case could be sufficient, without corroborating evidence, the BIA ruled, "if that testimony [was] believable, consistent, and sufficiently detailed to provide a plausible and coherent account of the basis for his fear."[40] In 1987, however, the US Supreme Court Case *I.N.S. v. Cardoza-Fonseca* (480 US 421) held that the "clear probability" standard for withholding differed from the "well-founded fear" standard used for asylum, presumably to make it more difficult to establish absolute entitlement to withholding of deportation. The court declined to define what a "well-founded fear" was, leaving it to the immigration courts to determine on a case-by-case basis. However, the court did reaffirm the ruling of *INS v. Stevic* (1984) that an alien must prove that it is "more likely than not" that he will be persecuted upon return.

Thus, an asylum seeker had a well-founded fear of persecution if (a) the applicant had a fear of persecution based on the race, religion, nationality, membership in a particular social group, or political opinion; (b) there was reasonable possibility of suffering such persecution if he or she were returned; and (c) he was unable to avail himself of the protection of that country because of such fear. Demonstrating that there was a pattern or practice of persecution of persons similarly situated to the applicant on account of race, religion, and so on, could be construed as evidence.[41]

Two decades later, as a result of the post-9/11 immigration reforms, asylum seekers encountered a heightened burden of proof. The REAL ID

Act of 2005 allowed judges to require corroborating evidence even with credible testimony. This placed an additional burden on the asylum seeker because, as legal scholar Donald Kerwin noted, survivors of persecution "cannot always establish a persecutor's motive, corroborate threats, or even prove past persecution: persecutors often succeed in hiding what they do and why they do it."[42] The BIA also made it much more difficult to prove membership in a "particular social group." *Matter of Acosta* (1985) had defined a "social group" as one whose members "share a common immutable characteristic." The immutable characteristic

> may be an innate one such as sex, color, or kinship ties, or in some circumstances it might be a shared past experience such as former military leadership or land ownership.... However, whatever the common characteristic that defines the group, it must be one that the members of the group either cannot change, or should not be required to change because it is fundamental to their individual identities or consciences.[43]

In subsequent rulings the BIA added greater specificity to this definition by requiring that the "immutable characteristics" grant members "social visibility" and "particularity," that is, that the members be perceived as a cohesive group by society. This was a heightened burden of proof, especially for those who deliberately hid their identities to remain inconspicuous to avoid persecution.[44]

These rulings have not helped standardize decisions in immigration courts. A 2008 report from the General Accountability Office (GAO) found significant variation in asylum outcomes across immigration courts and judges. From October 1994 through April 2007, for example, the GAO found that asylum applicants in San Francisco were twelve times more likely to be granted asylum than those in Atlanta. The GAO recommended that the EOIR use the report to identify immigration judges who might benefit from additional supervision and training.[45] Other studies recommended an expansion in the overall number of judges and the use of law clerks to assist with research and adjudication.[46] Indeed, because immigration judges have caseloads ranging from 1,200 to 1,500 cases a year (compared to the 480 criminal and civil cases for federal district judges), often working without law clerks or court reporters, they have little time for reflection or for editing or correcting a decision.[47] Under such circumstances, an asylum seeker's need for legal representation becomes all the more important. Attorneys and legal advocates assist asylum seekers to know their rights and to put together a substantiated and compelling claim.

Oscar Ramírez Castañeda learned firsthand the importance of legal representation. In late 2010, the Guatemalan Attorney General's Office launched an unprecedented campaign against human rights abusers, targeting those responsible for the massacres of the Guatemalan civil war. In the course of their investigations, public prosecutors discovered and tracked down Ramírez Castañeda, the sole survivor of a 1982 massacre in the village of Dos Erres, who was then an undocumented immigrant in the United States. After DNA evidence confirmed his identity and Ramírez Castañeda cooperated with Guatemalan investigators, he was provided with legal representation in the United States to legalize his status. His American attorneys offered compelling evidence that he faced retaliatory persecution—even death—at the hands of Guatemala's war criminals if repatriated back to his homeland, and in 2012 Ramírez Castañeda was granted asylum.[48]

Uwe and Hannelore Romeike, the evangelical Christians from Germany also benefited from legal representation. The Romeikes claimed that they were persecuted for homeschooling their seven children in their native Germany, where such education is prohibited by law. They settled in Morristown, Tennessee, the heart of the "Bible Belt," and requested asylum. The Virginia-based Home School Legal Defense Association (HSLDA) took up their asylum case, providing pro bono legal counsel and financial assistance. In 2010, an immigration judge based in Memphis granted the Romeikes' asylum. The BIA later overturned the judge's ruling, and the Sixth Circuit Court of Appeals denied the family an appellate hearing. With their clients now facing removal, the HSLDA attorneys prepared to take their case to the US Supreme Court. Christian and politically conservative groups around the country rallied to the family's support, using social media and conservative news outlets to rally support for their cause.[49] In March 2014, the Supreme Court announced that it would not hear the family's appeal for asylum. Within twenty-four hours of the announcement, the Department of Homeland Security informed the Romeikes that they would extend the family's "deferred action" status indefinitely. As long as they stayed out of trouble, they would not be deported to Germany.[50]

Such dramatic and high-profile cases are the exception. Most asylum seekers do not have attorneys in two countries working on their behalf, nor do they have well-endowed advocacy groups providing legal and financial assistance, or generating media attention and political will on their behalf. They are fortunate if they find anyone to defend their interests.

Challenges to Asylum in the Twenty-First Century

The asylum cases that make their way through US courts are fraught with moral and ethical uncertainty and raise a number of troubling questions. Cases are often highly politicized, especially when petitioners fall outside the traditional categories of persecution and must depend on advocates to appeal on their behalf. The following sections examine some of the challenges facing asylum adjudicators.

Fleeing Criminal Violence

Many of the asylum seekers who have come to the United States over the past decade have fled criminal violence. The largest number are from the Northern Triangle—Honduras, Guatemala, and El Salvador—a region barely recovered from civil war that by 2012 had the highest homicide rate per capita in the world. Murder rates surpassed civil war levels: in 2012, Honduras had a murder rate of 85.5 murders per 100,000 people, and El Salvador had a murder rate of 60 per 100,000 (the United States, by comparison, had 4.7 per 100,000).[51] Drug trafficking was the single largest driver of the criminal violence in the region. The World Bank reported that crime rates were more than 100 percent higher in drug-trafficking "hot spots" than in other areas.[52] However, other factors played a role in the social and political instability of these countries. Writing about the criminal violence in Honduras, Elizabeth Ferris called it "the toxic combination of weak governments, corruption, striking economic inequality, *narcotrafico*, the proliferation of arms, and the deportation of tens of thousands of Central Americans from the US, many of who recreated Los Angeles gang structures in the region."[53] Hal Brands, in turn, regarded the criminal violence in Guatemala as the legacy of the three-decade civil war that "left the country strewn with weapons ... initiated destabilizing refugee flows ... led to the growth of a predatory military elite skilled in corruption and intimidation ... [and which] exposed many Guatemalans to horrific bloodshed as a way of life."[54] Whatever the sources and reasons for the violence, the countries of Central America varied in their levels of institutional capacity and political will to confront organized crime and support institutional and social reforms.[55]

Although the groups engaged in criminal violence were complex, much of the journalistic and scholarly attention focused on organized gangs like the Mara Salvatruchas (MS-13) and Barrio Dieciocho (Eighteenth Street Gang) that expanded their numbers and influence in the region in large part because of aggressive American deportation policies.[56] The MS-13 was formed in Los Angeles in the 1980s by Salvadoran immigrant youths. Moving into traditional Mexican and Mexican American–dominated neighborhoods, these Salvadoran youths created their own gangs and *clicas* (subgroups) like MS-13 or joined existing gangs like the Eighteenth Street.[57] Beginning in the 1990s, the Justice Department adopted a more proactive policy of deporting those who had committed crimes in the United States, from minor infractions to more serious felonies. Those convicted of crimes who were undocumented or "legal" but noncitizen were deported after they completed their prison sentences. Members of street gangs were especially targeted in an effort to stem the violence that terrorized many low-income communities. Though deported to the countries of their birth, many deportees were unfamiliar with the culture and language of these countries, having been brought to the United States by their parents at a very young age. The conditions they encountered in Central America were conducive to the establishment of gangs. As the Washington Office on Latin America (WOLA) noted:

> After arriving in the country to which they had been deported, with few networks and sometimes little or no knowledge of Spanish, many gang members joined forces to establish gangs or joined existing gangs in their home countries, either in prison or on the streets. These deportee gang members, with US gang experience, are believed to have been a key catalyst for the evolution of *Mara Salvatrucha* and 18th Street gang into the dominant gangs that they are today in El Salvador, Guatemala, and Honduras.[58]

Consequently, a street gang that once counted a few thousand members in Los Angeles and other parts of California, spread across Central America and to other parts of the United States through cyclical migration.[59] In the Northern Triangle of Central America, the hundreds of *clicas* counted a total membership in the tens of thousands.

The transnational gangs were well armed and well funded. In 2007, a US federal grand jury indicted two MS-13 leaders for allegedly ordering murders in the United States from their prison cells in El Salvador.[60] The gangs engaged in extortion, immigrant and drug smuggling, and racketeering, and provided protection for the Mexican drug cartels. They retaliated violently against those who challenged their authority or encroached on their territory. Hal Brands called them the "new urban insurgency": irregular warfare that "aim[ed] not to overthrow established governments but to take control of a city, a neighborhood, or even a block at a time."[61] Citizens frustrated with the state's inability to protect them resorted to vigilante violence, hiring paramilitaries to eliminate those who threatened their families and communities.[62] Some states resorted to the zero-tolerance, or *mano dura* (the "iron fist"), policies: " 'Social cleansing' practices including extrajudicial killings, police violence, arbitrary or unlawful arrests and detention as well as inhumane prison conditions."[63] Thousands of youth were arrested and detained in already overburdened prison systems in Central America where the gang networks were at their strongest.[64]

The exact number of people displaced by gang-related and other criminal violence will never be known. Human rights activists who traveled through the region reported entire neighborhoods abandoned. Driven out of their communities, thousands fled to other parts of their country in search of safety; in the most desperate cases, they fled abroad. Those who remained behind paid "protection money" to the gangs who functioned as parallel governments, holding ad hoc tribunals, and determining where people could live and which businesses could operate.[65] The mass graves common during the civil wars once again became a feature of life in the region. Families sent their sons and daughters to the United States— often alone— to escape forced recruitment, reprisals, and sexual assault. Because of the transnational reach of these organizations, however, they did not always find the safety they sought.

Receiving asylum in the United States is difficult even though those who flee criminal violence share similarities with those who flee armed conflict. Gangs may not be motivated by a political ideology, but they operate in similar ways to other armed groups. The people who flee them also feel under siege. As scholar Elizabeth Ferris of the Brookings Institute has noted:

> We looked at profiles of people likely to be displaced by organized crime violence—gang members who wanted to leave the group, teachers trying to keep their students out of gangs, people (and their family members) resisting extortion, journalists, etc. The parallels were striking. Just as a soldier defecting from Assad's military or a

fighter defecting from FARC is in danger, so too are gang members who want to escape. Persecution for political reasons is grounds for refugee status, how about people standing up for their rights against the murders, kidnapping and extortion of criminal gangs? I struggled to find ways that this displacement is different from the more traditional reasons for flight, but I came up short.[66]

In 2010, the UNHCR developed guidelines for assessing asylum claims from people fleeing organized gangs.[67] "In areas where criminal activity is widespread and law enforcement is incapable of protecting people from gang violence," said the report, "a person expressing opposition to gangs will stand out from the rest of the community." These "gang-resisters" include individuals who refuse recruitment; young women and adolescent girls who refuse the sexual demands of gang members; business owners unable or unwilling to meet extortion; law enforcement agents targeted for reprisal; NGO workers, lawyers, clergy and church workers, and human rights activists who oppose gangs; and witnesses who have reported criminal activities or are otherwise perceived to be a threat.[68] Other victims include former and current gang members who face reprisals for trying to disassociate from the gangs; family members who are threatened as a way of forcing their kin to succumb to extortion or recruitment; and those who are caught in the crossfire of the rogue police and vigilante forces that target gangs.

In order to establish eligibility for asylum in gang-related cases, the asylum seeker has to demonstrate a relationship between past persecution, fear of future persecution, and claims to one of the five protected grounds for asylum (race, nationality, religion, membership in a particular social group, or political opinion).[69] Asylum seekers in gang-related cases usually claim that they were persecuted for their membership in a "particular social group," which is difficult to establish, as the circuit court cases from 2010 to 2012 demonstrate. In *Larios v. Holder* (608 F. 3d 105, 1st Cir. 2010), for example, the court held that Guatemalan youth who resisted gang recruitment were not socially visible and thus not "sufficiently particular" to constitute a social group. Likewise, *Zelaya v. Holder* (668 F. 3d 159, 4th Cir. 2012) also held that young Honduran males who refused to join gangs did not constitute a particular social group. Those who claimed membership in a more narrowly defined group that has a "shared past experience" were sometimes more successful. In *García v. Attorney General* (665 F. 3d 496, 3rd Cir. 2011), for example, the court ruled that civilian witnesses who have the "shared past experience" of assisting law enforcement against violent gangs in Guatemala are a statutorily protected social group. "It is a characteristic that members cannot change because it is based on their past conduct that cannot be undone," stated the court. "To the extent that members of this group can recant their testimony, they should not be required to do so."[70]

Since asylum is evaluated on a case-by-case basis, however, outcomes can vary from one court to the next. A negative ruling in a gang-related asylum case can have lethal consequences for the asylum seeker deported to his home country. One 2015 *New York Times* exposé reported that at least ninety migrants deported from the United States and Mexico had been killed over a twenty-one-month period.[71] Benito Zaldívar provides one tragic example. Zaldívar had resisted the recruitment efforts of the MS-13 since he was a very young boy. In 2003, when his grandmother died, he fled as a fifteen-year-old to the United States to rejoin his parents. Apprehended by the Border Patrol, he requested asylum. Seven years later, the Board of Immigration Appeals ordered Zaldívar removed from the United States. Eight weeks after his deportation, he was shot and killed by an MS-13 gunman. His father was unable to attend the funeral because of fears for his own safety.[72]

Twelve-year-old Santos Maldonado Canales was able to escape that fate. He attracted the attention of the National Center for Immigrant and Refugee Children. The NCIRC entrusted his case to a lawyer who was two years out of law school, spoke no Spanish, and had never argued an immigration case. After a ten-month legal battle, Santos's lawyer made a successful claim for asylum on the grounds that he was persecuted as the brother of someone murdered.[73] A year later, his mother and another brother also received asylum. While federal prosecutors initially challenged the verdict, they dropped the appeal in November 2010.

The number of Mexicans fleeing their country because of criminal violence and human rights abuses has also escalated over the past decade. During the period 2006- 2013, between ninety thousand and 106,000 people were killed in the ongoing Mexican drug cartel war.[74] Police officer José Alarcón fled Ciudad Juárez with his family in 2008 after a series of threats on his life. In his asylum claim he argued that he was a member of a persecuted social group as a police officer. The Mexican government, he argued, offered law enforcement officials little protection from the rival drug cartels that fight for control of the smuggling routes to the United States. The immigration judge rejected his request for asylum on the grounds that the dangers Alarcón faced in Ciudad Juárez were typical of the risks police officers have to take.[75] Alarcón's case is not unusual. Marisól Valles García, the twenty-year old police chief of Praxedis G. Guerrero, a town thirty-five miles from Ciudad Juárez, also requested asylum after her life was threatened by members of the Sinaloa and Juárez drug cartels. The town's previous police chief was tortured and decapitated.[76] Her case was still pending at the time of this writing.

Journalists are also particular targets for violence. Between 2000 and 2014, eighty-nine journalists were murdered, eighteen disappeared, and over a dozen fled to the United States, Canada, or Europe.[77] Emilio Gutiérrez Soto fled Ascención, Chihuahua, with his teenage son, after receiving death threats for publishing a series of articles on the human rights abuses committed by the Mexican military. Journalist Miguel Ángel López Solana of Veracruz also fled to the United States when he returned home to find his parents and brother murdered, and a fellow journalist decapitated.[78] López Solana, journalist Jorge Luis Aguirre, and rights activist Cipriana Jurado have received asylum, but their cases are exceptional.[79] The majority of Mexicans fleeing criminal violence are denied asylum. In FY2010, for example, only forty-nine of 3,231 (1.5%) asylum requests from Mexicans were successful compared to 3795 out of 10,087 (37.6%) Chinese requests. By 2013, Mexican citizens faced a ninety-one percent rejection rate but the number of asylum seekers from Mexico continued to grow.[80] By 2014, Mexico was second only to China in the number of asylum applications.

Unaccompanied Minors

In large part because of the spread of gangs and other forms of criminal violence, unaccompanied minors are one of the fastest growing populations of asylum seekers in the post–Cold War period. Children flee criminal or domestic violence, conscription in armies, indentured labor or slavery, rape and other forms of sexual abuse, poverty, and lack of opportunity. Perhaps the best known of these unaccompanied minors are the "Lost Boys" of Sudan. Orphaned by the war of 1983–2005, these children traveled hundreds of miles on foot to reach refugee camps in Ethiopia and Kenya. Four thousand of the estimated twenty thousand "Lost Boys" were eventually resettled in the United States; those under eighteen were fostered by American families.[81]

The number of children apprehended crossing the US-Mexico border without parents or guardians tripled from 2011 to 2014, in large part because of the criminal violence in the Northern Triangle.[82] Close to two hundred thousand unaccompanied children from Central America and Mexico were apprehended by the US Customs and Border Protection between October 2012 and March 2016.[83] Two-thirds of the children came from Honduras, Guatemala, and El Salvador, but dozens of countries were represented among the detainees.[84] Those who traveled from Central America experienced crime and violence along the transit routes. One 2015 study revealed that 52 percent of the minors had been robbed in transit, and 33 percent had been victims of extortion.[85] Young girls were especially vulnerable to abuse and violence.

The dramatic spike in unaccompanied children prompted President Obama to call the migration a "humanitarian crisis." As Marc Rosenblum of the Migration Policy Institute noted, "Images of an out-of-control border and waves of child refugees produced widespread anxiety across the United States, stoking a backlash in some communities as federal officials scrambled to find emergency housing in far flung locations."[86] To discourage minors from traveling, the Obama administration launched a public information campaign in Central America to warn against the dangers of overland travel and to dispel widely held beliefs that unaccompanied minors were automatically admitted to the United States. The White House once again resorted to creating an "in-country" refugee-/parole-processing program in El Salvador, Guatemala, and Honduras to assess applications from those who might have legitimate claims for asylum, but more importantly to discourage people from undertaking the overland journey to the United States. The Mexican government cooperated with the United States in the apprehension and deportation of undocumented immigrants in transit, prompting critics to charge that the minors were not receiving sufficient guarantees to petition for asylum, in violation of the international principle of *nonrefoulement*. All these strategies of deterrence worked temporarily: by the first half of 2015, the numbers of unaccompanied minors crossing the US-Mexico border had dropped by a third before spiking again in FY2016.[87]

Unaccompanied children from countries other than Mexico and Canada are generally exempt from expedited removal.[88] Prior to 2004, if unaccompanied minors did not have relatives in the United States, they awaited their immigration hearings in juvenile detention facilities or adult prisons. Since 2004, minors have not been able remain in DHS custody for more than seventy-two hours before being turned over to the Office of Refugee Resettlement, which runs the Unaccompanied Refugee Minor

Program (URMP).[89] ORR contracts with two voluntary agencies, the Lutheran Immigration and Refugee Service (LIRS) and the United States Conference of Catholic Bishops (USCCB), to manage the URMP. The LIRS or USCCB assigns the minors entrusted to their care to one of their affiliated agencies throughout the country, and these agencies provide support for housing, food, clothing, medical care, and other necessities. Some of the agencies also offer vocational training and English language instruction to facilitate independent living, as well as mental health services and legal assistance adjusting immigration status. The majority of unaccompanied minors are released to a family member or family friend while they wait for their cases to wend their way through the immigration courts. If the minors cannot be placed with relatives or a foster family, they are sent to shelters run by affiliated subcontractors like Catholic Charities. In FY2011, fifty-three shelters housed 6,560 unaccompanied minors; by 2013, the number of shelters had increased to eighty, housing 24,668. The FY2016 appropriation for this program was $948 million.[90]

Even though the cases of unaccompanied minors have been placed on a "priority docket," they still must wait months for their cases to be adjudicated. In 2015, individuals with immigration court cases waited on average 1,071 days—just under three years—for their first immigration hearing.[91] Like most adult asylum seekers, unaccompanied minors are dependent on pro bono representation from law firms, law school clinics, or advocacy groups to help them navigate the immigration bureaucracy. Nonprofits like Equal Justice America play an important role in providing legal counsel to the most vulnerable.[92] Immigration judges are required to ensure that minors under the age of eighteen understand the nature of the legal proceedings and can effectively respond to questions. The EOIR offers judges and court staff guidelines on courtroom modifications to create a nonadversarial setting: questioning in a child-sensitive manner, removing intimidating judicial robes, and making "common sense" adjustments such as allowing toys and booster seats.[93] However, because of the many evidentiary and procedural hurdles, legal representation is essential to secure asylum or "special immigrant juvenile" status. SIJ status offers minors under the age of twenty-one the possibility of permanent residency (green card) and work authorization if they cannot be reunited with their parents or legal guardians because of abuse, abandonment, or neglect, and if they risk persecution in their country of origin.[94] However, a 2015 study published by the Migration Policy Institute found that fewer than one in three unaccompanied minors in immigration court had access to legal counsel, and over 90 percent of children without legal representation were offered no relief from deportation.[95]

The growing number of unaccompanied minors has contributed to the backlog of the US immigration courts. The situation of unaccompanied minors raises difficult moral and ethical questions, however, that are not easy to resolve. Is the deportation of minors a violation of the *nonrefoulement* principle? Does the United States have a responsibility to offer refuge—even if only temporary status until the age of eighteen—if a young person's safety cannot be entrusted to the care of responsible parties in the home country?[96] At the very least, should the United States ensure that all children have legal representation?

Child Soldiers

According to international conventions and US Immigration law, only civilians can be refugees. Persons who have participated in war crimes, committed acts of terrorism, or violated human rights law in any way are excluded from protection.[97] During mass migrations, however, it is difficult to differentiate those persons who have committed serious human rights violations from those who have not, as Rwanda demonstrated. The post–Cold War violence worldwide has made it more and more difficult to differentiate the persecuted from the persecutors.[98]

Over the past two decades an estimated one million children have been conscripted by government armies, armed opposition groups, paramilitaries, and militias, in violation of the UN Convention on the Rights of the Child.[99] Forty percent of the world's armed organizations conscript children, but the most egregious use of child soldiers is found in Burundi, Colombia, the Democratic Republic of the Congo, Liberia, Myanmar, and Uganda. Over 80 percent of child soldiers are below the age of fifteen, with some soldiers as young as seven.[100] Armed groups target orphans in particular because they may be more willing to join to receive food and housing, but children have also been kidnapped into service or sold by their families. Not all of the children serve as actual combatants: children are also used as scouts, spies, messengers, minesweepers, bomb-makers, suicide bombers, cooks, and sexual slaves.[101] Children often witness or are forced (through drugging, psychological coercion, or threat of execution) to commit rape, beheadings, torture, and executions. If they survive their experience and can escape, they suffer the long-term effects of trauma for many years afterward.

A few hundred of these former child soldiers and child victims have secured asylum in the United States. Some have written, spoken, or testi-fied about their experiences to call attention to the plight of others in simi-lar circumstances. Ismeal Beah's memoir, *A Long Way Gone*, recounted the violence he inflicted and experienced as a boy soldier in Sierra Leone.[102] Grace Akallo, the founder and executive director of the United Africans for Women and Children Rights (UAWCR), wrote *Girl Soldier: A Story of Hope for Northern Ugandan Children*, in which she recounted her experi-ences in the Lord's Resistance Army (LRA) of Uganda.[103] Kassim Ouma, a junior middleweight boxing champion, has also spoken of his experiences with the National Resistance Army in Uganda, which kidnapped him at age five.[104] Track star Lopez Lomong, the US flag bearer at the opening ceremonies of the 2008 Olympics, was abducted at age six during the Sudanese civil war. One of the Lost Boys of Sudan, Lamong later spent ten years in a Kenyan refugee camp before he received refugee resettlement in New York.[105] Nongovernmental organizations such as Invisible Children and Child Soldiers International have called international attention to the plight of child soldiers.

As armies conscripted children to carry out missions, the US armed forces have had to deal with child soldiers captured on the battlefield.[106] International aid workers have also needed to respond to their requests for protection. Despite their youth and victimization, however, refuge in the United States or any other country is not guaranteed for such children. The Immigration and Nationality Act states that a person may not qualify as a "refugee" or receive asylum if the person "ordered, incited, assisted, or otherwise participated in the persecution of any person on account of race, religion, nationality, membership in a particular social group, or po-litical opinion."[107] Antiterrorist legislation passed in the wake of 9/11 also bars those who have offered "material support" to a known terrorist orga-nization.[108] Court decisions such as *Matter of Izatula* have ruled that con-scription into armies does not constitute as evidence of persecution.[109] In general, the immigration courts have protected the interests of the state, barring entry to those who are considered potentially dangerous, regard-less of age.

Critics of this policy argue that, as in criminal law, children under the age of eighteen should be assessed under different standards of culpability because their free will in decision-making is questionable. Even those who conscript voluntarily are, in actuality, coerced because of poverty, family or social pressures, or physical threat. Lawyers representing child soldiers in asylum cases have tried to argue that their clients had no intent to carry out military actions and did so under coercion and mental duress.[110]

In response to these realities, in 2008 Congress passed the Child Soldier Accountability Act (PL 110-340), which criminalized the recruitment or use of child soldiers and granted the United States the authority to arrest and prosecute, as well as to deport or deny entry to those who have engaged in such victimization. However, these measures focus on the prosecution of victimizers and offer few opportunities for its victims to find refuge in the United States, much less rehabilitation and reintegration into society.

Gender and Sexuality Cases

Gender is not a UN protected category, but immigrant rights organizations, human rights activists, and feminist advocates have long argued that gender violence is a form of persecution that warrants protection. Gender-related persecution comprises

> any type of violence that targets someone because of *gendered expectations* (such as forcing boys to join gangs or punishing women for their choices), *in gendered ways* (such as violence that includes sexual assault), or *due to nonconforming gender identities and sexual orientation* (such as police targeting lesbian, gay, bisexual, and transgender communities).[111]

The asylum courts do not always agree, however.

At age seventeen, Fauziya Kassindja fled her home in Togo to escape genital mutilation and a forced marriage. She fled first to Ghana, then Germany, and finally the United States, where she was detained in prisons in New Jersey and Pennsylvania for over a year. While she awaited the adjudication of her asylum case she was harassed, strip-searched, shackled and chained, and denied medical treatment. A law student working at a human rights clinic in Washington, DC, became aware of her case and, together with a law professor, mobilized widespread public support for their client. Articles on Kassindja appeared in the *Boston Globe* and in the *New York Times*. Two days after Kassindja's case appeared on the front page of the *New York Times*, she was released from jail. And two months after that, the Board of Immigration Appeals (BIA) overturned the decision of the immigration judge and granted her request for asylum based on her well-founded fear of persecution based on her membership in a particular social group: "young women of the Tchamba-Kunsuntu Tribe who have not had FGM [female genital mutilation], as practiced by that tribe, and who oppose the practice." Kassindja became the first person to receive asylum in the United States based on the threat of FGM. According to the Center for Gender and Refugee Studies, the 1996 Kassindja (also known as Kasinga) case became one of the most highly publicized asylum cases since the passage of the 1980 Refugee Act.[112] Her case was helped by the fact that, by the 1990s, international discussions of human rights increasingly included an acknowledgment of the rights of women in the public and private domestic spheres. During the early 1990s, CNN, ABC, the *New York Times*, and other television and print media outlets, as well as popular authors such as Gloria Steinem, Alice Walker, and Gloria Naylor, called national attention to the practice of FGM.[113]

In 2014, the World Health Organization estimated that 125 million girls and women in twenty-nine countries in Africa and Middle East had been subjected to genital mutilation. The practice encompasses a wide range of procedures that involve cutting off the clitoris, sewing shut the entrance to the vagina, and altering the remaining external genitalia. The practice is imposed on girls as young as infancy. The procedures can cause severe bleeding, scarring, and even death from infection. If girls survive the procedure, they might later experience problems urinating, develop cysts and infertility, experience excruciating pain during intercourse, and develop complications in childbirth.[114] The practice is considered a human rights violation by most Western nations. In US law, the practice is punishable by fine and imprisonment.

In *Matter of Kasinga* (1996) FGM was classified as a form of persecution that can act as the basis for an asylum claim or for the withholding of removal.[115] As in the Kasinga case, an applicant must demonstrate a well-founded fear of FGM (or a "clear probability" in the case of withholding of removal); and she must also establish membership in a particular social group, usually defined by both gender and ethnic or tribal affiliation.

The asylum offered Kasinga and other women in her situation offered protection from future FGM. An important question remained for the immigration courts, however: how does one consider asylum applicants who petition based on past experience of FGM, given that the practice is a one-time occurrence that negates the possibility of future infliction of mutilation. In their rulings, some courts have compared FGM to forced sterilization, a "continuing harm" that has lasting physical and emotional effects. As such, the past infliction of FGM creates both the presumption of either a well-founded fear of future persecution, which is a prerequisite for refugee status, or a probability of future harm, a requirement for obtaining withholding of removal.[116] In 2007, the BIA rejected this position in a decision known as *In re A-T*, ruling that FGM negated the possibility of future persecution. But a year later, the attorney general vacated this BIA decision (*Matter of A-T*), noting that FGM is not necessarily a one-time act; the applicant can still be threatened with severe future harm on account of being a member of a social group. Thus, a past infliction of FGM could be the basis for a well-founded fear of future persecution.[117]

In asylum claims involving issues of gender, sexuality, domestic violence, threat of honor killings, and FGM, petitioners usually claim "social group" membership as the protected category. While gender may appear to meet the "immutable characteristic" standard required of a "social group," the courts have been disinclined to recognize social groups defined solely by gender.[118] In FGM cases, for example, the "social group" requirement is satisfied through the applicant's gender in conjunction with some other characteristic such as ethnic or tribal membership. The courts also have required that social groups be "socially visible" and "particular" within the context of country conditions.

The lack of clarity in asylum statute regarding particularity and social visibility has opened the way for verdicts that are seemingly arbitrary. One study of 206 domestic violence cases from 1994 to 2012 found that judges ruled very differently in cases with nearly identical facts.[119] As one article reported:

> Essentially, each time a woman claims asylum for gender-related reasons, her attorney (if she has one) is building an asylum category from scratch or cobbling it together from other court cases. The result is a wildly inconsistent legal landscape where a female refugee's chances of asylum are largely based on luck.[120]

Johana Cece of Albania discovered the difficulties of proving social visibility in a gender-based claim. Cece, an unmarried woman, fled her country because she was threatened by a well-known criminal gang known for forcing women into prostitution rings, a gang that had apparent immunity from the law. After first relocating to another city in search of safety, she obtained a false Italian passport and arrived in the United States in 2002 under the Visa Waiver Program. In her asylum case she claimed membership in a particular social group, namely, single Albanian women targeted for sex trafficking. She also claimed that the state police would not offer her protection because she was an orthodox Christian in a largely Muslim state.

For the next eleven years, various US courts evaluated the circumstances of Cece's case. An immigration judge agreed that she belonged to persecuted social group and granted Cece asylum. DHS appealed the decision, and the Board of Immigration Appeals subsequently overturned the judge's ruling. Cece's lawyer then appealed to the Court of Appeals of the Seventh Circuit and, in 2013, a three-judge panel rejected the BIA's evaluation of the case and remanded the case back to the BIA for another review. However, even after remand, the BIA still rejected Cece's claims that she was a member of a persecuted social group, arguing that the group lacked immutable characteristics and social visibility: her social group was defined in large part by the past harm inflicted on its members and this social group membership did not exist independently of their vulnerability to traffickers. The Seventh Circuit then vacated the panel's opinion and agreed to rehear Cece's appeal en banc (before all the judges of the Seventh Circuit). The court ruled that Cece had proven membership in a recognizable social group (young Albanian women living alone at risk of becoming victims of sex trafficking), but remanded the case back to the BIA once again to determine whether she could have avoided persecution by relocating to another part of her country. In a strongly worded dissent to the majority opinion, however, Judge Frank Easterbrook argued that the decision unreasonably expanded asylum law to embrace "everyone threatened by criminals, rebels, or anyone else a nation's government does not control. This makes eligible for asylum everyone who faces a substantial risk of harm in his native land, no matter what the reason."[121]

According to the National Immigrant Justice Center, the ruling could indeed have "extremely positive implications for social group-based asylum cases, particularly those involving gender-based claims." By affirming that a shared past experience or status "has imparted some knowledge or labeling that cannot be undone," the court's decision assists those claiming persecution.[122] At the time of this writing, Cece's asylum was still not guaranteed, but her case had established a precedent that could potentially assist others claiming persecution based on membership in a particular social group, including victims of trafficking and those fleeing gang violence.[123]

Social group membership is also central to asylum cases involving persecution for reasons of sexuality. *Matter of Toboso-Alfonso* (1990) was the first major decision to establish that homosexuals are members of a particular social group for purposes of asylum and withholding of removal.[124] The petitioner in the case was a forty-year-old native and citizen of Cuba who was paroled into the United States in June 1980 during the Mariel boatlift. In 1985, when his parole was terminated and he was placed in removal proceedings, Toboso-Alfonso applied for asylum and withholding of deportation to Cuba on the grounds that he had faced—and would continue to face—persecution in Cuba because he was homosexual. In 1990, the BIA ruled that Toboso-Alfonso had established his membership in a particular social group in Cuba and had demonstrated that his freedom was threatened on account of his membership in that group. On June 14, 1994, Attorney General Janet Reno designated *Matter of Toboso-Alfonso* as precedent in all proceedings involving similar issues, thereby "opening the door to applications for asylum and withholding of removal based on sexual orientation."[125] Sexual identity was found to be immutable.[126]

Other court cases have further expanded the understanding of sexuality and sexual/gender identity as grounds for membership in a particular social group. In *Hernández-Montiel v. INS* (2000), the Ninth Circuit rejected the BIA's claim that Geovanni Hernández-Montiel's presentation of self as female was volitional, and thus the claimant could have avoided the persecution he fled. Hernández-Montiel's presentation as female was immutable and inherent to his identity, the court ruled, and he should not be required to change it. Thus the court ruled that "gay men in Mexico with female sexual identities" constituted a particular social group.[127] In *Amanfi v. Ashcroft* (2003), the court ruled that even imputed homosexual identity could constitute membership in a particular social group. In this case, an asylum seeker from Ghana claimed that he was repeatedly beaten by police on account of their perception that he was a homosexual, even though he did not identify as such. The Third Circuit remanded the case to the BIA, stating that "persecution 'on account of' membership in a social group . . . includes what the persecutor perceives to be the applicant's membership in a social group."[128]

Asylum statute recognizes sexual identity as immutable for purposes of establishing membership in a particular social group, but proving membership in the social group has been much more difficult to establish. The courts look not only for the petitioner's association with other individuals who belong to this social group, but also for characteristics that point to their social visibility and particularity. As legal scholar Deborah Morgan has noted, "The applicant must be 'gay enough' for the government to find that they have met their burden of proof. This often means that the applicant must mold aspects of their life and identity to fit US norms and expectations of what it means to be LGBT."[129] This presents a catch-22 situation since, in order to protect themselves from persecution in their homeland, individuals often hide their true sexual identity and they do not join or create organizations that might call attention to themselves. The proof the courts seek is often difficult to provide. In *Matter of Soto Vega* (2006), for example, the immigration judge and BIA found credible evidence that Jorge Soto Vega had been persecuted for being gay but ruled against his asylum because they felt he could live safely in Mexico if he concealed his identity. "I don't see anything in his appearance, his dress, his manner, his demeanor, his gestures, his voice, or anything of that nature that remotely approached some of the stereotypical things that society assesses to gays, whether those are legitimate or not," said the immigration judge. Soto Vega's lawyers challenged the ruling on the grounds that "asylum does not hinge on whether people can hide their religion, political beliefs, race or sexual orientation to avoid persecution." The Ninth Circuit remanded the case back to the BIA, which in turn remanded the case back to the immigration judge. In January 2007, Jorge Soto Vega was finally granted asylum. The immigration judge concluded that "no one should have to hide their sexual orientation to be safe."[130]

The political (and religious) leanings of judges are often demonstrated in court decisions: judges who believe that homosexuality is a personal choice rather than an immutable characteristic can reason that sexual identity can indeed be changed to avoid persecution.[131] One 2008 study found that while the success rates of sexuality-based asylum claims had improved since the first cases were argued, "Immigration officers and judges are still known to consider their homophobic or discriminatory beliefs in deciding the eligibility of LGBT applicants. Legal practitioners have observed that the success of their case hangs almost entirely upon the attitude ... of the adjudicator."[132]

In asylum cases involving gay, lesbian, bisexual, and transgender individuals, advocacy groups such as Lambda Legal and Immigration Equality have played a critical role. These organizations serve as a clearinghouse on LGBT asylum policy; provide legal services to asylum seekers already in the country; and provide training to lawyers who argue LGBT immigration cases. The New York–based Immigration Equality reported a 98 percent success rate for the closed cases it has represented.[133] Such assistance is invaluable since the experiences of LGBT asylum seekers illustrate that the current system often discriminates against those who do not conform to behavioral white norms. The federal government may demonstrate a greater willingness to recognize and protect sexual identity, but individual judges are not consistent in their rulings. Advocacy groups and the legal counsel they offer thus play a critical role in helping asylum seekers secure protection.

In 2014, the *Wall Street Journal* reported a significant jump in LGBT asylum applicants, mostly from Central America, a region hit hard by criminal violence. Close to one hundred LGBT individuals were murdered in Honduras from 2011 to 2014. According to the *WSJ*, LGBT migrants have become so visible among those apprehended along the US-Mexico border that in 2011 the Department of Homeland Security opened two detention centers specifically for this population—one in Pearsall, Texas, and the other in Santa Ana, California. In consultation with Immigration Equality, the Obama administration also issued a sixty-five-page guide and training manual to assist USCIS asylum officers in their interviews and assessments.[134]

If all asylum seekers must prove their "worthiness" of receiving protection, those with gender-related claims face particular obstacles. In her study of gender-based asylum claims, Meghana Nayak discussed the "framing" of worthiness in a system that does not recognize gender as a protected category: gender-related asylum seekers must demonstrate that they are autonomous, innocent, and nondeviant. Telling the right story is critical to the outcome of a case because the government uses these typologies, "frames," and preconceived notions of worthiness to justify the exclusion of those who do not meet expectations. Thus, lawyers and advocates are essential to crafting the narratives that will legitimize gender violence as a form of persecution.[135]

Victims of Trafficking

Since the early 1990s, millions of people worldwide have been "trafficked" for sweatshop labor, agricultural work, prostitution and sex tourism, forced marriage, and various forms of modern-day slavery. Trafficking has become a multi-billion-dollar industry. According to the United Nations, human trafficking is now the third most lucrative criminal enterprise after weapons and narcotics.[136] The actors engaged in human trafficking range from family-run organizations to transnational crime syndicates that add trafficking to their crime portfolios to subsidize other illegal activities.[137] In 1999, the first in-depth report on trafficking in the United States estimated approximately forty-five thousand to fifty thousand women and children were trafficked annually.[138]

In March 1998, President Clinton issued the presidential directive "Steps to Combat Violence Against Women and Trafficking in Women and Girls," as a follow-up to the 1994 Violence Against Women Act.[139] Clinton's directive marked the first time an administration had addressed the issue of trafficking, calling it a "fundamental human rights violation." A month later, at the United Nations Commission on Crime Prevention and Criminal Justice, the US delegation proposed the "Protocol to Prevent, Suppress and Punish Trafficking in Persons, Especially Women and Children," as a supplement to the UN Convention Against Transnational Organized Crime. The trafficking protocol had three principal goals: prevent and combat the trafficking of persons, especially women and children; offer victims protection and assistance; and promote international cooperation in law enforcement.[140]

The Protocol's definition of trafficking is broad. It defines trafficking as the

recruitment, transportation, transfer, harboring or receipt of persons, by means of the threat or use of force or other forms of coercion, of abduction, of fraud, of deception, of the abuse of power or of a position of vulnerability or of the giving or receiving of payments or benefits to achieve the consent of a person having control over another person, for the purposes of exploitation. Exploitation shall include, at a minimum, the exploitation or the prostitution of others or other forms of sexual exploitation, forced labor or services, slavery or practices similar to slavery, servitude or the removal of organs.[141]

The protocol made distinctions between trafficking and smuggling. People who are trafficked are presumed not to have given their consent and, once enslaved, are subject to isolation or limited movement. Those who are smuggled, by comparison, are assumed to have some degree of agency, having allowed themselves to be transported and are generally free to leave or change jobs. There is also a gender dimension to the distinctions between trafficking and smuggling, as legal scholar Jacqueline Bhabba writes: those who are smuggled are mostly assumed to be men, while victims of trafficking are "associated with the traditional targets of protective concern—women and children."[142] Indeed, the United Nations estimates that two-thirds of trafficking victims are women.[143]

The key issues in determining trafficking are coercion, fraud, and exploitation. Trafficking can start with a kidnapping, but more commonly, it starts with a broken agreement about the terms and conditions of employment. Not all trafficking is international; in some countries children are sold domestically for labor and household servitude and prostitution.[144] Trafficking also requires a vast network of people who profit at different stages of the exploitation:

> Many of the trade's foot soldiers, particularly at the recruiting end, are amateurs, opportunists, and even former victims. A Mafia boss in Kiev may be living on a cut of the proceeds from your exploitation, but your personal hell will very likely start ... with a betrayal by a friend or relative angling for a commission. You might even be sold into prostitution by the person sleeping next to you.[145]

Like the genocide convention, the Protocol on Trafficking required member states to criminalize such activities through the passage and enforcement of domestic legislation. It also mandated international cooperation to prevent and punish such activities. The Protocol urges states to provide for victims' physical, psychological, and social recovery, and facilitate their safe return to their country of residence when possible.[146] The US Congress responded to this mandate with the Victims of Trafficking and Violence Protection Act of 2000 (PL 106-386). Over the next decade the United States spent billions of dollars in prevention efforts overseas and in prosecution and protection efforts at home.[147]

Refugee and human rights activists identified potential problems with the law that played out over the next decade, in large part because the law was conceptually framed as a law enforcement issue rather than a human rights issue.[148] In order to receive protection, services, and benefits under the TVPA, victims must be willing to assist law enforcement in prosecuting their abusers, which many victims are reluctant to do because it makes their families back home vulnerable to retaliation from the international trafficking syndicates. Thus, victims are faced with two equally difficult choices: in order to receive protection they have to assist law enforcement, but for the safety of their families and communities, they choose to refrain from doing so. Some victims of trafficking are too traumatized by their experiences to assist law enforcement, and this perceived lack of cooperation makes them further vulnerable. Those who refuse—or are unable—to recount their experiences with law enforcement do not receive protection.

Refugee and human rights activists have also noted that US antitrafficking efforts focus almost exclusively on the sexually exploited.[149] According to the International Labor Organization, the commercial sex industry absorbs less than half of all trafficked labor, yet roughly 75 percent of the trafficking prosecutions in the United States are related to sex trafficking. This is not surprising, according to one author, since "rescuing prostitutes has historically been a popular philanthropic and religious mission" in the United States, especially among evangelical Christians and middle-class women, two of the principal drivers of antitrafficking policy, who tend to conflate sex trafficking with prostitution.[150] Nongovernmental organizations have urged the federal government to offer more protections to victims of labor exploitation. Children are especially vulnerable to labor (and sexual) exploitation but are the population least likely to receive protection because they can neither articulate their experience nor represent their interests. Instead, they are often labeled juvenile delinquents.[151]

Trafficking victims are allowed to remain in the United States through T and U visas, which offer three years of lawful temporary nonimmigrant status and employment authorization, after which the visa holder can apply for permanent residency. To qualify for the T visa, applicants must demonstrate that they were recruited, kidnapped, or deceived by a trafficker and then coerced and exploited in the United States. The U visa has a broader scope; applicants must prove that they suffered substantial physical or mental abuse as a result of certain types of crimes. Both visas require applicants to cooperate with the law enforcement officials who are investigating and prosecuting the crimes.[152] However, T visa applicants have yet another requirement: in order to remain in the United States, applicants must demonstrate that they would suffer "extreme hardship" or "extreme harm" if returned home (e.g., their government cannot protect them from retaliation; they would be socially stigmatized with devastating consequences for their future; or they require medical care that is only available in the United States).

The TVPA authorized only five thousand T visas and ten thousand U visas per year.[153] Advocates have urged the federal government to grant trafficking victims protection through asylum. This would encourage trafficking victims to come forward because it would release them from the responsibility of working with law enforcement and compromising the safety of their loved ones. The UNHCR has stated that human trafficking is a form of persecution, and "could be the basis of a refugee claim where the State has been unwilling or unable to provide protection."[154]

The majority of trafficking victims remain hidden from the general public, however, and either fail to seek protection from the United States out of fear or are prevented through coercion from doing so.

Building on the efforts of the Clinton administration, in 2002 President George W. Bush signed a presidential directive establishing the cabinet-level Interagency Task Force to Monitor and Combat Trafficking in Persons.[155] Between 2000 and 2008, the United States provided antitrafficking aid to governments, NGOs, and intergovernmental organizations, and sent law enforcement specialists overseas to advise countries with their anti-trafficking efforts.[156] Since passage of the TVPA (and the law's subsequent reauthorizations), and the establishment of the interagency task force, the US government has collected substantial data on trafficking. By 2013, the estimated number of foreign persons trafficked into the United States stood at 17,500, most believed to be from Latin America; an additional one hundred thousand US citizen children were believed to be victims of trafficking within the United States.[157] Trafficking victims were concentrated largely in California, New York, and Texas and performed a wide range of bonded or forced labor: prostitution, domestic work, agriculture, sweatshop labor, restaurant and hotel work, and pornography and other sex work.[158] Over a ten-year period—FY2002 to FY2012—the federal government received 5,202 applications for T-1 status (trafficking victims), and 3,269 of these applications were approved; 4,201 applied for derivative T status (family members of trafficking victims), and 3,302 were approved.[159] Hundreds of thousands of victims have been rescued, even if their future status in the United States remains unclear.[160] The Department of Homeland Security has negotiated partnerships with companies like Amtrak and Western Union, whose agents regularly interact with the immigrant public, to train them to identify and report potential victims.[161] The Human Smuggling and Trafficking Center also publishes case examples and scenarios to help the general public identify victims and assist in prosecution efforts.

Climate Refugees

Over the past two decades, natural and man-made disasters have had devastating consequences for millions of people. During one twelve-month period in 2004–2005, the earthquake in the Indian Ocean and resulting tsunami killed closed to three hundred thousand people and caused enormous ecological devastation in South and Southeast Asia, especially Sri Lanka, India, Indonesia, and Thailand. Hurricane Stan killed more than eleven hundred and caused flooding and mudslides in El Salvador and Guatemala that destroyed entire villages and disrupted agricultural production, exports, and livelihoods. An earthquake affected northern Pakistan and Kashmir, killing over one hundred thousand and displacing over three million from their homes. These three events alone had immediate consequences for immigration policies worldwide. As the Migration Policy Institute reported: "The tsunami, in migration terms, affected thousands of Burmese workers, both legal and illegal, in Thailand; delayed plans of numerous governments to deport Indonesians; spurred the Canadian and Australian governments to fast-track immigration paperwork for victims; and made thousands of orphaned children vulnerable to trafficking."[162]

Extreme weather events such as hurricanes, earthquakes, flooding, mudslides, and tsunamis, as well long-term environmental degradation through drought and desertification force people to migrate—both within their countries and across international borders. The devastation caused by Hurricane Mitch in 1998, for example, reinvigorated an external migration from Central America that had begun to taper off after the civil wars had ended. But in other cases, the full impact of environmental disasters is not felt until years later. Environmental catastrophes affect individual livelihoods, and ultimately local and regional economies. Populations made vulnerable by these disasters then compete for limited resources, exacerbating existing class, racial, and sectarian tensions. These tensions may then lead to civil strife or war, resulting in further displacement or migration. Several of the political crises that have generated refugees over the past three decades have had some environmental component. In these cases, extreme weather events had a catalytic effect on political conflict or served as "threat multipliers."[163] Recent conflicts in Darfur, Tunisia, Egypt, and Syria illustrate the social and political consequences of ecological disasters.[164]

Since 2005, the UNHCR and other nongovernmental organizations have played a more visible role in assisting populations displaced by environmental disasters and climate change, even though these populations do not technically fall under their mandate.[165] The United States provides international assistance through the Office of Foreign Disaster Assistance (OFDA) and through the Agency for International Development (AID). However, individuals who are displaced by environmental disasters do not qualify for refugee resettlement or asylum in the United States unless they can demonstrate that they face persecution because of one of the other traditional classes of protection. The United States does offer one legal recourse: foreign nationals in the United States who are unable to safely return to their country because of natural disaster (or armed conflict, or some other extraordinary situation) may qualify for temporary protected status, a status authorized by the Immigration Act of 1990.[166] In January 2014, nationals from eight countries—El Salvador, Haiti, Honduras, Nicaragua, Somalia, Sudan, South Sudan, and Syria—were potentially eligible for TPS. Two years later, five more countries had joined the list: Guinea, Liberia, Nepal, Sierra Leone, and Yemen. Eight of the countries had experienced environmental crises.

Recipients of temporary protected status are authorized to remain and work in the United States until the Departments of State and Homeland Security ascertain that conditions in their homeland have sufficiently improved to assure a safe return. However, these individuals occupy a liminal space in US society. They are allowed to temporarily stay but are denied the chance to become legal permanent residents or citizens. While most eventually transition off the TPS list, thousands of Salvadorans, Nicaraguans, and Honduran have held "temporary" status for over a decade. They have raised families, paid taxes, and invested in their host communities with limited opportunities to acquire full citizenship. These cases raise the very real possibility that the United States will have a population of "temporarily protected" residents within its borders who are both part of the nation and yet outside of it. At some point, long-term residents should be afforded the opportunity to be full citizens.

For generations, people have been uprooted from their homes and livelihoods as a result of natural disasters and ecological change. However, scientists warn that this uprooting will become increasingly common. Increased global temperatures are forecast to disrupt normal weather patterns, triggering stronger hurricanes and typhoons. They will contribute to rising sea levels, crop failures, freshwater shortages, wildfires, infrastructure breakdown and energy blackouts, and infectious disease outbreaks. The United Nations, the International Organization for Migration, and other agencies and nongovernmental organizations estimate that migration related to such conditions could reach as high as two hundred million by 2050. The United States will have to address significant increases in climate-related migration in the decades to come.[167]

The Immigrant Carceral State

UN guidelines state that the detention of asylum seekers is allowed on a "strictly limited basis" if it is "lawful and not arbitrary": "to verify identity;

to determine the elements on which the claim to refugee status or asylum is based; to deal with cases of deliberate fraud; or to protect the national security or public order." If asylum seekers must be detained, they are to be set apart from criminal detainees.[168]

US law, however, imposes no limits on the amount of time asylum seekers may stay in detention pending the adjudication of their claim, unless the asylum seeker is a minor. Neither the INS (in the pre-9/11 era) nor the DHS (in the post-9/11 era) has provided regular statistical data on how many asylum seekers have been detained. Refugee advocacy groups have documented cases of asylum seekers who have been detained for five years or longer, and who have been detained in jails and prisons with criminal populations, violating UN guidelines.[169]

Throughout the twentieth century, US immigration services detained immigrants who, for one reason or another, were regarded as undesirable. However, not until the 1980s did the detention of asylum seekers become standard procedure. By the mid-1980s, Haitians and Salvadorans were the two groups most likely to be detained in INS facilities. As more and more asylum seekers were detained, the flaws in the US immigration detention system became evident and pronounced. Violations of the rights of Central American refugees in detention prompted a number of lawsuits in the 1980s. *Castillo Núñez v. Boldin* (1982), for example, filed on behalf of Salvadorans and Guatemalans detained in Los Fresnos, Texas, charged that detainees were denied meaningful access to their legal counsel prior to and during legal proceedings. *Orantes-Hernández v. Smith* (1982) charged the INS with the use of coercive tactics to force detainees to accept "voluntary departure." *El Rescate Legal Services v. Executive Office of Immigration Review* (1989) charged the EOIR with failure to provide defendants with competent translators and complete interpretations of court proceedings in the Los Angeles, El Centro, and San Diego immigration courts.[170] In the landmark *Orantes-Hernández v. Meese* (1988), the court found that INS policies formed "a pattern and practice of illegal conduct which [was] approved, authorized and/or ratified by INS personnel at all levels." Judge David Kenyon mandated that specific procedures to be used by the INS when detaining, processing, and removing Salvadoran refugees.[171]

A decade later little had changed. During the late 1990s, representatives of Amnesty International visited dozens of INS facilities, local jails, and privately run detention centers where immigrant detainees were routinely held. Their 1999 report concluded that the US detention system was deeply flawed: "Until and unless US officials recognize their country's obligations under international law and take steps to change that system radically, abuses ... will inevitably continue."[172] Amnesty International identified three major problems: first, an inconsistency in policy and practice within and across INS districts; second, a failure to distinguish asylum seekers from other detainees as required by international standards; and third, the housing of asylum seekers in facilities designed for criminal convicts and run according to prison management philosophy. "Despite the USA's leading role in establishing the international human rights system," wrote the authors, "it has been reluctant to submit itself to international human rights law and to accept the same minimum standards for its own conduct that it demands from other countries."[173]

Since 1999, refugee advocacy groups have identified other problems that have emerged in the wake of 9/11. Since the detention system is under the purview of the Bureau of Immigration and Customs Enforcement (ICE), asylum seekers are isolated from those officials in the Bureau of Citizenship and Immigration Services (USCIS) that have the most expertise on asylum issues. This bureaucratic maze has resulted in a number of problems. Lawyers and refugee advocates often find it difficult to gain access to detention facilities, even to meet with their own clients. Detainees are frequently transferred from one facility to the next, sometimes across state lines, with no notification to their legal counsel or even their families. Access to translators and to medical care is inadequate, and some detainees are kept in solitary confinement or are shackled. Lawyers report that their clients have been physically, sexually, or verbally abused. These conditions are trying for any detainee, but they are especially difficult for asylum seekers escaping torture, harassment, or trauma. Until 2004, when the care and custody of children was finally transferred to the Office of Refugee Resettlement (ORR), unaccompanied minors were also held in such conditions.

The costs of detaining asylum seekers and immigrant detainees are significant. In 2004 the federal government spent $85 per day to detain a single person in detention; by 2014, the cost had risen to an estimated $164 per day.[174] Over four hundred thousand immigrants were detained in over 250 facilities around the country. DHS owns and operates its own facilities, but it also buys bed space in prisons and jails around the country. Close to 70 percent of all immigrant detainees are held in one of these contracted facilities.

The expansion—and privatization—of the immigration detention system over the past decade has created a multi-million-dollar industry where a handful of corporations have a financial investment and stake in perpetuating the detention of asylum seekers and other immigrants. In 2016, the Corrections Corporation of America (CCA), the largest detention contractor with Immigration and Customs Enforcement (ICE), and "the fifth-largest corrections system in the nation,"[175] operated fifteen immigration facilities with a total of 5,800 beds (and sixty facilities in all with over seventy thousand inmates). *Forbes* named CCA one of "America's Best Big Companies."[176] The GEO Group, the second largest contractor, operated seven immigration facilities with a total 7,183 beds. Private prison companies housed nearly half of all immigration detainees.[177] According to the National Immigration Forum, these facilities operated with little government oversight. (In March 2014, hundreds of detainees at a GEO-run detention center in Tacoma, Washington, went on a hunger strike to protest conditions at the facility.)[178] These private prison corporations, in turn, "[have] exerted their influence on legislators by lobbying for laws that detain immigrants more frequently and for longer periods of time." Over the past decade, the three corporations with the largest number of ICE contracts collectively spent at least forty-five million dollars on campaign donations and lobbyists at the state and federal levels.[179] GEO's profits allowed it to pay six million dollars for naming rights for a football stadium at Florida Atlantic University, until "heavy publicity to the company's shady dealings and past controversies" forced the company to withdraw its offer.[180]

One of the sad ironies of the post–Cold War era, then, is the increased reliance on incarceration as both a deterrent and a form of securitization. During the Cold War, asylum seekers fled from carceral states in the hopes of finding freedom in the West, but now asylum seekers flee to carceral states. In addition to the automatic detention of asylum seekers, migrants also face criminal prosecution for immigration-related activities such as document fraud, marriage fraud, and repeated unlawful entry. As a result, criminal law and procedure has converged with immigration law and procedure into a new field legal scholar Juliet Stumpf has called "crimmigration."[181]

The federal government could provide community-based alternatives to detention that are more humane and more cost-effective. According to the Detention Watch Network, some community-based programs cost as little as twelve dollars a day and yet yield a 93 percent appearance rate in immigration courts.[182] Any future immigration and asylum reform package will need to address the issue of incarceration.

In the post–Cold War era, the asylum system is one of the branches of the immigration bureaucracy that has been most amended and yet is still in need of reform. Numerous scholars, advocates, and policymakers have offered recommendations for making the asylum system more responsive, consistent, and fair. Some recommend that asylum officers have law degrees, be given more time to adjudicate decisions, and receive continuous specialized training;[183] or they urge the government to reevaluate the procedural barriers that discourage many from seeking asylum.[184] Human Rights First, for example, offered a lengthy list of recommendations that included limiting the use of expedited removal since the process "lacks sufficient safeguards to ensure asylum seekers are not mistakenly deported."[185]

Others have argued for harsher measures and penalties to protect against "frivolous" asylum claims that financially strain government coffers and backlog the immigration bureaucracy. The conservative Center for Immigration Studies, for example, urged DHS to "renew its commitment" to the detention of asylum seekers; require a three-year waiting period before asylum seekers can adjust their status to legal permanent resident; and give "careful consideration" to the circumstances that might merit the termination of asylee or refugee status, or the denial of legal permanent residence.[186]

In 1986, long before concerns about terrorism altered the asylum bureaucracy, a report published by the US Committee for Refugees cautioned Americans on the need to craft an immigration policy grounded in a human rights approach:

Opponents of generosity toward asylum seekers may argue that international agreements are not binding on the United States. They may contrive ways, within the ambiguities of law, to maintain policies that keep asylum seekers out. They may appeal to the need to stem the flow of illegal immigrants. But all this tragically misses the point. The United States should bring its treatment of asylum seekers into conformity with its own laws, with international law, and with the humanitarian principles underlying them, not only because it is the law, but because it is right. Perhaps not all who seek asylum are truly in need of protection. But the right to seek asylum must be secure, and asylum decisions must be fair, in order to assure protection to those who are threatened by violent death, intolerance, or persecution.[187]

Three decades later, such advice has never been more important.

Conclusion

THE UNITED STATES has been the top refugee resettlement nation for many years accepting, on average, 59,000 refugees per year since 2004.[1] The United States has also granted asylum to an average of 24,500 individuals per year since 2004.[2] The United States' role in the world is changing, however, and there is no guarantee that the country will continue to honor its international obligation to provide refuge to even a small share of the world's displaced populations. Within weeks of his inauguration, President Donald J. Trump, who had campaigned on the promise of the "extreme vetting" of refugees, had reduced the refugee quota for FY2017 by more than half, from 110,000 to 50,000; imposed a 120-day moratorium on refugee admissions; and barred Syrian refugees indefinitely.

But as the case studies in this book have shown, the executive branch is not the sole architect of refugee policy. Various historical actors and organizations have played a role in formulating, implementing, and influencing refugee policies in the post–Cold War era. These actors and organizations are likely to continue to shape policy in the immediate future. Indeed, as this book went to press, HIAS and the International Refugee Assistance Project (formerly the Iraqi Refugee Assistance Project) had filed a motion asking for an injunction on Trump's executive order. "We cannot remain silent as Muslim refugees are turned away just for being Muslim," said one HIAS spokesman, "just as we could not stand idly by when the US turned away Jewish refugees fleeing Germany during the 1930s and 40s."[3]

The chapters in this book examined the various actors and interests that have shaped refugee policy since the end of the Cold War. Chapter 1 discussed the tensions between Congress and the White House during the transitional years of the late 1980s and early 1990s, as officials struggled to define a coherent and consistent refugee policy for the post–Cold War era. A wide range of domestic actors emerged to influence policy, advocating and lobbying on behalf of particular populations whose rights they felt had been denied or ignored. The experiences of the Soviet refuseniks, the Chinese university students, and the Haitian and Cuban boat people illustrated how advocates can elicit positive responses from the executive and legislative branches of government, and create opportunities for refuge even when facing popular and institutional resistance.

Chapter 2 examined the challenges of responding to populations displaced by genocide. In the aftermath of the Holocaust, "Never again" has become the rallying cry of human rights activists around the world, and yet genocide and crimes against humanity have continued to occur with sobering frequency in the post–Cold War era. Students of history might assume that populations displaced by genocidal governments would be prioritized for refugee resettlement, but the case studies in this chapter highlighted the obstacles that have blocked their admission to the United States. Politics, ethnicity, race, and religion have influenced American perceptions of refugees' overall "worthiness," which, in turn, have shaped policy decisions about military intervention and humanitarian assistance, as well as opportunities for parole or refugee status. Refugee advocates have had to convince government officials—and a reluctant American population—that assistance is in the national interest; when they have failed to do so, refugees have suffered the consequences.

The third chapter discussed the bureaucracy that vets and processes refugee applications. In the aftermath of the terrorist attacks of 1993 and 2001, the Clinton and Bush administrations, working with Congress, restructured the immigration bureaucracy to more effectively block the entry of terrorists. Many of the officials who implemented immigration policies were eventually placed within a new cabinet-level Department of Homeland Security. This restructuring raised legitimate questions about whether the United States could effectively meet its humanitarian obligations if refugee determinations were made in an office entrusted to police and reinforce borders. The drop in refugee and asylum admissions after 9/11 suggested that the United States was failing to meet its humanitarian obligations. Refugees, especially those from Iraq, Afghanistan, and Syria, suffered the consequences of the new national security state policies. In the post-9/11 era, refugee advocates have become even more important actors in the debates about refugee admissions, reminding Americans of their humanitarian obligations, especially to those who come from areas of the world where US foreign policy had played a role in displacing populations.

The fourth chapter discussed the vast asylum bureaucracy, comprised of multiple official administrative levels, to demonstrate the complex legal world asylum seekers have navigated in the post–Cold War era. Many of the asylum seekers discussed in this chapter fell outside the traditionally defined categories of persecution, and their struggles to secure some type of protected status raised important questions about who is deserving of admission. Once again advocates and lawyers played critical roles in making asylum seekers visible and prying open the door to the United States.

These various case studies have demonstrated that governmental actors must exercise leadership and political will to allow refugees and asylum seekers to gain entry. Despite the reputation and self-image of the United States as a haven for the oppressed, Americans have always questioned whether refugee and immigrant admissions serve the national interest.[4] In the crafting of refugee policy, policymakers have rarely had a strong mandate from their constituents, and they have often made the decision to grant refuge at great political cost. During periods of strong popular resistance to refugee admissions, advocates (many of them nongovernmental actors) have been especially critical in expanding public debate because, as Margaret Keck and Kathryn Sikkink have written, advocates multiply the voices that are heard in the domestic and international arenas: "[They] argue, persuade, strategize, document, lobby, pressure, and complain. . . . [They] open channels by bringing alternative visions and information."[5] Many of those who have been admitted as refugees (or who have received asylum or some other protected status) in the post–Cold War era would never have been considered for admission just a few decades earlier, but their advocates have mobilized political support for them.

The case studies in this book also portend some of the challenges that lie ahead for American policymakers, advocates, asylum officials, and judges, as they try to exercise leadership in the face of popular and institutional opposition to the admission of refugees. For policymakers, the major challenge will be deciding the size of the refugee quota and the priorities in selecting candidates for admission to the United States. In light of debates on Capitol Hill in recent years, they may also have to decide which branch of government should be responsible for refugee policy in the future. Should refugee policy continue to be determined by the White House, in consultation with Congress, as it has been for decades? Or should refugee policy—like immigration policy in general—be the purview of Congress? What implications might such a reconfiguration have for refugee admissions in the future? In assisting populations at risk, should government officials consider alternatives to refugee status to expand the number of people who have a chance to find safety and live meaningful and productive lives?

For the officials of the State Department, Homeland Security, and the judiciary, who vet, process, and evaluate refugee referrals and asy-lum adjudications each year, the major challenge will be streamlining the admissions process to offer prompt protection to those at risk, while main-taining the proper safeguards to protect the American public from foreign actors who want to cause the nation harm. Government officials will also need to evaluate their deterrence and detention policies to ensure that fun-damental human rights are protected. Is there a way to reform deterrence practices such as "expedited removal" to minimize the chances that legiti-mate refugees will be sent back to face life-threatening conditions in their homeland? Are there alternatives to mandatory and indefinite detention that will inflict less injury on refugees who wait for resolutions of their case?

For advocates, the major challenge will be to raise public consciousness about refugees—and the conditions that produce them—so that fears and cultural biases do not negatively influence assessments of who is "worthy" of admission to the United States. Lawyers will continue to be critical to this endeavor. In the immigration courts, asylum seekers are not entitled to the same due process guarantees available to those in the criminal court system, so they are heavily dependent on the counsel and representation that lawyers offer them to navigate the administrative and legal labyrinth. Unfortunately, most asylum seekers navigate the bureaucracy without the benefit of legal counsel, undermining their chances of finding refuge in the United States.

These and other challenges are predicated on the idea that the United States should continue to offer separate tracks for refugee and asylum admissions, which, as shown here, has been the case after the Cold War. Although the political and economic motivations for migration have often gone hand in hand, the United States has recognized that refu-gees are a particular type of migrant in need of humanitarian protection, and that they require a separate—and more rapid—track for admission. Consequently, although today the vetting of refugees takes, on average, eighteen to twenty-four months, and only a tiny fraction of applicants ever receive one of the coveted refugee visas, the waiting period for admission for those privileged few is shorter than for many green-card applicants.[6]

The definition of "refugee" on which US law has been based in the post–Cold War era, while more inclusive in practice than during the Cold War, continues to exclude a wide range of people from consideration. Scholars have offered alternative definitions of "refugee" that more accurately reflect the realities of displacement in today's world and the ethical stakes involved. Matthew J. Gibney has offered one of the most inclusive definitions, defining refugees as "those people who require a new state of residence, either temporarily or permanently, because if forced to return or to stay at home they would, as a result of either the inadequacy or brutality of their state, be persecuted or seriously jeopardize their physical security or vital subsistence needs."[7] In the current political climate in the United States, it is unlikely that policymakers will engage in a reevaluation of the refugee definition. The popular impulse is to reduce entry rather than to expand the possibilities or eligibility for entry. Americans expect stronger borders even though they do not want the "big government"—or the taxes—that are necessary to create and enforce those stronger borders.

This book has focused on one country's response to the challenge of refugees. As generous as US policy has been—accepting over 4.5 million refugees and asylees since 1946—the figure is a tiny fraction of those who have been in need of humanitarian assistance.[8] The countries that border areas of political conflict—the so-called second or transition countries where refugees flee to first—have faced an even greater challenge because of geography. Countries that border areas of conflict bear the brunt of assisting displaced populations, and they are often the least equipped to do so. Jordan, Pakistan, Lebanon, Tanzania, and Kenya are among the countries that have carried the weight of refugee crises in the first decades of the twenty-first century, and some of their refugee camps have larger populations than some US cities. Fewer than 1 percent of refugees worldwide have been resettled to third countries like the United States.[9]

Because of the scale of migrations, the countries that border areas of crisis have often confined refugees to camps, and in these camps refugees face their own set of challenges. They are denied a chance to work, practice professions, run businesses, own property, choose their place of residence, move about freely, or make other basic choices about their day-to-day lives. The education and medical care offered to them has been rudimentary at best. They cannot become citizens. Their safety has been compromised, and they have been made vulnerable to trafficking and other forms of organized crime. At times, even the United Nations peace-keepers entrusted with their safety have been complicit in their victimiza-tion.[10] Millions have spent a decade or more in these so-called temporary settlements (which refugee advocates call "warehousing"), and many have been forced to raise their children and grandchildren in liminal political spaces that have become permanent settlements. Many Americans, geo-graphically removed from areas of crisis, and suffering from what Senator Alan Simpson once called "compassion fatigue," have ignored their plight or felt helpless to do anything about it.[11]

In December 2000, the United Nation's General Assembly declared June 20 World Refugee Day. Each year, as late June approaches, the number of op-eds on refugee issues increases exponentially as politicians, scholars, clergy, aid workers, and journalists have reflected on the cour-age and resilience of refugees, lamented the failure of the international community to prevent their displacement, and appealed for more fund-ing to address humanitarian crises. Perhaps the only point these writers have agreed on is the heroism of relief workers on the front lines of hu-manitarian crises, who have worked under dire conditions, with limited resources, and at great risk to their own safety. These aid workers have implemented the policies crafted by states and nongovernmental organ-izations, even though they might not agree with them. Since 1989, the UNHCR and other refugee relief organizations have sought durable solu-tions to humanitarian crises with ever-diminishing resources.[12] They have convinced the host societies to continue accommodating refugees, even though many of these countries have not signed the UN Convention and Protocol on Refugees and have not been able to count on assistance from the countries that have signed these international agreements. Scholars Guy Goodwin-Gil and Selim Can Sazak have noted in *Foreign Affairs*,

> Every state that admits refugees acts on behalf of the international community in defense of fundamental human rights principles. In turn, asylum states are entitled to expect the support of others, whether it is through financial, political, or material aid, or ideally, through more active efforts to mitigate the problems that create refugees in the first place. Tragically, such support is rare.

Contributions from donor countries have met less than half of the UNHCR's assessed needs. "If the international community is to address [humanitarian] challenges," Goodwin-Gill and Can Sazak have written, "it must take the issue of state responsibility more seriously—both in terms of those who create refugees, and by supporting those that bear the financial burden of hosting them."[13] These authors have offered one controversial proposal for addressing these financial challenges: allow refugee-receiving nations—or "competent international institutions"—to draw on the assets of refugee-producing nations for financial compensation. Such a policy would require states to provide for the material support of the refugees they created and help "square the circle of justice."[14]

Undoubtedly, many will take issue with this proposal, citing multiple reasons why imposing duties on refugee-producing nations is impractical. However, current conditions are unsustainable and require creative solutions. The financial cost to relief agencies and to receiving nations is simply too great, especially when crises become protracted and the quick repatriation of refugees cannot be guaranteed.

The number of refugees and displaced persons grows larger with each passing year. By late 2014, 59.5 million people were displaced from their homes by war and violence, and 19.5 million had crossed international borders and become refugees. According to the United Nations, 1 out of every 122 people worldwide is a refugee, displaced person, or asylum seeker, and the number is growing. Repatriation was at an all-time low in 2014, and displacement lasted, on average, twenty-five years.[15] In many refugee families, one generation or more has been born in refugee camps or in exile. On the geopolitical stage, the influx of hundreds of thousands of refugees into a country in a short period of time has exacerbated popular resentments, fueled political and sectarian conflicts, and created new humanitarian crises. Solutions that allow refugees to rebuild their lives in peace and safety—and to return home—are in short supply.

On the individual state level, the costs of resettlement have been exorbitant, making nations unlikely to accommodate a fair share of refugees. The UNHCR and other refugee relief agencies have depended on wealthy donor nations like the United States for funding and for assistance in the resettlement of refugees. In the post–Cold War era, the United States has tried to make refugee camps abroad more tolerable by providing refugee relief organizations with considerable funding so that they can offer refugees food, medicine, water, and tents for housing, and ensure their survival; but Americans are reluctant to offer more opportunities for resettlement.[16] Domestic interests have trumped international obligations, especially in democracies like the United States where politicians have been responsive to the constituents that elect them to office. Refugee crises have been far removed from the day-to-day realities of their constituents, and it is only when asylum seekers have begun to arrive at their borders that citizens are moved to act. Even then these citizens have been quick to feel under siege from an influx of refugees, expressing not only compassion but also fear.

Ideally, the best assistance the United States and the rest of the international community can offer refugees is to address the conditions that made them refugees in the first place. Since many consider this a utopian aspiration, the most feasible options require creating more opportunities for resettlement and increasing humanitarian assistance. Until refugees can return home—and some may never be able to return home—they are dependent on donor nations and on the goodwill of populations in the countries that welcome them.

Notes

INTRODUCTION

1. This assessment is based on the public opinion polls compiled by the Roper Center for Public Opinion Research at Cornell University, https://ropercenter-cornell-edu.proxy.library.cornell.edu/.

2. Michael Barnett offers a useful distinction: "Human rights relies on the discourse of rights, humanitarianism on a discourse of needs. Human rights focuses on legal discourse and frameworks, whereas humanitarianism shifts attention to moral codes and sentiments. Human rights typically focuses on the long-term goal of eliminating the causes of suffering, humanitarianism on the urgent goal of keeping people alive." See Barnett, *Empire of Humanity: A History of Humanitarianism* (Ithaca, NY: Cornell University Press, 2011), 16.

3. For a theoretical discussion of framing and communicating human rights norms see Margaret E. Keck and Kathryn Sikkink, *Activists beyond Borders: Advocacy Networks in International* Politics (Ithaca, NY: Cornell University Press, 1998); Thomas Risse-Kappen, Steve C. Ropp, and Kathryn Sikkink, *The Power of Human Rights: International Norms and Domestic Change* (Cambridge: Cambridge University Press, 1999); and Alison Brysk, *Speaking Rights to Power: Constructing Political Will* (New York: Oxford University Press, 2013).

4. The traditional historiography argues that a separate track for refugee admissions emerges only after World War II. Julian Lim and Evan Taparata argue that there is evidence of a refugee policy in the nineteenth century and early twentieth century. See Julian Lim, "Immigration, Asylum, and Citizenship: A More Holistic Approach," *California Law Review* 101.4 (2013): 1013–1078; and Evan Taparata, "No Asylum for Mankind: The Creation of Refugee Law and Policy in the United States, 1787–1924" (PhD diss., University of Minnesota, forthcoming).

5. Carl J. Bon Tempo, *Americans at the Gate: The United States and Refugees during the Cold War* (Princeton, NJ: Princeton University Press, 2008); Gil Loescher and John A. Scanlan, *Calculated Kindness: Refugees and America's Half-Open Door, 1945*

to the Present (New York: Free Press, 1986). Many other historical studies have focused on particular refugee populations such as the Hungarians, the Cubans, the Haitians, the Vietnamese and other Southeast Asians, and the policies that facilitated their entrance.

6. "1952 Immigration and Nationality Act," http://library.uwb.edu/static/USimmigration/1952_immigration_and_nationality_act.html.

7. "The Migration and Refugee Assistance Act of 1962 (PL 87-510)," https://www.govtrack.us/congress/bills/87/hr8291/text.

8. See the text of the 1965 Immigration and Nationality Act at http://library.uwb.edu/static/USimmigration/1965_immigration_and_nationality_act.html. The numerical allotment was set at 6 percent of overall admissions. The Middle East was defined as the territory between and including Libya on the west, Turkey on the north, Pakistan on the east, and Saudi Arabia and Ethiopia on the south.

9. The 1951 Convention limited the focus of assistance to European refugees in the aftermath of World War II. The 1967 Protocol removed these temporal and geographic restrictions. The United States did not sign the 1951 Convention, but it did sign the 1967 Protocol.

10. UNHCR, "Text of the 1951 Convention and the 1967 Protocol," http://www.unhcr.org/pages/49da0e466.html.

11. The goal was to establish "a permanent and systematic procedure for the admission [of refugees] of special humanitarian concern to the United States." "The 1980 Refugee Act (PL 96-212)," https://www.gpo.gov/fdsys/pkg/STATUTE-94/pdf/STATUTE-94-Pg102.pdf. The 1951 UN Convention defined a refugee as "a person who owing to a well-founded fear of being persecuted for reasons of race, religion, nationality, membership of a particular social group or political opinion, is outside the country of his nationality and is unable or, owing to such fear, is unwilling to avail himself of the protection of that country or who, not having a nationality and being outside the country of his former habitual residence as a result of such events, is unable or, owing to such fear, is unwilling to return to it." UNHCR, "Definitions and Obligations," http://www.unhcr.org.au/basicdef.shtml.

12. See Andorra Bruno, "Refugee Admissions and Resettlement Policy," Congressional Research Service, March 6, 2014, http://www.fas.org/sgp/crs/misc/RL31269.pdf.

13. "The 1980 Refugee Act (PL 96-212)," https://www.gpo.gov/fdsys/pkg/STATUTE-94/pdf/STATUTE-94-Pg102.pdf.

14. US Department of State, "US Refugee Admissions Program (USRAP) Frequently Asked Questions," May 31, 2013, http://www.state.gov/j/prm/releases/factsheets/2013/210135.htm. ORR is considered the heart of the US Refugee Admissions Program (USRAP). This temporary assistance is currently set at thirty to ninety days. Refugees are expected to go to work within six months of arrival in the United States. Refugees may apply for legal permanent residency after one year

of residence, and may apply for citizenship after five years. If their airfare to the United States is not paid by the family or sponsoring organization, the government grants a loan to the refugee applicant, which must be repaid to the government.

15. Bruno, "Refugee Admissions."

16. See, for example, Monique Laney, *German Rocketeers in the Heart of Dixie: Making Sense of the Nazi Past during the Civil Rights Era* (New Haven: Yale University Press, 2015). American policies allowed former Nazis to enter the United States to prevent the Soviets and Eastern bloc countries from using their expertise against the United States and its allies.

17. The period from 1989 to 1992 marks the end of the Cold War. During these years, the Berlin Wall—the physical symbol of the Cold War—was torn down and Germany was unified once again; the powerful Union of Soviet Socialist Republics dissolved; and Poland, Hungary, and other countries in Central and Eastern Europe abandoned their one-party communist governments (or re-emerged as separate nations). In an address before the joint houses of Congress on September 11, 1990, President George Herbert Walker Bush spoke of the "new world order" about to be born, "freer from the threat of terror, stronger in the pursuit of justice, and more secure in the quest for peace." The coming age, he said, would be "an era in which the nations of the world, East and West, North and South, can prosper and live in harmony.... A world where the rule of law supplants the rule of the jungle. A world in which nations recognize the shared responsibility for freedom and justice. A world where the strong respect the rights of the weak." George H.W. Bush, "Address before a Joint Session of Congress (September 11, 1990)," http://millercenter.org/president/bush/speeches/speech-3425.

18. Diana Tietjens Meyers, "Rethinking Coercion for a World of Poverty and Transnational Migration," in *Poverty, Agency, and Human Rights*, ed. Diana Tietjens Meyers (Oxford: Oxford University Press, 2014), 68–91.

19. According to the Office of the Historian of the State Department, the Clinton administration took office in 1993 "against the backdrop of an unprecedented increase in the number of the world's democracies during the previous two decades—from 30 in 1974 to about 110 in 1993." Office of the Historian, US Department of State, *History of the Department of State during the Clinton Presidency 1993–2001*, January 2001, 3, http://www.clintonlibrary.gov/.

20. Henry Kamm, "Yugoslav Refugee Crisis Europe's Worst since 40's," *New York Times*, July 24, 1992, http://www.nytimes.com/1992/07/24/world/yugoslav-refugee-crisis-europe-s-worst-since-40-s.html.

21. UNHCR, "Chronology: 1991 Gulf War Crisis," March 20, 2003, http://www.unhcr.org/en-us/subsites/iraqcrisis/3e798c2d4/chronology-1991-gulf-war-crisis.html.

22. Human Rights Watch, "Numbers," *Leave None to Tell the Story: Genocide in Rwanda*, https://www.hrw.org/reports/1999/rwanda/

23. Lois McHugh, Joyce Vialet, and Ruth Ellen Wasem, *Refugee Policy in a Changing World* (Washington, DC: Congressional Research Service, April 8, 1997), 3.

24. UNHCR, "Figures at a Glance," http://www.unhcr.org/en-us/figures-at-a-glance.html.

25. Barry N. Stein and Frederick C. Cuny, "Refugee Repatriation during Conflict: Protection and Post-Return Assistance," *Development in Practice* 4.3 (1994): 173–187.

26. Prepared Statement of J. Stapleton Roy, Assistant Secretary of State for Intelligence and Research, *Current and Projected National Security Threats to the United States, Hearing before the Select Committee on Intelligence of the US Senate, 106th Congress, Second Session, February 2, 2000*, 7.

27. Office of the Historian, *Department of State during Clinton Presidency*, 73–74.

28. For an excellent history of humanitarianism see Barnett's *Empire of Humanity*. Although the book is not a history of nongovernmental organizations, Barnett offers an especially useful discussion of the UNHCR's changing role and mandate over time.

29. The United States has considered applicants for refugee status for admission if they fall within one of the three processing "priorities": Under Priority-1 (P-1) the UNHCR or another nongovernmental organization identifies compelling reasons for emergency resettlement; Priority-2 cases are of special humanitarian interest to the United States; and Priority-3 cases represent the immediate family members of refugees already in the United States. For several decades, P-3 applicants have dominated refugee admissions, just as immediate family members have dominated immigration admissions overall.

30. UNHCR, "Asylum Seekers," http://www.unhcr.org/pages/49c3646c137.html.

31. "The United States Refugee Admissions Program (USRAP) Consultation and Worldwide Processing Priorities," https://www.uscis.gov/humanitarian/refugees-asylum/refugees/united-states-refugee-admissions-program-usrap-consultation-worldwide-processing-priorities. See also Refugee Council USA, "Eligibility," http://www.rcusa.org/eligibility/.

32. See, for example, Bon Tempo, *Americans at the Gate*; Loescher and Scanlan, *Calculated Kindness*.

33. Myriam Dunn Cavelty and Victor Mauer, introduction to *The Routledge Handbook of Security Studies*, ed. Myriam Dunn Cavelty and Victor Mauer (Milton Park, Abingdon, Oxon: Routledge, 2010), 1–3. The study of security and securitization is one of the most dynamic areas for research and publishing in the field of international relations. According to Cavelty and Mauer, the number of students in the field has grown since 9/11 and the global War on Terror; and security studies is also a growth market in the academic book market.

34. Ibid. There is a lack of consensus about what security actually means. Security can be approached in either strategic or critical terms: as a value or condition to be achieved, or as a knowledge, discourse, technology, or practice. See Phil

Williams, "Organized Crime, Drug Trafficking and Trafficking in Women," and Jef Huysmans and Vicki Squire, "Migration and Security," both essays in Cavelty and Mauer, *Handbook of Security Studies.*

35. Edward Newman has written that refugees were "an inevitable and peripheral consequence—although not a cause—of conflict, insecurity, and instability . . . [and a] humanitarian issue separate from the security agenda." See Edward Newman, "Refugees, International Security, and Human Vulnerability: Introduction and Survey," in *Refugees and Forced Displacement: International Security, Human Vulnerability, and the State*, ed. Edward Newman and Joanne van Selm (Tokyo: United Nations University Press, 2003), 11–12. Other scholars have examined how migration exacerbates the insecurity of states. See, for example, Carl-Friedrich Schleussner, Jonathan F. Donges, Reik V. Donner, and Hans Joachim Schellnhuber, "Armed-Conflict Risks Enhanced by Climate-Related Disasters in Ethnic Fractionalized Countries," *Proceedings of the National Academy of Sciences* 113.33 (2016): 9216–9221.

36. Schleussner et al., "Armed-Conflict Risks." International relations scholars Jef Huysmans and Vicki Squire have noted that the study of migration, the traditional purview of socioeconomic history, sociology, and anthropology, became important to security studies because scholars sought to "develop an alternative narrative [after] the fall of the Iron Curtain and the breakup of the Soviet Union had destabilized the dominant script." Migration emerged as an issue in security studies because of the geopolitical dislocation associated with the end of the Cold War and the new globalization. See Huysmans and Squire, "Migration and Security," 169.

37. Gregor Noll, "Securitizing Sovereignty? States, Refugees, and the Regionalization of International Law," in Newman and van Selm, *Refugees and Forced Displacement*, 280; Huysmans and Squire, "Migration and Security," 173–174.

38. Newman, "Refugees, International Security," 16. See also Alex J. Bellamy, "Humanitarian Intervention," in Cavelty and Mauer, *Handbook of Security Studies.*

39. Noll, "Securitizing Sovereignty," 279. Bellamy, "Humanitarian Intervention," 428–429. International consensus has emerged around the principle called "the responsibility to protect"—an idea first developed in 2001 by the International Commission on Intervention and State Sovereignty—which holds that states have the responsibility to protect its citizens and, when they fail to do so, the responsibility transfers to the international community (as represented by the UN Security Council). According to Bellamy, this principle raised the "thorny issue" of what to do when the Security Council failed to intervene. "R2P" was discussed by the ICISS in 2001 but omitted entirely from the international commitment to R2P in 2005. See "The Responsibility to Protect: A Report of the International Commission on Intervention and State Sovereignty," December 2001, http:// responsibilitytoprotect.org/ICISS%20Report.pdf.

40. Thierry Balzacq, "Constructivism and Securitization Studies," in Cavelty and Mauer, *Handbook of Security Studies*, 59. See also Philippe Bourbeau, *The Securitization of Migration: A Study of Movement and Order* (New York: Routledge, 2011). Linguistic utterances, writes Philippe Bourbeau, are always produced in particular contexts, and the social properties of these contexts "endow speech acts with a differential value system" (2).

41. Huysmans, and Squire, "Migration and Security," 171.

42. Ariane Chebel d'Appollonia, *Migrant Mobilization and Securitization in the US and Europe: How Does It Feel to Be a Threat?* (New York: Palgrave Macmillan, 2015), 6–9, 15. The War on Terror "has no definitive time horizon," writes d'Appollonia, so the "management of ethnic diversity" has become an important tool in countering the perceived threat posed by different types of migrants. See also Anna Sampaio, *Terrorizing Latina/o Immigrants: Race, Gender, and Immigration Politics in the Age of Security* (Philadelphia: Temple University Press, 2015). According to Sampaio, efforts at securitization may appear racially neutral "but in reality work to rearticulate and reinscribe forms of racial and gender hierarchy." Domestic security measures construct internal enemies predicated on ethnic and racial profiling to justify the rapid expansion of state authority (11).

43. I am especially indebted to the scholarly work of Margaret Keck and Kathryn Sikkink, who have demonstrated how advocates "multiply the voices that are heard in international and domestic policies": "These voices argue, persuade, strategize, document, lobby, pressure, and complain. The multiplication of voices is imperfect and selective . . . but in a world where the voices of states have predominated, networks open channels by bringing alternative visions and information into international debate." Keck and Sikkink, *Activists beyond Borders*, ix–x. According to the authors, half of all international nongovernmental social change organizations work on three areas: human rights, women's rights, and the environment.

44. Ibid., 2–3.

45. Ibid., 12. The idea that human rights should be an integral part of foreign policy and international relations is new, write Keck and Sikkink: "As recently as 1970, the idea that the human rights of citizens of any country are legitimately the concern of people and governments everywhere was considered radical. Transnational advocacy networks played a key role in placing human rights on foreign policy agendas" (79). See also Norman J. Ornstein and Shirley Elder Lyons, *Interest Groups, Lobbying, and Policymaking* (Washington, DC: Congressional Quarterly Press, 1978), 82. According to the authors, "interest group behavior" can try to reach political objectives "through face-to-face communications [with legislators], or [working] indirect[ly] through political aides, mass media, or appeals to public opinion. Influence can be particular (a specific vote on a specific bill) or diffuse (general attitudes towards a subject area or the welfare of a group). Group

strategies may be 'inside,' focusing on members or staff of a political body, 'outside,' focusing on grassroots opinion and pressure, or a combination of the two." A 1986 congressional report on lobbying groups remarked that interest group success "was increasingly dependent on the group's ability to attract and hold media attention. As media outlets increase, particularly as the numbers of television channels increase, greater programming variety and less uniformity in political views could dilute media appeals." See also US Congress, *Congress and Pressure Groups: Lobbying in a Modern Democracy: A Report* (Washington, DC: Government Printing Office, 1986), 63.

46. Austin Sarat and Stuart A. Scheingold, eds., *Cause Lawyers and Social Movements* (Stanford, CA: Stanford Law and Politics, 2006), 1.

47. Ibid., 4–9.

CHAPTER 1

1. See Boris Mozorov, ed., *Documents on Soviet Jewish Emigration* (Portland, OR: Frank Cass, 1999); Sana Krasikov, "Declassified KGB Study Illuminates Early Years of Soviet Jewish Emigration," *Jewish Daily Forward*, December 14, 2007, http://forward.com/articles/12254/declassified-kgb-study-illuminates-early-years-of-/. See also Annelise Orleck, *The Soviet Jewish Americans* (Westport, CT: Greenwood Press, 1999), 53.

2. Orleck, *The Soviet Jewish Americans*, 54.

3. Michael Sherbourne, a London high school teacher, first coined the term as an English-language equivalent for the Russian word *otkaznik* ("person denied the right to emigrate"). Gal Beckerman, *When They Come for Us, We'll Be Gone: The Epic Struggle to Save Soviet Jewry* (New York: Houghton Mifflin, 2010), 355; Rosa Doherty, "Soviet Jewry Campaigner Michael Sherbourne Dies," *Jewish Chronicle Online*, June 23, 2014, http://www.thejc.com/news/uk-news/120008/soviet-jewry-campaigner-michael-sherbourne-dies.

4. Yossi Klein Halevi, "Glory," *New Republic*, November 25, 2010, http://www.newrepublic.com/article/books-and-arts/magazine/79086/soviet-union-jews-movement.

5. Ibid.

6. The organization was founded by Yaakov (Jacob) Birnbaum, the grandson of Nathan Birnbaum, the author of the term "Zionism." The SSSJ was eventually renamed the Center for Russian Jewry with Student Struggle for Soviet Jewry. In the late 1970s, the organization was renamed yet again—the Center for Russian and East European Jewry.

7. Douglas Martin, "Jacob Birnbaum, Civil Rights Champion of Soviet Jewry, Dies at 88, *New York Times*, April 19, 2014, http://www.nytimes.com/2014/04/20/nyregion/jacob-birnbaum-champion-of-soviet-jews-dies-at-88.html?_r=0. See also "Columbia's Forgotten Human Rights Beacon," *Current*, Winter 2007,

http://www.columbia.edu/cu/current/articles/spring2008/from-the-editors.
html.

8. Halevi, "Glory"; Elie Wiesel, *The Jews of Silence: A Personal Report on Soviet Jewry*
(New York: Schocken, 1987).

9. "Historical Note," *Guide to the Records of Chicago Action for Soviet Jewry*, http://
digifindingaids.cjh.org/?pID=1485864#a2.

10. Christopher Smith, "In Memory of Sister Ann Gillen," *Congressional Record*,
March 3, 1995, https://www.congress.gov/crec/1995/03/03/CREC-1995-03-03-
pt1-PgE516-2.pdf. In 1979, Sister Ann Gillen, the executive director of the task
force, offered her own freedom to the Soviet Union in exchange for the release
of long-time refusenik Ira Nudel. In 1982, Sister Ann was one of three human
rights leaders to serve an historic writ of habeas corpus on the Soviet consul in
Washington, DC, for Andrei Sakharov.

11. "Helsinki Accord: Declaration of Human Rights," https://chnm.gmu.edu/1989/
items/show/245. Of particular concern to this network of human rights activists
was the Soviet's violation of two rights affirmed by the Helsinki Accords: the
right to travel and the right to family reunification.

12. Sarah B. Snyder, *Human Rights Activism and the End of the Cold War: A Transnational
History of the Helsinki Network* (New York: Cambridge University Press, 2011).
According to Sarah B. Snyder, the Helsinki process and the transnational network of human rights activists contributed to the transformation of Europe, and
made human rights an integral component of international relations.

13. Orleck, *The Soviet Jewish Americans*, 54–55; David Newman, "Borderline
Views: Remembering the Soviet Refuseniks," *Jerusalem Post*, April 22, 2013;
Krasikov, "Declassified KGB Study." See also Janna Kaplan, "Remembering
Refuseniks," December 18, 2011, http://people.brandeis.edu/~jannakap/writ-
ings_copernicus.html.

14. Krasikov, "Declassified KGB Study."

15. Ibid. Of the twenty-five thousand leaving in 1972, for example, only 13.5 percent
had a college education. Only twenty-six had a doctoral degree. The majority
came from Georgia, Lithuania, and Latvia. See also Orleck, *The Soviet Jewish
Americans*, 51. According to Orleck, "Soviet popular hostility toward the Jews was
fueled by reports that Soviet Jews attended state-funded universities in numbers
far out of proportion to their percentage of the population."

16. The 1974 Jackson-Vanik amendment states that "products from any nonmar-
ket economy country shall not be eligible to receive nondiscriminatory treatment [most-favored nation status]" if the president determines that the country
denied its citizens the right or opportunity to emigrate. Sam Kliger, "The
Jackson-Vanik Amendment and US-Russian Relations," presentation at Kennan
Institute Conference, February 4, 2010, http://www.wilsoncenter.org/event/
the-jackson-vanik-amendment-and-us-russian-relations. See also John Quigley,
"Most-Favored-Nation Status and Soviet Emigration: Does the Jackson-Vanik

Amendment Apply," *Loyola of Los Angeles International and Comparative Law Review* 543 (1989): 543–548, http://digitalcommons.lmu.edu/ilr/vol11/iss3/4.

17. Statement of Jewel S. LaFontant, US Coordinator for Refugee Affairs, in *Processing of Soviet Refugees: Joint Hearing before the Subcommittee on Europe and the Middle East of the Committee on Foreign Affairs and the Subcommittee on Immigration, Refugees, and International Law of the Committee on the Judiciary, House of Representatives, 101st Congress, First Session, September 14, 1989* (Washington, DC: Government Printing Office, 1990), 12–13.

18. Orleck, *The Soviet Jewish Americans*, 58, 64–65. The arrival of one hundred thousand Soviet Jews in Israel had created tensions with the Soviet Union's Arab allies, so exit permits were restricted once again.

19. "President Ronald Reagan and the Jews," *Jewish Ledger*, February 2001, http://www.jewishledger.com/2011/02/president-ronald-reagan-and-the-jews/.

20. Ibid. See also "S. 2308—99th Congress: A Bill to Authorize the President of the United States to Award Congressional Gold Medals to Anatoly and Avital Sharansky," https://www.govtrack.us/congress/bills/99/s2308.

21. "Remarks on Signing the Bill of Rights Day and Human Rights Day and Week Proclamation," December 9, 1983, http://www.regan.utexas.edu/archives/speeches/1093/120983a.htm.

22. Jack Matlock, "Who Won the Cold War? And Who Will Win Now?" *Washington Post*, March 16, 2014, B4.

23. In a 1983 White House meeting with American Jewish leaders, for example, Reagan told his audience, "Those of us who believe in better relations with the Soviet Union, yet, at the same time, value freedom and human decency, we've made it plain now we want deeds, not rhetoric and repression from the new Soviet leadership. We've had enough of words. There's no better way for them to begin than by releasing the prisoners of conscience in Siberia and restoring Jewish emigration to the levels of the late 1970s." "Remarks at a White House Meeting with Jewish leaders," February 2, 1983, http://www.presidency.ucsb.edu/ws/?pid=40661.

24. The CHRC worked "in the defense of all rights codified in the United Nations Universal Declaration of Human Rights." In 2008, in memory of Representative Lantos, the House of Representatives unanimously adopted HR 1451, the "Tom Lantos Human Rights Commission Establishment Resolution," to institutionalize the bipartisan caucus and rename it in Lantos's honor. In 2014 US senators Chris Coons and Mark Kirk launched the Senate Human Rights Caucus.

25. "S. 2308—99th Congress: A Bill to Authorize the President of the United States to Award Congressional Gold Medals to Anatoly and Avital Sharansky."

26. Interview with Corey Parker, chief legislative assistant for Edward Kennedy, October 20, 2008, in Edward M. Kennedy Oral History Project, Miller Center, University of Virginia, http://millercenter.org/oralhistory/interview/carey_parker_10-20-2008. According to Parker, Kennedy and US ambassador Jack

Matlock served as the principal backchannels because they did not agree with the hawkish positions of Secretary of Defense Caspar Weinberger and other members of the Reagan administration.

27. "Interview with Boris and Natalya Katz," February 15, 2009, http://millercenter.org/oralhistory/interview/boris_and_natalya_katz. Soviet refuseniks Boris and Natalya Katz recounted how schoolchildren and others wrote on their behalf and convinced Senator Edward Kennedy to advocate for their release from the Soviet Union. Kennedy met with Boris Katz and other dissidents in Moscow and later, when Katz was allowed to emigrate, assisted the Katz family to secure visas to the United States via Vienna, and find employment in Boston. See also "Interview with Galina Veremkroit (formerly Nizhnikov)," February 17, 2009, http://millercenter.org/oralhistory/interview/galina_veremkroit.

28. "Remarks to Soviet Dissidents at Spaso House in Moscow," May 30, 1988; "Reagan Meets with Refuseniks, Presses Soviet on Human Rights," *Jewish Telegraphic Agency*, May 31, 1988; Kengor, "The Liberator: Ronald Reagan and Soviet Jewry."

29. Orleck, *The Soviet Jewish Americans*, 68–69.

30. George de Lama, "Reagan Urges Soviet Freedoms," *Chicago Tribune*, May 28, 1988, http://articles.chicagotribune.com/1988-05-28/news/8801030035_1_kiev-and-leningrad-reagan-and-gorbachev-soviet-security-officials.

31. Doris Meissner, "'Refugee' is a Misnomer for Soviet Armenian Emigres," *Los Angeles Times*, June 8, 1988, http://articles.latimes.com/1988-06-08/local/me-3777_1_soviet-armenians.

32. In 2002, there were an estimated one million Armenian Americans, concentrated largely in Massachusetts and California. During the final decades of the twentieth century, they advocated for or against a wide range of issues: economic support to the state of Armenia; blocking aid to rival Azerbaijan; stalling an arms deal with Turkey; and support for official US government recognition of the Armenian genocide of 1915–1922. See Heather S. Gregg, "Divided They Conquer: The Success of Armenian Ethnic Lobbies in the US," Rosemary Rogers Working Paper Series, Working Paper No. 13, August 2002, http://web.mit.edu/cis/www/migration/pubs/rrwp/13_divided.pdf. See also "Soviet Jewry: Welcome, up to a Point," *Economist*, September 9, 1989, 26; Robert Pear, "Soviet Armenians Let In Improperly, US Officials Says," *New York Times*, May 29, 1988, http://www.nytimes.com/1988/05/29/world/soviet-armenians-let-in-improperly-us-officials-say.html; Robert Reinhold, "Armenians in US Split on Visa Issue," *New York Times*, July 9, 1988, http://www.nytimes.com/1988/07/09/world/armenians-in-us-split-on-visa-issue.html.

33. Appendix 1 in *Processing of Soviet Refugees*, 154.

34. Ibid., 158.

35. Statement of Jewel S. LaFontant, *Processing of Soviet Refugees*, 4–5.

36. Ibid., 2, 14; Appendix 1 in *Processing of Soviet Refugees*, 154; Testimony of Gerald L. Coyle, *Processing of Soviet Refugees*, 27.

37. "Soviet Jewry: Welcome, Up to a Point," 26.

38. Statement of Gerald Coyle, *Processing of Soviet Refugees*, 21–22.

39. Norman Kempster and Lee May, "US Refugee Policy Still Keeps Out 99% of the Oppressed," *Los Angeles Times*, March 4, 1989, http://articles.latimes.com/1989-03-04/news/mn-31_1_u-s-refugee-policy.

40. Fred A. Lazin, "Refugee Resettlement and 'Freedom of Choice': The Case of Soviet Jewry," *Center for Immigration Studies*, July 2005, http://cis.org/RefugeeResettlement-SovietJewry.

41. Letter, Richard Gephardt and William O. Lipinski to George Bush, September 7, 1989, #71114, Box 9, WHORM: Immigration/Naturalization, Bush Presidential Records, George H. W. Bush Presidential Library; letter, Janet G. Mullins to Charles E. Schumer, April 4, 1989, Box 8, WHORM: Immigration/Naturalization, Bush Presidential Records.

42. Despite the liberalization of Soviet emigration policy, some restrictions remained in place: individuals with specialized skills or who once had access to sensitive state information were not allowed to emigrate for a period of years. Kempster and May, "US Refugee Policy"; John M. Goshko, "Special Category to Be Sought to Admit 30,000 Emigres," *Washington Post*, March 1, 1989, http://www.washingtonpost.com/archive/politics/1989/03/01/special-category-to-be-sought-to-admit-30000-emigres/0a601ace-8955-4307-8d6e-d8bd8104c0d4/.

43. "Refugee, Asylum Policy under Fire in 1989," *CQ Almanac 1989*, 273–279, http://library.cqpress.com/cqalmanac/cqal89-1138734.

44. Statement of Jewel S. LaFontant, *Processing of Soviet Refugees*, 2–3.

45. Ibid., 16.

46. Ibid., 7.

47. Ibid., 5.

48. Letter, James A. Budeit to Lynn Singer, n.d., Box 1, WHORM: Immigration/Naturalization, Bush Presidential Records; "Soviet Jewry: Welcome, Up to a Point," 26.

49. "Background on Soviet Refugee Processing by the Immigration and Naturalization Service," in "File Immigration, Romanians," A1 1091, Box 783, Office of the Attorney General, RG 60, General Records of the Department of Justice, National Archives and Research Administration (NARA). See also George Bush, National Security Directive 27, October 2, 1989; letter, James A. Budeit to the Chicago Coalition for Immigrant and Refugee Protection, November 8, 1989, #081989, Box 2, WHORM: Immigration/Naturalization, Bush Presidential Records.

50. Appendix 3, "Background Information on Soviet Emigrants, Prepared by the Department of State (Submitted by Rep. Howard Berman [D-California])," in *Processing of Soviet Refugees*, 171.

51. Letter, James A. Budeit to Bernard Cardinal Law, February 6, 1990, #104141, Box 10, WHORM: Immigration/Naturalization, Bush Presidential Records. See also letter, Bernard Cardinal Law to George Bush, March 20, 1990, #126119, Box 11, WHORM: Immigration/Naturalization, Bush Presidential Records; Testimony of Curtis W. Kamman, Deputy Assistant Secretary of State for European and Canadian Affairs, in *Eastern European Refugees: Hearing before the Subcommittee on Immigration, Refugees, and International Law of the Committee on the Judiciary, House of Representatives, 101st Congress, First Session, November 2, 1989* (Washington, DC: Government Printing Office, 1990), 15–16.

52. Jews and certain Christian groups from the Soviet Union, and certain refugees from Vietnam, Laos, and Cambodia, were the first beneficiaries of this amendment to the Foreign Operations Appropriations Act (PL 101-167). A 2004 amendment—the Specter amendment—extended protection to refugees from Iran—mostly Christians but also Jews, Baha'is, Zoroastrians, and other persecuted minorities, whose cases were to be adjudicated under the Lautenberg amendment's reduced evidentiary standard. Subsequent laws extended the Lautenberg amendment, as amended by the Specter amendment, through 2014. Bruno, "Refugee Admissions"; US Refugee Resettlement Program Watchdog Group, "What Was the Morrison-Lautenberg Amendment of 1989? Should It Be Renewed?" December 1, 2011, http://forefugees.com/2011/12/01/what-was-the-morrison-lautenberg-amendment-of-1989; Hebrew Immigrant Aid Society, "The 20th Anniversary of the Lautenberg Amendment," http://www.hias.org/en/post/hias-blog/20th-anniversary-lautenberg-amendment.

53. Letter, W. Lee Rawls to Charles Grassley, July 3, 1991, "File Asylum 1991," A1 1091, Box 605, Office of the Attorney General, RG 60 General Records of the Department of Justice, NARA. See also Bruno, "Refugee Admissions," 7; and Joyce Vialet, *Refugee Admissions and Resettlement Policy: Facts and Issues* (Washington, DC: Congressional Research Service, December 6, 1999), 4, http://www.cnie.org/nle/crsreports/population/pop-6.cfm.

54. Letter, Ben Zion Leuchter to Bush, May 21, 1990, #144259, Box 11, WHORM: Immigration/Naturalization, Bush Presidential Records. See also the comments of representatives of the Hebrew Immigrant Aid Society (HIAS) and the Christian evangelical group World Relief in Goshko, "Special Category."

55. Statement of Jewel S. LaFontant, *Processing of Soviet Refugees*, 7.

56. Letter, James A. Budeit to Lynn Singer.

57. Douglas Waller, "A World Awash in Refugees," *Newsweek*, October 9, 1989, 44; "Refuseniks and Other Refugees," *New York Times*, April 12, 1989, A24.

58. Statement of Gerald Coyle, *Eastern European Refugees*, 33.

59. Ibid., 34–35.

60. Statement of Princeton Lyman, Director, Bureau for Refugee Programs, *Eastern European Refugees*, 26–27.

61. "Cable Regarding Austria's Economic Situation Due to Its Liberal Emigration Policies," July 18, 1988, Declassified Documents Reference System, Gale Digital Collections, http://gdc.gale.com/products/declassified-documents-reference-system/.

62. See, for example, the concerns expressed by Louis L. Lote of the Committee of Translyvania, *Eastern European Refugees*, 102.

63. Stephen Green, "What Happens If the 'Wall' Comes Down?" *Christian Science Monitor*, June 9, 1989, 18.

64. In West Germany, over 260,000 Eastern Europeans took refuge during the first nine months of 1989, and the German government became increasingly unwilling to support anyone but the 145,000 East Germans. East Germans were offered citizenship, social security and retirement benefits, job training, priority for housing, and subsistence housing. Statement of Nancy R. Kingsbury, Director, Foreign Economics Assistance Issues, National Security and International Affairs Division, General Accountability Office, *Eastern European Refugees*, 50.

65. East Germany was excluded from this list since West Germany regarded East Germans as fellow citizens who would be reincorporated into the political fold. While Poles were allocated over a third of the Eastern European refugee quota in FY1989 (3,607), a year later they received only a small fraction of the quota. 8,950 Eastern European admissions were determined by presidential "emergency determination." The other slots went to Romanians (3,182), Hungarians (1,075), Czechs (925), Bulgarians (111), Albanians (47), and Yugoslavs (1). Statement of Princeton Lyman, *Eastern European Refugees*, 23; see also Testimony of Curtis W. Kamman, *Eastern European Refugees*, 15–16, 22–23.

66. Statement of Princeton Lyman, *Eastern European Refugees*, 26–27.

67. Letter, Gene McNary to Bruce A. Morrison, May 25, 1990, #A1 1091, Asylum 1990, Box 741, Office of the Attorney General, RG 60, General Records of the Department of Justice, NARA. As an example of the news media's suspicions, see "In Florida, Comaneci Offers Only Partial Explanations," *New York Times*, December 6, 1989, D32.

68. An excellent discussion of Polish immigrants and Polish Americans—whom the author calls *Polonia*—can be found in Helena Znaniecka Lopata, *Polish Americans*, 2nd ed. (New Brunswick, NJ: Transaction, 1994). In a supplemental chapter in the 1994 edition written by Mary Patrice Erdmans, called "Recent Political Action on Behalf of Poland: The Interrelationships among Polonia's Cohorts 1978–1990," the author writes that New York State had the largest number of Poles, but Chicago had the largest city concentration of Poles. In 1980, 10 percent of the eight million Americans who claimed Polish ancestry lived in Illinois, and roughly 90 percent of these lived in the Chicago metropolitan area (213–214).

69. Erdsmans in Lopata, *Polish Americans*, 214–218, 232–235. When the Polish government scheduled elections in June 1989, many of these refugees (who were now US citizens) participated in the electoral process through absentee ballot.

70. Ibid., 222.

71. Letter, Rep. Dan Rostenkowski to Jack Brooks, November 9, 1989, #9729, Box 2, WHORM: Immigration/Naturalization, Bush Presidential Records.

72. Letter, Richard Gephardt and William O. Lipinski to George Bush, September 7, 1989; Opening Statement of Bruce A. Morrison, *Eastern European Refugees*, 2.

73. See, for example, Letter, Frank Wolf to Princeton Lyman, October 8, 1989, and letter, Frank Wolf to Lawrence Eagleburger, April 9, 1990, in "File Immigration, Romanians," in A1 1091, Box 783, Office of the Attorney General, RG 60 General Records of the Department of Justice, NARA.

74. Statement of Rev. Msgr. Nicholas DiMarzio, Executive Director, Migration and Refugee Services, US Catholic Conference, *Eastern European Refugees*, 50.

75. Letter, Paul C. Odrobina to George Bush, December 21, 1989, #100576, Box 10, Bush WHORM: Immigration/Naturalization, Bush Presidential Records; see also Statement of Thaddeus Kontek, Chairman, Refugee Committee, Polish American Congress, and Statement of Janusz Krzyzanowski, Executive Vice-President, Polish American Immigration and Relief Committee, *Eastern European Refugees*, 78–85 and 108–111.

76. See *Romanian Adoptions: Hearing before the Subcommittee on International Law, Immigration, and Refugees of the Committee on the Judiciary, House of Representatives, 102nd Congress, First Session, June 5, 1991* (Washington, DC: Government Printing Office, 1991).

77. Letter, Alan K. Simpson and Strom Thurmond to George Bush, May 31, 1989, Box 9, WHORM: Immigration/Naturalization, Bush Presidential Records.

78. Pear, "Soviet Armenians Let In Improperly."

79. Memorandum, Dick Thornburgh to Gene McNary, April 24, 1990, "File Immigration, Russians," A1 1091, Box 783, Office of the Attorney General, RG 60, General Records of the Department of Justice, NARA. Romanians were briefly included in this category in the FY1991 refugee admissions.

80. Heritage Foundation, "Preparing America for the Wave of Russian Immigrants," March 6, 1991, http://www.heritage.org/research/reports/1991/03/preparing-america-for-the-wave-of-russian-immigrants. Between 1881 and 1921 two million Russian and Polish Jews left for the United States, constituting the first wave of Russian Jewish migration. After World War II, small numbers of Soviet Jews who had served in the Red Army joined more than one hundred thousand Holocaust survivors in the second wave of immigration. See Orleck, *The Soviet Jewish Americans*, 13.

81. Department of Homeland Security, table 24, "Refugee Arrivals into the United States by Selected Country of Chargeability: Fiscal Years 1990–2000," *Fiscal Year Statistical Yearbook, Refugees/Asylees*, http://www.dhs.gov/publication/

fiscal-year-2000-statistical-yearbook-refugeesasylees. From 1975 to 2001, 573,000 refugees from the former Soviet Union were resettled in the United States. "The White House, Jackson-Vanik and Russia Fact Sheet," http://georgewbush-whitehouse.archives.gov/news/releases/2001/11/20011113-16.html. The closing of the Vienna-Rome pipeline did have the effect of increasing migration to Israel: almost four hundred thousand migrated to Israel between 1989 and 1992. Lazin, "Refugee Resettlement."

82. Orleck, *The Soviet Jewish Americans*, 14. According to Orleck, seven hundred thousand Soviet Jews emigrated to Israel between 1987 and 1998; and one hundred thousand migrated to Germany, Australia, and Canada (72).

83. Department of Homeland Security, table 24, "Refugee Arrivals into the United States by Selected Country of Chargeability: Fiscal Years 1990–2000."

84. The annual refugee quotas identified certain groups that might be granted refugee status, if otherwise qualified, even though they might still reside within their country of nationality: persons from Cuba and Vietnam frequently appeared on this list.

85. In this text I have chosen to list the name in Chinese format, with the surname appearing first, even though the *Congressional Record* uses the Western format. Statement of Heping Shi, *Alleged Intimidation and Harassment of Chinese Citizens in the United States: Hearing before the Subcommittee on Human Rights and International Organizations, and on Asian and Pacific Affairs of the Committee on Foreign Affairs, House of Representatives, 101st Congress, Second Session, June 19, 1990* (Washington, DC: Government Printing Office, 1991), 42.

86. *The Tiananmen Papers*, compiled by Zhang Liang, ed. Andrew J. Nathan and Perry Link (New York: Public Affairs, 2001), xi.

87. Jeffrey T. Richelson and Michael L. Evans, eds., "Tiananmen Square 1989: The Declassified History," National Security Archive Electronic Briefing Book No. 16, June 1, 1999, http://nsarchive.gwu/NSAEBB/NSAEBB16/; see also "Document 6: IPAC Daily Intelligence Summary 10–87, China: Hu Yaobang Resigns (17 January 1987)," National Security Archive Electronic Briefing Book No. 16, http://www2.gwu.edu/~nsarchiv/NSAEBB/NSAEBB16/#d6.

88. During the period October 1934 to October 1935 of the communist revolution, the communist armies were forced to retreat to the north and west to avoid the armies of the Kuomintang (Chinese Nationalist Party). These retreats are collectively known as the "Long March."

89. The "May Fourth Movement" takes its name from the protests of May 1919 in response to the Treaty of Versailles, which transferred Germany's territorial rights in China to the Japanese. Chinese called for returning China to its former international position, which many felt would only be secured by abandoning Chinese traditional culture and adopting Western notions of equality and democracy.

90. Nick Kristof and Sheryl WuDunn of the *New York Times* won the 1990 Pulitzer Prize for international reporting for their coverage of the Tiananmen prodemocracy demonstrations. See also Bill Keller, "Gorbachev Visits Beijing for Start of Summit Talks," *New York Times*, May 15, 1989, http://www.nytimes.com/1989/05/15/world/gorbachev-visits-beijing-for-start-of-summit-talks.html.

91. Jonathan D. Spence, *The Search for Modern China*, 3rd ed. (New York: Norton, 2013), 661.

92. *The Tiananmen Papers*, 436–437; Richelson and Evans, "Tiananmen Square 1989"; "Document 13: Secretary of State's Morning Summary for June 4, 1989, China: Troops Open Fire," National Security Archive Electronic Briefing Book No. 16, http://www2.gwu.edu/~nsarchiv/NSAEBB/NSAEBB16/#d6; see also Philip J. Cunningham, *Tiananmen Moon: Inside the Chinese Student Uprising of 1989* (Lanham, MD: Rowman and Littlefield, 2009).

93. Richelson and Evans, "Tiananmen Square 1989"; "Document 29: Secretary of State's Morning Summary for June 21, 1989, China: Swift Justice," National Security Archive Electronic Briefing Book No. 16, http://www2.gwu.edu/~nsarchiv/NSAEBB/NSAEBB16/#d6.

94. Jon Meacham, *Destiny and Power: The American Odyssey of George Herbert Walker Bush* (New York: Random House, 2015), 373.

95. "The President's News Conference, 8 June 1989," online by Gerhard Peters and John T. Woolley, *The American Presidency Project*, http://www.presidency.ucsb.edu/ws/?pid=17128.

96. Meacham, *Destiny and Power*, 373.

97. Ibid., 373–374.

98. Ibid., 374–375.

99. Congressional Research Service, "Report on Current and Possible Future Sanctions Against the PRC," January 26, 1990, included in *Chinese Students in America and Human Rights in China: Hearing before the Subcommittee on Immigration and Refugee Affairs of the Committee on the Judiciary, US Senate, 101st Congress, Second Session on H.R. 2712, January 23, 1990* (Washington, DC: Government Printing Office, 1991), 109–113.

100. "The President's News Conference," June 8, 1989. The Fang Lizhi case contributed to US-China tensions over the next year. Secret negotiations brokered by Henry Kissinger facilitated Fang's emigration in June 1990. See also "Fang Lizhi, Chinese Physicist and Seminal Dissident, Dies at 76," *New York Times*, April 7, 2012, http://www.presidency.ucsb.edu/ws/index.php?pid=17128.

101. Fang Lizhi recounts his experiences in his memoir, *The Most Wanted Man in China: My Journey from Scientist to Enemy of the State*, trans. Perry Link (New York: Henry Holt, 2016).

102. Ruth Ellen Wasem, "Chinese Students and Other Chinese in the US: Immigrant Issues and Options," Congressional Research Service, June 23, 1989, 2–3, HTTP://congressional.proquest.com/congressional/docview/t21.d22.

crs-1989-epw-0066?accountid=10267. Other sources reported lower figures, ranging from twenty-five thousand to forty thousand Chinese students in the United States. INS figures did not take into account those who may have left the United States before their visas expired (and returned).

103. Statement of Congressman Matthew G. Martinez in Support of HR 2712 in *Immigration Status of Chinese Nationals Currently in the United States: Hearing before the Subcommittee on Immigration, Refugees, and International Law of the Committee on the Judiciary, House of Representatives, 101st Congress, First Session, on H.R. 2929, H.R. 2712, H.R. 2722, and H.R. 2726, July 20, 1989* (Washington, DC: Government Printing Office, 1989), 217.

104. *Immigration Status of Chinese Nationals Currently in the United States*, 1.

105. Most of them would not be able to receive legal permanent residency until passage of the Hart-Celler Act of 1965. See Madeline Y. Hsu, "The Disappearance of America's Cold War Chinese Refugees, 1948–1966." *Journal of American Ethnic History* 31.4 (2012): 12–33. See also Madeline Y. Hsu, "Befriending the 'Yellow Peril': Chinese Students and Intellectuals and the Liberalization of US Immigration Laws, 1950–1965," *Journal of American-East Asian Relations* 16.3 (2009): 139–162.

106. Hsu, "Befriending the 'Yellow Peril,'" 153; see also Hsu, "Disappearance."

107. According to Wasem, the INS granted EVD status to Poles who entered the United States prior to July 21, 1984; Ethiopians who arrived before June 30, 1980; and Afghans who arrived in 1989. EVD status was also given to Nicaraguans (July 3, 1979, to September 28, 1980), Iranians (April 16, 1979, to December 13, 1979), and Ugandans (June 8, 1978, to September 30, 1986). Other countries whose nationals benefitted from a status similar to EVD include Cambodia, Chile, Cuba, Czechoslovakia, Dominican Republic, Hungary, Laos, Romania, and Vietnam. See Wasem, "Chinese Students," 4.

108. *Immigration Status of Chinese Nationals Currently in the United States*, 1.

109. Statement of Professor Bill Ong Hing, ibid., 180–181.

110. In August 1988, Attorney General Edwin Meese issued a memorandum requiring immigration judges in asylum cases to consider "reasonable" claims of persecution from Chinese nationals who refused to end a pregnancy or undergo sterilization. Katherine Bishop, "Officials Debate Asylum for Chinese Fleeing Abortion Policy," *New York Times*, April 3, 1989, http://www.nytimes.com/1989/04/03/us/officials-debate-asylum-for-chinese-fleeing-abortion-policy.html. See also CRS summary, "Bill Summary and Status, 101st Congress (1989–1990), HR 2712," http://thomas.loc.gov/cgi-bin/bdquery/D?d101:4:./temp/~bdjpzv:@@@D&summ2=5&|/home/LegislativeData.php?n=BSS;c=101|. Several other bills were introduced in the House to address some aspect of the Tiananmen crisis. Bruce Morrison introduced HR 2929, which offered temporary protected status to nationals of any country residing temporarily in the United States on nonimmigrant visas at the time of the occurrence of

armed conflict or catastrophic environmental disaster in their home country. Temporary protected status was written into the 1990 Immigration Act.

111. Letter, William Armstrong, Edward Kennedy, et al. to President Bush, November 28, 1989; memorandum, Richard Darman to George Bush, November 30, 1989, Box 2, WHORM: Immigration/Naturalization, Bush Presidential Records.

112. Alan K. Simpson, "The China Bill: Uphold the President," *Washington Post*, January 25, 1990, A27.

113. Memorandum, Richard Darman to George Bush, November 30, 1989.

114. A. Doak Barnett, "Increasingly, Bush Seems Right on China," *New York Times*, January 21, 1990, E21.

115. Carl Shusterman, "Amnesty for Chinese Students in the US," *Christian Science Monitor*, June 7, 1990, 19.

116. Cal Thomas, "Playing Checkers with Chinese Students' Lives," November 30, 1989, https://news.google.com/newspapers?nid=348&dat=19891201&id=bBJ NAAAAIBAJ&sjid=jTUDAAAAIBAJ&pg=6876,84050&hl=en.

117. Mary McGrory, "Playing the Nixon Card," *Washington Post*, November 30, 1989, A2.

118. Thomas Oliphant, "China's Meaningless Gestures," *Boston Globe*, January 12, 1990, 15; "Will Mr. Bush Kowtow?" *Washington Post*, November 30, 1989, A26.

119. Letter, Vartan Gregorian et al. to George Bush, November 28, 1989, Box 11, WHORM: Immigration/Naturalization, Bush Presidential Records.

120. Independent Federation of Chinese Students and Scholars, Press Release, "Chinese Students Are Thankful to Congress for a Bill of Protection Yet Concerned About the Intention of President Bush," n.d., #98003, Box 10, WHORM: Immigration/Naturalization, Bush Presidential Records.

121. Letter, Xiaoquan Liu to President George Bush, November 28, 1989, #98003, Box 10, WHORM: Immigration/Naturalization, Bush Presidential Records.

122. "Statement on the Disapproval of the Bill Providing Emergency Chinese Immigration Relief," November 30, 1989, online by Gerhard Peters and John T. Woolley, *The American Presidency Project*, http://www.presidency.ucsb.edu/ws/?pid=17884.

123. "January 26, 1990 Report on Current and Possible Future Sanctions against the PRC," included in *Chinese Students in America and Human Rights in China*, 112–113.

124. Ibid., 2.

125. Ibid., 36.

126. Ibid., 4.

127. Ibid., 5, 26.

128. The Justice Department provided PRC nationals with an irrevocable waiver of the foreign residence requirement that they could exercise until January 1, 1994. The foreign residence requirement was waived for all PRC aliens in the United States as of December 1, 1989. All PRC aliens who were

in lawful status as of June 5, 1989, were to be considered to have main-
tained lawful status for the purposes of adjustment or change of nonimmigrant status. The INS also established an outreach program to assist PRC
aliens in the United States and inform them of available options. During
that four-year period, Chinese students had the right to an immigrant visa
or to an adjustment or change of status. Letter, Richard Thornburgh to
George Bush, January 16, 1990, #104852, Box 10, WHORM: Immigration/
Naturalization, Bush Presidential Records. See also "Executive Order
12711—Policy Implementation with Respect to Nationals of the People's
Republic of China," April 11, 1990, online by Gerhard Peters and John T.
Woolley, *The American Presidency Project*, http://www.presidency.ucsb.edu/
ws/?pid=23556.

129. Bush, "Memorandum of Disapproval," n.d.

130. *Alleged Intimidation and Harassment of Chinese Citizens in the United States*, 1.

131. Ibid., 2.

132. Ibid., 6–7.

133. Ibid., 19.

134. Ibid., 26.

135. Ibid., 29.

136. Chinese Student Protection Act of 1992, http://www.gpo.gov/fdsys/pkg/
STATUTE-106/pdf/STATUTE-106-Pg1969.pdf. See also Donald M. Kerwin,
"The Faltering US Refugee Protection System: Legal and Policy Responses to
Refugees, Asylum Seekers, and Others in Need of Protection," *Refugee Survey
Quarterly* 31.1 (2012): 26.

137. "Recognizing the 17th Anniversary of the Massacre at Tiananmen Square,"
Congressional Record 152, No. 74 (June 12, 2006), http://www.gpo.gov/fdsys/
pkg/CREC-2006-06-12/html/CREC-2006-06-12-pt1-PgH3729.htm.

138. *Statistical Yearbook of the Immigration and Naturalization Service* (Washington,
DC: The Service, 1997), 83.

139. *Yearbook of Immigration Statistics* (Washington, DC: Office of Immigration
Statistics, 2013), 40–45; Ruth Ellen Wasem, "US Immigration Policy on Asylum
Seekers," Congressional Research Service, May 5, 2005, 13–15.

140. Wei Jingsheng, "Don't Believe China's Promises," *New York Times*, May 4, 2012,
http://www.nytimes.com/2012/05/05/opinion/dont-believe-chinas-promises.
html?ref=topics.

141. Michael Forsythe, "From Exiled Students, Sympathy for One Who Chose
Another Path," *New York Times*, June, 3, 2014, http://sinosphere.blogs.nytimes.
com/2014/06/03/from-exiled-students-sympathy-for-one-who-chose-another-
path/?ref=topics&_r=0; Austin Ramzy, "25 Years Later, Student Leaders
Witness Freedoms Fought for at Tiananmen," *New York Times*, June 4, 2014,
http://www.nytimes.com/2014/06/06/world/asia/25-years-later-student-
leaders-witness-freedoms-fought-for-in-tiananmen.html?ref=topics.

142. Andrew Jacobs, "Tiananmen's Most Wanted," *New York Times*, June 3, 2014, http://sinosphere.blogs.nytimes.com/2014/06/03/tiananmens-most-wanted/?ref=topics. Chai Ling wrote a memoir of her experiences: *A Heart for Freedom: The Remarkable Journey of a Young Dissident. Her Daring Escape, and Her Quest to Free China's Daughters* (Carol Stream, IL: Tyndale House, 2011); see also Li Lu's memoir, *Moving the Mountain: My Life in China from the Cultural Revolution to Tiananmen Square* (London: Macmillan, 1990).

143. George H. W. Bush, Proclamation 6367, "Refugee Day, 1991," October 28, 1991, http://www.gpo.gov/fdsys/pkg/STATUTE-105/pdf/STATUTE-105-Pg2739.pdf.

144. Ibid.; see also President George H. W. Bush, Proclamation 636, http://sinosphere.blogs.nytimes.com/2014/06/03/tiananmens-most-wanted/?ref=topics.

145. George P. Shultz, "Proposed Refugee Admissions for FY 1989," *Department of State Bulletin* 8, no. 2140 (November 1988): 12.

146. "Convention Regarding the Specific Aspects of Refugee Problems in Africa," http://www.africa-union.org/Official_documents/Treaties_%20Conventions_%20Protocols/Refugee_Convention.pdf.

147. Refworld, "Cartagena Declaration on Refugees, Colloquium on the International Protection of Refugees in Central America, Mexico and Panama," http://www.refworld.org/docid/3ae6b36ec.html.

148. Linda S. Peterson, *Central American Migration: Past and Present* (Washington, DC: Center for International Research, US Bureau of the Census, 1986), 3.

149. "An Ugly Choice," *Philadelphia Inquirer*, January 29, 1989, http://articles.philly.com/1989-01-29/news/26123804_1_refugee-status-refugee-ceiling-soviet-emigres.

150. For a discussion of the Central American refugee crisis see María Cristina García, *Seeking Refuge: Central American Migration to Mexico, the United States, and Canada* (Berkeley: University of California Press, 2006).

151. Ibid., 88–90.

152. Cheryl Little and Charu Newhouse al-Sahli, *Haitian Refugees: A People in Search of Hope* (Miami: Florida Immigrant Advocacy Center), May 1, 2004, 1, http://www.aijustice.org/haitian_refugees_a_people_in_search_of_hope.

153. Chiamaka Nwosu and Jeanne Batalova, "Haitian Immigrants in the United States," Migration Policy Institute, May 29, 2014, http://www.migrationpolicy.org/article/haitian-immigrants-united-states.

154. Stuart Taylor Jr., "Deciding How to Stop Haitians—and Why," *New York Times*, November 1, 1981, 4.

155. Loescher and Scanlan, *Calculated Kindness*, 80; Norman L. Zucker and Naomi Flink Zucker, *Desperate Crossings: Seeking Refuge in America* (New York: M.E. Sharpe, 1996), 69.

156. Margot Hornblower, "Freedom for Haitian Refugees, Probe of Detention Policy Urged," *Washington Post*, April 22, 1982, A8.

157. Loescher and Scanlan, *Calculated Kindness*, 84.

158. Gil Loescher and John Scanlan, "Human Rights, US Foreign Policy, and Haitian Refugees," *Journal of Interamerican Studies and World Affairs* 26.3 (1984): 340.

159. *Haitian Refugee Center v. Smith*, 676 F.2d 1023 (5th Cir. 1982), http://openjurist. org/676/f2d/1023.

160. Maria Cristina García, *Havana USA: Cuban Exiles and Cuban Americans in South Florida* (Berkeley: University of California Press, 1996), 46–80.

161. Arthur C. Helton, "Establishing a Comprehensive Scheme for Refugee and Migration Emergencies in the Caribbean Region: Lessons from Recent Haitian and Cuban Emergencies," in *Free Markets, Open Societies, Closed Borders? Trends in International Migration and Immigration Policy in the Americas*, ed. Max J. Castro (Coral Gables, FL: North-South Center Press, 1999), 249. See also Frederick J. Conway, "Haiti and Refugees," in *Immigration and Asylum: From 1900 to the Present*, vol. 1, ed. Matthew J. Gibney and Randall Hansen (Santa Barbara, CA: ABC-CLIO, 2005), 283; Zucker and Zucker, *Desperate Crossings*, 78.

162. Bill Frelick, *Refugees at Our Border: The US Response to Asylum Seekers* (Washington, DC: American Council for Nationalities Service, 1989), 12; see also "Haitian Refugee Center v. Garcey," http://www.leagle.com/decision/19851996600FSupp1396_11796.xml/HAITIAN%20REFUGEE%20 CENTER,%20INC.%20v.%20GRACEY.

163. Jana K. Lipman, "'The Fish Trusts the Water, and It Is in the Water That It Is Cooked': The Caribbean Origins of the Krome Detention Center," *Radical History Review* 115 (2013): 115–141.

164. *Louis v. Nelson*, 544 F. Supp. 973 (S.D. Fla. 1982), http://law.justia.com/cases/ federal/district-courts/FSupp/544/973/1686455/.

165. Frelick, *Refugees at Our Border*, 15, 18.

166. Nwosu and Batalova, "Haitian Immigrants." In 2012, the Haitian immigrant population stood at 606,000, constituting 1.5 percent of the foreign-born population. After the 2010 earthquake claimed the lives of tens of thousands, the United States granted temporary protected status (TPS) to fifty-eight thousand Haitians in the United States at the time of the earthquake.

167. "White House Press Release, 29 July 1992," Box 7f, July 29–31, 1992 (OTS 274), Bush Presidential Records. Helton, "Establishing a Comprehensive Scheme," places the number at 38,000 (249).

168. Helton, "Establishing a Comprehensive Scheme," 249.

169. Bush issued the executive order while vacationing at his home in Kennebunkport, Maine.

170. Barbara Crossette, "UN Official Rebukes US on Haitians," *New York Times*, May 27, 1992, A3.

171. This assessment is based on public opinion polls conducted during 1992 compiled by the Roper Center for Public Opinion Research at Cornell University, https://ropercenter-cornell-edu.proxy.library.cornell.edu/.

172. Letter, Rep. Charles B. Rangel to George Bush, October 29, 1991, #282596, Box 5, WHORM: Immigration/Naturalization, Bush Presidential Records.

173. Ibid.

174. Tom Squitieri, "Haitian Boat People Forced to Return Home," *USA Today*, November 19, 1991, 5A.

175. Tom Squitieri and Deborah Sharp, "Fleeing Haitians Caught in Political Net," *USA Today*, November 21, 1991, 1A.

176. "Refugee, Asylum Policy under Fire in 1989," 273–279.

177. Letter, Dante B. Fascell, William Lehman, and Larry Smith to George Bush, July 17, 1991, #256033, Box 5, WHORM: Immigration/Naturalization, Bush Presidential Records.

178. Letter, W. Lee Rawls, Assistant Attorney General to Representative Dante B. Fascell, November 19, 1991, #256033, Box 5, WHORM: Immigration/Naturalization, Bush Presidential Records.

179. Letter, Janet G. Mullins, to Charles Rangel, February 12, 1992, #282596, Box 5, WHORM: Immigration/Naturalization, Bush Presidential Records. For a discussion of the Haitians' economic motivations and charges of persecution upon return see letter, Brunson McKinley to Marie Dennis, n.d., #332842, WHORM: Country Files, CO-64, Bush Presidential Records.

180. Letter, Ileana Ros-Lehtinen to George Bush, July 17, 1991, #256055, Box 5, WHORM: Immigration/Naturalization, Bush Presidential Records.

181. Letter, W. Lee Rawl to Ileana Ros-Lehtinen, December 13, 1991, #256055, Box 5, WHORM: Immigration/Naturalization, Bush Presidential Records.

182. This professional corps was established when the INS issued a "final asylum rule" on the 1980 Refugee Act on July 27, 1990. Gregg A. Beyer, "Reforming Affirmative Asylum Processing in the United States: Challenges and Opportunities," *American University International Law Review* 9.4 (1994): 43–78.

183. William Raspberry, "A Fair Shake for Haitian Refugees; Protect American Interests without Abandoning American Values," *Washington Post*, November 22, 1991, A25.

184. See Alex Stepick and Dale Frederick Swartz, *Haitian Refugees in the US* (London: Minority Rights Group, 1982); Kevin R. Johnson, "Race, the Immigration Laws, and Domestic Race relations: A 'Magic Mirror' into the Heart of Darkness," *Indiana Law Journal* 73, no. 4 (1997-1998): 1111.

185. Letter, Jacques A. Despinosse to George Bush, 5 August 1991, # 263010, Box 5, WHORM: Immigration/Naturalization, Bush Presidential Records.

186. "Haitian Americans Demonstrate in Times Square, *New York Times*, April 7, 1992, B6.

187. See, for example, Letter, Marie Dennis, Maryknoll Society Justice and Peace Office to President George Bush, June 8, 1992, #332842, WHORM: Country Files, CO-64, Bush Presidential Records.

188. African Activist Archive, "TransAfrica," http://africanactivist.msu.edu/organization.php?name=TransAfrica. TransAfrica was founded in 1977 as an African American lobby on Africa and the Caribbean. See also Garry Lee and Molly Sinclair, "Refugees Policy Protested; 95 Supporters of Haitians Arrested outside White House," *Washington Post*, September 10, 1992, A9.

189. Letter, Brunson McKinley to Marie Dennis, n.d.

190. Ibid.

191. Zucker and Zucker, *Desperate Crossings*, 109.

192. Excerpts and samples of these news reports can be found in *Haitian Asylum-Seekers: Hearing before the Subcommittee on International Law, Immigration, and Refugees of the Committee on the Judiciary, House of Representatives, 103rd Congress, Second Session, on H.R. 3663, H.R. 4114, and H.R. 4264, June 15, 1994* (Washington, DC: Government Printing Office, 1994).

193. *Haitian Centers Council, Inc. v. McNary*, 807 F. Supp. 928 (E.D.N.Y. 1992), http://law.justia.com/cases/federal/district-courts/FSupp/807/928/1968058/.

194. *Haitian Centers Council, Inc. v. Sale*, 817 F. Supp. 336 (E.D.N.Y. 1993), http://law.justia.com/cases/federal/district-courts/FSupp/817/336/1459400/; see also Leslie A. Benton and Glenn T. Ware, "Haiti: A Case Study of the International Response and the Efficacy of Nongovernmental Organizations in the Crisis," *Emory International Law Review* 12.2 (1998): 851–934.

195. Zucker and Zucker, *Desperate Crossings*, 113.

196. Lydia Martin, "Marchers Demand Justice for Haitians," *Miami Herald*, February 8, 1993, A1; Mark Stencel, "Clinton's Pledges," *Washington Post*, January 20, 1993, A19.

197. Desda Moss, "Fasting Haiti Activist Hospitalized," *USA Today*, May 5, 1994, 2A.

198. Bills HR 3663, 4114, and 4264 of the 103rd Congress.

199. Moss, "Fasting Haiti Activist Hospitalized," 2A.

200. Americas Watch, National Coalition for Haitian Refugees, and Jesuit Refugee Services, *No Port in a Storm: The Misguided Use of In-Country Refugee Processing Center in Haiti*, September 1993, 5.

201. Thomas L. Friedman, "US to Release 158 Haitian Detainees," *New York Times*, June 10, 1993, A12.

202. The White House did take a proactive approach toward the Haitian junta. The administration barred the entry into the United States of individuals associated with the regime, ordered that their assets in the United States be frozen, and blocked financial transactions with members of the junta. The administration also worked with the OAS to tighten the multinational embargo on Haiti, and it secured financial and material sanctions on Haiti from the United Nations Security Council. On June 30, 1993, Clinton issued Executive Order No. 12853 to prohibit the sale or supply from the United States of petroleum, petroleum products, arms, or related materiel (or the carrying of such materials on US-registered vessels). Finally, in September 1994, the administration

sent American military forces to occupy Haiti in advance of UN troops. See Harold Hongju Koh, "The 'Haiti Paradigm' in United States Human Rights Policy" (1994), Faculty Scholarship Series, Paper 2092, http://digitalcommons. law.yale.edu/ff_papers/2092; "Press Briefing by William Gray, Special Advisor to the President on Haiti," July 5, 1994, online by Gerhard Peters and John T. Woolley, *The American Presidency Project.*

203. Sadako Ogata, *The Turbulent Decade: Confronting the Refugee Crises of the 1990s* (New York: Norton, 2005), 24. The UN high commissioner made the United States' treatment of Haitian refugees the top agenda item during her first meeting with Bill Clinton on May 12, 1994. See also Roberto Suro, "US Concedes Time Limits to Get Haitian Refugee Deal," *Washington Post*, June 16, 1994, https:// www.washingtonpost.com/archive/politics/1994/06/16/us-concedes-time-limits-to-get-haitian-refugee-deal/8cbc65c7-ef85-4a4e-8b21-355ca12ddb14/.

204. Helton, "Establishing a Comprehensive Scheme," 250. Most of these countries agreed to accommodate Haitians for a period of up to six months.

205. Ogata, *Turbulent Decade*, 24.

206. United States Coast Guard, "Alien Migrant Interdiction," http://www.uscg. mil/hq/cg5/cg531/AMIO/FlowStats/FY.asp. See also US Department of State, "Fact Sheet: US Relations with Haiti," February 11, 2013, http://www.state.gov/ r/pa/ei/bgn/1982.htm.

207. See Department of Homeland Security, table 26, "Number of Individuals Granted Asylum by Asylum Officer by Nationality, Fiscal Years 1990–2000," and table 24, "Refugee Arrivals into the United States by Selected Countries of Chargeability," *Fiscal Year Statistical Yearbook, Refugees/Asylees.*

208. "Haitian Refugee Immigration Fairness Act of 1998," https://www.govtrack. us/congress/bills/105/s1504. HRIFA was added to the FY1999 Omnibus Consolidated and Emergency Supplemental Appropriations Act (PL 105-277) at the close of the 105th Congress. The law allowed Haitians to file for an adjustment of status until March 31, 2000. After that date, only dependents of primary applicants could apply. The Legal Immigration Family Equity (LIFE) Act later amended HRIFA, making eligible some people previously ineligible for adjustment of status. Applications for readjustment of status had to be submitted by June 19, 2001.

209. See García, *Havana USA*, chapter 2.

210. During the 1980s Cuba was almost completely dependent on Soviet subsidies and trade—receiving up to $4.5 billion in subsidies annually, and three-quarters of its imports from the Soviet Union.

211. Susan Kaufmann Purcell, "Collapsing Cuba," *Foreign Affairs* 71.1 (1991): 131–145.

212. The Cuban Democracy Act sanctioned countries that traded with Cuba, prohibiting their vessels from unloading freight in the United States for 180 days

after docking in a Cuban port. "Cuban Democracy Act of 1992," http://www. govtrack.us/congress/bills/102/h55323.

213. García, *Havana USA*, 79.

214. White House Press Secretary, "Press Briefing by Attorney General Janet Reno," August 19, 1994.

215. Gallup / CNN / *USA Today* Poll, September 1994 (survey question), USGALLUP.807020.Q18, Gallup Organization (producer), Cornell University, Ithaca, NY, Roper Center for Public Opinion Research, iPOLL (distributor).

216. Cuban scholars later estimated that as many as a million people would have emigrated in the mid-1990s. See Jorge Duany, "Cuban Communities in the United States: Migration Waves, Settlement Patterns and Socioeconomic Diversity," *Pouvoirs dans la Caraïbe*, October 30, 2010, http://plc.revues.org/464. Duany cites these two sources: Antonio Aja Díaz, Guillermo C. Milán Acosta, and Marta Díaz Fernández, "La emigración cubana de cara al futuro: estimación de su potencial migratorio y algunas reflexiones en torno a la representación de los jóvenes en su composición," in *Anuario CEAP 1995: Emigración Cubana*, ed. Centro de Estudios de Alternativas Políticas, Universidad de La Habana, 142–163; Rodríguez Chávez Ernesto, "El flujo emigratorio cubano, 1984–1995: balance y perspectivas," paper presented at the workshop "The Caribbean Diaspora: The Present Context and Future Trends," University of Puerto Rico, Río Piedras, May 2, 1997.

217. Thomas David Jones and Judith Hippler Bello, "Cuban American Bar Association, Inc. v. Christopher. 43 F.3d 1412. Haitian Refugee Center, Inc. v. Christopher. 43 F.3d 1431," *American Journal of International Law* 90.3 (1996): 477–483.

218. In 2013 the Cuban government enacted a series of reforms to allow Cuban citizens to reside abroad for up to twenty-four months without losing their residency status or property. This change in policy only served to encourage more migration from Cuba, leading to widespread resentment in the United States that the Cuban government was once again dictating US immigration policy, taking advantage of the "fast-tracking" of Cuban immigrants who arrived through regular or irregular channels for the state's political and economic gain. Migration served as a means of exporting dissent, as well as gaining much-needed remittances. Cubans in the United States sent $2 billion in remittances to the island in 2013 alone. See "Americans Send $2 Billion a Year to Cuba," *CNN Money*, December 17, 2014, http://money.cnn.com/2014/12/17/news/ economy/cuba-remittances/. See also USCIS, "Cuban Medical Professional Parole (CMPP) Program," https://www.uscis.gov/humanitarian/humanitarian-parole/cuban-medical-professional-parole-cmpp-program; and USCIS, "The Cuban Family Reunification Parole Program," https://www.uscis.gov/humanitarian/humanitarian-parole/cuban-family-reunification-parole-program

219. Chicago Council on Foreign Relations, Gallup/CCFR Survey of American Public Opinion and US Foreign Policy 1995, October 1994 (survey question), USGALLUP.94CFRP.R19H, Gallup Organization (producer), Cornell University, Ithaca, NY, Roper Center for Public Opinion Research, iPOLL (distributor).

220. US Committee for Refugees, *Despite a Generous Spirit: Denying Asylum in the United States* (Washington, DC: American Council for Nationalities Service, 1986), 39.

CHAPTER 2

1. Raphael Lemkin, a Holocaust survivor, lost forty-nine members of his family to the Nazis. Despite his tireless advocacy on behalf of the genocide convention, Lemkin was not invited by the Senate subcommittee to testify in the congressional hearings on ratification. Samantha Power, *A Problem from Hell: America and the Age of Genocide* (New York: Harper Perennial, 2007), 68–69. See also William Schabas, "Genocide and Crimes against Humanity: Clarifying the Relationship," in *The Genocide Convention: The Legacy of Sixty Years*, ed. H. G. van der Wilt, J. Vervliet, G. K. Sluiter, and J. Th. M. Houwink ten Cate (Boston: Martinus Nijhoff, 2012), 3–14.

2. Keck and Sikkink, *Activists beyond Borders*, 82. See also William Korey, "Raphael Lemkin: The Unofficial Man," *Midstream*, June–July 1989, 45–46, cited in Keck and Sikkink, *Activists beyond Borders*, 82. Influenced as a boy by the massacre of Armenians in Turkey, Lemkin became convinced in the 1930s that the Nazis would carry out a similar campaign against the Jews. As early as 1933, at a conference sponsored by the League of Nations in Madrid, Lemkin proposed an international treaty making "destruction of national, religious, and ethnic groups" an international crime. The proposal was defeated.

3. Schabas, "Genocide and Crimes," 4–6; see also Power, *A Problem from Hell*, chapter 4.

4. United Nations Convention on the Prevention and Punishment of Genocide, http://www.hrweb.org/legal/genocide.html.

5. Schabas, "Genocide and Crimes," 4.

6. Power, *A Problem from Hell*, 64.

7. Proxmire was elected in a special election in 1957. His first vote in office was for the 1957 Civil Rights Act. On October 18, 1988, he cast his 10,252nd consecutive roll-call vote—a record that still stands today. He is more infamously known for the monthly "Golden Fleece Award" that he awarded to agencies that exemplified wasteful spending. US Senate, "August 27, 1957, Senator William Proxmire," https://www.senate.gov/artandhistory/history/minute/Senator_William_Proxmire.htm. See also "Senator Proxmire's Monument." *New York Times*, October 21, 1988, 1, http://search.proquest.com/docview/110437005?accountid=10267;

and Irvin Molotsky, "Bill Banning Genocide Still Snagged in the Senate," *New York Times*, September 27, 1988, http://www.nytimes.com/1988/09/27/world/bill-banning-genocide-still-snagged-in-senate.html.

8. United Nations Treaty Collection, "Chapter IV Human Rights, Convention on the Prevention and Punishment of the Crime of Genocide," https://treaties.un.org/pages/ViewDetails.aspx?src=TREATY&mtdsg_no=IV-1&chapter=4&lang=en#EndDec.

9. The law also set forth criminal penalties (a fine of $500,000 and/or imprisonment for up to five years) for directly and publicly inciting an act of genocide. See also 18 USC § 1091, http://www.law.cornell.edu/uscode/text/18/1091.

10. Statement of Trisha Katson, Director of Legislative Affairs, Liberty Lobby, *Genocide Convention Implementation Act: Hearing before the Subcommittee on Immigration, Refugees, and International Law of the Committee on the Judiciary, House of Representatives, 100th Congress, Second Session, on H.R. 807, March 16, 1988* (Washington, DC: Government Printing Office, 1988), 99.

11. Statement of Richard Schifter, *Genocide Convention Implementation Act*, 16.

12. Statement of William Proxmire, *Genocide Convention Implementation Act*, 8–9.

13. The site was chosen because Chicago had a large Jewish population with special interest in the genocide bill. Steven V. Roberts, "Reagan Signs Bill Ratifying UN Genocide Pact," *New York Times*, November 5, 1988, http://www.nytimes.com/1988/11/05/opinion/reagan-signs-bill-ratifying-un-genocide-pact.html.

14. Samantha Power, "Never Again: The World's Most Unfulfilled Promise," *Frontline*, n.d., http://www.pbs.org/wgbh/pages/frontline/shows/karadzic/genocide/neveragain.html.

15. Ibid.

16. This term was drawn from Samantha Power's *A Problem from Hell*.

17. McHugh, Vialet, and Wasem, *Refugee Policy*, 2.

18. Ibid.

19. Office of the Historian, *Department of State during Clinton Presidency*, 66, http://www.clintonlibrary.gov/.

20. Ibid., 61.

21. Ibid., 62.

22. Meacham, *Destiny and Power*, 467. Hussein never surrendered to coalition forces, however, which President Bush later considered one of the greatest failures of the war.

23. Peter W. Galbraith, "Refugees from War in Iraq: What Happened in 1991 and What May Happen in 2003," Migration Policy Institute Policy Brief, February 2003, 2, http://www.google.com/url?sa=t&rct=j&q=&esrc=s&source=web&cd=17&ved=0CEgQFjAGOAo&url=http%3A%2F%2Fwww.migrationpolicy.org%2Fpubs%2FMPIPolicyBriefIraq.pdf&ei=qotaVNGUIIrasATJnoC4Cw&usg=AFQjCNEgbCB52z_CC7_ZCCBvFZPa_C_33Q&bvm=bv.78677474,d.cWc.

24. Marion Farouk-Sluglett and Peter Sluglett, "The Historiography of Modern Iraq," *American Historical Review* 96.5 (1991): 1408–1421.

25. Galbraith, "Refugees from War," 4.

26. Meacham, *Destiny and Power*, 467.

27. *US Refugee Programs for 1992: Annual Refugee Consultations: Hearing before the Committee on the Judiciary, United States Senate, 102nd Congress, First Session, September 24, 1991* (Washington, DC: Government Printing Office, 1992), 15, 176.

28. Congressional Record Daily Edition, "House Leadership Congressional Delegation to assess Iraqi Refugee Crisis, April 18–22, 1991," April 23, 1991, http://congressional.proquest.com:80/congressional/docview/t17.d18.c45211fc0b0019bb?accountid=10267.

29. *Aftermath of War: The Persian Gulf Refugee Crisis: A Staff Report Prepared for the Use of the Subcommittee on Immigration and Refugee Affairs of the Committee on the Judiciary, United States Senate, 102nd Congress, First Session* (Washington, DC: Government Printing Office, 1991), 2.

30. Ibid., v.

31. Joseph Sassoon, *The Iraqi Refugees: The New Crisis In the Middle East* (London: I.B. Tauris, 2009), 9. According to Sassoon, accurate statistics are unavailable because of the government's control and manipulation of information.

32. Pieced together by the British after World War I from three Ottoman provinces, Iraq was politically and economically controlled by the Sunnis, who occupied the top posts in society. The Shia majority was composed largely of poor laborers. Iraq's borders separated Iraqi Kurds from Kurds in Turkey, Iran, and Syria. Kurdish rebels fought for independence or autonomy as early as 1922. Major Kurdish uprisings occurred from 1974 to 1975 and from 1983 to 1988. Middle East Watch, *Human Rights in Iraq* (New Haven: Human Rights Watch Books, 1990), 1–2. See also Power, *A Problem from Hell*, 175.

33. Helen Fein, *Human Rights and Wrongs: Slavery, Terror, Genocide* (Boulder, CO: Paradigm Publishers, 2007), 112; Power, *A Problem from Hell*, 186. The Anfal, wrote Fein, "can be seen as the endpoint of more than twenty years of government discrimination, disempowerment, and displacement of the Kurds" (113).

34. George Black, *Genocide in Iraq: The Anfal Campaign against the Kurds* (New York: Human Rights Watch, 1993), 323–324, cited in Power, *A Problem from Hell*, 232; Sassoon, *Iraqi Refugees*, 9.

35. Sassoon, *Iraqi Refugees*, 10.

36. See, for example, Document 25: Department of State, Office of the Assistant Secretary for Near Eastern and South Asian Affairs Action Memorandum from Jonathan T. Howe to Lawrence S. Eagleburger, "Iraqi Use of Chemical Weapons" (includes Cables Entitled "Deterring Iraqi Use of Chemical Weapons" and "Background of Iraqi Use of Chemical Weapons"), November 21, 1983, in National Security Archive Briefing Booklet No. 82, *Shaking Hands with Saddam*

Hussein: The US Tilt Toward Iraq, 1980-1984, ed. Joyce Battle, February 25, 2003, http://www2.gwu.edu/~nsarchiv/NSAEBB/NSAEBB82/. See also Middle East Watch, *Human Rights in Iraq*, 105–106.

37. Middle East Watch urged the Bush administration to pursue a number of policies: terminate all commodity and export credits; cease the export of any technology that might contribute to Iraq's military capabilities or arms development; publicly condemn the Iraqi government for its human rights abuses; and call on the United Nations to censure Iraq. *Human Rights in Iraq*, 131–132.

38. Iraq severed relations with the United States in protest over US support of Israel in the 1967 Six-Day War. Interest sections were established in 1972, but Iraq rejected all overtures for full diplomatic relations. Serious reverses in the Iran-Iraq war, and the Soviet Union's decision to stop supplying heavy arms to Iraq, forced the Hussein government to reconsider.

39. Middle East Watch, *Human Rights in Iraq*, 106–107.

40. Ibid., 106–107.

41. Power, *A Problem from Hell*, 191.

42. Ibid., 191.

43. Middle East Watch, *Human Rights in Iraq*, 104–105.

44. The conference sought to discuss and strengthen the 1925 Geneva Protocol barring the use of chemical weapons. Kurdish representatives were not allowed to participate in the conference on procedural grounds that only states could attend. See ibid., 112–114.

45. American farmers exported one million tons of wheat to Iraq each year; and Iraq was the ninth largest purchaser of US farm products. Power, *A Problem from Hell*, 231–233.

46. "Iraq," *Human Rights Watch World Report 1989*, http://www.hrw.org/reports/1989/WR89/Iraq.htm.

47. Power, *A Problem from Hell*, 236.

48. *Aftermath of War*, 11.

49. "House Leadership Congressional Delegation to Assess Iraqi Refugee Crisis"; *US Refugee Programs for 1992: Annual Refugee Consultations*, 127.

50. *US Refugee Programs for 1991: Hearing before the Committee on the Judiciary, United States Senate, 101st Congress, Second Session, on the Proposed US Refugee Resettlement Admissions Program for Fiscal Year 1991, October 3, 1990* (Washington, DC: Government Printing Office, 1991), 123; *Aftermath of War*, 1; Middle East Watch, *Human Rights in Iraq*, vii–viii.

51. Resolution 688 "condemned the repression of the Iraqi civilian population and demanded Iraq remove the threat to international peace and security and allow immediate access to international humanitarian organizations." Ogata, *Turbulent Decade*, 36. The text of the resolution can be found at United Nations, "Security Council Resolutions—1991," http://www.un.org/Docs/scres/1991/scres91.htm.

52. National Security Council, Unclassified Memorandum," Final Fact Sheet," April 11, 1991; "House Leadership Congressional Delegation to Assess Iraqi Refugee Crisis, April 18–22, 1991."

53. *Aftermath of War*, 9.

54. Power, *A Problem from Hell*, 241; Ogata, *Turbulent Decade*, 43.

55. Ogata, *Turbulent Decade*, 43.

56. *Aftermath of War*, 9.

57. National Security Council, Unclassified Memorandum, "Final Fact Sheet," April 11, 1991, Staff and Office Files: National Security Affairs, Nancy Bearg Dyke, Box 36, Bush Presidential Records, George H. W. Bush Presidential Library; Memorandum, Nancy B. Dyke to Robert M. Gates, "Points for Pickering to Make to UNSYG," April 25, 1991, Staff and Office Files: National Security Affairs, Nancy Bearg Dyke, Box 37, Bush Presidential Records.

58. Ogata reported that she met with President Bush and Secretary of Defense Dick Cheney in June 1991, when the last of the Iraqi-Turkish border mountain camps were closed, to urge that US troops remain in northern Iraq, but the president declined the request for fear that his administration would be accused of having imperialist designs. Ogata reports that her visits to the White House and the Pentagon during this period were "unprecedented." Ogata, *Turbulent Decade*, 42–43.

59. *US Refugee Program for 1993: Annual Refugee Consultations: Hearing before the Committee on the Judiciary, US Senate, 102nd Congress, Second Session, July 23, 1992* (Washington, DC: Government Printing Office, 1993), 62.

60. Bill Frelick, "The Dangers of 'Safe Havens' for Kosovo," *Refuge* 18.3 (1999): 33–34; The List Project to Resettle Iraqi Allies, "Iraq 1996," http://thelistproject.org/history/iraq-1996/.

61. Gallup Organization, Gallup Poll, April 1991 (survey question), USGALLUP.122027.Q6, Cornell University, Ithaca, NY, Roper Center for Public Opinion Research, iPOLL.

62. *US Refugee Programs for 1992*, 128.

63. Ibid.; Department of Homeland Security, table 24, "Refugee Arrivals into the United States by Selected Country of Chargeability: Fiscal Years 1990–2000."

64. *US Refugee Programs for 1994: Annual Refugee Consultations: Hearing before the Committee on the Judiciary, US Senate, 103rd Congress, First Session, September 23, 1993* (Washington, DC: Government Printing Office, 1994), 76; see also Department of Homeland Security, table 24, "Refugee Arrivals into the United States by Selected Country of Chargeability: Fiscal Years 1990–2000."

65. At thirty million, the Kurds are regarded as the largest stateless population in the world. See "The Kurdish Project," http://thekurdishproject.org/latest-news/us-kurdish-relations/nashville-growing-community-of-kurdish-americans/. Perhaps the best-known Kurdish American (who immigrated from Turkey and is not a refugee) is Hamdi Ulukaya, the founder and CEO

of the yogurt company Chobani. Ulukaya is involved in raising money for Kurdish refugees.

66. See, for example, Vesna Pešić, *Serbian Nationalism and the Origins of the Yugoslav Crisis* (Washington, DC: US Institute of Peace, 1996).

67. V. P. Gagnon Jr., *The Myth of Ethnic War: Serbia and Croatia in the 1990s* (Ithaca, NY: Cornell University Press, 2004), 178–179.

68. Ibid., 180–181; V. P. Gagnon Jr., "Yugoslavia in 1989 and after," *Nationalities Papers* 38.1 (2010): 23–39.

69. Slavenka Drakulić, *They Would Never Hurt a Fly: War Criminals on Trial in The Hague* (New York: Viking, 2004), 1.

70. Valerie Bunce, *Subversive Institutions: The Design and the Destruction of Socialism and the State* (Cambridge: Cambridge University Press, 1999), 73.

71. Gagnon, "Yugoslavia in 1989," 28–29.

72. Gagnon, *Myth of Ethnic War*, 60.

73. See, for example, Bunch, *Subversive Institutions*.

74. Gagnon, *Myth of Ethnic War*, 63–64.

75. Ibid., 71–72.

76. Gagnon, "Yugoslavia in 1989," 24.

77. According to Adam Lebor, Slobodan Milošević had no interest in keeping Slovenia in the federation because it had no Serbs and thus had no territorial claims there. Milošević struck a deal with Slovenian president Milan Kučan: Serbia recognized Slovenian self-determination in return for Slovenia's recognition of Serbs' rights to form part of a Greater Serbia. Adam Lebor, *Milosevic: A Biography* (New Haven: Yale University Press, 2004), 132–137.

78. Power, *A Problem from Hell*, 247; *Human Rights Watch World Report 1992: Yugoslavia*, January 1, 1992, http://www.refworld.org/docid/467fca581e.html.

79. "Statement by Press Secretary Fitzwater on Humanitarian Assistance to Refugees in Yugoslavia and the Caucasus," May 28, 1992, online by Gerhard Peters and John T. Woolley, *The American Presidency Project*, http://www.presidency.ucsb.edu/ws/?pid=21012. See also *War Crimes in Bosnia Hercegovina* (New York: Human Rights Watch, 1992) and *World Refugee Survey, 1995* (Washington, DC: US Committee for Refugees, 1995).

80. Power, *A Problem from Hell*, 251. See also Chloe Kay, "Contemporary Russian-Serbian Relations: Interviews with Youth from Political Parties in Belgrade and Vojvodina," *School of Russian and Asian Studies*, August 24, 2014, http://www.sras.org/russia_serbia_relations_youth. Milošević expected Russia, a permanent member of the Security Council, to come to its defense; but as a recently reconstituted state, Russia was still too weakened to prevent any action against Serbia until later in the decade, in the Kosovo crisis.

81. Power, *A Problem from Hell*, 288.

82. Ibid., 282–283.

83. George H. W. Bush, "Statement on Humanitarian Assistance to Bosnia, "October 2, 1992, http://www.gpo.gov/fdsys/pkg/PPP-1992-book2/pdf/PPP-1992-book2-doc-pg1738.pdf; *Bosnian Refugees: Hearing before the Subcommittee on International Operations and Human Rights of the Committee on International Relations, House of Representatives, 104th Congress, First Session, September 28, 1995* (Washington, DC: Government Printing Office, 1996), 4.

84. Power, *A Problem from Hell*, 285.

85. Anthony Lewis, "Yesterday's Man," *New York Times*, August 3, 1992, A19.

86. Anthony Lewis, "Clinton Fiddles While Bosnia Burns," *Baltimore Sun*, March 29, 1993, http://articles.baltimoresun.com/1993-03-29/news/1993088201_1_serbs-yugoslav-army-bosnia.

87. Power, *A Problem from Hell*, 324.

88. Cited in James M. McCormick, *American Foreign Policy and Process*, 2nd ed. (Itasca, IL: FE Peacock Publishers, 1992), 530. See also Power, *A Problem from Hell*, 324–325.

89. See Bill Frelick, "The Death March from Srebrenica," *Refugee Reports* 16, no. 7 (July 31, 1995).

90. Gerard Toal, "Srebrenica at 20 Years: How Do We Study Genocide?" *Washington Post*, July 11, 2015, http://www.washingtonpost.com/rweb/politics/srebrenica-at-20-years-how-do-we-study-genocide/2015/07/11/af9ca041ee73f815a029b88e-3ae375b6_story.html?tid=kindle-app.

91. The peacekeepers were part of the UN Protective Force (UNPROFOR). See *Bosnian Refugees*, 2.

92. Office of the Historian, *Department of State during Clinton Presidency*, 62.

93. Statement of Lionel A. Rosenblatt, Refugees International, in *Bosnian Refugees*, 8.

94. Power, *A Problem from Hell*, 440.

95. The USCR issued a recommendation that the UN General Assembly draft a Convention on Refugees of War and Civil Strife. Bill Frelick, *Yugoslavia Torn Asunder: Lessons for Protecting Refugees from Civil War* (Washington, DC: American Council for Nationalities Service, 1992), 18–19, 25. See also Bill Frelick, *Reversal of Fortune: Yugoslavia's Refugee Crisis since the Ethnic Albanian Return to Kosovo* (Washington, DC: US Committee for Refugees, 2000), 16–17. Regarding draft evaders/deserters and conscientious objectors, the *UN Handbook on Procedures and Criteria for Determining Refugee Status* stated, "Where, however, the type of military action with which an individual does not want to be associated, is condemned by the international community as contrary to basic rules of human conduct, punishment for desertion or draft evasion could . . . in itself be regarded as persecution." http://www.unhcr.org/publ/PUBL/3d58e13b4.pdf.

96. Frelick, *Yugoslavia Torn Asunder*, 21.

97. For a discussion of this migration see William Zimmerman, *Open Borders, Nonalignment, and the Political Evolution of Yugoslavia* (Princeton, NJ: Princeton University Press, 1987), 74–105.

98. Frelick, *Yugoslavia Torn Asunder*, 10–11, 13.

99. Testimony of Bill Frelick, US Committee for Refugees, in *Bosnian Refugees*, 70.

100. Ibid., 59.

101. Ibid., 64.

102. The US Committee for Refugees reported that there were 1.5 million inter-ethnic (Croat-Serb) marriages in Yugoslavia, and that the intolerance generated by the wars put enormous pressures on these families to separate. Frelick, *Yugoslavia Torn Asunder*, 30. See also *Bosnian Refugees*, 11.

103. Testimony of Bill Frelick, *Bosnian Refugees*, 64–67.

104. Six percent of those admitted by the US were Serb; 4.7 percent were Croat; and 4.2 were members of some other group. *Bosnian Refugees*, 8.

105. Ibid., 19.

106. Testimony of Semir Tanovic in ibid., 50–52.

107. Testimony of Bill Frelick in *Bosnian Refugees*, 78.

108. Hisako Matsuo, "Bosnian Refugee Resettlement in St. Louis, Missouri," in Peter Waxman and Val Colic-Peisker, eds., *Homeland Wanted: Interdisciplinary Perspectives on Refugee Resettlement in the West* (New York: Nova Scotia Publishers, 2005), 109.

109. Reed Coughlan and Judith Owens-Manley, *Bosnian Refugees in America: New Communities, New Cultures* (New York: Springer, 2006), 9, 28. In 2006, refugees constituted about 12 percent of Utica's population of over 60,651, the fourth highest per capita refugee population in the country. Refugees from the former Soviet Union, Vietnam, and Bosnia constitute 85 percent of the refugee population (Bosnians were roughly 40 percent). Resettlement services for Bosnians, as for most refugee groups, varied across locales. Utica was among the most generous of the host communities, providing not only housing, food, healthcare, and clothing for the standard six months, as is generally the case for refugees, but also offering numerous opportunities for job and language training, and classes for orientation to the US. Nonprofit groups such as the Mohawk Valley Resource Center for Refugees worked with the Lutheran Immigration and Refugee Service to identify refugees for resettlement in their community, and by 2014 Bosnians were the largest refugee group in Utica. See Susan Hartman, "A New Life for Refugees, and the City They Adopted," *New York Times*, August 10, 2014, http://www.nytimes.com/2014/08/11/nyregion/a-new-life-for-refugees-and-the-city-they-adopted.html?_r=0.

110. Eric Lichtblau, "US Seeks to Deport Bosnians over War Crimes," *New York Times*, February 28, 2015, http://www.nytimes.com/2015/03/01/world/us-seeks-to-deport-bosnians-over-war-crimes.html?_r=0.

111. President Clinton appointed Senator Robert Dole (R-Kansas) to serve as the chairman of the International Commission on Missing Persons, entrusted with locating the tens of thousands still unaccounted for victims of the wars in the former Yugoslavia.

112. See Lois McHugh, *Bosnia-Former Yugoslavia: Refugee Repatriation and Humanitarian Assistance under the Peace Agreement* (Washington, DC: Congressional Research Service, 1996).

113. *World Refugee Survey 1998—Bosnia and Herzegovina*, January 1, 1998, http://www.refworld.org/docid/3ae6a8ab10.html.

114. Kenneth Anderson, *Yugoslavia, Crisis in Kosovo: A Report from Helsinki Watch and the International Helsinki Federation for Human Rights* (New York: Helsinki Watch, 1990), 1.

115. Julie Mertus, Vlatka Mihelić, and Jeri Laber, *Open Wounds: Human Rights Abuses in Kosovo* (New York: Human Rights Watch, 1993).

116. Gagnon, *Myth of Ethnic War*, 124–125.

117. US Department of State, *Ethnic Cleansing in Kosovo: An Accounting*, December 1999, http://www.state.gov/www/global/human_rights/kosovoii/homepage.html.

118. Mary H. Cooper, "Foreign Affairs: 'We Have a Hard Life Here,'" *CQ Weekly*, May 8, 1999, 1094–1095, http://library.cqpress.com.proxy.library.cornell.edu/cqweekly/WR19990508-19KOSOVOREFUGEE001.

119. *The Kosovo Refugee Crisis: Hearing before the Subcommittee on Immigration of the Committee on the Judiciary, US Senate, 106th Congress, First Session, on the Current Kosovo Refugee Situation and the Scope and Adequacy of the Response of the United States and the International Community, April 14, 1999* (Washington, DC: Government Printing Office, 2000), 30.

120. William J. Clinton, "Videotaped Remarks by the President to the Serbian People," March 25, 1999, http://clinton6.nara.gov/1999/03/1999-03-25-videotaped-remarks-by-the-president-to-the-serbian-people.html.

121. The White House Office of the Press Secretary, "President Clinton and Secretary of Defense Cohen Statement on Kosovo," April 5, 1999, 4, http://www.ess.uwe.ac.uk/Kosovo/Kosovo-Current_News12.htm.

122. Ibid., 1.

123. See, for example, Noam Chomsky, *The New Military Humanism: Lessons from Kosovo* (Monroe, ME: Common Courage Press, 1999).

124. Power, *A Problem from Hell*, 446; Office of the Historian, *Department of State during Clinton Presidency*. See also "Statement on Kosovo," March 24, 1999, http://millercenter.org/president/speeches/speech-3932.

125. Power, *A Problem from Hell*, 448–451, 466.

126. UNHCR, "Daily Press Briefing of Office of Spokesman for Secretary-General," April 1, 1999, http://www.un.org/News/briefings/docs/1999/19990401.db040199.html.

127. Roberta Cohen and David A. Korn, "Refugees and Internally Displaced: Some Lessons from the Kosovo Crisis," *Refuge* 18.3 (1999): 37.

128. NATO deliberately bombed the Chinese embassy in Belgrade when it was discovered that it was being used to transmit Yugoslav army communications. See "NATO Bombed Chinese Deliberately," *Guardian*, October 16, 1999, http://www.theguardian.com/world/1999/oct/17/balkans.

129. Office of the Historian, *Department of State during Clinton Presidency.*

130. United Nations Office of Spokesman for the Secretary-General, "Daily Press Briefing, 31 March 1999," http://www.un.org/News/briefings/docs/1999/19990331.db033199.html.

131. President Bill Clinton, "Statement on Kosovo," March 24, 1999, http://miller-center.org/president/speeches/speech-3932.

132. Lydia Saad, "Americans Support Active Role for US in World Affairs, but Don't View Ethnic Conflicts as Critical to US Interests," *Gallup News Service*, http://www.gallup.com/home.aspx?ref=b; Mark Gillespie, "Crisis in Kosovo: Questions and Answers about American Public Opinion," *Gallup News Service*, http://www.gallup.com/home.aspx?ref=b.

133. "President Clinton and Secretary of Defense Cohen Statement on Kosovo, April 5, 1999, 5–6.

134. Hillary Rodham Clinton, "Talking It Over," May 5, 1999, http://clinton4.nara.gov/textonly/WH/EOP/First_Lady/html/columns/hrc050599.html.

135. Frelick, *Reversal of Fortune*, 16, 22–23. See also Cooper, "Foreign Affairs," 1094. Kosovar refugees who fled into Serbia or Montenegro were regarded as "internally displaced" rather than refugees, and thus were of lower priority for refugee resettlement. European allies assisted in resettlement efforts. By May 1999, Germany had accepted almost 10,000 refugees, followed by Turkey (6,259), Norway (2,476) and France (2,354).

136. Frelick, *Reversal of Fortune*, 16–17.

137. Office of the Press Secretary, "Remarks by the President and Chancellor Schroeder of Germany in Discussion with Kosovar Refugees and Their Families," May 6, 1999, http://clinton6.nara.gov/1999/05/1999-05-06-remarks-by-the-president-in-roundtable-with-refugees.html.

138. Joyce Vialet, *Refugee Admissions and Resettlement Policy: Facts and Issues* (Washington, DC: Congressional Research Service, 1999), 3–4, http://www.cnie.org/nle/crsreports/population/pop-6.cfm. During the first decade of the twenty-first century, an estimated eight hundred thousand Kosovars returned to their homes under NATO protection. Before they could return home to rebuild their homes, institutions, and communities, however, NATO peacekeepers and humanitarian agencies had to clear the land mines left by Serb and KLA forces; repair roads, bridges and other forms of rural and urban infrastructure; and ensure that there was sufficient food, water, and shelter for the returning populations. Once back in Kosovo the repatriates found it hard to

prove previous residency since the widespread bombings had resulted in the destruction of many public and private records. As in Bosnia, the resentments and recriminations among neighbors also made reaccommodation difficult. Unfortunately, UN and NATO peacekeepers failed to expeditiously identify and apprehend those who committed the most egregious war crimes, contributing to the fear and anxiety that these assassins would reemerge to kill the returnees. See Office of the Press Secretary, "Remarks by the President to the Kosovar Refugees," June 12, 1999, http://clinton5.nara.gov/textonly/WH/New/html/19990612b.html.

139. See *Erasing History: Ethnic Cleansing in Kosovo* (Washington, DC: Department of State, 1999) and US Department of State, *Ethnic Cleansing in Kosovo*. See also Office of the Historian, *Department of State during Clinton Presidency*, 81.

140. See *Still Waiting: Bringing Justice for War Crimes, Crimes against Humanity, and Genocide in Bosnia and Herzegovina's Cantonal and District Courts* (New York: Human Rights Watch, 2008). The trials at the district and cantonical level proceeded at an even slower pace because of the lack of witness protection; the limited cooperation between prosecutors and police; the lack of harmonization of the legal codes used in war crimes trials at the state and entity level; and the lack of staffing and prosecutorial knowledge.

141. Changes in the domestic political opposition—and in US policy toward the regime—created the conditions that facilitated his removal from office and the installation of a democratic government. For a detailed discussion of the 2000 election see Valerie Bunce and Sharon L Wolchik's *Defeating Authoritarian Leaders in Postcommunist Countries* (Cambridge: Cambridge University Press, 2011), 85–113.

142. Kathryn Sikkink, *The Justice Cascade: How Human Rights Prosecutions Are Changing World Politics* (New York: Norton, 2011), 5.

143. Trevor Hughes, "Serbian PM Forced to Flee Ceremony Marking Srebrenica Massacre," *USA Today*, July 11, 2015, http://www.usatoday.com/story/news/world/2015/07/11/tens-thousands-20-srebrenica-massacre/30006595/.

144. Hamilton, "Refugee Women."

145. McHugh, Vialet, and Wasem, *Refugee Policy*, 2.

146. Rwanda and Burundi were German colonies from 1897 to 1916. In 1918, Belgium assumed the administration of the colonies as trusteeship territories on behalf of the first League of Nations and eventually the United Nations. *The State of the World's Refugees, 2000: Fifty Years of Humanitarian Action* (Oxford: Oxford University Press, 2000), 47; *Rwanda: Genocide and the Continuing Cycle of Violence: Hearing before the Subcommittee on International Operations and Human Rights of the Committee on International Relations, House of Representatives, 105th Congress, Second Session, May 5, 1998* (Washington, DC: Government Printing Office, 1998), 3–4.

147. *The State of the World's Refugees, 2000: Fifty Years of Humanitarian Action*, 49.

148. Ibid., 52.

149. The UNHCR was invited to participate in the drafting of the OAU Convention. *The State of the World's Refugees, 2000: Fifty Years of Humanitarian Action*, 55–57.

150. Gérard Prunier, *The Rwandan Crisis: History of a Genocide* (Kampala: Fountain Publishers, 1999), 63; Ogata, *Turbulent Decade*, 172–173.

151. Kristin Scalzo, "The Rwandan Refugee Crisis: Before the Genocide," National Security Archive Electronic Briefing Book No. 464, March 31, 2014, http://nsarchive.gwu.edu/NSAEBB/NSAEBB464.

152. Peace Pledge Union, "Rwanda 1994," http://www.ppu.org.uk/genocide/g_rwanda4.html; Outreach Programme on the Rwandan Genocide and the United Nations, "Rwanda: A Brief History of the Country," http://www.un.org/en/preventgenocide/rwanda/education/rwandagenocide.shtml.

153. Prunier, *The Rwanda Crisis*, 234.

154. Ogata, *Turbulent Decade*, 175–176.

155. Prunier, *The Rwanda Crisis*, 238–239, 249.

156. Ibid., 248–249, 256–257.

157. Ibid., 259–261.

158. The Aegis Trust and other nonprofit organizations are now collecting the stories of rescuers, perpetrators, and survivors to inform the new generation of Rwandans (half the country's population was born after the genocide of 1994) of this painful past. National Public Radio, "Remembering Rwandans Who Followed Their Conscience," http://www.npr.org/sections/parallels/2014/04/08/300508669/remembering-rwandans-who-followed-their-conscience. See also "The Aegis Trust," http://www.aegistrust.org/ and "The Genocide Archive of Rwanda," http://www.genocidearchiverwanda.org.rw/index.php/Category:Rescuer_Testimonies.

159. Hyacinth Mascarenhas, "Twelve Portraits of Heroic Rwandans Who Stood Up to Their Country's Genocide," *World Mic*, April 9, 2014.

160. Philip Gourevitch was the first to write about Rusesagagina in his book *We Wish to Inform You That Tomorrow We Will Be Killed with Our Families: Stories from Rwanda* (New York: Farrar, Straus and Giroux, 1998). Some have disputed the Rusesagagina story. One of these critiques can be found in Edouard Kayihura and Kerry Zukus, *Inside the Hotel Rwanda: What Really Happened and Why it Matters Today* (Dallas, TX: BenBella Books, 2014).

161. United Nations High Commissioner for Refugees, *The State of the World's Refugees 1997–1998: A Humanitarian Agenda* (Oxford: Oxford University Press, 1997), 20.

162. Gérard Prunier, *Africa's World War: Congo, the Rwandan Genocide, and the Making of a Continental Catastrophe* (New York: Oxford University Press, 2009), 24–25.

163. Ibid., 27.

164. Prunier, *The Rwandan Crisis*, 302.

165. Ray Wilkinson, "Heart of Darkness," *Refugees Magazine* 110 (December 1, 1997), http://www.unhcr.org/print/3b6925384.html; Prunier, *Africa's World War*, 24–25.

166. Prunier, *Africa's World War*, 25.

167. *Rwanda: Genocide and the Continuing Cycle of Violence*, 1; Wilkinson, "Heart of Darkness."

168. Wilkinson, "Heart of Darkness."

169. Prunier, *Africa's World War*, 30.

170. In March 1998, during a visit of several African nations, Clinton met with family members of the Rwandan victims. "We in the United States and the world community did not do as much as we could have and should have done to try to limit what occurred in Rwanda in 1994," said the president. He admitted to three errors: not acting quickly to halt the killings; failing to label the slaughter "genocide"; and permitting the refugee camps in Zaire to become havens for Hutu killers. See James Bennet, "Clinton Declares US, with World, Failed Rwandans," *New York Times*, March 26, 1998, http://www.nytimes.com/1998/03/26/world/clinton-in-africa-the-overview-clinton-declares-us-with-world-failed-rwandans.html. See also Dana Hughes, "Rwanda, and What Bill Clinton Left Out When He Criticized Obama on Syria," *ABC News*, http://abcnews.go.com/blogs/politics/2013/06/rwanda-and-what-bill-clinton-left-out-of-criticism-of-obama-on-syria/.

171. Douglas Jehl, "Officials Told to Avoid Calling Rwanda Killings 'Genocide,'" *New York Times*, June 10, 1994, http://www.nytimes.com/1994/06/10/world/officials-told-to-avoid-calling-rwanda-killings-genocide.html.

172. PBS *Frontline*, "Interview with Alison Des Forges," http://www.pbs.org/wgbh/pages/frontline/shows/ghosts/interviews/desforges.html.

173. Alison Des Forges, *The Killing Campaign: The 1994 Genocide in Rwanda* (New York: Human Rights Watch, 1998); Tim Weiner, "Critics Say US Ignored C.I.A. Warnings of Genocide in Rwanda," *New York Times*, March 26, 1998, http://www.nytimes.com/1998/03/26/world/clinton-africa-blood-bath-critics-say-us-ignored-cia-warnings-genocide-rwanda.html; Bennet, "Clinton Declares." See also letter from Senators Paul Simon and Jim Jeffords to President Clinton, May 13, 1994, inserted into the *Congressional Record*, 140, no. 72 (June 10, 1994), http://www.gpo.gov/fdsys/pkg/CREC-1994-06-10/html/CREC-1994-06-10-pt1-PgS35.htm.

174. *Rwanda: Genocide and the Continuing Cycle of Violence*, 29–30; see also Philip Gourevitch, "The Genocide Fax," *New Yorker*, May 11, 1998, http://www.newyorker.com/magazine/1998/05/11/the-genocide-fax. See also declassified documents in the National Security Archive, "The US and the Genocide in Rwanda, 1994," http://nsarchive.gwu.edu/NSAEBB/NSAEBB53/.

175. Office of the Historian, *Department of State during Clinton Presidency*, 61. See also Presidential Decision Directive/NSC-25," May 3, 1994, http://www.

clintonlibrary.gov/_previous/Documents/2010%20FOIA/Presidential%20 Directives/PDD-25.pdf.

176. Herman Cohen, "Getting Rwanda Wrong," *Washington Post*, June 3, 1994, inserted into the *Congressional Record*, 140, no. 72 (June 10, 1994), http://www. gpo.gov/fdsys/pkg/CREC-1994-06-10/html/CREC-1994-06-10-pt1-PgS35.htm.

177. Anthony Lewis, "World without Power," *New York Times*, July 25, 1994, A15.

178. Michael N. Barnett, *Eyewitness to a Genocide: The United Nations and Rwanda* (Ithaca, NY: Cornell University Press, 2003), 12. Barnett's book is an examination of the institutional culture that facilitated genocide.

179. *Frontline*, "America's Response to Genocide," http://www.pbs.org/wgbh/ pages/frontline/shows/ghosts/themes/response.html.

180. Ibid.

181. Dallaire recounted his years in Rwanda, and the personal cost he suffered as a result. See Roméo A. Dallaire and Brent Beardsley, *Shake Hands with the Devil: The Failure of Humanity in Rwanda* (Toronto: Random House Canada, 2003). See also "Racism of Rwanda," *Washington Times*, March 31, 2004, http://www.washingtontimes.com/news/2004/mar/31/20040331-093452-5434r/?page=all.

182. Pat Towell, "Senate Follows Clinton's Lead with $243.4 Billion Bill," *CQ Weekly*, August 13, 1994, 2361–2367, http://library.cqpress.com/cqweekly/ WR103405346 (9 June 2015); James Risen, "Clinton Defends US Action on Rwanda," *Los Angeles Times*, July 24, 1994, http://articles.latimes.com/print/ 1994-07-24/news/mn-19398_1_relief-effort.

183. Benton and Ware, "Haiti."

184. Heather M. Fleming, "Foreign Aid: US Steps Up Rwandan Relief as Lawmakers Assail Pace," *CQ Weekly*, July 30, 1994, 2158, http://library.cqpress. com.proxy.library.cornell.edu/cqweekly/WR103405139 (June 9, 2015).

185. Office of the Historian, *Department of State during Clinton Presidency*, 5; "African Growth and Opportunity Act," http://trade.gov/agoa/.

186. Office of the Historian, *Department of State during Clinton Presidency*, 5.

187. US Department of Homeland Security, table 23, "Refugee Approvals and Arrivals by Geographic Area of Chargeability: Fiscal Years 1990-2000," http:// www.dhs.gov/fiscal-year-2000-statistical-yearbook-2.

188. Migration Policy Institute, "Characteristics of the African Born in the United States," http://www.migrationinformation.org/datahub/countrydata. cfm?ID=366.

189. Table 24, "Refugee Arrivals into the United States by Selected Country of Chargeability: Fiscal Years 1990–2000."

190. US Department of Homeland Security, table 26, "Number of Individuals Granted Asylum by INS Asylum Officers by Nationality, Fiscal Years 1994–2000," http://www.dhs.gov/fiscal-year-2000-statistical-yearbook-2.

191. Immigration and Naturalization Service, "Termination of Designation of Rwanda Under Temporary Protected Status Program After Final 6-Month

Extension," *Federal Register* 62, no. 118 (June 19, 1997), http://www.justice.gov/eoir/vll/fedreg/1996_1997/fr19jn97-92.pdf.

192. Immigration and Customs Enforcement, "ICE's Top 10 High Profile Removals," July 2, 2013, http://www.ece.gov/news/releases/1307/130702washingtondc.htm (13 January 2014); Immigration and Customs Enforcement, "ICE Deports Rwandan Wanted for Committing War Crimes during 1994 Genocide," January 29, 2011, http://www.ice.gov/news/releases/1101/110129chicago.htm.

193. Jocelyne Sambira, "Rwandan Genocide Survivors Struggle to Rebuild Their Lives," *Africa Renewal Online*, http://www.un.org/africarenewal/web-features/rwanda-genocide-survivors-struggle-rebuild-their-lives.

194. After the post-9/11 restructuring of the immigration bureaucracy, the Human Rights Violators and War Crimes Unit (HRVWCU) of the Bureau of Immigration and Customs Enforcement (ICE) was charged with identifying human rights violators who sought to evade justice by fleeing to the United States. By 2013, ICE's Homeland Security Investigations were investigating more than two thousand cases from ninety-five different countries, including Rwanda, Haiti, the former Yugoslavia, and El Salvador. Immigration and Customs Enforcement, "ICE Deports Rwandan"; "Rwandan Woman Gets 10 Years in US Prison for Lying about Genocide," *Chicago Tribune*, July 15, 2013, http://articles.chicagotribune.com/2013-07-15/news/sns-rt-us-usa-newhampshire-genocide-20130715_1_southern-rwandan-town-beatrice-munyenyezi-prudence-kantengwa; Immigration and Customs Enforcement, "Rwandan National Sentenced to 21 Months for Immigration Fraud," http://www.ice.gov/news/releases/1210/121001boston.htm; "ICE Deports Convicted Rwandan to Serve Sentence for Role in 1994 Genocide," December 21, 2011, http://www.ice.gov/news/releases/1112/111221detroit.htm.

195. Leona Johnson, "Rwanda Survivor Tells Her Story of Genocide in Hopes of Raising Awareness," June 6, 2011, http://blog.cleveland.com/metro//print.html; Howard Reich, "A Young Survivor of Genocide Takes Her Message around the World," *Chicago Tribune*, October 5, 2012, http://articles.chicago-tribune.com/2012-10-05/entertainment/ct-ent-1009-chicago-ideas-clemantine-wamariya-20121005_1_chicago-ideas-week-rwandan-town-genocide.

196. "Rwandan Genocide Survivor Speaks at Livingstone College," *Salisbury Post*, March 15, 2012, http://www.salisburypost.com/article/20120315/SP0103/303159996/.

197. Sambira, "Rwandan Genocide Survivors"; Genocide Survivors Foundation, https://genocidesurvivorsfoundation.org/who-we-are/our-founder/.

198. Imaculée Ilibagiza and Steve Erwin, *Left to Tell: Finding God amidst the Rwandan Holocaust* (Carlsbad, CA: Hay House, 2006). See also her website, http://immaculee.com/.

199. *Rwanda: Genocide and the Continuing Cycle of Violence: Hearing before the Subcommittee on International Operations and Human Rights of the Committee on*

International Relations, House of Representatives, 105th Congress, second session, May 5, 1998, 2.

200. "Racism of Rwanda," *Washington Times*, March 31, 2004, http://www.washingtontimes.com/news/2004/mar/31/20040331-093452-5434r/?page=all.

CHAPTER 3

1. UNHCR, "War Stokes Further Growth in Forced Displacement in the First Half of 2014," January 7, 2015, http://www.unhcr.org/54ac24226.html.
2. Ibid.
3. Bill Frelick, "Iraqi Refugees' Plight Grows as US Dawdles," *Human Rights Watch*, June 12, 2007, http://www.hrw.org/news/2007/06/12/iraqi-refugees-plight-grows-us-dawdles.
4. Ibid.
5. Daniel Benjamin and Steven Simon, *The Age of Sacred Terror* (New York: Random House, 2002), 7. See also "FBI 100: First Strike: Global Terror in America," February 26, 2008, http://www.fbi.gov/news/stories/2008/february/tradebom_022608; Jesse Greenspan, "Remembering the 1993 World Trade Center Bombing," *History*, February 26, 2013, http://www.history.com/news/remembering-the-1993-world-trade-center-bombing. See also Federal Bureau of Investigation, *Terrorism in the United States, 1999: 30 Years of Terrorism, A Special Retrospective Edition*, http://gateway.proquest.com/openurl?url_ver=Z39.88-2004&res_dat=xri:dnsa&rft_dat=xri:dnsa:article:CTE01226.
6. Gabriel Weimann, "Virtual Packs of Lone Wolves: How the Internet Made 'Lone Wolf' Terrorism a Misnomer," https://medium.com/p/17b12f8c455a; Federal Bureau of Investigation, *Terrorism in the United States*, 15–16; see also Thomas H. Kean and Lee Hamilton, *The 9/11 Commission Report: Final Report of the National Commission on Terrorist Attacks upon the United States* (Washington, DC: National Commission on Terrorist Attacks upon the United States, 2004), 72–73.
7. Greenspan, "Remembering the Bombing."
8. A fifteen-page list of rules limits Yousef's contact with relatives, lawyers, and other inmates, and restricts his access to newspapers and magazines to keep him from receiving coded messages. Matt Smith, "'93 WTC Plotter Ramzi Yousef Wants Contact Ban Lifted," *CNN*, February 18, 2013, http://www.cnn.com/2013/02/17/us/terrorist-prison/index.html; "Ramzi Yousef, 1993 World Trade Center Bombing Culprit, Sues to Get Out of Solitary Confinement," *Huffington Post*, February 18, 2013, http://www.huffingtonpost.com/2013/02/18/ramzi-yousef-solitary-confinement_n_2712293.html.
9. Janice Kephart, "Immigration and Terrorism: Moving beyond the 9/11 Staff Report on Terrorist Travel," *Backgrounder*, September 2005, http://www.cis.org/articles/2005/kephart.html; Greenspan, "Remembering the Bombing."

10. James C. McKinley Jr., "Islamic Leader on US Terrorist List Is in Brooklyn," *New York Times*, December 16, 1990, http://www.nytimes.com/1990/12/16/nyregion/islamic-leader-on-us-terrorist-list-is-in-brooklyn.html.

11. Richard A. Clarke, *Against All Enemies: Inside America's War on Terror* (New York: Free Press, 2004), 77–79; Douglas Jehl, "The Twin Towers; Rahman Errors Admitted," *New York Times*, March 7, 1993, http://www.nytimes.com/1993/03/07/nyregion/the-twin-towers-rahman-errors-admitted.html.

12. Cited in John L. Martin, "Immigration Reform Gains Momentum," *Center for Immigration Studies*, August 1993, http://www.cis.org/articles/1993/back593.html.

13. Williams, "Organized Crime," 149. According to Phil Williams, some scholars of security studies dismiss transnational organized crime as a threat to national and international security, and view military threat as the only true threat. According to such skeptics, transnational organized crime arrived on the agenda only because of the paucity of military challenges after the end of the Cold War.

14. According to Robert S. Leiken, "The Canadian border is more attractive to Muslim [jihadists] because of the large Canadian Muslim presence, the support networks created by indulgent asylum and other immigration policies in Canada." Robert S. Leiken, *Bearers of Global Jihad? Immigration and National Security after 9/11* (Washington, DC: Nixon Center, 2004), 131, http://www.mafhoum.com/press7/193S23.pdf.

15. Office of the Press Secretary, "Remarks by the President, Vice President, and the Attorney General during Immigration Policy Announcement," July 27, 1993, http://www.clintonlibrary.gov/assets/storage/Research%20-%20Digital%20Library/rascosubject/Box%20014/612956-immigration-info-92-93-3.pdf. See also Thomas L. Friedman, "Clinton Seeks More Powers to Stem Illegal Immigration," *New York Times*, July 28, 1993, A13.

16. Susan Hegger, "Many in US Concerned over Immigration," *St. Louis Dispatch*, September 3, 1993, 4B.

17. Seth Mydans, "Poll Finds Tide of Immigration Brings Hostility, *New York Times*, June 27, 1993, A1; Hegger, "Many in US Concerned."

18. Postelection polls showed the Cuban refugee crisis and the high cost of vehicle renewal tags were the two issues that most undercut support for Clinton's reelection in 1980. Clinton wrote in his memoir: "With all my other problems and mistakes, if I had been free of either of these two issues, I would have won. But if I hadn't been defeated, I probably never would have become President. It was a near-death experience, but an invaluable one, forcing me to be more sensitive to the political problems inherent in progressive politics: the system can absorb only so much change at once; no one can beat all the entrenched interests at the same time; and if people think you've stopped listening, you're sunk." Clinton was later reelected governor of Arkansas in 1982. The Mariel boatlift also affected how he later dealt with the Cuban *balsero* crisis of 1994.

See President Bill Clinton's recounting of the Mariel boatlift and his re-election campaign in Bill Clinton, *My Life* (New York: Knopf, 2004), 274–278, 279, 280, 282–287. See also Mirta Ojito, "The Long Voyage from Mariel Ends," *New York Times*, January 16, 2005, http://www.nytimes.com/2005/01/16/weekinreview/16ojito.html?_r=0.

19. Richard C. Paddock and Katherine Edwards, "300 Illegal Chinese Immigrants Arrested," *Los Angeles Times*, June 3, 1993, http://articles.latimes.com/1993-06-03/news/mn-42768_1_san-francisco; Mike Argento, "Golden Venture 20 Years Later Today," *York Daily Record*, June 6, 2013, http://www.ydr.com/ci_23362804/golden-venture-20-years-later-many-lives-remain. Of the 286 workers, 111 were deported; the rest were granted asylum, paroled, or otherwise permitted to remain in the United States.

20. "Remarks . . . during Immigration Policy Announcement," July 27, 1993.

21. See, for example, HR 1355 (103): Exclusion and Asylum Reform Amendments of 1993, http://www.govtrack.us/congress/bills/103/hr1355.

22. The commission was charged "to review and evaluate the implementation and impact of US immigration policy and to transmit to Congress reports of its findings and recommendations." The first report, *US Immigration Policy: Restoring Credibility: A Report to Congress, 1994 Executive Summary* (Washington, DC: The Commission, 1994), *US Immigration Policy: Restoring Credibility*, was released in September 1994. A second interim report, *Legal Immigration: Setting Priorities* was released in 1995. Two final reports were released in 1997: *US Refugee Policy: Taking Leadership. A Report to Congress* (Washington, DC: US Commission on Immigration Reform, 1997), *US Refugee Policy: Taking Leadership* and *Becoming an American. Immigration and Immigrant Policy. 1997 Executive Summary* (Washington, DC: US Commission on Immigration Reform, 1997); *Becoming an American: Immigration and Immigrant Policy*; see also Immigration Policy, Center, "The US Commission on Immigration Reform: The Jordan Commission," http://www.immigrationpolicy.org/just-facts/us-commission-immigration-reform-1990-1997-%E2%80%9Cjordan-commission%E2%80%9D.

23. "HR 3610—104th Congress: Omnibus Consolidated Appropriations Act, 1997," http://www.govtrack.us/congress/bills/104/.

24. Battered women and children under the age of eighteen were exempted from these penalties, as were the spouses and children of US citizens and permanent residents if they could demonstrate that their deportation would result in extreme hardship for the citizen or permanent resident.

25. The Welfare Reform Act is officially titled "The Personal Responsibility and Work Opportunity Reconciliation Act of 1996 (PL 104-193)." See Elena Kagan Collection, Domestic Policy Council Files, "President Clinton and Vice President Gore, Working on Behalf of the Hispanic Community," Box 034, Folder 001, http://www.clintonlibrary.gov/_previous/KAGAN%20DPC/DPC%2031-38/1829_DOMESTIC%20POLICY%20COUNCIL%20BOXES%2031-38.pdf.

26. "North American Free Trade Agreement (NAFTA)," http://www.ustr.gov/trade-agreements/free-trade-agreements/north-american-free-trade-agreement-nafta.

27. Clinton Administration History Project, *A History of the US Department of Justice during the Clinton Administration, 1993–2001* (Washington, DC, 2001), 79–80, http://www.clintonlibrary.gov/assets/DigitalLibrary/AdminHistories/Box%20 011-020/Box%20014/1225098-justice-1.pdf.

28. *A History of the US Department of Justice during the Clinton Administration*, 82.

29. Lorena Figueroa, "Hold the Line: Experts Say Operation Did More Harm Than Good," *El Paso Times*, September 30, 2013, http://www.elpasotimes.com/portlet/article/html/imageDisplay.jsp?contentItemRelationshipId=5445403; Kay Recede, "'Operation Hold the Line,' 20 Years Later," *KDBC*, September 19, 2013, http://www.kdbc.com/news/operation-hold-line-20-years-later.

30. Benjamin and Simon, *Age of Sacred Terror*, 13–14.

31. *Patterns of Global Terrorism 2001* (Washington, DC: US Department of State, May 2002), i, http://www.state.gov/documents/organization/10286.pdf.

32. Ibid., xii–xiii.

33. Ibid., xvi. The US State Department recognizes that no definition of terrorism has gained universal acceptance. Title 22 of the United States Code, § 2656(d), defines terrorism as "premeditated, politically motivated violence perpetrated against noncombatant targets by subnational groups or clandestine agents, usually intended to influence an audience." The State Department also recognizes that domestic terrorism "is probably a more widespread phenomenon than international terrorism."

34. Ibid., vi.

35. Kean and Hamilton, *The 9/11 Commission Report*, 369.

36. Richard A. Clarke, among many others, has argued that the Bush administration planned to wage war on Iraq even before September 11; fabricated or misrepresented intelligence reports about the weapons of mass destruction; and mismanaged the war, which "cost thousands of American lives and more than 100,000 Iraqi lives and disfigured, dismembered or traumatized tens of thousands of Americans." Richard A. Clarke, "Never Forget: Our Invasion of Iraq Was a Breach of Trust," *Huffington Post*, March 19, 2013, http://www.huffingtonpost.com/richard-a-clarke/iraq-war-anniversary_b_2904285.html.

37. "Enhanced interrogation" became a euphemism for activities some consider torture, or at the very least a violation of the Geneva Conventions on the treatment of prisoners and the UN Convention on Torture: painful stress conditions, humiliation, hypothermia, sensory deprivation of light and sound, waterboarding, and the use of dogs for intimidation. See Daniel B. Prieto, "War about Terror: Civil Liberties and National Security after 9/11," Council on Foreign Relations, February 2009, 23–24, http://www.cfr.org/terrorism-and-the-law/war-terror/p18373. Abuses by soldiers, military contractors, and intelligence officers at the Abu Ghraib prison in Iraq and at Guantánamo came to light.

38. Alison Parker and Jamie Fellner, "Above the Law: Executive Power after September 11 in the United States," https://www.hrw.org/legacy/wr2k4/8.htm.

39. Susan Gzesh, "America's Human Rights Challenge: International Human Rights Implications of US Immigration Enforcement Actions Post-September 11, September 2006, 10, www.migrationpolicy.org/pubs/Americas_Human_Rights_Challenge_1006.pdf.

40. Although the Patriot Act's most controversial provisions had sunset clauses, Congress amended or reauthorized them from 2004 to 2006. In 2011, President Barack Obama signed the Patriot Sunset Extension Act (PL 112-14), which extended for four years, two of the more controversial provisions: roving electronic surveillance (wiretaps), and the search of business and other records.

41. Prieto, "War about Terror," 1. Domestic cleavages were evident in public opinion polls. Prieto writes that 56 percent of Republicans thought that US counterterrorism policies had not gone far enough to protect the United States, while 47 percent of Democrats thought counterterrorism policies were too restrictive of civil liberties. Sixty-six percent of Republicans felts that the torture of terrorist suspects was often or sometimes justified; while 60 percent of Democrats felt that torture was rarely or never justified.

42. Ibid., 15; Donald Kerwin, "The Use and Misuse of 'National Security' Rationale in Crafting US Refugee and Immigration Policies," *International Journal of Refugee Law* 17.4 (2005): 763; Gzesh, "America's Human Rights Challenge," 11.

43. "USA Patriot Act" is an acronym for the "Uniting and Strengthening America by Providing Appropriate Tools Required to Intercept and Obstruct Terrorism Act of 2001." See American Civil Liberties Union, "Bush's Spin on the War on Terror," September 12, 2006, https://www.aclu.org/national-security/bushs-spin-war-terror. See also Julian Sánchez, "The Reauthorization of the Patriot Act," *Cato Institute*, March 9, 2011, http://www.cato.org/publications/congressional-testimony/reauthorization-patriot-act. For a text of the bill see https://www.congress.gov/bill/107th-congress/house-bill/3162.

44. Parker and Fellner, "Above the Law." These surveillance powers included the ability to investigate the business records, library files, and other data of citizens and noncitizens alike, which critics argued violated basic civil liberties.

45. The news media first reported on the existence of this program in 2005; by then the emails and telephone calls of some five hundred individuals had been monitored. Until media disclosure in 2005, the Bush White House limited congressional briefings on the program to the bipartisan leadership of both houses of Congress, the ranking members of both congressional intelligence committees, and the leadership of the Senate Appropriations Committee Defense Subcommittee. See Prieto, "War about Terror," 49–50.

46. These actions were made unlawful by the 1996 Antiterrorism and Effective Death Penalty Act. The act made it a criminal offense to provide funds or other material support to such organizations; required US financial institutions to

block the funds of the group; and made members of these groups both ineligible for US visas and subject to deportation if in the United States. See *Patterns of Global Terrorism 2001*, viii.

47. In 2002, for example, the American Civil Liberties Union filed suit against the Denver Police Department in federal court on behalf of several hundred political activists. Among the activists were members of the Chiapas Coalition, a nonprofit group that promoted "peaceful resolution of ongoing conflicts in the Mexican state by facilitating free trade networks and educational exchanges." The ACLU's investigation revealed that the DPD had produced and stored more than thirty-five hundred criminal intelligence files in a newly formed electronic database. Under investigation were a number of internationally known celebrities and activists, and well-established nongovernmental organizations such as the American Friends Service Committee and Amnesty International. Their files were shared with the FBI, the INS, and TSA. The "ascension of state authority" and surge in securitization began much earlier, however: the ACLU discovered that the preponderance of files were created prior to 9/11 and the USA Patriot Act. See chapter 1 of Sampaio, *Terrorizing Latina/o Immigrants*.

48. See, for example, this article on labor shortages in the United States: "Demand for Workers to Rise in 3rd Quarter," *Washington Post*, May 21, 2000, A22.

49. Kean and Hamilton, *The 9/11 Commission Report*, 353–357. See also Kerwin, "Use and Misuse."

50. Kerwin, "Use and Misuse," 752.

51. Kean and Hamilton, *The 9/11 Commission Report*, 383. See also Ariane Chebel d'Appollonia, *Frontiers of Fear: Immigration and Insecurity in the United States and Europe* (Ithaca, NY: Cornell University Press, 2012), 2–3; *Final Report of the Senate Select Committee on Intelligence and the House Permanent Select Committee on Intelligence Joint Inquiry into the Terrorist Attacks of September 11, 2001*, December 2002, http://fas.org/irp/congress/2002_rpt/911rept.pdf.

52. Kean and Hamilton, *The 9/11 Commission Report*, 384.

53. Leiken, *Bearers of Global Jihad*, 6, 146–147. Leiken wrote: "Those entering with fraudulent documents are next in line. Terrorists stealing across the Mexican border come last, virtually nil. The Canadian border is more expedient for jihadis thanks to Islamic support networks fostered by indulgent Canadian asylum policies. And terrorists like the shoe bomber Richard Reid and Zacarias Moussaoui came from 'visa waiver' countries (countries which do not require a visa for travel to the US, such as the E.U. countries). Moreover, especially in Western Europe but also in Lackawanna, N.Y. terrorists were citizens, immigrants of the second generation."

54. Ibid., 127.

55. Parker and Fellner, "Above the Law."

56. Ibid. See also Eleanor Acer and Archana Pyati, *In Liberty's Shadow: US Detention of Asylum Seekers in the Era of Homeland Security* (New York: Human Rights First, 2004), 21.

57. Gzesh, "America's Human Rights Challenge," 8, 11.

58. "America's Disappeared: Seeking International Justice for those Detained after September 11, an ACLU Report," January 2004, cited in Gzesh, "America's Human Rights Challenge," 19 n. 56.

59. *The September 11 Detainees: A Review of the Treatment of Aliens Held on Immigration Charges in Connection with the Investigation of the September 11 Attacks* (Washington, DC: US Dept. of Justice, Office of the Inspector General, 2003), http://www.justice.gov/oig/special/0306/index.htm.

60. OIR Report as summarized in Gzesh, "America's Human Rights Challenge," 19.

61. Prieto, "War about Terror," 17; Gzesh, "America's Human Rights Challenge," 18 n. 51, 19. Gzesh reports that some community-based and legal services organizations have placed the total number of detainees at three thousand.

62. Gzesh, "America's Human Rights Challenge," 21–22. The ACLU and the Center for Constitutional Rights brought two federal cases to contest all these practices, which resulted in two contradictory decisions—one ordering access and the other upholding secrecy.

63. Ibid., 19.

64. Ibid., 45; Sampaio, *Terrorizing Latina/o Immigrants*, 5–7.

65. Kerwin reports that in the two years after the 9/11 attacks, there were 341 terrorism convictions, but only 16 convictions resulted in sentences of more than five years. The median sentence for an international terrorism conviction was fourteen days. The Transactional Records Access Clearinghouse, "Criminal Terrorism Enforcement since the 9/11/01 Attacks: A TRAC Special Report," December 8, 2003, cited in Kerwin, "Use and Misuse," 761–762.

66. For an in-depth discussion of the impact of securitization on immigrants from the Americas see Sampaio, *Terrorizing Latino/a Immigrants*. See also See Daniel Kanstroom, *Deportation Nation: Outsiders in American History* (Cambridge, MA: Harvard University Press, 2007), 245. Kanstroom argues that deportation has functioned primarily as a labor control device, "a kind of extra tool in the hands of large businesses (and for that matter, American families seeking nannies, gardeners, and so forth) to provide a cheap, flexible, and largely rightless labor supply." Deportation has facilitated the selective enforcement against particular racial and ethnic groups.

67. Department of Justice, "Statement of Barbara Comstock, Director of Public Affairs, Regarding the Inspector General's Report on 9/11 Detainees," June 2, 2003, cited in Parker and Fellner, "Above the Law."

68. The DHS was "the largest restructuring of executive-branch functions since the establishment of the Department of Defense after World War II." Marc R. Rosenblum, "US Immigration Policy since 9/11: Understanding the Stalemate over Comprehensive Immigration Reform," Migration Policy Institute, 2011, 4, www.migrationpolicy.org. See also Department of Homeland Security, "Homeland Security Act of 2002," http://www.dhs.gov/homeland-security-act-2002. The

primary mission of the DHS is to "a) prevent terrorist attacks within the United States; b) reduce the vulnerability of the United States to terrorism; and c) minimize the damage, and assist in the recovery, from terrorist attacks that do occur within the United States."

69. Gzesh, "America's Human Rights Challenge," 42.

70. This analogy appears in Catherine Solyom, "US Drops Red, White, and Blue Curtain," *Gazette* (Canada), August 27, 2004, A2.

71. Arthur E. Dewey, "Immigration after 9/11: The View from the United States," April 3, 2003, http://2001-2009.state.gov/g/prm/rls/2003/37906.htm.

72. "The United States Refugee Admissions Program (USRAP) Consultation and Processing Priorities," https://www.uscis.gov/humanitarian/refugees-asylum/refugees/united-states-refugee-admissions-program-usrap-consultation-worldwide-processing-priorities. See also Refugee Council USA, "Eligibility," http://www.rcusa.org/eligibility/.

73. The Real ID Act of 2005 established federally mandated requirements for state drivers' licenses, essentially making them a national identification card. State driver's licenses had to be tamper-proof. Applicants for driver's licenses were required to provide a birth certificate, passport, or other legitimate identification document as proof of identity and to help verify legal status in the United States. DHS secretary Janet Napolitano (Obama administration) delayed implementing the Real ID Act in late 2009. However, in 2013, the Obama administration announced that all states would have to be in compliance by 2017. Some states have opposed implementation of the law because of the cost. Civil libertarians have opposed the national ID card because of the collection of personal information into a national database, and the invasion of privacy that represents. The Real ID Act also expands the evidentiary support required for a successful asylum petition.

74. Kerwin, "Use and Misuse," 756.

75. *Denial and Delay: The Impact of the Immigration Law's "Terrorism Bars" on Asylum Seekers and Refugees in the United States* (Washington, DC: Human Rights First, 2009), 1–2, 11.

76. Ibid., 4–5.

77. Operation Liberty Shield increased maritime patrols, airport security, border surveillance and screening; enhanced rail security and airspace control; and designed cybersecurity measures. "Statement by Homeland Security Secretary Tom Ridge: Operation Liberty Shield," March 17, 2003, http://www.jewishfederations.org/page.aspx?id=40778.

78. Forty-three people were detained as a result of this policy. Acer and Pyati, *In Liberty's Shadow*, 24–25.

79. Lawyer's Committee for Human Rights, "Refugees, Asylum Seekers and the New Department of Homeland Security: Initial Concerns and Preliminary Recommendations," March 2003, 8; Donald Kerwin, "Undermining

Antiterrorism: When National Security and Immigration Policy Collide," *America*, June 23–30, 2003, 13.

80. Leiken, *Bearers of Global Jihad*, 131; Canada Border Services Agency, "North American Partnerships: Working with the United States, Smart Border Declaration," http://www.cbsa-asfc.gc.ca/agency-agence/partner-partenaire-eng.html.

81. García, *Seeking Refuge*, 142–144; Kerwin, "Use and Misuse," 757.

82. Sampaio, *Terrorizing Latino/a Immigrants*, 7–11. According to Sampaio, securitization measures may appear racially neutral, "but in reality work to rearticulate and reinscribe forms of racial and gender hierarchy" (10).

83. National Conference on State Legislatures, "Border Protection, Antiterrorism and Illegal Immigration Control Act of 2005 | H.R. 4437," http://www.ncls.org/research/immigration/summary-of-the-sensenbrenner-immigration-bill.aspx.

84. Bureau of Immigration and Customs Enforcement, "Secure Communities," https://www.ice.gov/secure-communities#tab1.

85. "The Great Expulsion," *The Economist*, February 8, 2014, http://www.economist.com/news/briefing/21595892-barack-obama-has-presided-over-one-largest-peacetime-outflows-people-americas. According to Sampaio, as the number of apprehensions and detentions escalated, and particularly as more women and children were held in detention facilities, the reports of sexual harassment and other forms of gendered violence increased. See *Terrorizing Latino/a Immigrants*.

86. United States Customs and Border Protection, "Border Patrol Overview," http://www.cbp.gov/border-security/along-us-borders/overview.

87. "The Great Expulsion."

88. Belen Fernandez, "The Creeping Expansion of the Border Patrol," *Al Jazeera America*, May 7, 2014, http://america.aljazeera.com/opinions/2014/5/border-patrol-immigrationmilitarizationhomelandsecurity.html.

89. Department of Homeland Security, table 16, "Individuals Granted Asylum Affirmatively or Defensively: Fiscal Years 1990 to 2010," *Yearbook of Immigration Statistics*, 2010, http://www.dhs.gov/publication/yearbook-immigration-statistics-2010-refugees-and-asylees.

90. TRAC Immigration Project, "Asylum Denial Rate Reaches All Time Low: FY 2010 Results, a Twenty-Five Year Perspective," http://trac.syr.edu/immigration/reports/240/. See also Nina Bernstein and Marc Santora, "Asylum Seekers Treated Poorly, US Panel Says," *New York Times*, February 8, 2005, http://www.nytimes.com/2005/02/08/nyregion/asylum-seekers-treated-poorly-us-panel-says.html.

91. Daniel Swanwick, "Foreign Policy and Humanitarianism in US Asylum Adjudication: Revisiting the Debate in the Wake of the War on Terror," *Georgetown Immigration Law Journal* 21 (2007): 129, http://scholarship.law.georgetown.edu/spps_papers/4.

92. The case of the Mir family was first reported in "Afghan Refugee Family Halted by 9/11 Finally Heads to a New Life in the USA," *UNHCR*, February 11, 2004, http://www.unhcr.org/402a2c474.html.

93. Citizenship and Immigration Services Ombudsman, "Recommendation Regarding the Adjudication of Applications for Refugee Status," April 14, 2010, http://www.dhs.gov/ombudsman-recommendation- adjudication-applications-refugee-status.

94. Anthropologist Alessandro Monsutti has argued that migration is a calculated decision for many Afghans, a means through which to establish and expand social networks that will contribute to the economic welfare of the family. Migration has become so common, he argues, that it could be considered a rite of passage for young men. See *War and Migration: Social Networks and Economic Strategies of the Hazaras of Afghanistan* (New York: Routledge, 2005).

95. Rhoda Margesson, "Afghan Refugees: Current Status and Future Prospects," Congressional Research Service, January 26, 2007, 2–3, https://www.fas.org/sgp/crs/row/RL33851.pdf.

96. Hiram A. Ruiz, "Afghanistan: Conflict and Displacement 1978 to 2001," *Forced Migration Review* 13 (June 2002): 8. See also Margesson, "Afghan Refugees," 4. Margesson reported that by 2007 roughly half of the Afghans in were born in Pakistan, and over 80 percent had lived in Pakistan for over two decades.

97. Ruiz, "Afghanistan," 8.

98. In 2004, an estimated 250,000 landmines remained from this war. Charles Recknagel, "Afghanistan: Land Mines Left from Afghan-Soviet War Leave Bitter Legacy," *Radio Free Europe*, February 13, 2004, http://www.rferl.org/content/article/1051546.html. The defense industry estimated one hundred thousand landmines. See "Landmines in Afghanistan a Decades-Old Danger," *Defense Industry Daily*, February 1, 2010, http://www.defenseindustrydaily.com/Landmines-in-Afghanistan-A-Decades-Old-Danger-06143/. See also Margesson, "Afghan Refugees," 16–17.

99. Roberta Cohen, "Afghanistan and the Challenges of Humanitarian Action in Time of War," *Forced Migration Review* 13 (June 2002): 23–24, http://www.fmreview.org/FMRpdfs/FMR13/fmr13.9.pdf. See also Joanne van Selm, "Perceptions of Afghan Refugees," in *Global Responses to Terrorism: 9/11, Afghanistan and Beyond*, ed. Mary Buckley and Rick Fawn (New York: Routledge, 2003).

100. Department of Homeland Security, "Fact Sheet: News about the War against Terror," November 16, 2002, http://www.dhs.gov/xnews/releases/press_release_0007.shtm; Margesson, "Afghan Refugees," 2–3. According to Iranian government statistics, approximately 920,000 Afghans were living in Iran as of May 2006, primarily in urban areas.

101. US Department of State, "Afghanistan (11/08)," http://www.state.gov/outofdate/bgn/afghanistan/112064.htm.

102. Nicholas van Hear, "Refugee Diasporas, Remittances, Development, and Conflict," *Migration Information Source*, June 2003, http://www.migrationinformation.org/Feature/display.cfm?ID=125.

103. Margesson, "Afghan Refugees," summary.

104. Dewey, "Immigration after 9/11."

105. Van Selm, "Perceptions of Afghan Refugees," 265–266.

106. Ibid., 268.

107. Department of Homeland Security, table 14, "Refugee Arrivals by Region and Country of Nationality: Fiscal Years 2000 to 2009," https://www.dhs.gov/immigration-statistics/yearbook/2009. See also "Memorandum on FY 2009 Refugee Admissions Numbers and Authorizations of In-Country Refugee Status," Presidential Determination No. 2008-29, http://findarticles.com/p/articles/mi_m2889/is_39_44/ai_n30933031/.

108. Matthew Garcia, "Afghan Refugees Risked Their Lives but Are Frustrated by Resettlement in US," *Kansas City Star*, March 6, 2009 republished in *Common Dreams*, http://www.commondreams.org/news/2009/03/07/afghan-refugees-risked-their-lives-are-frustrated-resettlement-us.

109. The Omnibus Appropriations Act of 2009 (PL 111-118) and the National Defense Authorization Act for Fiscal Year 2008 (PL 110-181).

110. Bethany Matta, "Afghan Interpreters Demand Promised US Visas," *Aljazeera*, October 1, 2014, http://www.aljazeera.com/indepth/features/2014/09/afghan-interpreters-demand-promised-us-visas-201492811253296233.html; Kevin Sieff, "In Afghanistan, Interpreters Who Helped US in War Denied Visas; US Says They Face No Threat," *Washington Post*, November 10, 2013, http://www.washingtonpost.com/world/in-afghanistan-interpreters-who-helped-us-in-war-denied-visas-us-says-they-face-no-threat/2013/11/10/af7acfc8-4180-11e3-b028-de922d7a3f47_story.html; see also Bureau of Consular Affairs, Department of State, "Special Immigrant Visas for Afghans Who Were Employed by/on Behalf of the US Government," http://www.travel.state.gov/content/visas/english/immigrate/types/afghans-work-for-us.html.

111. Secretary of State John Kerry, "Additional Visas Authorized for the Afghan Special Immigrant Visa Program," August 1, 2014, http://kabul.usembassy.gov/uso-080114.html; US Department of State, "Afghan SIV Program Update," http://travel.state.gov/content/visas/en/immigrate/afghans-work-for-us.html.

112. Through the Lawyer's Committee for Human Rights (now Human Rights First) Helton established the Refugee Protection Program, which provides free legal help for those who seek refuge in the United States. In 1994 he founded and directed the Forced Migration Project and the Open Society Institute. Helton is the author of *The Price of Indifference: Refugees and Humanitarian Action in the New Century* (New York: Oxford University Press, 2002). Loescher is an internationally recognized expert on refugees currently teaching at the Refugee

Studies Centre at Oxford University. Both Helton and Loescher were in Iraq to study the humanitarian consequences of the war. See Gil Loescher, "Living after Tragedy: The UN Baghdad Bomb, One Year On," *Open Democracy*, http://www.opendemocracy.net/conflict/article_2050.jsp.

113. PBS *Frontline*, "The Iraq War: How We Spent $800 Billion (and Counting)," March 18, 2013, http://www.pbs.org/wgbh/pages/frontline/iraq-war-on-terror/the-iraq-war-how-we-spent-800-billion-and-counting/.

114. Seymour Hersh, "Torture at Abu Ghraib," *New Yorker*, May 10, 2004, http://www.newyorker.com/archive/2004/05/10/040510fa_fact?currentPage=all; "Abu Ghraib, Ten Years Later," *New York Times*, April 22, 2014, http://www.nytimes.com/2014/04/23/opinion/abu-ghraib-10-years-later.html;   Mark Mazzetti and James Risen, "Blackwater Said to Pursue Bribes to Iraq after 17 Died," *New York Times*, November 10, 2009, http://www.nytimes.com/2009/11/11/world/middleeast/11blackwater.html?_r=0.

115. "France Says the Name 'ISIS' Is Offensive, Will Use "Daesh' Instead," *The Week*, September 17, 2014, http://theweek.com/speedreads/446139/france-says-name-isis-offensive-call-daesh-instead.

116. CNN, "Home and Away: Iraq and Afghanistan War Casualties," http://www.cnn.com/SPECIALS/war.casualties/; "Half-Million Iraqis Died in the War, New Study Says," *National Geographic*, October 15, 2013, http://news.nationalgeographic.com/news/2013/10/131015-iraq-war-deaths-survey-2013/.

117. Kerry Sheridan, "Iraq Death Toll Reaches 500,000 since the Start of the US-led Invasion, New Study Says," *World Post*, October 15, 2013, http://www.huffingtonpost.com/2013/10/15/iraq-death-toll_n_4102855.html. The survey and study can be found at Amy Hagopian et al., "Mortality in Iraq Associated with the 2003–2011 War and Occupation: Findings from a National Cluster Sample Survey," *PLOS Medicine*, October 15, 2013, doi:10.1371/journal.pmed.1001533. See also Salman Rawaf, "The 2003 Iraq War and Avoidable Death Toll," *PLOS Medicine*, October 15, 2013, http://journals.plos.org/plosmedicine/article?id=10.1371/journal.pmed.1001532.

118. Rhoda Margesson, Jeremy M. Sharp, and Andorra Bruno, "Iraqi Refugees and Internally Displaced Persons: A Deepening Humanitarian Crisis?," *Congressional Research Service*, August 15, 2008, 1–2, https://www.fas.org/sgp/crs/mideast/RL33936.pdf.

119. UNHCR, "Guterres Urges Greater Support for Countries Hosting Iraqi Refugees," February 7, 2007, http://www.unhcr.org/45ca06284.html, September 20, 2013.

120. "UNHCR Iraq Factsheet," http://reliefweb.int/sites/reliefweb.int/files/resources/4c9084e49.pdf.

121. United States Commission on International Freedom, *Iraq: Urgent Action Needed to Protect Religious Minorities*, March 12, 2007, cited in Kelly O'Donnell and Kathleen Newland, "The Iraqi Refugee Crisis: The Need for Action,"

Migration Policy Institute, 2008, 8, http://www.migrationpolicy.org/research/iraqi-refugee-crisis-need-action.

122. Gil Loescher, Alexander Betts, and James Milner, *The United Nations High Commissioner for Refugees (UNHCR): The Politics and Practice of Refugee Protection into the 21st century* (New York: Routledge, 2008), 35–36.

123. O'Donnell and Newland, "The Iraqi Refugee Crisis," 1. By 2005, Jordan had closed its borders; and a fourth country, Saudi Arabia, made plans to build a 560-mile fence along the Iraq border to keep out "illegal migrants" and insurgents.

124. José Riera and Andrew Harper, "Iraq: The Search for Solutions," *Forced Migration Review*, June 2007, 10–13 cited in Benjamin R. Banta, "Just War Theory and the 2003 Iraq War Forced Displacement," *Journal of Refugee Studies* 21.3 (2008): 275; Margesson, Sharp, and Bruno, "Iraqi Refugees," 6.

125. Margesson, Sharp, and Bruno, "Iraqi Refugees," updated August 15, 2008, 7–8; see also *Managing Chaos: The Iraqi Refugees of Jordan and Syria and Internally Displaced Persons in Iraq. Staff Trip Report to the Committee on Foreign Relations, US Senate, 110th Congress, Second Session* (Washington, DC: Government Printing Office, 2008), 3–5, https://www.gpo.gov/fdsys/pkg/CPRT-110SPRT41773/pdf/CPRT-110SPRT41773.pdf.

126. Margesson, Sharp, and Bruno, "Iraqi Refugees," updated August 15, 2008, 11.

127. "Fact Sheet: Iraqi Refugee Processing," March 11, 2008. Beginning in May 2007, the Departments of Homeland Security and State worked cooperatively to administer the overseas component of the US Refugee Admissions Program (USRAP). The Department of State's Bureau of Population, Refugees and Migration (PRM) assumed the overall management of the USRAP: it proposed admissions ceilings and processing priorities; handled the intake of refugee referrals from the UNHCR and the US embassies; and prescreened the applicants. Within the DHS, the USCIS interviewed the refugee applicants and adjudicated the applications for refugee status. The USCIS and the PRM shared the responsibility for initiating the security checks.

128. The Bush administration identified several categories of Iraqi applications to be fast-tracked for processing: those employed by the US government in Iraq, by a media or nongovernmental organization headquartered in the United States, or by an organization associated with the US mission in Iraq that received US government funding.

129. US Department of State, Ellen Sauerbrey Remarks to USCIRF, *Sectarian Violence and the Refugee Crisis in Iraq*, September 19, 2007, cited in O'Donnell and Newland, "The Iraqi Refugee Crisis," 9.

130. Nir Rosen, "The Flight from Iraq," *New York Times*, May 13, 2007, 10.

131. Sassoon, *Iraqi Refugees*, 110–111.

132. Jame Baker, Lee H. Hamilton, et al., "The Iraq Study Group Report," http://media.usip.org/reports/iraq_study_group_report.pdf.

133. *The Plight of Iraqi Refugees: Hearing before the Committee on the Judiciary, US Senate, 110th Congress, First Session, January 16, 2007* (Washington, DC: Government Printing Office, 2007).

134. Ibid., 21–22.

135. Ibid., 19–20.

136. Tim Arango, "Visa Delays Put Iraqis Who Aided US in Fear," *New York Times,* July 12, 2011, http://www.nytimes.com/2011/07/13/world/middleeast/13baghdad.html?hp&_r=0.

137. Letter from Elissa Massimino, Human Rights First, et al. to Stephen J. Hadley, National Security Advisor, December 12, 2007, http://www.humanrightsfirst.org/wp-content/uploads/pdf/08103-asy-iraqi-refugees-hadley.pdf; see also O'Donnell and Newland, "The Iraqi Refugee Crisis," 19.

138. *Neglected Responsibilities: The US Response to the Iraqi Refugee Crisis: Joint Hearing before the Subcommittee on the Middle East and South Asia and the Subcommittee on International Organizations, Human Rights, and Oversight of the Committee on Foreign Affairs, House of Representatives, 110th Congress, Second Session, March 11, 2008* (Washington, DC: Government Printing Office, 2008), 1.

139. On June 3, 2008, the administration clarified that fiscal year 2008 would be the first year that the five thousand SIVs were available for use. It also permitted Iraqis who had applied before September 30, 2008 to access the five thousand SIVs allotted by the act for FY2008. The older program for Iraqi and Afghan translators who worked with the US government—authorized by Section 1059 of the National Defense Authorization Act for Fiscal Year 2006 (PL 109-163)— remained in place. The act provided for fifty SIVs in FY2006; it was amended on June 15, 2007 (PL 110-36) to provide for five hundred SIVs for FY2007 and FY2008. The annual SIV allotment under Section 1059 reverted to fifty in FY2009. See Human Rights First, "Promises to the Persecuted: The Refugee Crisis in Iraq Act of 2008," April 2009, http://www.humanrightsfirst.org/wp-content/uploads/pdf/090428-RP-iraqi-progress.pdf.

140. "Letter to President Bush: US Should Lead Response to Iraqi Refugee Crisis," January 2, 2008, http://www.refintl.org/policy/letter/letter-president-bush-us-should-lead-response-iraqi-refugee-crisis.

141. O'Donnell and Newland, "The Iraqi Refugee Crisis," 24.

142. Kirk Johnson, former USAID coordinator in Fallujah, founded the List Project to Resettle Iraqi Allies to coordinate pro bono legal counsel to Iraqis who had assisted the United States and were now refugees or IDPs. Johnson first began compiling a list of Iraqis in need of resettlement in 2006—after his own medical evacuation from Iraq—when former Iraqi colleagues began contacting him to plead for assistance. In February 2007, Johnson presented his list to Congress and began a media campaign to call attention to the plight of the Iraqi allies. By April 2008, his list contained over one thousand

names. Eight law firms committed themselves to offer pro bono counsel. See "Timeline of Major Events in the Iraqi Refugee Crisis and the List Project," http://thelistproject.org/the-refugee-crisis/timeline-of-events/. In 2008, five Yale law students—Becca Heller, Jon Finer, Mike Breen, Steve Poellot, and Kate Brubacher—founded the Iraqi Refugee Assistance Project (IRAP), which brought together over a thousand lawyers and law students across the country to provide pro bono legal assistance to Iraqi and Afghan refugee and SIV applicants. Through their op-eds and other media presentations, their testimony before Congress, their briefings to the State Department and the National Security Council, the IRAP has continually called attention to the plight of refugees and displaced persons. By 2013, the IRAP had successfully resettled more than fifteen hundred refugees in the United States, Australia, Canada, Ireland, Sweden, the Netherlands, and Germany. IRAP now has chapters at law schools around the country. See http://refugeerights.org/our-work/our-team/.

143. *Neglected Responsibilities*, 3.

144. Sassoon, *Iraqi Refugees*, 112–113.

145. *Managing Chaos*, v.

146. US Department of State, "The United States Humanitarian Assistance for Displaced Iraqis," October 5, 2007, http://www.state.gov/r/pa/prs/ps/2007/oct/93319.htm; Margesson, Sharp, and Bruno, "Iraqi Refugees," updated August 15, 2008, 14–15; Daniel C. Martin, "Refugees and Asylees: 2009," April 2010, 3, http://www.dhs.gov/files/statistics/publications/yearbook.shtm; Departmental Homeland Security, table 14, "Refugees arrivals by Region and Country of Nationality, http://www.dhs.gov/publication/yearbook-immigration- statistics-2010-refugees-and-asylees.

147. USCIS, "Iraqi Refugee Processing Fact Sheet," June 6, 2013, http://www.uscis.gov/humanitarian/refugees-asylum/refugees/iraqi-refugee-processing-fact-sheet. Iraqi refugees and their family members could also apply directly to the USRAP program without a UNHCR referral if they had worked for the US government, a US contractor, or a US-based media organization or NGO. USCIS sent officers to interview refugee applicants in Jordan, Egypt, Turkey, Lebanon, and—when the Assad government permitted it—Syria. Before 2012, the majority of cases processed by the USRAP were referrals from UNHCR; after 2012, the majority of applications processed were either direct applications or I-130 petitions filed by Iraqis in the United States for their relatives. As in other refugee processing around the world, decisions about eligibility were made on a case-by-case basis. The USCIS officer interviewed the applicant to confirm his or her biographical data; determine whether the applicant had suffered persecution or had a well-founded fear of future persecution on the basis of race, religion, nationality, membership in a particular social group, or political opinion; and whether he or she was admissible on security or other

grounds. If the applicant was "firmly resettled" in another country, the application was rejected.

148. Packer's highly acclaimed play *Betrayed* explored the dire situation of US-affiliated Iraqis. See George Packer, "Iraqi Refugees: A Debt Defaulted," *New Yorker*, July 29, 2011, http://www.newyorker.com/online/blogs/george-packer/2011/07/iraqi-refugees.html. See also Arango, "Visa Delays"; Charles Isherwood, "Seduced and Abandoned by Promises of Freedom, *New York Times*, February 7, 2008, http://www.nytimes.com/2008/02/07/theater/reviews/07betr.html?pagewanted=all&_r=0.

149. See Iraqi Refugee Assistance Project, http://refugeerights.org/stories/.

150. Becca Heller, "The US Should Not Abandon Those Who Helped in Iraq," *Washington Post*, June 19, 2014, http://www.washingtonpost.com/opinions/the-us-should-not-abandon-those-who-helped-in-iraq/2014/06/19/70e6c84e-f624-11e3-a3a5-42be35962a52_story.html; Sali's story is also recounted in Iraqi Refugee Assistance Project, "Report to Supporters, 2012–2013," 10, http://refugeerights.org/wp-content/uploads/2013/11/IRAP_DonorReport_2013_release.pdf.

151. "Report to Supporters, 2012–2013," 10.

152. The checks may have been mandated in response to the arrest of two Iraqi immigrants (non-SIV holders) in Kentucky on charges of sending weapons to insurgent groups. According to the USCIS website, "In May 2007, DHS announced and implemented an administration-coordinated, enhanced background and security check process for Iraqi refugees applying for resettlement in the United States. The security check regime, including both biographic and biometric checks, [was] enhanced periodically over the last several years as new opportunities and interagency partnerships with the law enforcement and intelligence communities [were] identified. These enhancements are a reflection of the commitment of DHS and other agencies to conduct the most thorough checks possible to prevent dangerous individuals from gaining access to the United States through the refugee program. No case is finally approved until results from all security checks have been received and analyzed." USCIS, "Iraqi Refugee Processing Fact Sheet," August 23, 2013, http://www.uscis.gov/taxonomy/term/6424/feed.

153. Natalie Ondiak and Brian Katulis, *Operation Safe Haven Iraq 2009: An Action Plan for Airlifting Endangered Iraqis Linked to the United States* (Washington, DC: Center for American Progress, January 2009), http://cdn.americanprogress.org/wp-content/uploads/issues/2009/01/pdf/iraqi_refugees.pdf.

154. Iraqi Refugee Assistance Project, "Report to Supporters, 2012–2013," 4; Sassoon, *Iraqi Refugees*, 110–113; see also Arango, "Visa Delays."

155. They joined the 130,665 Iraqi refugees who migrated during the same period. Department of State, Bureau of Population, Refugees, and Migration, "Refugee and Special Immigrant Visa Arrivals by Placement State, Nationality of Iraq,"

http://www.wrapsnet.org/Reports/AdmissionsArrivals/tabid/211/Default.aspx.

156. "US Department of State, "Special Immigrant Visas for Iraqis—Who were Employed by/on Behalf of the US Government," https://travel.state.gov/content/visas/en/immigrate/iraqis-work-for-us.html.

157. A small security contingent was to remain in the country after 2016 to support the US embassy in Kabul. Office of the Press Secretary, "Fact Sheet: Bringing the US War in Afghanistan to a Responsible End," May 27, 2014, http://www.whitehouse.gov/the-press-office/2014/05/27/fact-sheet-bringing-us-war-afghanistan-responsible-end.

158. "NATO and Afghanistan," http://www.nato.int/cps/en/natolive/69772.htm; United States Institute of Peace, "Afghanistan: The Current Situation," http://www.usip.org/afghanistan-the-current-situation.

159. "NATO and Afghanistan"; United States Institute of Peace, "Afghanistan: The Current Situation." In 2002, only nine hundred thousand children attended school, all of them boys as per Taliban mandate.

160. Ernesto Lindoño and Kevin Sieff, "Afghans Vote in Historic Election Amid, Attacks, Allegations of Fraud," *Washington Post*, June 14, 2014, http://www.washingtonpost.com/world/afghans-vote-in-historic-election-amid-attacks-fraud-allegations/2014/06/14/7de2deca-4509-4838-b5e9-b2d16898a046_story.html.

161. UNHCR, "2015 UNHCR Country Operations Profile-Afghanistan," http://www.unhcr.org/pages/49e486eb6.html; UNHCR, "Afghan Solutions Strategy," http://www.unhcr.org/pages/4f9016576.html.

162. Amnesty International, "Humanitarian Efforts Failing the Hundreds of Thousands Forced to Flee Ethnic Cleansing in Northern Iraq," August 11, 2014, http://www.amnestyusa.org/news/news-item/humanitarian-efforts-failing-the-hundreds-of-thousands-forced-to-flee-ethnic-cleansing-in-northern-i. Kevin Clarke, "Amnesty International Report Details ISIS Abuses," *America*, September 3, 2014, http://americamagazine.org/content/all-things/amnesty-international-report-details-isis-abuses.

163. Lisa Schlein, "UNHCR: Kurdish Region Overwhelmed by Influx of Displaced," *Voice of America*, August 12, 2014, http://www.voanews.com/content/unhcr-kurdish-region-overhelmed-by-influx-of-displaced-from-northern-iraq/2411419.html; Vivian Salama and Sameer N. Yacoub, "UN Says Iraq Humanitarian Crisis at Highest Level," *Washington Times*, August 13, 2014, http://www.washingtontimes.com/news/2014/aug/13/un-says-iraq-humanitarian-crisis-at-highest-level/?page=all.

164. Raheem Salman and Isabel Coles, "US Bombs Islamic State after Obama Call to Prevent Iraq 'Genocide," *Reuters*, August 8, 2014, http://www.reuters.com/article/2014/08/08/us-iraq-security-idUSKBN0G808J20140808.

165. Anne Barnard, "Death Toll from War in Syria Now 470,000, Group Finds," *New York Times*, February 11, 2016, http://www.nytimes.com/2016/02/12/world/middleeast/death-toll-from-war-in-syria-now-470000-group-finds.html?_r=0.

166. Internal Displacement Monitoring Centre, "Syria," http://www.nytimes.com/2016/02/12/world/middleeast/death-toll-from-war-in-syria-now-470000-group-finds.html?_r=0.

167. BBC News, "Aleppo Battle: Raids of Syria City 'Likely a War Crime,' UN Says," December 15, 2016, http://www.bbc.com/news/world-middle-east-38320647.

168. UNHCR, "Syrian Refugees in Lebanon Now Surpass One Million," http://www.unhcr.org/533c15179.html.

169. UNHCR, "Jordan," http://www.unhcr.org/pages/49e486566.html.

170. UNHCR, "Turkey," http://www.unhcr.org/cgi-bin/texis/vtx/page?page=49e48e0fa7f&submit=GO; UNHCR, "Iraq," http://www.unhcr.org/cgi-bin/texis/vtx/page?page=49e486426&submit=GO.

171. UNHCR, "Some 3,300 People a Day Still Arriving on Lesvos," November 13, 2015, http://www.unhcr.org/5645eb7f9.html.

172. UNHCR, "Europe: Syrian Asylum Applications," http://data.unhcr.org/syrian-refugees/asylum.php.

173. Rick Noack, "Germany Said It Took in More Than 1 Million Refugees Last Year. It Didn't," *Washington Post*, September 30, 2016; Paul Hockenos, "Nothing Can Take Down Angela Merkel—Except 800,000 Refugees," *Foreign Policy*, October 22, 2015, http://foreignpolicy.com/2015/10/22/nothing-can-take-down-angela-merkel-except-800000-refugees-germany-cdu-pegida/.

174. Lauren Collins, "The Children's Odyssey," *New Yorker*, February 27, 2017; BBC, "Migrant Crisis: Migration to Europe Explained in Graphics," January 28, 2016, http://www.bbc.com/news/world-europe-34131911.

175. Eurostat, "Asylum Statistics Explained," http://ec.europa.eu/eurostat/statistics-explained/index.php/Asylum_statistics.

176. "Sweden and Finland Planning Deportation of Refugees, Germany to Tighten Asylum Rules," *HNGN*, January 29, 2016, http://www.hngn.com/articles/174302/20160129/sweden-finland-planning-deportation-refugees-germany-tighten-asylum-rules.htm; Lizzie Dearden, "Denmark Approves Controversial Refugee Bill Allowing Police to Seize Asylum Seekers' Cash and valuables," *Independent*, January 26, 2016, http://www.independent.co.uk/news/world/europe/denmark-approves-controversial-refugee-bill-allowing-police-to-seize-asylum-seekers-cash-and-a6834581.html. See also Arno Tanner, "Overwhelmed by Refugee Flows, Scandinavia Tempers Its Warm Welcome," February 10, 2016, http://www.migrationpolicy.org/article/overwhelmed-refugee-flows-scandinavia-tempers-its-warm-welcome.

177. Eyk Henning and Matthias Goldschmidt, "Germany's Merkel Expects Syrian Refugees to return Home after War," *Wall Street Journal*, January 31, 2016,

http://www.wsj.com/articles/germanys-merkel-expects-syrian-refugees-to-return-home-after-war-1454184419.

178. Eleanor Acer, "America Has Resettled 121 of Syria's 2m Refugees: We Must Do Better—Now," *Guardian*, April 2, 2014, http://www.theguardian.com/commentisfree/2014/apr/02/america-syria-refugee-resettlement-do-better-now.

179. Howard LaFranchi, "World Refugee Day: UN Calls Syria 'Worst Humanitarian Disaster' since Cold War," *Christian Science Monitor*, June 20, 2013, http://www.csmonitor.com/USA/Foreign-Policy/2013/0620/World-Refugee-Day-UN-calls-Syria-worst-humanitarian-disaster-since-cold-war. See also Omar Dahi, "Syria in Crisis: The Politics of the Refugee Crisis," *Dissent*, Winter 2014, http://www.dissentmagazine.org/article/syria-in-fragments-the-politics-of-the-refugee-crisis.

180. Anne Gearan, "Little Room for Syrian Refugees," *Washington Post*, December 28, 2013, A1, A8.

181. "Testimony by Jan Egeland, *Syria after Geneva: Next Steps for US Policy: Hearing before the Committee on Foreign Relations, US Senate, 113th Congress, Second Session, March 26, 2014* (Washington, DC: Government Publishing Office, 2015).

182. Acer, "America Has Resettled."

183. Office of the White House, "How We're Welcoming Syrian Refugees While Ensuring Our Own Safety," November 17, 2015, https://www.whitehouse.gov/blog/2015/11/17/how-were-welcoming-syrian-refugees. Pew Research Center, "US Admits Record Numbers of Muslim Refugees in 2016," October 5, 2016, http://www.pewresearch.org/fact-tank/2016/10/05/u-s-admits-record-number-of-muslim-refugees-in-2016/.

184. Government of Canada, "#Welcome Refugees: Key Figures," http://www.cic.gc.ca/english/refugees/welcome/milestones.asp, January 2, 2017.

185. Arnie Seipel, "30 Governors Call for Halt to US Resettlement of Syrian Refugees," November 17, 2015, http://www.npr.org/2015/11/17/456336432/more-governors-oppose-u-s-resettlement-of-syrian-refugees. The Democratic presidential nominee, Hillary Clinton, promised to increase the refugee quotas to accommodate a minimum of sixty-five thousand Syrian refugees. See Ishaan Tharoor, "Trump and Pence's Opposition to Syrian Refugees Is Based on a Huge Lie," *Washington Post*, October 5, 2016, https://www.washingtonpost.com/news/worldviews/wp/2016/10/05/the-huge-lie-at-the-heart-of-trump-and-pences-opposition-to-syrian-refugees/?utm_term=.b48553fa17e0; Michell Lee, "Fact Check: Pence on Clinton's Plan for Accepting Syrian Refugees," *Washington Post*, October 4, 2016, https://www.washingtonpost.com/politics/2016/live-updates/general-election/real-time-fact-checking-and-analysis-of-the-vice-presidential-debate/fact-check-pence-on-clintons-plan-for-accepting-syrian-refugees/?utm_term=.45830b2668e0.

186. Acer, "America Has Resettled."

187. It gave $2.9 billion in aid to Syria alone from March 2011 to October 2014. USAID, "Syria," http://www.usaid.gov/crisis/syria.

CHAPTER 4

1. Tristana Moore, "Homeschooling: German Family Gets Political Asylum in the US," *Time*, March 2, 2010, http://content.time.com/time/magazine/article/0,9171,1968099,00.html.

2. Scott Calvert, "A Child's Life, a Lawyer's Humanity," *Baltimore Sun*, September 27, 2009, http://articles.baltimoresun.com/2009-09-27/news/0909260154_1_santos-salvador-asylum.

3. Todd Bensman, "Can a Mexican Cop Find Asylum in North Texas?," *D Magazine*, November 2009, http://www.dmagazine.com/publications/d-magazine/2009/november/can-a-mexican-cop-find-asylum-in-north-texas.

4. Department of Homeland Security, table 16, "Asylum Cases Filed with USCIS District Directors and Asylum Officers, Fiscal Years 1973–2003," *Yearbook of Immigration Statistics*, 2003, http://www.dhs.gov. See also US Committee for Refugees, "Refugee Reports: 2004 Statistical Issue," 25, no. 9 (December 31, 2004).

5. Department of Homeland Security, table 16, "Asylum Cases Filed with USCIS District Directors and Asylum Officers, Fiscal Years 1973–2003." See also Department of Homeland Security, table 25, "Asylum Cases Filed with District Directors and Asylum Officers, Fiscal Years 1973–2003," *Yearbook of Immigration Statistics*, 2001, http://www.dhs.gov; Department of Homeland Security, "Asylees," *Yearbook of Immigration Statistics*, 2003, 47, http://www.dhs.gov.

6. Approval rates increased after the 1991 settlement of the class action suit *American Baptist Churches v. Thornburgh* (760 F. Supp. 796), which resulted in the filing (or reopening) of thousands of asylum claims from El Salvador and Guatemala. I discuss North American responses to this migration in my study *Seeking Refuge*.

7. Andrew Ian Schoenholtz, Philip G. Schrag, and Jaya Ramji-Nogales, *Lives in the Balance: Asylum Adjudication by the Department of Homeland Security* (New York: New York University Press, 2014), 7.

8. An asylum officer or immigration judge can offer asylum. An immigration judge is the only official who can grant withholding of removal, and this status is given only to those who can demonstrate a 50 percent chance of persecution if returned to the homeland. The person granted WOR must file a yearly renewal fee. The person is eligible for some types of social services but cannot travel outside the United States. See Immigration Equality, "Withholding of Removal and CAT," http://www.immigrationequality.org/get-legal-help/our-legal-resources/asylum/withholding-of-removal-and-cat/.

9. In US immigration law a person can file for asylum "affirmatively" or "defensively." Those in the United States on a temporary visa could apply for asylum through the Immigration and Naturalization Service (after 2002, they applied through the US Citizenship and Immigration Services). These are known as the "affirmative" cases for asylum. The asylum officer reviews applications, interviews the applicants, and decides whether the applicants meet the requirements for asylum. If the asylum officer denies an asylum application, and the applicant is placed in removal proceedings, the applicant can request withholding of removal before an immigration judge. An applicant who requests asylum as an unauthorized (illegal) immigrant, files a "defensive" application (to prevent removal from the United States by securing asylum). Defensive cases are always heard by an immigration judge. The same legal test applies to both affirmative and defensive asylum applications: applicants must show they have a well-founded fear of persecution based on race, religion, nationality, political opinion, or membership in a particular social group. However, establishing a well-founded fear is more difficult in defensive cases, as this chapter demonstrates.

10. Schoenholtz, Schrag, and Ramji-Nogales, *Lives in the Balance*, 1–2.

11. US Committee for Refugees, *Refugees at Our Border: The US Response to Asylum Seekers* (American Council for Nationalities Service, 1989), 20.

12. The Universal Declaration of Human Rights, http://www.un.org/en/documents/udhr/index.shtml#a14.

13. The UN Conference on Territorial Asylum failed to establish an international right to asylum. See Guy S. Goodwin-Gill, *The Refugee in International Law* (New York: Oxford University Press, 1983).

14. Department of Homeland Security, table 25, "Asylum Cases Filed with District Directors and Asylum Officers, Fiscal Years 1973–2003," *Yearbook of Immigration Statistics*, 2001.

15. Asylum approval rates in the 1980s ranged from 18 to 54 percent. See ibid.

16. Ibid.

17. American Immigration Law Center, "History of the United States Asylum Officer Corps," http://www.ailc.com/services/asylum/history.htm#E.

18. Ashley Dunn, "Political Asylum Cases Swamp INS: A Surge of Applications by Central Americans and Haitians and a Critical Staffing Shortage Are Delaying Hearings in Thousands of Cases," *Los Angeles Times*, April 10, 1992, http://articles.latimes.com/1992-04-10/local/me-207_1_political-asylum.

19. Department of Justice, "Asylum Reform: Five Years Later," February 1, 2000, http://www.uscis.gov.

20. Ibid.; Ashley Dunn, "Political Asylum Cases."

21. For a discussion of the historical construction of the legal/illegal dichotomy see Mae M. Ngai, *Impossible Subjects: Illegal Aliens and the Making of Modern America* (Princeton, NJ: Princeton University Press, 2004).

22. As Jef Huysmans and Vicki Squire have noted, "A continuous and intensive circulation of [such] discourses … can change the dominant language through

which migration is approached.... A language that employs metaphors such as 'floods' legitimates a stronger focus on border controls." Huysmans and Squire, "Migration and Security," 173.

23. Another feature of the law is the "safe third country option" (see chapter 3). On their way to the United States, asylum seekers often traveled through countries that were signatories to the UN Refugee Convention/Protocol and which, presumably, offered some degree of protection to refugees. Some, like the Central American asylum seekers, traveled on foot through safe third countries like Costa Rica and Mexico on their overland journeys to the United States, while others changed planes in safe third countries. Modeled after similar European agreements, IIRIRA's safe third country option was designed to encourage asylum seekers to file wherever they arrived first to prevent a variation of "asylum shopping." In order to return an asylum seeker to a safe third country, however, the United States had to negotiate a reciprocal agreement with the third party. In 2002, the United States negotiated such a memorandum of agreement with Canada as part of the "smart border" initiatives in the wake of 9/11. The MOA drew vocal criticism from Canadian refugee advocates, however, who argued that the agreement affected larger numbers of asylum seekers bound for Canada than for the United States since flights were more likely to stop in US cities on the way to Canada than vice versa, and overland journeys required travel through the United States. Since asylum seekers had a better chance of securing asylum in Canada deporting them to the United States to file their petitions was inhumane, they argued. The MOA remained in place, but by January 2014 no other "safe third country" agreement had been negotiated. See García, *Seeking Refuge*, 142–144.

24. United States Commission on International Religious Freedom, *Report on Asylum Seekers in Expedited Removal*, vol. 2 (February 2005), 20–23, cited in Kerwin, "Use and Misuse," 758. Kerwin also discusses a confidential UNHCR report that concluded that US inspectors failed to provide certified translators for asylum seekers who did not speak English; improperly notified consulates about the identity and detention of immigrants seeking asylum; and in fourteen cases, mistakenly concluded that the asylum seekers were not entitled to apply for asylum.

25. US Citizenship and Immigration Services, "Questions and Answers: Credible Fear Screening," http://www.uscis.gov/humanitarian/refugees-asylum/asylum/questions-answers-credible-fear-screening; US Citizenship and Immigration Services, "Obtaining Asylum in the United States," http://www.uscis.gov/humanitarian/refugees-asylum/asylum/obtaining-asylum-united-states.

26. Acer and Pyati, *In Liberty's Shadow*, 8.

27. Lawyer's Committee for Human Rights, "Refugees, Asylum Seekers and the New Department of Homeland Security: Initial Concerns and Preliminary Recommendations," March 2003, 10, https://www.humanrightsfirst.org/wp-content/uploads/pdf/refs_032503.pdf. See also Acer and Pyati, *In Liberty's Shadow*, 8.

28. Bill Frelick and Brian Jacek, "Immigration Reform Overlooks Asylum-Seekers," *Los Angeles Times*, April 25, 2013, http://articles.latimes.com/2013/apr/25/opinion/la-oe-frelickjacek-asylum-immigration-20130425. According to Frelick and Jacek, the clock stopped any time the government determined that the applicant delayed the proceedings but "in practice, it [was] unclear precisely what stop[ped] and restart[ed] the clock." In 2011, the clock had stopped at some point for 262,025 people—92 percent of all pending cases.

29. As Kerwin writes, this delay poses a risk to the psychological health of the asylum seeker. It also threatens the safety of family members who remained abroad, who cannot be sponsored to come to the United States until their spouse or parent is a legal resident. Donald Kerwin, *The Faltering US Refugee Protection System: Legal and Policy Responses to Refugees, Asylum Seekers and Others in Need of Protection*, Migration Policy Institute, May 2011, 14, http://www.migrationpolicy.org/pubs/refugeeprotection-2011.pdf.

30. American Immigration Council, "Court Approves Settlement in National Class Action Lawsuit on Work Authorization for Asylum Seekers," November 5, 2013, http://www.americanimmigrationcouncil.org/newsroom/release/court-approves-settlement-national-class-action-lawsuit-work-authorization-asylum-s. See also Human Rights Initiative, "Federal District Judge Approves Settlement in Class Action Lawsuit on Employment Authorization for Asylum Applicants," http://www.hrionline.org/federal-district-judge-approves-settlement-in-class-action-lawsuit-on-employment-authorization-for-asylum-applicants/.

31. A study of fourteen hundred cases by the Lawyer's Committee for Civil Rights found that the BIA granted asylum, withholding of removal, and/or Convention Against Torture relief in less than 5 percent of these cases. Reported in Acer and Pyati, *In Liberty's Shadow*, 26.

32. Transactional Records Access Clearinghouse (TRAC) Immigration Project, "Asylum Denial Rate Reaches All Time Low: FY 2010 Results, a Twenty-Five Year Perspective," http://trac.syr.edu/immigration/reports/240/. See also Julian Aguilar, "Analysis Reveals Asylum Records of Judges," *New York Times*, July 30, 2011, http://www.nytimes.com/2011/07/31/us/31ttasylum.html?pagewanted=all&_r=0.

33. Nadwa Mossaad, "Refugees and Asylees: 2014," *Annual Flow Report*, 6, https://www.dhs.gov/sites/default/files/publications/Refugees%20%26%20Asylees%20Flow%20Report%202014_508.pdf.

34. American Civil Liberties Union, "American Exile: Rapid Deportations That Bypass the Courtroom," December 2014, 1, 3, https://www.aclu.org/feature/american-exile.

35. Ibid., 32–33. For another evaluation see US Commission on International Religious Freedom, "Report on Asylum Seekers in Expedited Removal (2005)," vols. 1 and 2, and the 2007 follow-up "Report Card." Available at www.uscirf.gov.

36. *Cardoza-Fonseca*, 480 US at 448 (1987), cited in Yule Kim, "Female Genital Mutilation as Persecution: When Can It Constitute a Basis for Asylum and Withholding of Removal?," Congressional Research Service, updated October 10, 2008, 6, http://congressionalresearch.com/RL34587/document.php.

37. Withholding of removal is a temporary status and does not lead to LPR status, or provide derivative asylum status to family members. While withholding applicants need not demonstrate persecution based on one of the five categories (race, religion, etc.), they must demonstrate that "more often than not" they suffer torture or some other form of persecution. United States Citizenship and Immigration Services, "I-589, Application for Asylum and for Withholding of Removal," 1–2, http://www.uscis.gov/sites/default/files/files/form/i-589instr.pdf.

38. When a legal proceeding does not have adverse parties (claimant versus defendant), the procedural phrase used is "In re" or "In the Matter of." See *Matter of Acosta*, Interim #2986 Decision (BIA, March 1, 1985), 441, http://www.justice.gov/eoir/vll/intdec/vol19/2986.pdf.

39. *Matter of Mogharrabi*, Interim decision #3028 (BIA, June 12, 1987), http://www.justice.gov/eoir/vll/intdec/vol19/3028.pdf.

40. Ibid.; see also "Burden of Proof for Applicants of Refugee Status," Attorney General Order No. 1391-90, January 23, 1990, in *Chinese Students in America and Human Rights in China: Hearing before the Subcommittee on Immigration and Refugee Affairs of the Committee on the Judiciary, US Senate, 101st Congress, Second Session on H.R. 2712 . . . January 23, 1990* (Washington, DC: Government Printing Office, 1991), 84.

41. Ruth Ellen Wasem, "US Immigration Policy on Asylum Seekers," Congressional Research Service, May 5, 2005, 7, http://www.fas.org/sgp/crs/misc/RL32621.pdf; Kim, "Female Genital Mutilation," 7.

42. Kerwin, *Faltering Refugee Protection System*, 21.

43. *Matter of Acosta*, 19 I&N Dec, 211, 233 (BIA 1985).

44. See references to In re AME and JCU, 24 I&N Dec. 69 (BIA 2007) in University of Pennsylvania School of Law Immigration Clinic, Memo, May 4, 2007, http://www.uscrirefugees.org/2010Website/5_Resources/5_4_For_Lawyers/5_4_1%20Asylum%20Research/5_4_1_1_General_Asylum_Information/SocialVisibilityMemo.pdf; see also Kim, "Female Genital Mutilation," 11; Kerwin, *Faltering Refugee Protection System*, 21; and Jennifer Hess, "Social Visibility and Particularity in Asylum: *Gaitan v Holder* and the Ironic Requirement of Social Perception to Avoid Persecution," *Boston College Journal of Law and Social Justice* 33.3 (2013): 27–38.

45. See US General Accountability Office, *US Asylum System: Significant Variation Existed in Asylum Outcomes across Immigration Courts and Judges* (Washington, DC, September 2008).

46. See Jaya Ramji-Nogales, Andrew Ian Schoenholtz, and Philip G. Schrag, eds., *Refugee Roulette: Disparities in Asylum Adjudication and Proposals for Reform*

(New York: New York University Press, 2009); see also the asylum reports of the Transactional Resource Action Clearinghouse (TRAC) at Syracuse University, http://trac.syr.edu/phptools/reports/reports.php.

47. Anna O. Law, *The Immigration Battle in American Courts* (Cambridge: Cambridge University Press, 2010), 177. See also Eli Saslow, "In a Crowded Immigration Court, a Future Decided in Seven Minutes," *Washington Post*, February 3, 2014, http://www.washingtonpost.com/national/in-a-crowded-immigration-court-seven-minutes-to-decide-a-familys-future/2014/02/02/518c3e3e-8798-11e3-a5bd-844629433ba3_story.html.

48. Sebastian Rotella and Ana Arana, "Finding Oscar: Massacre, Memory and Justice in Guatemala," *ProPublica*, http://www.propublica.org/article/finding-oscar-massacre-memory-and-justice-in-guatemala; "Guatemala Massacre Survivor Wins Political Asylum in the United States," *JCS Immigration Law*, September 30, 2012, http://jcsla.wordpress.com/2012/09/.

49. Conservative HQ, "Home Schoolers Uwe and Hannelore Romeike Need Your Help NOW!," March 21, 2013, http://www.conservativehq.com/article/12670-home-schoolers-uwe-and-hannelore-romeike-need-your-help-now.

50. Moore, "Homeschooling"; Andrew Evans, "Homeschoolers Seeking Religious Freedom to Appeal Asylum Rejection," *Washington Free Beacon*, July 16, 2013, http://freebeacon.com/homeschoolers-seeking-religious-freedom-to-appeal-asylum-rejection/; Ben Waldron, "Homeschooling German Family Allowed to Stay in the US," *ABC News*, March 5, 2014, http://abcnews.go.com/US/home-schooling-german-family-allowed-stay-us/story?id=22788876.

51. By comparison, the US murder rate is 4.7 per 100,000. See Elizabeth Ferris, "Criminal Violence and Displacement: Notes from Honduras," Brookings-LSE Project in Internal Displacement, November 8, 2013, http://www.brookings.edu/blogs/up-front/posts/2013/11/08-honduras-violence-displacement-ferris; Vanda Felbab-Brown, "Crime as a Mirror of Politics: Urban Gangs in Indonesia," *Brookings Foreign Policy Trip Reports*, February 6, 2013, http://www.brookings.edu/research/reports/2013/02/06-indonesia-gangs-felbabbrown; Hal Brands, "Crime, Violence, and the Crisis in Guatemala: A Case Study in the Erosion of the State," Strategic Studies Institute, US Army War College, May 2010, http://strategicstudiesinstitute.army.mil/pdffiles/PUB986.pdf.

52. Press release, "Crime and Violence: A Staggering Toll on Central American Development," April 7, 2011, http://www.worldbank.org/en/news/press-release/2011/04/07/crime-violence-staggering-toll-central-american-development. See also Cynthia Arnson and Eric L. Olson, eds., *Organized Crime in Central America: The Northern Triangle*, Woodrow Wilson Center Reports on the Americas No. 29, http://www.wilsoncenter.org/sites/default/files/LAP_single_page.pdf.

53. Ferris, "Criminal Violence and Displacement."

54. Brands, "Crime, Violence," 12–13.

55. Arnson and Olson, *Organized Crime*, 12.

56. There is no universally recognized definition of a "gang," but the UNHCR uses the term to denote the "relatively durable, predominantly *street-based groups of young people* for whom crime and violence is integral to the group's identity." See UNHCR, "Guidance Note on Refugee Claims Relating to Victims of Organized Gangs," March 2010, 1, 1 n. 3, http://www.refworld.org/docid/4bb21fa02.html.

57. Washington Office on Latin America (WOLA), "Why a Resource Manual on Central American Gangs?," *Central American Gang-Related Asylum: A Resource Guide*, May 2008, 2, http://www.wola.org/publications/central_american_gang_related_asylum_guide; Thomas Boerman, "Central American Gang Related Asylum Cases: Background, Leverage Points and the Use of Expert Witnesses," *Immigration Daily*, http://www.ilw.com/articles/2009,125-boerman.shtm.

58. WOLA, "Why a Resource Manual on Central American Gangs?" *Central American Gang-Related Asylum: A Resource Guide*, 2.

59. Robert J. Lopez, Rich Connell, and Chris Kraul, "Gang Uses Deportation to Its Advantage to Flourish in the US," *Los Angeles Times*, October 30, 2005, http://www.latimes.com/news/local/la-me-gang30oct30,0,6717943.story#axzz2tKO9Yov0.

60. Brands, "Crime, Violence," 27.

61. Ibid., 7.

62. Ibid., 36–37.

63. UNHCR, "Guidance Note on Refugee Claims Relating to Victims of Organized Gangs," 3.

64. WOLA, "Why a Resource Manual?," 5.

65. Tracy Wilkinson, "After Broken Gang Truce, El Salvador Sees Deadliest Month in Ten Years," *Los Angeles Times*, April 18, 2015, http://www.latimes.com/world/mexico-americas/la-fg-el-salvador-gangs-20150418-story.html#page=1.

66. Elizabeth Ferris, "Gangs, Violence and Displacement in Central America," Brookings-LSE Project in Internal Displacement, November 7, 2013, http://www.brookings.edu/blogs/up-front/posts/2013/11/07-central-america-armed-conflict-displacement-ferris.

67. See UNHCR, "Guidance Note on Refugee Claims Relating to Victims of Organized Gangs."

68. Ibid.

69. Washington Office on Latin America (WOLA), "Elements of Successful Legal Arguments for Gang-Related Asylum," *Central American Gang-Related Asylum: A Resource Guide*, May 2008, 3, http://www.wola.org/sites/default/files/downloadable/Central%20America/past/CA%20Gang-Related%20Asylum.pdf.

70. See USCRI, "Gang-Related Asylum Resources," http://www.refugees.org/resources/for-lawyers/asylum-research/gang-related-asylum-resources/.

71. Sonia Nazario, "The Refugees at Our Door," *New York Times*, October 10, 2015, http://www.nytimes.com/2015/10/11/opinion/sunday/the-refugees-at-our-door.html?smprod=nytcore-iphone&smid=nytcore-iphone-share&_r=2.

72. Julia Preston, "Losing Asylum, Then His Life," *New York Times*, June 28, 2010, http://www.nytimes.com/2010/06/29/us/29asylum.html?pagewanted=all&_r=0.

73. Calvert, "A Child's Life."

74. Frederick Reese, "America's Asylum Requests," *Mint Press News*, August 22, 2013, http://www.mintpressnews.com/americas-asylum-requests-how-do-you-prove-that-you-live-in-fear/167473/.

75. Melissa del Bosque, "Juarez Police Officer Denied Asylum," *Texas Observer*, February 8, 2011, http://www.texasobserver.org/juarez-officer-denied-us-asylum/.

76. "'Bravest Woman in Mexico' Seeks Asylum in the United States," *CNN.com*, March 23, 2011, http://www.cnn.com/2011/WORLD/americas/05/23/mexico.female.police.chief/index.html; "Mexico Drug War Refugees Face Long Odds for Asylum," *Fox News*, July 2, 2012, http://www.foxnews.com/world/2012/07/02/mexico-drug-war-refugees-face-long-odds-for-asylum.html Vales García, a criminology student at the University of Guadalajara, was the only person willing to accept the position of police chief.

77. Marcela Turati, "Death Threats, Then Red Tape," *New York Times*, June 21, 2014, http://www.nytimes.com/2014/06/22/opinion/sunday/exiled-mexican-journalists-face-red-tape-and-doubt-in-us.html?_r=0.

78. Ibid. See also Aguilar, "Analysis Reveals Asylum Records."

79. Patricia Giovine, "More Mexicans Fleeing the Drug War Seek Asylum," *Reuters*, July 19, 2011, http://www.reuters.com/article/2011/07/19/us-usa-mexico-asylum-idUSTRE76I6P020110719; Luis Hernández Navarro, "Mexicans Are Uneasy about America's Outsourced War on Drugs," *Guardian*, June 14, 2011, http://www.theguardian.com/commentisfree/2011/jun/14/mexican-drug-war.

80. Human rights advocates argue that immigration judges hold Mexican plaintiffs to a much higher threshold, in part because of fears of straining US-Mexico diplomatic relations. One retired immigration judge commented: "There is a real sense in the executive branch of our government that the relationship needs to be as smooth as possible and as a result if you read the state department's human rights reports on México, which are part of the evidence that are used by asylum adjudicators, you'll find that it's a very delicately frayed description of democracy in México. The problems that affect human rights in México are handled gingerly." Andrew Carpenter, "Mexican Asylum Seekers Disproportionately Rejected," *Latin America Working Group*, August 24, 2011, http://www.lawg.org/action-center/lawg-blog/69-general/914-mexican-asylum-seekers-disproportionately-rejected; Reese, "America's Asylum Requests."

81. See, for example, Public Broadcasting System, "Lost Boys of Sudan," http://www.pbs.org/pov/lostboysofsudan/.

82. Marc R. Rosenblum, "Unaccompanied Child Migration to the United States: The tension between Protection and Prevention," Migration Policy Institute, April 2015, 3,

http://www.migrationpolicy.org/research/unaccompanied-child-migration-united-states-tension-between-protection-and-prevention.

83. US Customs and Border Protection, "United States Border Patrol Southwest Family Unit Subject and Unaccompanied Alien Children Apprehensions Fiscal Year 2016," https://www.cbp.gov/newsroom/stats/southwest-border-unaccompanied-children/fy-2016; see also Sara Pierce, "Unaccompanied Child Migrants in US Communities, Immigration Court, and Schools," Migration Policy Institute, October 2015, http://www.migrationpolicy.org/research/unaccompanied-child-migrants-us-communities-immigration-court-and-schools.

84. Migration Policy Institute, Panel Discussion: "Children on the Run: An Analysis of First-Hand Accounts from Children Fleeing Central America," March 12, 2014, http://www.migrationpolicy.org/multimedia/children-run-analysis-first-hand-accounts-children-fleeing-central-america; Anna González-Barrera and Jens Manuel Krogstad, "With Help from Mexico, Number of Child Migrants Crossing US Border Falls," *Pew Research Center*, April 28, 2015, http://www.pewresearch.org/fact-tank/2015/04/28/child-migrants-border/. See also the following journalistic accounts: David Agren, "Central American Minors Risk All in Journeys North," *USA Today*, June 13, 2014, 6A; Laura Meckler and Jeffrey Sparshott, "Obama Directs Officials to Lead Relief for Children Crossing Borders," *Wall Street Journal*, June 2, 2014, http://online.wsj.com/articles/obama-directs-officials-to-lead-relief-for-children-crossing-border-1401749935; Ian Gordon, "Why Are More and More Children Walking across the Border?," *Mother Jones*, December 23, 2013, http://www.motherjones.com/politics/2013/12/unaccompanied-children-immigrants-surge-central-america-mexico.

85. Rosenblum, "Unaccompanied Child Migration," 5.

86. Ibid., 6.

87. US Customs and Border Protection, "Southwest Border Unaccompanied Alien Children Statistics FY 2016," http://www.cbp.gov/newsroom/stats/southwest-border-unaccompanied-children/fy-2016.

88. The Trafficking Victims Protection Reauthorization Act of 2008 (TVPRA) allows minors from countries other than Mexico and Canada to appear before an immigration judge to petition for humanitarian relief from removal. Children from Mexico and Canada are subject to a separate set of procedures.

89. Teenage children without proper identification are sometimes deported because they are incorrectly determined to be adults based on dental and wrist examinations. In the absence of identification papers, Immigration and Customs Enforcement (ICE) relies on such examinations, even though their reliability has been challenged by medical authorities. See Lawyer's Committee for Human Rights, "Refugees, Asylum Seekers and the New Department of Homeland Security: Initial Concerns and Preliminary Recommendations," March 2003, 11.

90. Office of Refugee Resettlement, "Unaccompanied Children Frequently Asked Questions," http://www.acf.hhs.gov/programs/orr/unaccompanied-children-frequently-asked-questions. See also Gordon, "More Children Walking."

91. Pierce, "Unaccompanied Child Migrants."

92. "Equal Justice America," https://www.equaljusticeamerica.org/.

93. US Department of Justice, Executive Office for Immigration Review, "Operating Policies and Procedures Memorandum 07-01: Guidelines for Immigration Court Cases Involving Unaccompanied Alien Children," May 22, 2007, http://www.justice.gov/sites/default/files/eoir/legacy/2007/05/22/07-01.pdf.

94. SJI visa holders can never petition for a green card for their parents, and they cannot petition for a green card for their siblings until they become US citizens. "Special Immigrant Juvenile Status," https://www.uscis.gov/green-card/special-immigrant-juveniles/special-immigrant-juveniles-sij-status.

95. Rosenblum, "Unaccompanied Child Migration," 7–8.

96. National Immigrant Justice Center, "Policy Brief: Unaccompanied Immigrant Children," January 14, 2014, https://immigrantjustice.org/sites/immigrantjustice.org/files/NIJC%20Policy%20Brief%20-%20Unaccompanied%20Immigrant%20Children%20FINAL%20Winter%202014.pdf.

97. UNHCR, "Protecting Refugees: Questions and Answers," February 1, 2002, http://www.unhcr.org/3b779dfe2.html.

98. Wasem, "US Immigration Policy on Asylum Seekers," 2.

99. The generally accepted international definition of "child" is every person under the age of 18. See Memorandum from Jeff Weiss, Acting Director, Office of International Affairs, Department of Justice, "Guidelines for Children's Asylum Claims," December 10, 1998, 1, http://www.nlada.org/Training/Train_Civil/Equal_Justice/2007_Materials/109_2007_Kerwin_handout7.

100. Eben Kaplan, "Child Soldiers around the World," *Council on Foreign Relations*, December 2, 2005, http://www.cfr.org/human-rights/child-soldiers-around-world/p9331; United Nations, "Child Soldiers," http://www.un.org/cyberschoolbus/briefing/soldiers/soldiers.pdf.

101. Kaplan, "Child Soldiers."

102. Ishmael Beah, *A Long Way Gone: Memoirs of a Boy Soldier* (London: Harper Perennial, 2007).

103. Faith J. H. McDonnell and Grace Akallo, *Girl Soldier: A Story of Hope for Northern Uganda's Children* (Grand Rapids, MI: Chosen, 2007); "United Africans for Women and Children Rights," http://www.africanwomenrights.org/.

104. Ugandan Diaspora Team, "Ugandan Boxer, Former Child Soldier, Kassim Ouma 'The Dream,'" April 5, 2011, http://www.ugandandiaspora.com/ugandan-boxer-former-child-soldier-kassim-ouma-the-%E2%80%9Cthe-dream%E2%80%9D; Uzodinma Iweala, "'I Used to Carry a Gun, Now I Use My Gloves,'" *Guardian*, July 28, 2007, http://www.theguardian.com/sport/2007/jul/29/boxing.features; Bernard Fernández, "Ouma fighting memories

as child soldier in Uganda," *ESPN*, December 7, 2006, http://sports.espn. go.com/sports/boxing/news/story?id=2689218.

105. Lomong was kidnapped at age six to be a soldier but managed to escape. He is one of the thousands of refugees known as the "Lost Boys" of Sudan. Jessica Ellis, "Lopez Lomong: From War Child to US Olympics Star," *CNN*, August 9, 2012, http://edition.cnn.com/2012/08/06/sport/lopez-lomong-lost-boy/ index.html; Lopez Lomong and Steve Haas, "Running for My Life: A True Story," *Huffington Post*, August 3, 2012, http://www.huffingtonpost.com/lopez-lomong/running-for-my-life-a-tru_b_1739059.html.

106. Child soldiers who have fought in Afghanistan and Iraq are especially suspect. By 2008, the United States had detained over twenty-five hundred juveniles as enemy combatants, one hundred in Afghanistan and twenty-four hundred in Iraq. Leonard Birdsong, "Child Soldiers Seeking Asylum/ between a Rock and a Hard Place," *Birdsong's Law Blog*, January 26, 2011, http://birdsongslaw.com/.

107. "Immigration and Nationality Act," http://www.uscis.gov/iframe/ilink/ docView/SLB/HTML/SLB/act.html.

108. 18 U.S. Code § 2339B, "Providing Material Support or Resources to Designated Foreign Terrorist Organizations," https://www.law.cornell.edu/uscode/text/ 18/2339B.

109. *Matter of Izatula*, 20 I&N (BIA 1990), http://www.justice.gov/sites/default/ files/eoir/legacy/2012/08/14/3127.pdf.

110. Raio G. Krishnayya, "No Way Out: Representing Child Soldiers in Asylum Cases and Alternate Solutions to the Strict Liability Exclusion under the 'Persecution of Others' Clause," Indianapolis, IN, Center for Victim and Human Rights, 2009, 23, http://www.cvhr.org/Immigration-Law-Asylum-of-Child-Soldiers.pdf.

111. Meghana Nayak, *Who Is Worthy of Protection? Gender-Based Asylum and US Immigration Politics* (New York: Oxford University Press, 2015), 2.

112. Center for Gender and Refugee Studies, "Matter of Kasinga (1996)," http:// cgrs.uchastings.edu/our-work/matter-kasinga-1996.

113. For a discussion of this shift in the human rights discourse see Kelly J. Shannon, "The Right to Bodily Integrity," in Akira Iriye, Petra Goedde, and William I. Hitchcock, eds., *The Human Rights Revolution: An International History* (New York: Oxford University Press, 2012).

114. World Health Organization, "Female Genital Mutilation," updated February 2014, http://www.who.int/mediacentre/factsheets/fs241/en/.

115. *Matter of Kasinga*, 21 I. & N. Dec.357, 365 (BIA 1996).

116. Kim, "Female Genital Mutilation," 17–18.

117. 24 I&N Dec. 296 (BIA 2007), 24, http://www.justice.gov/eoir/vll/intdec/vol24/ 3584.pdf; I&N Dec. 617 (A.G. 2008), http://www.justice.gov/eoir/vll/intdec/ vol24/3622.pdf. See also Kim, "Female Genital Mutilation," 16–17, 21.

118. See, for example, *Gómez v. INS*, 947 f.2d 660,664 (2d Cir. 1991) as cited in Kim, "Female Genital Mutilation," 11. Kim writes that the closest a court has come to acknowledging gender as sufficient in itself to constitute a social group was *Fatin v. INS*. (12 F.3d 1240). The court held that "while gender could be used as the sole characteristic to link members of a particular social group, to do so would require the applicant to also show that sex was the sole reason for the persecution" (14).

119. The study was conducted by attorney Blaine Bookey at the Hastings Center for Gender and Refugee Studies at the University of California and reported in Molly Redden, "A Sex Trafficking Victory That Shows Just How Broken the System Is," *New Republic*, August 29, 2013, http://www.newrepublic.com/article/114512/obama-should-fix-gender-based-asylum-claims-he-leaves-office.

120. Ibid.

121. Reese, "America's Asylum Requests"; Warren Richey, "Asylum: Court Decision on Albanian Woman Could Create Showdown on US Rules," *Christian Science Monitor*, August 9, 2013, http://www.csmonitor.com/USA/Justice/2013/0809/Asylum-Court-decision-on-Albanian-woman-could-create-showdown-on-US-rules.

122. National Immigrant Justice Center, "Cece v. Holder," http://immigrantjustice.org/litigation/blog/cece-v-holder-0#.VZbeReejQ-8.

123. In a similar case, *Perdomo v. Holder*, the Ninth Circuit expanded the possibilities for asylum for women fleeing countries that permit femicide. The case involved thirty-four-year-old Lesly Yajayra Perdomo of Guatemala, who arrived in the United States in 1991, at age fifteen, and requested asylum based on membership in a persecuted social group: namely, Guatemalan women between the ages of fourteen and forty who face a high risk of murder. Over five thousand women have been murdered in Guatemala since 2001. Law enforcement offers little protection to victims of domestic abuse, sexual assault, torture, and other forms of violence. Both an immigration judge and the BIA rejected Perdomo's petition for asylum. The Ninth Circuit, however, found merit in her case and remanded it back to the BIA "to determine in the first instance whether women in Guatemala constitute a particular social group, and if so, whether [the respondent] has demonstrated a fear of persecution 'on account of' her membership in such a group." The BIA, in turn, remanded the case back to the immigration judge. Like Cece's case, the Perdomo case has significant consequences for thousands of women in asylum adjudication. *Perdomo v. Holder*. 611 F.3d 662 (9th Circ. 2010), http://www.readbag.com/cgrs-uchastings-pdfs-9th-circuit-decision-perdomo. "Asylum Victory for Guatemalan Women," *Courthouse News Service*, July 13, 2010, http://www.courthousenews.com/2010/07/13/28785.htm; Amy Lieberman, "Appeals Case Gives Hope to Guatemalan Refugees," *We News*, October 3, 2010, http://womensenews.org/print/8320.

124. *Matter of Toboso-Alfonso* (BIA, 1990), http://www.refworld.org/docid/3ae6b6b84.html.

125. Dorothy A. Harbeck and Ellen L. Buckwalter, "Asking and Telling: Identity and Persecution in Sexual Orientation Asylum Claims," *Immigration Law Advisor*, 2, no. 9 (September 2008), 2, http://www.justice.gov/eoir/vll/ILA-Newsleter/ILA%20Vol%202/vol2no9.pdf.

126. The advocacy group "Immigration Equality" updates its website with relevant case law to assist asylum seekers and their attorneys. Immigration Equality, "Asylum Decisions," http://immigrationequality.org/issues/law-library/asylum-decisions/.

127. *Hernandez-Montiel v. INS*, 225 F.3d 1084 (9th Cir. 2000), http://www1.umn.edu/humanrts/refugee/hernandez_v_ins-2000.html.

128. *Amanfi v. Ashcroft*, 328 F.3d 719 (3rd Cir. 2003), http://openjurist.org/328/f3d/719/amanfi-v-ashcroft; see also Harbeck and Showalter, 2.

129. Deborah Morgan, "Not Gay Enough for the Government: Racial and Sexual Stereotypes in Sexual Orientation Asylum Cases," *Law and Sexuality* 15 (2006): 136; see also Swetha Sridharan, "The Difficulties of US Asylum Claims Based on Sexual Orientation," *Migration Information Source*, October 29, 2008, http://www.migrationpolicy.org/article/difficulties-us-asylum-claims-based-sexual-orientation/.

130. Lambda Legal, "Soto Vega v. Gonzales," http://www.lambdalegal.org/in-court/cases/soto-vega-v-gonzales.

131. Andrew Calvario, "Advocacy Groups in Creating, Influencing, and Changing Asylum and Refugee Policy," Cornell University, October 4, 2011.

132. Sridharan, "Difficulties of US Asylum."

133. Joel Millman, "If You're Seeking Asylum, It Helps to Be Gay," *Wall Street Journal*, June 14, 2014, A1.

134. The guide is called "Guidance for Adjudicating Lesbian, Gay, Bisexual, Transgender, and Intersex (LGBTI) Refugee and Asylum Claims." See Millman, "If You're Seeking Asylum," A10.

135. Nayak, *Who Is Worthy*, 32.

136. William Finnegan, "The Countertraffickers," *New Yorker*, May 5, 2008, 47.

137. See Alison Siskin and Liana Sun Wyler, "Trafficking in Persons: US Policy and Issues for Congress," Congressional Research Service, February 27, 2013, http://www.fas.org/sgp/crs/row/RL34317.pdf.

138. Women's Commission for Refugee Women and Children, "The US Response to Human Trafficking: An Unbalanced Approach," May 2007, 10, http://www.humantrafficking.org/uploads/publications/ustraff.pdf.

139. The Violence against Women Act declared certain forms of violence against women federal crimes. "Memorandum on Steps to Combat Violence Against Women and Trafficking in Women and Girls," March 11, 1998, http://www.gpo.gov/fdsys/pkg/WCPD-1998-03-16/pdf/WCPD-1998-03-16-Pg412.pdf; Office of the Historian, *Department of State during Clinton Presidency*, 78.

140. The trafficking protocol was one of two of the so-called Palermo Protocols, the other of which addressed smuggling. The protocol built on previous international instruments including the Convention on the Rights of the Child (1990) that addressed the abduction, sale, and trafficking of children, but which the United States had not yet signed; and the Convention on the Elimination of All Forms of Discrimination against Women (1981) that addressed sexual and labor exploitation, which the US had signed but not yet ratified.

141. United Nations Convention Against Transnational Organized Crime and the Protocols Thereto, http://www.unodc.org/documents/treaties/UNTOC/Publications/TOC%20Convention/TOCebook-e.pdf.

142. Jacqueline Bhabba, "Trafficking, Smuggling, and Human Rights," *Migration Information Source*, March 1, 2005, http://www.migrationpolicy.org/article/trafficking-smuggling-and-human-rights/. For the federal government's distinctions between trafficking and smuggling see Human Smuggling and Trafficking Center, "Fact Sheet: Distinctions Between Human Smuggling and Human Trafficking," January 2005, https://www.hsdl.org/?view&did=23324.

143. United Nations Office on Drugs and Crime, "'Put Yourself in My Shoes': A Human Trafficking Victim Speaks Out," http://www.unodc.org/unodc/en/frontpage/2012/November/put-yourself-in-my-in-my-shoes-a-human-trafficking-victim-speaks-out.html.

144. Bhabba, "Trafficking, Smuggling"; Finnegan, "The Countertraffickers," 46; Siskin and Wyler, "Trafficking in Persons," 1–2.

145. Finnegan, "The Countertraffickers," 46–47.

146. Office of the Historian, *Department of State during Clinton Presidency*, 78; Women's Commission for Refugee Women and Children, "US Response to Trafficking."

147. The law also reauthorized the Violence against Women Act (2000). Further protections for trafficking victims were offered through the Trafficking Victims Protection Reauthorization Act of 2003 (HR 2620), the Trafficking Victims Protection Reauthorization Act of 2005 (HR 972), the Trafficking Victims Protection Reauthorization Act of 2008 (HR 7311). See also Women's Commission for Refugee Women and Children, "US Response to Trafficking."

148. According to the Women's Commission for Refugee Women and Children, the TVPA originated in federal prosecutors having limited ability to prosecute involuntary servitude and slavery cases. See "US Response to Trafficking," 10.

149. Siskin and Wyler, "Trafficking in Persons," 2; Women's Commission for Refugee Women and Children, "US Response to Trafficking," 1, 14–15.

150. The 2003 reauthorization of the TVPA provided for cutting off aid to NGOs and governments that supported or advocated for the legalization of prostitution. Finnegan, "The Countertraffickers," 54.

151. Kristin M. Finklea, Adrienne L. Fernandes-Alcantara, and Alison Siskin, "Sex Trafficking of Children in the United States: Overview and Issues for

Congress," Congressional Research Service, August 15, 2012, http://www.fas.
org/sgp/crs/misc/R41878.pdf.

152. Minor children and those unable to cooperate because of psychological or physical trauma are exempted.

153. Department of Homeland Security, "U Visa Law Enforcement Certification
Resource Guide for Federal, State, Local, Tribal and Territorial Law
Enforcement." PL 106-386, 114 Stat. 1464–1548 (2000), http://www.dhs.gov/
xlibrary/assets/dhs_u_visa_certification_guide.pdf.

154. UNHCR, *Guidelines on International Protection: Gender Related Persecution*
(2002).

155. In July 2004, the attorney general and the secretaries of the Departments of
State and Homeland Security signed a charter to establish a Human Smuggling
and Trafficking Center (HSTC) to serve as the federal clearinghouse and intel-
ligence center for all federal agencies addressing issues of smuggling, traffick-
ing, and the potential use of smuggling routes by terrorists. Office of the Press
Secretary, "Trafficking in Persons National Security Presidential Directive,"
February 25, 2003, http://www.fas.org/irp/offdocs/nspd/trafpers.html;
Finklea, Fernandes-Alcantara, and Siskin, "Sex Trafficking of Children," 18.

156. Finnegan, "The Countertraffickers," 54.

157. Siskin and Wyler, "Trafficking in Persons"; Clare Ribando Seelke, "Trafficking
in Persons in Latin America and the Caribbean," Congressional Research
Service, July 15, 2013, 1, http://www.fas.org/sgp/crs/row/RL33200.pdf.

158. Women's Commission for Refugee Women and Children, "US Response to
Trafficking," 10–11; Siskin and Wyler, "Trafficking in Persons," 19–21, 35–36.

159. Siskin and Wyler, "Trafficking in Persons," 21.

160. Between 2006 and 2011, for example, the thirty-one groups that form part of
the Western New York Human Trafficking Task Force claimed to have rescued three hundred thousand victims. Annette Jimenez, "Modern-Day Slavery
Decried," *Catholic Courier*, October 2011, 10.

161. Worldwide, the number of trafficking victims is even larger. In 2013, the
Department of State estimated that as many as twenty-seven million people
worldwide may be trafficking victims (the largest number are in Africa and
Europe). The United Nations Office on Drugs and Crime (UNODC) estimated
that 58 percent of all trafficking cases worldwide involved sex trafficking, while
36 percent involved labor trafficking. Twenty-seven percent of all trafficking victims were children used for "child sex tourism, forced child begging, domestic
servitude, and … in armed conflicts as soldiers, porters, cooks, messengers,
and sex slaves." In the wake of the 2010 earthquake and hurricane that affected
Haiti, for example, an estimated seventy-three boys and girls were smuggled
or trafficked into the Dominican Republic to work as maids, cooks, and prostitutes; the average cost of buying a child or a teenager was eighty dollars. See
Department of Homeland Security, "DHS and Western Union Announce

New Alliance to Combat Human Trafficking," November 6, 2013, http://www.
dhs.gov/news/2013/11/06/dhs-and-western-union-announce-new-alliance-
combat-human-trafficking; Seelke, "Trafficking in Persons," 1; Siskin and
Wyler, "Trafficking in Persons," 7–8; Maria Elena Salinas, "Trafficking Another
Disaster in Hard-Hit Haiti," *Denver Post*, November 27, 2010, http://www.den-
verpost.com/ci_16719655.

162. Migration Policy Institute, "Top 10 Migration Issues of 2005 Issue #10: Record
Numbers Displaced by Natural Disasters," *Migration Information Source*,
December 1, 2005, http://www.migrationpolicy.org/article/top-10-migration-
issues-2005-issue-10-record-numbers-displaced-natural-disasters/.

163. One study noted, "[While] we find no indications that environmental disasters directly trigger armed conflicts, our results imply that disasters might act
as a threat multiplier in several of the world's most conflict prone regions."
Schleussner et al., "Armed-Conflict Risks."

164. Eric Holthaus, "'Climate Change War' is Not a Metaphor," *Grist*, April 21, 2014,
http://grist.org/climate-energy/climate-change-war-is-not-metaphor/?utm_
source=facebook&utm_medium=update&utm_campaign=socialflow.

165. Carolina Fritz, "Climate Change and Migration: Sorting through Complex
Issues without the Hype," *Migration Information Source*, March 4, 2010, 7,
http://www.migrationpolicy.org/article/climate-change-and-migration-sorting-
through-complex-issues-without-hype/; Diane Bates, "Environmental Refugees?
Classifying Human Migrations Caused by Environmental Change," *Population
and Environment* 23.5 (2002): 465–477; Norman Myers, "Environmental
Refugees," *Population and Environment* 19.2 (1997): 167–182; Idean Salehyan,
"The New Myth about Climate Change," *Foreign Policy*, August 14, 2007, http://
www.foreignpolicy.com/articles/2007/08/13/the_new_myth_about_climate_
change.

166. US Citizenship and Immigration Services, "What Is TPS?," http://www.uscis.
gov/humanitarian/temporary-protected-status-deferred-enforced-departure/
temporary-protected-status#What%20is%20TPS?

167. Fritz, "Climate Change and Migration," 1–2.

168. Amnesty International, *Lost in the Labyrinth: Detention of Asylum-Seekers*,
September 1999, 2. A brief summary of this 1999 report is available at http://
www.amnesty.org/en/library/asset/AMR51/115/1999/en/ca61a6c6-e0e6-
11dd-aaeb-414a3b04625c/amr511151999en.html. The detention of asylum
seekers is discussed in the 1951 Convention, the International Covenant on
Civil and Political Rights (ICCPR), the Convention Against Torture and Other
Cruel, Inhuman or Degrading Treatment or Punishment (Convention Against
Torture), and the Convention on the Rights of the Child. Nontreaty standards
that have been adopted by consensus by UN member states include the UN
Standard Minimum Rules for the Treatment of Prisoners; the UN Body of
Principles for the Protection of All Persons Under Any Form of Detention or

Imprisonment; and the UN Rules for the Protection of Juveniles Deprived of their Liberty.

169. In February 2004, the Lawyer's Committee filed a FOIA request for information relating to the detention and parole of asylum seekers, including information required to be provided to Congress. At the time the study went to press, the DHS had not provided this information. Acer and Pyati, *In Liberty's Shadow*, 13–14.

170. García, *Seeking Refuge*, 108–109.

171. US Committee for Refugees, *Refugees at Our Border: The US Response to Asylum Seekers* (American Council for Nationalities Service, 1989), 19; see also University of Michigan Law School, Civil Rights Litigation Clearinghouse, "Case Profile: Orantes-Hernández v. Meese," http://www.clearinghouse.net/detail.php?id=10185.

172. Amnesty International, *Lost in the Labyrinth*, 2.

173. Ibid.

174. Detention Watch Network, "About the US Detention and Deportation System," http://www.detentionwatchnetwork.org/resources. See also Acer and Pyati, *In Liberty's Shadow*, 38; National Immigration Forum, "The Math of Immigration Detention: Runaway Costs for Immigration Detention Do Not Add Up to Sensible Policies," August 2013, 1, http://www.immigrationforum.org/images/uploads/mathofimmigrationdetention.pdf.

175. Corrections Corporation of America, "Who We Are," http://cca.com/who-we-are.

176. Scott DeCarlo, "America's Best Big Companies," December 22, 2008, http://www.forbes.com/2008/12/22/best-big-companies-biz-cz_sd_bigcompanies08_1222land.html.

177. National Immigration Forum, "Math of Immigration Detention," 7.

178. Jonathan Kaminsky, "Immigrant Detainees in Wash. on Hunger Strike," *Washington Post*, March 9, 2014, A8.

179. Of the thirty-six cosponsors of Arizona's controversial S.B. 1070 law, thirty received campaign contributions from private prison lobbyists. Justice Policy Institute, "Gaming the System" (June 22, 2011), 30, cited in National Immigration Forum, "Math of Immigration Detention," 1.

180. Roger Sherman, "FAU Drops GEO Group Stadium Deal amid Controversy: Say Bye to Owlcatraz," *SBNation*, April 2, 2013, http://www.sbnation.com/college-football/2013/4/2/4017440/fau-stadium-geo-group-prison-company.

181. Juliet Stumpf, "The Crimmigration Crisis: Immigrants, Crime, and Sovereign Power," *American University Law Review* 56.2 (2006–2007): 367–420. See also Juliet P. Stumpf, "Doing Time: Crimmigration Law and the Perils of Haste," *UCLA Law Review* 58.6 (2010–2011): 1705–1748; and Alissa Ackerman and Rich Furman, *The Criminalization of Immigration: Contexts and Consequences* (Durham: Carolina Academic Press, 2014). See also César Cuauhtémoc García

Hernández, *Crimmigration Law* (Chicago: American Bar Association, 2015); Julie A. Dowling, and Jonathan Xavier Inda, eds., *Governing Immigration through Crime: A Reader* (Stanford, CA: Stanford Social Sciences, an imprint of Stanford University Press, 2013).

182. Detention Watch Network, "US Detention and Deportation."
183. See, for example, Schoenholtz, Schrag, and Ramji-Nogales, *Lives in the Balance.* See also the authors' edited collection *Refugee Roulette.*
184. See, for example, Kerwin, *Faltering Refugee Protection System.*
185. For a full list of recommendations see Human Rights First, *How to Repair the US Asylum and Refugee Resettlement Systems,* December 2012, https://www. humanrightsfirst.org/wp-content/uploads/pdf/asylum_blueprint.pdf.
186. Dan Cadman, "Asylum in the United States," *Center for Immigration Studies Backgrounder,* March 2014, http://cis.org/asylum-system-checks-balances-dismantled.
187. US Committee for Refugees, *Despite a Generous Spirit: Denying Asylum in the United States* (American Council for Nationalities Service, 1986), 45–46.

CONCLUSION

1. The estimates are based on figures from the *Yearbook of Immigration Statistics,* table 13, "Refugee Arrivals," https://www.dhs.gov/immigration-statistics/ yearbook/2015; UNHCR, "Resettlement in the United States," http://www. unhcr.org/en-us/resettlement-in-the-united-states.html; in 2015, for example, the United States accommodated more refugees than the other four leading nations—Canada, Australia, Norway, and the United Kingdom. UNHCR, "Resettlement Fact Sheet 2015," http://www.unhcr.org/en-us/524c31a09.
2. American Immigration Council, "Fact Sheet: Asylum in the United States," August 22, 2016, https://www.americanimmigrationcouncil.org/research/ asylum-united-states.
3. Bonnie Malkin, "Donald J. Trump Compares Syrian Refugees to Poisoned Skittles," *Guardian,* September 20, 2016, https://www.theguardian.com/us-news/2016/sep/20/donald-trump-jnr-compares-refugees-poisoned-skittles-twitter-reacted; Deborah Amos, "For Refugees and Advocates, an Anxious Wait for Clarity on Trump's Policy," November 15, 2016, http://www.npr.org/sections/ parallels/2016/11/15/502010346/for-refugees-and-advocates-an-anxious-wait-for-clarity-on-trumps-policy; HIAS, "HAS v. Trump: Why We're Suing," February 7, 2017, https://www.hias.org/blog/hias-v-trump-why-were-suing.
4. María Cristina García, "America Has Never Actually Welcomed the World's Huddled Masses," *Washington Post,* November 20, 2015, https://www.wash-ingtonpost.com/opinions/america-has-never-actually-welcomed-the-worlds-huddled-masses/2015/11/20/6763fad0-8e71-11e5-ae1f-af46b7df8483_story. html?utm_term=.8a2d3fa456d4.

5. Keck and Sikkink, *Activists beyond Borders*, ix–x.

6. US Department of State, "US Refugee Admissions Program," https://www.state.gov/j/prm/ra/admissions/; The White House, "Infographic: The Screening Process for refugee Entry into the United States," November 20, 2015, https://www.whitehouse.gov/blog/2015/11/20/infographic-screening-process-refugee-entry-united-states. An immigration visa is not guaranteed to any applicant. It may take certain categories of applicants from the top immigrant-sending countries like Mexico and the Philippines as long as two decades to receive permission to immigrate to the United States. Suzy Khimm, "How Long Is the Immigration 'Line'? As Long as 24 Years," *Washington Post*, January 31, 2013, https://www.washingtonpost.com/news/wonk/wp/2013/01/31/how-long-is-the-immigration-line-as-long-as-24-years/?utm_term=.27ca7e0baa5c.

7. Matthew Gibney, "Liberal Democratic States and Responsibilities to Refugees," *American Political Science Review* 93 (March 1999): 170–171.

8. Ruth Ellen Wasem, "US Immigration Policy on Asylum Seekers," Congressional Research Service, January 25, 2007, 2. Data from the period 2001–2014 was compiled from the *Yearbook of Immigration Statistics*, https://www.dhs.gov/immigration-statistics/yearbook.

9. US Department of State, Bureau of Population, Refugees, and Migration, "What We Do," http://www.state.gov/g/prm/c25756.htm. The refugees and asylees that the United States has accepted also represent a small percentage of the immigrants admitted overall—less than 10 percent.

10. See, for example, Colum Lynch, "The Whistleblower: The Movie the UN Would Prefer You Didn't See," *Foreign Policy*, June 29, 2011, http://foreignpolicy.com/2011/06/29/the-whistleblower-the-movie-the-u-n-would-prefer-you-didnt-see/; Lauren Wolfe, "The UN Is Not Serious about Its Peacekeeper Rape Problem," *Foreign Policy*, August 13, 2015, http://foreignpolicy.com/2015/08/13/bangui-un-car-minusca-sexual-violence-rape/; Kevin Sieff, "The Growing UN Scandal over Sex Abuse and 'Peacekeeper Babies,'" *Washington Post*, February 27, 2016, http://www.washingtonpost.com/sf/world/2016/02/27/peacekeepers/.

11. "US Immigration Dilemma: Is There Too Much 'Compassion?,'" *Christian Science Monitor*, December 9, 1980.

12. See, for example, Elizabeth Ferris, "World Refugee Day: Honoring Refugees, Resolving to Prevent Further Displacement," June 20, 2013, http://www.brookings.edu/blogs/up-front/posts/2013/06/20-world-refugee-day-ferris. UNHCR officials pursue three basic solutions to refugee crises—voluntary repatriation, integration in host societies, or resettlement. While the details of these so-called durable solutions are worked out, aid workers must meet refugees' immediate needs: housing, food, water, and medical care.

13. Guy S. Goodwin-Gill and Selim Can Sazak, "Footing the Bill: Refugee-Creating States' Responsibility to Pay," July 29, 2015, https://www.foreignaffairs.com/articles/africa/2015-07-29/footing-bill.

14. The suggested policy had international precedent. Following the first Gulf War in 1991, the UN Security Council cited Chapter VII of the UN Charter to hold Iraq liable for losses that resulted from its unlawful invasion and occupation of Kuwait. The UN created a compensation fund to be financed through a percentage of Iraq's oil exports. Ibid.

15. UNHCR, "Facts and Figures about Refugees," http://www.unhcr.org.uk/about-us/key-facts-and-figures.html; "On World Refugee Day, UN Chief Appeals for Hearts to be Open to Refugees Elsewhere," http://www.un.org/apps/news/story.asp?NewsID=51208#.Vb_E8rejQTk; UNHCR, "Worldwide Displacement Reaches All-Time High as War and Persecution Increases," June 18, 2015, http://www.unhcr.org/en-us/news/latest/2015/6/558193896/worldwide-displacement-hits-all-time-high-war-persecution-increase.html.

16. In 2012, for example, the United States provided more humanitarian aid than any other nation: $3.8 billion, or 29.4 percent of all humanitarian aid. Jon Greenberg, "Obama: US Is Largest Donor for Displaced persons, Refugee Relief," *Politifact*, November 17, 2015, http://www.politifact.com/truth-o-meter/statements/2015/nov/17/barack-obama/obama-us-largest-donor-displaced-personsrefugee-re/.

Bibliography

ARCHIVAL COLLECTIONS
George H. W. Bush Presidential Library

White House Office of Records Management Subject File
    Alphabetical File, 1989–1993
    Subject File CO—Countries
    Subject File FA—Foreign Affairs
    Subject File HU—Human Rights
    Subject File—International Organizations
    Subject File IM—Immigration
    Subject File PR—Public Relations

Staff and Office Files
    Office to the Chief of Staff to the President
        Papers of James A. Baker, III
    Office of Communications
        Papers of David Demarest
        Papers of Kathy Jeavons
    Correspondence Office
        Papers of Jan Burmeister
        Correspondence re: China [1989–1993]
        Correspondence re: Persian Gulf 1990–1991
    Office of Intergovernmental Affairs
        Papers of Cliff Alderman
        Papers of Debra Anderson
        Papers of Barbara Kilberg

Office of Legislative Affairs
    East Wing (EW) Congressional Files [1989–1993]
Office of the Assistant to the President for National Security Affairs
        Declassified National Security Directives (NSD's) and National Security
            Reviews (NSR's) [1989–1993]
        Papers of Nicholas A. Burns
    Papers of Richard Clarke
    Papers of Lorne Craner
    Papers of Nancy Bearg Dyke
    Papers of Robert M. Gates
    Papers of Charles A. Gillespie, Jr.
    Papers of Richard N. Haass
    Papers of Jane Hull
    Papers of Robert L. Hutchings
    Papers of Virginia Lampley
    Papers of John McShane
    Papers of William T. Pryce
    Papers of Condoleeza Rice
    Papers of Brent Scowcroft
    Papers of Nicholas Rostow
    Papers of Michael A. Sheehan
Office of the Press Secretary
    Daily Press Briefings 1989–1993
    Daily Press Releases 1989–1993
    News Summaries 1989–1993
    Press Briefings and Releases 1989–1993
    Subject File [1989–1993]
    Weekly Compilation of Presidential Documents 1989–1993
Office of Public Liaison
    Papers of Charles Bacarisse
    Papers of Sarah DeCamp
    Papers of David Demarest
    Papers of Clayton Fong
    Papers of Leigh Ann Metzger
    Papers of Shiree Sanchez
    Papers of Charles James Schaefer
    Papers of Sichan Siv
    Papers of Scott Sutherland
    Papers of Douglas Wead
    Papers of Lindley H. White

MILLER CENTER, UNIVERSITY OF VIRGINIA

Edward M. Kennedy Oral History Collection
William J. Clinton Presidential History Project
George H.W. Bush Presidential History Project
George W. Bush Presidential History Project
Ronald Reagan Presidential History Project

NATIONAL ARCHIVES AND RECORDS ADMINISTRATION,
COLLEGE PARK, MD

General Records of the Department of Justice
    Office of the Attorney General, RG 60

A 1091
Box 605
    Asylum 1991
    Attorney General 1991
Box 620
    Congressional Correspondence
Box 637
    Immigration, General
Box 638
    Immigration, Krome
    Immigration, Temporary Protected Status
    Immigration, Vietnamese
Box 722
    Immigration Act of 1990
    Immigration reform and Control Act 1986
Box 741
    Asylum 1990
Box 783
    Immigration, Chinese
    Immigration, General
    Immigration, Romanians
    Immigration, Russians
Box 784
    Immigration, Temporary Protected Status
        P 101
Box 17
    Papers of Gene McNary

NATIONAL SECURITY ARCHIVE

Electronic Briefing Books
   China and East Asia
      Tiananmen at 25 Years
      The US "Tiananmen Papers"
      Tiananmen Square 1989
   The September 11 Sourcebooks
   Volume 1: Terrorism and US Policy
   Humanitarian Interventions
      Srebrenica conference documents detail path to genocide
      Rwanda Pullout Driven by Clinton White House, UN Equivocation
      Rwanda reexamined
      Rwanda: The Failure of the Arusha Accords
      Rwandan Refugee Crisis: Before the Genocide
      Warnings of Catastrophes
      The US and Genocide in Rwanda 1994
Digital National Security Archive

RONALD REAGAN PRESIDENTIAL LIBRARY

White House Office of Records Management Subject File
   Subject File CO—Countries
   Subject File FA—Foreign Affairs
   Subject File IM—Immigration/Naturalization

WILLIAM JEFFERSON CLINTON PRESIDENTIAL LIBRARY

Clinton Digital Library
   Audiovisual Collections
      Audio Recordings of the White House Communications Agency
      Video Recordings of the White House Television Office
   Bosnian Declassified Records
   White House Staff and Office Collections
      National Security Council
         Office of Records Management-Presidential Decisions Directives
         Office of Records Management-Presidential Review Directives
         Speechwriting Offices

Roper Center for Public Opinion Research, Cornell University

PERIODICALS AND ONLINE NEWS SOURCES

Christian Science Monitor
El Paso Times
Gallup News Service
The Guardian
History
Huffington Post
Los Angeles Times
Miami Herald
New York Times
New Yorker
Newsweek
Reuters
Time
Washington Post
Washington Times

SELECT SOURCES

Acer, Eleanor, and Archana Pyati. *In Liberty's Shadow: US Detention of Asylum Seekers in the Era of Homeland Security.* New York: Human Rights First, 2004.

Ackerman, Alissa, and Rich Furman. *The Criminalization of Immigration: Contexts and Consequences.* Durham: Carolina Academic Press, 2014.

"The Aegis Trust." http://www.aegistrust.org/.

"African Growth and Opportunity Act." http://trade.gov/agoa/.

Aftermath of War: The Persian Gulf Refugee Crisis. A Staff Report Prepared for the Use of the Subcommittee on Immigration and Refugee Affairs of the Committee on the Judiciary, United States Senate, 102nd Congress, First Session. Washington, DC: Government Printing Office, 1991.

Alleged Intimidation and Harassment of Chinese Citizens in the United States: Hearing before the Subcommittee on Human Rights and International Organizations, and on Asian and Pacific Affairs of the Committee on Foreign Affairs, House of Representatives, 101st Congress, Second Session, June 19, 1990. Washington, DC: Government Printing Office, 1991.

American Civil Liberties Union. "American Exile: Rapid Deportations That Bypass the Courtroom." December 2014. https://www.aclu.org/feature/american-exile.

American Civil Liberties Union. "Bush's Spin on the War on Terror." September 12, 2006. https://www.aclu.org/national-security/bushs-spin-war-terror.

American Immigration Council. "Court Approves Settlement in National Class Action Lawsuit on Work Authorization for Asylum Seekers." November 5,

2013. http://www.americanimmigrationcouncil.org/newsroom/release/court-approves-settlement-national-class-action-lawsuit-work-authorization-asylum-s.

American Jewish Historical Society. "Historical Note." *Guide to the Records of Chicago Action for Soviet Jewry.* http://digifindingaids.cjh.org/?pID=1485864.

Americas Watch. *Silencing a People: The Destruction of Civil Society in Haiti.* New York: Human Rights Watch, February 1993.

Americas Watch, National Coalition for Haitian Refugees, and Jesuit Refugee Services. *No Port in a Storm: The Misguided Use of In-Country Refugee Processing Center in Haiti.* September 1993.

Amnesty International. "Humanitarian Efforts Failing the Hundreds of Thousands Forced to Flee Ethnic Cleansing in Northern Iraq." August 11, 2014. http://www.amnestyusa.org/news/news-item/humanitarian-efforts-failing-the-hundreds-of-thousands-forced-to-flee-ethnic-cleansing-in-northern-i.

Amnesty International. *Lost in the Labyrinth: Detention of Asylum-Seekers.* September 1999. http://www.amnesty.org/en/library/asset/AMR51/115/1999/en/ca61a6c6-e0e6-11dd-aaeb-414a3b04625c/amr511151999en.html.

Anderson, Kenneth. *Yugoslavia, Crisis in Kosovo: A Report from Helsinki Watch and the International Helsinki Federation for Human Rights.* New York: Helsinki Watch, 1990.

Arnson, Cynthia, and Eric L. Olson, eds. *Organized Crime in Central America: The Northern Triangle.* Woodrow Wilson Center Reports on the Americas No. 29, http://www.wilsoncenter.org/sites/default/files/LAP_single_page.pdf.

Baker, James, Lee H. Hamilton, et al. "The Iraq Study Group Report." http://media.usip.org/reports/iraq_study_group_report.pdf.

Banta, Benjamin R. "Just War Theory and the 2003 Iraq War Forced Displacement." *Journal of Refugee Studies* 21.3 (2008): 261–284.

Barnett, Michael N. *Empire of Humanity: A History of Humanitarianism.* Ithaca, NY: Cornell University Press, 2011.

Barnett, Michael N. *Eyewitness to a Genocide: The United Nations and Rwanda.* Ithaca, NY: Cornell University Press, 2003.

Barnett, Michael N., and Martha Finnemore. *Rules for the World: International Organizations in Global Politics.* Ithaca, NY: Cornell University Press, 2004.

Bass, Gary Jonathan. *Freedom's Battle: The Origins of Humanitarian Intervention.* New York: Knopf, 2008.

Bates, Diane. "Environmental Refugees? Classifying Human Migrations Caused by Environmental Change." *Population and Environment* 23.5 (2002): 465–477.

Beah, Ishmael. *A Long Way Gone: Memoirs of a Boy Soldier.* London: Harper Perennial, 2007.

Beckerman, Gal. *When They Come for Us, We'll Be Gone: The Epic Struggle to Save Soviet Jewry.* New York: Houghton Mifflin, 2010.

Becoming an American: Immigration and Immigrant Policy. 1997 Executive Summary. Washington, DC: US Commission on Immigration Reform, 1997.

Benjamin, Daniel, and Steven Simon. *The Age of Sacred Terror*. New York: Random House, 2002.

Benton, Leslie A., and Glenn T. Ware. "Haiti: A Case Study of the International Response and the Efficacy of Nongovernmental Organizations in the Crisis." *Emory International Law Review* 12.2 (1998): 851–934.

Beyer, Gregg A. "Reforming Affirmative Asylum Processing in the United States: Challenges and Opportunities." *American University International Law Review* 9.4 (1994): 43–78.

Bhabba, Jacqueline. "Trafficking, Smuggling, and Human Rights." *Migration Information Source*. March 1, 2005. http://www.migrationpolicy.org/article/trafficking-smuggling-and-human-rights/.

Birdsong, Leonard. "Child Soldiers Seeking Asylum between a Rock and a Hard Place." *Birdsong's Law Blog*, January 26, 2011. http://birdsongslaw.com/.

Black, George. *Genocide in Iraq: The Anfal Campaign against the Kurds*. New York: Human Rights Watch, 1993.

Boerman, Thomas. "Central American Gang Related Asylum Cases: Background, Leverage Points and the Use of Expert Witnesses." *Immigration Daily*. http://www.ilw.com/articles/2009,125-boerman.shtm.

Bohmer, Carol, and Amy Shuman. *Rejecting Refugees: Political Asylum in the 21st Century*. London: Routledge, 2008.

Bon Tempo, Carl J. *Americans at the Gate: The United States and Refugees during the Cold War*. Princeton, NJ: Princeton University Press, 2008.

Bosnian Refugees: Hearing before the Subcommittee on International Operations and Human Rights of the Committee on International Relations, House of Representatives, 104th Congress, First Session, September 28, 1995. Washington, DC: Government Printing Office, 1996.

Bourbeau, Philippe. *The Securitization of Migration: A Study of Movement and Order*. Milton Park, Abingdon, Oxon: Routledge, 2011.

Brands, Hal. "Crime, Violence, and the Crisis in Guatemala: A Case Study in the Erosion of the State." Strategic Studies Institute, US Army War College, May 2010. http://strategicstudiesinstitute.army.mil/pdffiles/PUB986.pdf.

Bruno, Andorra. "Refugee Admissions and Resettlement Policy." Congressional Research Service, March 6, 2014, http://www.fas.org/sgp/crs/misc/RL31269.pdf.

Brysk, Alison. *Speaking Rights to Power: Constructing Political Will*. New York: Oxford University Press, 2013.

Buckley, Mary, and Rick Fawn, eds. *Global Responses to Terrorism: 9/11, Afghanistan and Beyond*. New York: Routledge, 2003.

Bunce, Valerie. *Subversive Institutions: The Design and the Destruction of Socialism and the State*. Cambridge: Cambridge University Press, 1999.

Bunce, Valerie, and Sharon L. Wolchik. *Defeating Authoritarian Leaders in Postcommunist Countries*. Cambridge: Cambridge University Press, 2011.

Buruma, Ian. *Bad Elements: Chinese Rebels from Los Angeles to Beijing*. New York: Random House, 2001.

Bush, George H. W. "Executive Order 12711—Policy Implementation with Respect to Nationals of the People's Republic of China." April 11, 1990. Online by Gerhard Peters and John T. Woolley, *The American Presidency Project*. http://www.presidency.ucsb.edu/ws/?pid=23556.

Buzan, Barry, Ole Wæver, and Jaap de Wilde. *Security: A New Framework for Analysis*. Boulder, CO: Lynne Rienner, 1998.

Cadman, Dan. "Asylum in the United States." *Center for Immigration Studies Backgrounder*. March 2014. http://cis.org/asylum-system-checks-balances-dismantled.

Carpenter, Andrew. "Mexican Asylum Seekers Disproportionately Rejected." *Latin America Working Group*, August 24, 2011. http://www.lawg.org/action-center/lawg-blog/69-general/914-mexican-asylum-seekers-disproportionately-rejected.

Castro, Max J. *Free Markets, Open Societies, Closed Borders? Trends in International Migration and Immigration Policy in the Americas*. Coral Gables, FL: North-South Center Press, 1999.

Center for Gender and Refugee Studies. "Matter of Kasinga (1996)." http://cgrs.uchastings.edu/our-work/matter-kasinga-1996.

Chai Ling. *A Heart for Freedom: The Remarkable Journey of a Young Dissident, Her Daring Escape, and Her Quest to Free China's Daughters*. Carol Stream, IL: Tyndale House, 2011.

Chebel d'Appollonia, Ariane. *Frontiers of Fear: Immigration and Insecurity in the United States and Europe*. Ithaca, NY: Cornell University Press, 2012.

Chebel d'Appollonia, Ariane. *Migrant Mobilization and Securitization in the US and Europe: How Does It Feel to Be a Threat?* New York: Palgrave Macmillan, 2015.

Chinese Students in America and Human Rights in China: Hearing before the Subcommittee on Immigration and Refugee Affairs of the Committee on the Judiciary, US Senate, 101st Congress, Second Session on H.R. 2712, January 23, 1990. Washington, DC: Government Printing Office, 1991.

Chomsky, Noam. *The New Military Humanism: Lessons from Kosovo*. Monroe, ME: Common Courage Press, 1999.

Clarke, Richard A. *Against All Enemies: Inside America's War on Terror*. New York: Free Press, 2004.

Clarke, Kevin. "Amnesty International Report Details ISIS Abuses." *America*, September 3, 2014. http://americamagazine.org/content/all-things/amnesty-international-report-details-isis-abuses.

Clinton, Bill. *My Life*. New York: Alfred A. Knopf, 2004.

Clinton Administration History Project. *A History of the US Department of Justice during the Clinton Administration, 1993–2001*. Washington, DC, 2001. http://www.clintonlibrary.gov/assets/DigitalLibrary/AdminHistories/Box%20011-020/Box%20014/1225098-justice-1.pdf.

Cohen, Roberta. "Afghanistan and the Challenges of Humanitarian Action in Time of war." *Forced Migration Review* 13 (June 2002): 23–28. http://www.fmreview.org/FMRpdfs/FMR13/fmr13.9.pdf.

Cohen, Roberta, and David A. Korn. "Refugees and Internally Displaced: Some Lessons from the Kosovo Crisis." *Refuge* 18.3 (1999): 37.

Collins, Lauren. "The Children's Odyssey." *New Yorker*, February 27, 2017.

"Columbia's Forgotten Human Rights Beacon." *The Current*, Winter 2007. http://www.columbia.edu/cu/current/articles/spring2008/from-the-editors.html.

Cooper, Mary H. "Foreign Affairs: 'We Have a Hard Life Here.'" *CQ Weekly*, May 8, 1999, 1094–1095. http://library.cqpress.com.proxy.library.cornell.edu/cqweekly/WR19990508-19KOSOVOREFUGEE001.

Coughlan, Reed, and Judith Owens-Manley. *Bosnian Refugees in America: New Communities, New Cultures*. New York: Springer, 2006.

Crisis in Central Africa: Hearing before the Subcommittee on African Affairs of the Committee on Foreign Relations, US Senate, 103rd Congress, Second Session, July 26, 1994. Washington, DC: Government Printing Office, 1995.

Cunningham, Philip J. *Tiananmen Moon: Inside the Chinese Student Uprising of 1989*. Lanham, MD: Rowman & Littlefield, 2009.

Current and Projected National Security Threats to the United States: Hearing before the Select Committee on Intelligence of the US Senate, 106th Congress, Second Session, February 2, 2000. Washington, DC: Government Printing Office, 2000.

Dahi, Omar. "Syria in Crisis: The Politics of the Refugee Crisis." *Dissent*, Winter 2014. http://www.dissentmagazine.org/article/syria-in-fragments-the-politics-of-the-refugee-crisis.

Dallaire, Roméo A., and Brent Beardsley. *Shake Hands with the Devil: The Failure of Humanity in Rwanda*. Toronto: Random House Canada, 2003.

Department of Defense Briefing on the Situation in Rwanda: Hearing before the Committee on Armed Services, US Senate, 103rd Congress, Second Session, July 25, 1994. Washington, DC: Government Printing Office, 1995.

Des Forges, Alison. *The Killing Campaign: The 1994 Genocide in Rwanda*. New York: Human Rights Watch, 1998.

Des Forges, Alison. *"Leave None to Tell the Story": Genocide in Rwanda*. New York: Human Rights Watch, 1999.

Detention Watch Network. "About the US Detention and Deportation System." http://www.detentionwatchnetwork.org/resources.

Dewey, Arthur E. "Immigration after 9/11: The View from the United States." April 3, 2003. http://2001-2009.state.gov/g/prm/rls/2003/37906.htm.

DeWind, Josh, and Renata Segura. *Diaspora Lobbies and the US Government: Convergence and Divergence in Making Foreign Policy*. New York: New York University Press, 2014.

Dowling, Julie A., and Jonathan Xavier Inda, eds. *Governing Immigration through Crime: A Reader*. Stanford, CA: Stanford Social Sciences, an imprint of Stanford University Press, 2013.

Drakulić, Slavenka. *They Would Never Hurt a Fly: War Criminals on Trial in The Hague.* New York: Viking, 2004.

Duany, Jorge. "Cuban Communities in the United States: Migration Waves, Settlement Patterns and Socioeconomic Diversity." *Pouvoirs dans la Caraïbe,* October 30, 2010. http://plc.revues.org/464.

Dunn Cavelty, Myriam, and Victor Mauer, eds. *The Routledge Handbook of Security Studies.* Milton Park, Abingdon, Oxon: Routledge, 2010.

Eastern European Refugees: Hearing before the Subcommittee on Immigration, Refugees, and International Law of the Committee on the Judiciary, House of Representatives, 101st Congress, First Session, November 2, 1989. Washington, DC: Government Printing Office, 1990.

Einolf, Christopher J. *The Mercy Factory: Refugees and the American Asylum System.* Chicago: I.R. Dee, 2001.

Farouk-Sluglett, Marion, and Peter Sluglett. "The Historiography of Modern Iraq." *American Historical Review* 96.5 (1991): 1408–1421.

Federal Bureau of Investigation. "First Strike: Global Terror in America." February 26, 2008. http://www.fbi.gov/news/stories/2008/february/tradebom_022608.

Federal Bureau of Investigation. *Terrorism in the United States, 1999: 30 Years of Terrorism. A Special Retrospective Edition.* http://gateway.proquest.com/openurl?url_ver=Z39.88-2004&res_dat=xri:dnsa&rft_dat=xri:dnsa:article:CTE01226.

Fein, Helen. *Human Rights and Wrongs: Slavery, Terror, Genocide.* Boulder, CO: Paradigm Publishers, 2007.

Felbab-Brown, Vanda. "Crime as a Mirror of Politics: Urban Gangs in Indonesia." *Brookings Foreign Policy Trip Reports.* February 6, 2013. http://www.brookings.edu/research/reports/2013/02/06-indonesia-gangs-felbabbrown.

Ferris, Elizabeth. "Criminal Violence and Displacement: Notes from Honduras." *Brookings-LSE Project in Internal Displacement.* November 8, 2013. http://www.brookings.edu/blogs/up-front/posts/2013/11/08-honduras-violence-displacement-ferris.

Ferris, Elizabeth. "Gangs, Violence and Displacement in Central America." *Brookings-LSE Project in Internal Displacement.* November 7, 2013. http://www.brookings.edu/blogs/up-front/posts/2013/11/07-central-america-armed-conflict-displacement-ferris.

Ferris, Elizabeth. "World Refugee Day: Honoring Refugees, Resolving to Prevent Further Displacement." *Brookings Institute.* June 20, 2013. http://www.brookings.edu/blogs/up-front/posts/2013/06/20-world-refugee-day-ferris.

Fiddian-Qasmiyeh, Elena, Gil Loescher, Katy Long, and Nando Sigona, eds. *The Oxford Handbook of Refugee and Forced Migration Studies.* Oxford: Oxford University Press, 2014.

Final Report of the Senate Select Committee on Intelligence and the House Permanent Select Committee on Intelligence Joint Inquiry into the Terrorist Attacks of September 11, 2001. December 2002. http://fas.org/irp/congress/2002_rpt/911rept.pdf.

Finklea, Kristin M., Adrienne L. Fernandes-Alcantara, and Alison Siskin. "Sex Trafficking of Children in the United States: Overview and Issues for Congress." Congressional Research Service. August 15, 2012. http://www.fas.org/sgp/crs/misc/R41878.pdf.

Fleming, Heather M. "US Steps Up Rwandan Relief as Lawmakers Assail Pace." *CQ Weekly*, July 30, 1994, 2158. http://library.cqpress.com.proxy.library.cornell.edu/cqweekly/WR103405139.

Franz, Barbara. *Uprooted and Unwanted: Bosnian Refugees in Austria and the United States*. College Station: Texas A&M Press, 2005.

Frelick, Bill. "The Dangers of 'Safe Havens' for Kosovo." *Refuge* 18.3 (August 1999): 33–34.

Frelick, Bill. "Iraqi Refugees' Plight Grows as US Dawdles." *Human Rights Watch*. June 12, 2007. http://www.hrw.org/news/2007/06/12/iraqi-refugees-plight-grows-us-dawdles.

Frelick, Bill. *Refugees at Our Border: The US Response to Asylum Seekers*. Washington DC: American Council for Nationalities Service, 1989.

Frelick, Bill. *Reversal of Fortune: Yugoslavia's Refugees Crisis since the Ethnic Albanian Return to Kosovo*. Washington, DC: US Committee for Refugees, 2000.

Frelick, Bill. "Special Issue: The Death March from Srebrenica." *Refugee Reports* 16, no. 7 (July 31, 1995).

Frelick, Bill. *Yugoslavia Torn Asunder: Lessons for Protecting Refugees from Civil War*. Washington, DC: American Council for Nationalities Service, 1992.

Fritz, Carolina. "Climate Change and Migration: Sorting through Complex Issues without the Hype." *Migration Information Source*. March 4, 2010. http://www.migrationpolicy.org/article/climate-change-and-migration-sorting-through-complex-issues-without-hype/.

Gagnon, V. P., Jr. *The Myth of Ethnic War: Serbia and Croatia in the 1990s*. Ithaca, NY: Cornell University Press, 2004.

Gagnon, V.P., Jr. "Yugoslavia in 1989 and after." *Nationalities Papers* 38.1 (2010): 23–39.

Galbraith, Peter W. "Refugees from War in Iraq: What Happened in 1991 and What May Happen in 2003." *Migration Policy Institute Policy Brief*, February 2003. http://www.google.com/url?sa=t&rct=j&q=&esrc=s&source=web&cd=17&ved=0CEgQFjAGOAo&url=http%3A%2F%2Fwww.migrationpolicy.org%2Fpubs%2FMPIPolicyBriefIraq.pdf&ei=qotaVNGUIIrasATJnoC4Cw&usg=AFQjCNEgbCB52z_CC7_ZCCBvFZPa_C_33Q&bvm=bv.78677474,d.cWc.

Gall, Carlotta. *The Wrong Enemy: America in Afghanistan, 2001–2014*. Boston: Houghton Mifflin Harcourt, 2014.

García, Maria Cristina. *Havana USA: Cuban Exiles and Cuban Americans in South Florida, 1959–1994*. Berkeley: University of California Press, 1996.

García, María Cristina. *Seeking Refuge: Central American Migration to Mexico, the United States, and Canada*. Berkeley: University of California Press, 2006.

García Hernández, César Cuauhtémoc. *Crimmigration Law*. Chicago: American Bar Association, 2015.

Gatrell, Peter. *The Making of the Modern Refugee*. Oxford: Oxford University Press, 2013.

"The Genocide Archive of Rwanda." http://www.genocidearchiverwanda.org.rw/index.php/Category:Rescuer_Testimonies.

Genocide Convention Implementation Act: Hearing before the Subcommittee on Immigration, Refugees, and International Law of the Committee on the Judiciary, House of Representatives, 100th Congress, Second Session, on H.R. 807 . . . March 16, 1988. Washington, DC: Government Printing Office, 1988.

Gerard, Alison. *The Securitization of Migration and Refugee Women*. London: Routledge, Taylor & Francis Group, 2014.

Gibney, Matthew J. "Liberal Democratic States and Responsibilities to Refugees." *American Political Science Review* 93 (March 1999): 169–181.

Gibney, Matthew J., and Randall Hansen, eds. *Immigration and Asylum: From 1900 to the Present*. Vol. 1. Santa Barbara, CA: ABC-CLIO, 2005.

Golash-Boza, Tanya Maria. *Immigration Nation: Raids, Detentions, and Deportations in Post-9/11 America*. Boulder, CO: Paradigm Publishers, 2012.

Goldhagen, Daniel Jonah. *Worse Than War: Genocide, Eliminationism, and the Ongoing Assault on Humanity*. New York: Public Affairs Books, 2009.

Goldstein, Kenneth M. *Interest Groups, Lobbying, and Participation in America*. Cambridge: Cambridge University Press, 1999.

González-Barrera, Anna, and Jens Manuel Krogstad. "With Help from Mexico, Number of Child Migrants Crossing US Border Falls." *Pew Research Center*. April 28, 2015. http://www.pewresearch.org/fact-tank/2015/04/28/child-migrants-border/.

Goodwin-Gill, Guy S. *The Refugee in International Law*. New York: Oxford University Press, 1983.

Goodwin-Gill, Guy S., and Selim Can Sazak. "Footing the Bill: Refugee-Creating States' Responsibility to Pay." July 29, 2015. https://www.foreignaffairs.com/articles/africa/2015-07-29/footing-bill.

Green, Nancy L., and François Weil. *Citizenship and Those Who Leave: The Politics of Emigration and Expatriation*. Urbana: University of Illinois Press, 2007.

Greenhill, Kelly M. *Weapons of Mass Migration: Forced Displacement, Coercion, and Foreign Policy*. Ithaca, NY: Cornell University Press, 2010.

Greenspan, Jesse. "Remembering the 1993 World Trade Center Bombing." *History*, February 26, 2013. http://www.history.com/news/remembering-the-1993-world-trade-center-bombing.

Gourevitch, Philip. *We Wish to Inform You That Tomorrow We Will Be Killed with Our Families: Stories from Rwanda*. New York: Farrar, Straus and Giroux, 1998.

Gzesh, Susan. "America's Human Rights Challenge: International Human Rights Implications of US Immigration Enforcement Actions Post-September 11." September 2006. www.migrationpolicy.org/pubs/Americas_Human_Rights_Challenge_1006.pdf.

Hagopian, Amy, et al. "Mortality in Iraq Associated with the 2003–2011 War and Occupation: Findings from a National Cluster Sample Survey." *PLoS Medicine*, October 15, 2013. doi:10.1371/journal.pmed.1001533.

Haitian Asylum-Seekers: Hearing before the Subcommittee on International Law, Immigration, and Refugees of the Committee on the Judiciary, House of Representatives, 103rd Congress, Second Session, on H.R. 3663, H.R. 4114, and H.R. 4264, June 15, 1994. Washington, DC: Government Printing Office, 1994.

Hamilton, Heather N. "Refugee Women, UNHCR, and the Great Lakes Crisis." http://www.freewebs.com/hbhamilton/Women%20Refugees%20Great%20Lakes.pdf.

Harbeck, Dorothy A., and Ellen L. Buckwalter. "Asking and Telling: Identity and Persecution in Sexual Orientation Asylum Claims." *Immigration Law Advisor* 2, no. 9 (September 2008). http://www.justice.gov/eoir/vll/ILA-Newsleter/ILA%20Vol%202/vol2no9.pdf.

Harman, Jane. "Not a War on Terror, a War on an Ideology." *Wilson Center*. September 17, 2014. http://wilsoncenter.org/article/not-war-terror-war-ideology?mkt_tok=3RkMMJWWfF9wsRouuanNZKXonjHpfsX56u4vWKOxlMI%2F0ER3fOvrPUfGjI4ATMVkNK%2BTFAwTG5toziV8R7LEJc1tzMAQXRXh.

Hauerwas, Stanley, and Frank Lentricchia. *Dissent from the Homeland: Essays after September 11.* Durham, NC: Duke University Press, 2003.

Hebrew Immigrant Aid Society. "The 20th Anniversary of the Lautenberg Amendment."301301http://www.hias.org/en/post/hias-blog/20th-anniversary-lautenberg-amendment.

Helsinki Watch. *Detained, Denied, Deported: Asylum Seekers in the United States.* New York: Helsinki Watch, 1989.

Helton, Arthur C. *The Price of Indifference: Refugees and Humanitarian Action in the New Century.* Oxford: Oxford University Press, 2002.

Heritage Foundation. "Preparing America for the Wave of Russian Immigrants." March 6, 1991. http://www.heritage.org/research/reports/1991/03/preparing-america-for-the-wave-of-russian-immigrants.

Hersh, Seymour. "Torture at Abu Ghraib." *New Yorker*, May 10, 2004. http://www.newyorker.com/archive/2004/05/10/040510fa_fact?currentPage=all.

Hess, Jennifer. "Social Visibility and Particularity in Asylum: *Gaitan v. Holder* and the Ironic Requirement of Social Perception to Avoid Persecution." *Boston College Journal of Law and Social Justice* 33.3 (2013): 27–38.

Hsu, Madeline Y. "Befriending the 'Yellow Peril': Chinese Students and Intellectuals and the Liberalization of US Immigration Laws, 1950–1965." *Journal of American-East Asian Relations* 16.3 (2009): 139–162.

Hsu, Madeline Y. "The Disappearance of America's Cold War Chinese Refugees, 1948–1966." *Journal of American Ethnic History* 31.4 (2012): 12–33.

Hula, Kevin W. *Lobbying Together: Interest Group Coalitions in Legislative Politics.* Washington, DC: Georgetown University Press, 1999.

Human Rights First. *Denial and Delay: The Impact of the Immigration Law's "Terrorism Bars" on Asylum Seekers and Refugees in the United States.* Washington, DC: Human Rights First, 2009.

Human Rights Initiative. "Federal District Judge Approves Settlement in Class Action Lawsuit on Employment Authorization for Asylum Applicants." http://www.hrionline.org/federal-district-judge-approves-settlement-in-class-action-lawsuit-on-employment-authorization-for-asylum-applicants/.

Human Rights Watch. *Human Rights in Iraq.* New Haven: Yale University Press, 1990.

Human Rights Watch. "Iraq." *Human Rights Watch World Report 1989.* http://www.hrw.org/reports/1989/WR89/Iraq.htm.

Human Rights Watch. *Still Waiting: Bringing Justice for War Crimes, Crimes against Humanity, and Genocide in Bosnia and Herzegovina's Cantonal and District Courts.* New York: Human Rights Watch, 2008.

Human Rights Watch World Report 1992: Yugoslavia. http://www.refworld.org/docid/467fca581e.html.

The Human Smuggling and Trafficking Center. "Fact Sheet: Distinctions between Human Smuggling and Human Trafficking." January 2005. https://www.hsdl.org/?view&did=23324.

Huysmans, Jef. *The Politics of Insecurity: Fear, Migration, and Asylum in the EU.* London: Routledge, 2006.

Ilibagiza, Immaculée, and Steve Erwin. *Left to Tell: Discovering God amidst the Rwandan Holocaust.* Carlsbad, CA: Hay House, 2006.

Immigration and Naturalization Service. *Statistical Yearbook of the Immigration and Naturalization Service.* Washington, DC: The Service, 1997.

Immigration Equality. "Asylum Decisions." http://immigrationequality.org/issues/law-library/asylum-decisions/.

Immigration in the National Interest Act of 1995: Hearing before the Subcommittee on Immigration and Claims of the Committee on the Judiciary, House of Representatives, 104th Congress, First Session, on H.R. 1915 ... June 29, 1995. Washington, DC: Government Printing Office, 1996.

Immigration Status of Chinese Nationals Currently in the United States: Hearing before the Subcommittee on Immigration, Refugees, and International Law of the Committee on the Judiciary, House of Representatives, 101st Congress, First Session, on H.R. 2929, H.R. 2712, H.R. 2722, and H.R. 2726, July 20, 1989. Washington, DC: Government Printing Office, 1989.

International Organization for Migration. "Facts and Figures." http://www.iom.int/jahia/Jahia/about-migration/facts-and-figures/lang/en.

Iraqi Refugee Assistance Project. http://refugeerights.org/stories/.

Iriye, Akira., Petra Goedde, and William I. Hitchcock, eds. *The Human Rights Revolution: An International History.* New York: Oxford University Press, 2012.

Irwin, Julia. *Making the World Safe: The American Red Cross and a Nation's Humanitarian Awakening.* New York: Oxford University Press, 2013.

Johnson, Kevin R. "Race, the Immigration Laws, and Domestic Race Relations: A 'Magic Mirror' into the Heart of Darkness." *Indiana Law Journal* 73.4 (1997–1998): 1111–1159.

Jones, Thomas David, and Judith Hippler Bello. "Cuban American Bar Association, Inc. v. Christopher. 43 F.3d 1412. Haitian Refugee Center, Inc. v. Christopher. 43 F.3d 1431." *American Journal of International Law* 90.3 (1996): 477–483.

Kanstroom, Daniel. *Deportation Nation: Outsiders in American History.* Cambridge, MA: Harvard University Press, 2007.

Kaplan, Ebe. "Child Soldiers around the World." *Council on Foreign Relations.* December 2, 2005. http://www.cfr.org/human-rights/child-soldiers-around-world/p9331.

Kaplan, Janna. "Remembering Refuseniks." December 18, 2011. http://people.brandeis.edu/~jannakap/writings_copernicus.html.

Kay, Chloe. "Contemporary Russian-Serbian Relations: Interviews with Youth from Political Parties in Belgrade and Vojvodina." *School of Russian and Asian Studies.* August 24, 2014. http://www.sras.org/russia_serbia_relations_youth.

Kayihura, Edouard, and Kerry Zukus. *Inside the Hotel Rwanda: What Really Happened and Why It Matters Today.* Dallas, TX: BenBella Books, 2014.

Kean, Thomas H., and Lee Hamilton. *The 9/11 Commission Report: Final Report of the National Commission on Terrorist Attacks upon the United States.* Washington, DC: National Commission on Terrorist Attacks upon the United States, 2004.

Keck, Margaret E., and Kathryn Sikkink. *Activists beyond Borders: Advocacy Networks in International Politics.* Ithaca, NY: Cornell University Press, 1998.

Kenney, David Ngaruri, and Philip G. Schrag. *Asylum Denied: A Refugee's Struggle for Safety in America.* Berkeley: University of California Press, 2008.

Kephart, Janice. "Immigration and Terrorism: Moving beyond the 9/11 Staff Report on Terrorist Travel." *Backgrounder*, September 2005. http://www.cis.org/articles/2005/kephart.html.

Kerwin, Donald M. "The Faltering US Refugee Protection System: Legal and Policy Responses to Refugees, Asylum Seekers, and Others in Need of Protection." *Migration Policy Institute Report.* March 2011. http://www.migrationpolicy.org/research/faltering-us-refugee-protection-system.

Kerwin, Donald M. "Undermining Antiterrorism: When National Security and Immigration Policy Collide." *America*, June 23–30, 2003.

Kerwin, Donald M. "The Use and Misuse of 'National Security' Rationale in Crafting US Refugee and Immigration Policies." *International Journal of Refugee Law* 17.4 (2005): 749–763.

Kim, Yule. "Female Genital Mutilation as Persecution: When Can It Constitute a Basis for Asylum and Withholding of Removal?" Congressional Research Service. Updated October 10, 2008. http://congressionalresearch.com/RL34587/document.php.

Kliger, Sam. "The Jackson-Vanik Amendment and US-Russian Relations." Presentation at Kennan Institute Conference, February 4, 2010. http://www.wilsoncenter.org/event/the-jackson-vanik-amendment-and-us-russian-relations.

Koh, Harold Hongju. "The 'Haiti Paradigm' in United States Human Rights Policy." Faculty Scholarship Series, Paper 2092, 1994. http://digitalcommons.law.yale.edu/ff_papers/2092.

The Kosovo Refugee Crisis: Hearing before the Subcommittee on Immigration of the Committee on the Judiciary, US Senate, 106th Congress, First Session, on the Current Kosovo Refugee Situation and the Scope and Adequacy of the Response of the United States and the International Community, April 14, 1999. Washington, DC: Government Printing Office, 2000.

Krishnayya, Raio G. "No Way Out: Representing Child Soldiers in Asylum Cases and Alternate Solutions to the Strict Liability Exclusion under the 'Persecution of Others' Clause." Indianapolis, IN: Center for Victim and Human Rights, 2009. http://www.cvhr.org/Immigration-Law-Asylum-of-Child-Soldiers.pdf.

Lambda Legal. "Soto Vega v. Gonzales." http://www.lambdalegal.org/in-court/cases/soto-vega-v-gonzales.

Laney, Monique. *German Rocketeers in the Heart of Dixie: Making Sense of the Nazi Past during the Civil Rights Era.* New Haven: Yale University Press, 2015.

Law, Anna O. *The Immigration Battle in American Courts.* Cambridge: Cambridge University Press, 2010.

Lawyer's Committee for Human Rights. *Refugee Women at Risk: Unfair US Laws Hurt Asylum Seekers.* New York: Lawyer's Committee for Human Rights, 2002.

Lawyer's Committee for Human Rights. "Refugees, Asylum Seekers and the New Department of Homeland Security: Initial Concerns and Preliminary Recommendations." March 2003. https://www.humanrightsfirst.org/wp-content/uploads/pdf/refs_032503.pdf.

Lazin, Fred. "Refugee Resettlement and 'Freedom of Choice': The Case of Soviet Jewry." *Backgrounder*, July 2005. http://www.cis.org/print/RefugeeResettlement-SovietJewry.

LeBor, Adam. *Milosevic: A Biography.* New Haven: Yale University Press, 2004.

Leiken, Robert S. *Bearers of Global Jihad? Immigration and National Security after 9/11.* Washington, DC: Nixon Center, 2004. http://www.mafhoum.com/press7/193S23.pdf.

Li, Lu. *Moving the Mountain: My Life in China from the Cultural Revolution to Tiananmen Square.* London: Macmillan, 1990.

Lim, Julian. "Immigration, Asylum, and Citizenship: A More Holistic Approach." *California Law Review* 101.4 (2013): 1013–1078.

Lipman, Jana K. "'The Fish Trusts the Water, and It Is in the Water That It Is Cooked': The Caribbean Origins of the Krome Detention Center." *Radical History Review* 115 (2013): 115–141.

Lizhi, Fang. *The Most Wanted Man in China: My Journey from Scientist to Enemy of the State*. Translated by Perry Link. New York: Henry Holt, 2016.

Loescher, Gil. "Living after Tragedy: The UN Baghdad Bomb, One Year On." *Open Democracy*. http://www.opendemocracy.net/conflict/article_2050.jsp.

Loescher, Gil, and John A. Scanlan. *Calculated Kindness: Refugees and America's Half-Open Door, 1945 to the Present*. New York: Free Press, 1986.

Loescher, Gil, and John A. Scanlan. "Human Rights, US Foreign Policy, and Haitian Refugees." *Journal of Interamerican Studies and World Affairs* 26.3 (1984): 313–366.

Loomis, Burdett A., Peter L. Francia, and Dara Z. Strolovitch. *Guide to Interest Groups and Lobbying in the United States*. Washington, DC: CQ Press, 2012.

Lopata, Helena Znaniecka. *Polish Americans*. 2nd ed. New Brunswick, NJ: Transaction Publishers, 1994.

Managing Chaos: The Iraqi Refugees of Jordan and Syria and Internally Displaced Persons in Iraq: Staff Trip Report to the Committee on Foreign Relations, United States Senate, 110th Congress, Second Session. Washington, DC: Government Printing Office, 2008.

Margesson, Rhoda. "Afghan Refugees: Current Status and Future Prospects." Congressional Research Service. January 26, 2007. https://www.fas.org/sgp/crs/row/RL33851.pdf.

Margesson, Rhoda, Jeremy M. Sharp, and Andorra Bruno. "Iraqi Refugees and Internally Displaced Persons: A Deepening Humanitarian Crisis?" Congressional Research Service. August 15, 2008. https://www.fas.org/sgp/crs/mideast/RL33936.pdf.

Martin, Daniel C., and James E. Yankey. *Refugees and Asylees: 2013*. Washington, DC: Department of Homeland Security, August 2014. http://www.dhs.gov/sites/default/files/publications/ois_rfa_fr_2013.pdf.

Martin, John L. "Immigration Reform Gains Momentum." *Center for Immigration Studies*. August 1993. http://www.cis.org/articles/1993/back593.html.

Mascarenhas, Hyacinth. "Twelve Portraits of Heroic Rwandans Who Stood Up to Their Country's Genocide." *World Mic*. April 9, 2014. https://mic.com/articles/87211/12-portraits-of-heroic-rwandans-who-stood-up-to-their-country-s-genocide#.dVgpkECOt.

McCormick, James M. *American Foreign Policy and Process*. 2nd ed. Itasca, IL: FE Peacock Publishers, 1992.

McDonnell, Faith J. H., and Grace Akallo. *Girl Soldier: A Story of Hope for Northern Uganda's Children*. Grand Rapids, MI: Chosen, 2007.

McHugh, Lois. *Bosnia-Former Yugoslavia: Refugee Repatriation and Humanitarian Assistance under the Peace Agreement*. Washington, DC: Congressional Research Service, 1996.

McHugh, Lois. "International Disasters: How the United States Responds." Congressional Research Service. April 17, 2001. http://digital.library.unt.edu/ark:/67531/metacrs6985/.

McHugh, Lois, Joyce Vialet, and Ruth Ellen Wasem. *Refugee Policy in a Changing World*. Washington DC: Congressional Research Service, April 8, 1997.

Meacham, Jon. *Destiny and Power: The American Odyssey of George Herbert Walker Bush*. New York: Random House, 2015.

Meierhenrich, Jens, ed. *Genocide: A Reader*. New York: Oxford University Press, 2014.

Mertus, Julie, Vlatka Mihelić, and Jeri Laber. *Open Wounds: Human Rights Abuses in Kosovo*. New York: Human Rights Watch, 1993.

Meyers, Diana Tietjens, ed. *Poverty, Agency, and Human Rights*. Oxford: Oxford University Press, 2014.

Migration Policy Institute. "Top 10 Migration Issues of 2005 Issue #10: Record Numbers Displaced by Natural Disasters." *Migration Information Source*. December 1, 2005. http://www.migrationpolicy.org/article/top-10-migration-issues-2005-issue-10-record-numbers-displaced-natural-disasters/.

Monsutti, Alessandro. *War and Migration: Social Networks and Economic Strategies of the Hazaras of Afghanistan*. New York: Routledge, 2005.

Morgan, Deborah. "Not Gay Enough for the Government: Racial and Sexual Stereotypes in Sexual Orientation Asylum Cases." *Law and Sexuality* 15 (2006): 135–175.

Morozov, Boris. *Documents on Soviet Jewish Emigration*. Portland, OR: Frank Cass, 1999.

Myers, Norman. "Environmental Refugees." *Population and Environment* 19.2 (1997): 167–182.

National Conference on State Legislatures. "Border Protection, Antiterrorism and Illegal Immigration Control Act of 2005 | H.R. 4437." http://www.ncsl.org/research/immigration/summary-of-the-sensenbrenner-immigration-bill.aspx.

National Immigrant Justice Center. "Cece v. Holder." http://immigrantjustice.org/litigation/blog/cece-v-holder-0#.VZbeReejQ-8.

National Immigrant Justice Center. "Policy Brief: Unaccompanied Immigrant Children." January 14, 2014. https://immigrantjustice.org/sites/immigrantjustice.org/files/NIJC%20Policy%20Brief%20-%20Unaccompanied%20Immigrant%20Children%20FINAL%20Winter%202014.pdf.

National Immigration Forum. "The Math of Immigration Detention: Runaway Costs for Immigration Detention Do Not Add Up to Sensible Policies." August 2013. http://www.immigrationforum.org/images/uploads/mathofimmigrationdetention.pdf.

National Public Radio. "Remembering Rwandans Who Followed Their Conscience." http://www.npr.org/sections/parallels/2014/04/08/300508669/remembering-rwandans-who-followed-their-conscience.

National Security Considerations in Asylum Applications: A Case Study of Six Iraqis. Hearing before the Subcommittee on Technology, Terrorism, and Government Information of the Committee on the Judiciary, United States Senate, 105th

Congress, Second Session, October 8, 1998. Washington, DC: Government Printing Office, 1999.

Nayak, Meghana. *Who Is Worthy of Protection? Gender-Based Asylum and US Immigration Politics.* New York: Oxford University Press, 2015.

Neglected Responsibilities: The US Response to the Iraqi Refugee Crisis: Joint Hearing before the Subcommittee on the Middle East and South Asia and the Subcommittee on International Organizations, Human Rights, and Oversight of the Committee on Foreign Affairs, House of Representatives, 110th Congress, Second Session, March 11, 2008. Washington, DC: Government Printing Office, 2008.

Newman, Edward, and Joanne van Selm, eds. *Refugees and Forced Displacement: International Security, Human Vulnerability, and the State.* Tokyo: United Nations University Press, 2003.

Ngai, Mae M. *Impossible Subjects: Illegal Aliens and the Making of Modern America.* Princeton, NJ: Princeton University Press, 2004.

Nizich, Ivana. *War Crimes in Bosnia-Hercegovina.* New York: Human Rights Watch, 1992.

"North American Partnerships: Working with the United States, Smart Border Declaration." http://www.cbsa-asfc.gc.ca/agency-agence/partner-partenaire-eng.html.

North Atlantic Treaty Organization. "NATO and Afghanistan." http://www.nato.int/cps/en/natolive/69772.htm.

Nwosu, Chiamaka, and Jeanne Batalova, "Haitian Immigrants in the United States." *Migration Policy Institute.* May 29, 2014. http://www.migrationpolicy.org/article/haitian-immigrants-united-states.

Office of Immigration Statistics, Department of Homeland Security. *Yearbook of Immigration Statistics.* Washington, DC: Department of Homeland Security, Office of Immigration Statistics, 2003.

Office of Immigration Statistics, Department of Homeland Security. *Yearbook of Immigration Statistics.* Washington, DC: Department of Homeland Security, Office of Immigration Statistics, 2013.

Office of the Historian, United States Department of State. *History of the Department of State during the Clinton Presidency, 1993–2001,* January 2001. http://www.clintonlibrary.gov/.

Office of the Inspector General, US Department of Justice. *The September 11 Detainees: A Review of the Treatment of Aliens Held on Immigration Charges in Connection with the Investigation of the September 11 Attacks.* Washington, DC: US Department of Justice, Office of the Inspector General, 2003.

Ogata, Sadako. *The Turbulent Decade: Confronting the Refugee Crises of the 1990s.* New York: Norton, 2005.

Ondiak, Natalie, and Brian Katulis. *Operation Safe Haven Iraq 2009: An Action Plan for Airlifting Endangered Iraqis Linked to the United States.* Washington, DC: Center for American Progress, January 2009. http://cdn.americanprogress.org/wp-content/uploads/issues/2009/01/pdf/iraqi_refugees.pdf.

Orleck, Annelise. *The Soviet Jewish Americans.* Westport, CT: Greenwood Press, 1999.

Ornstein, Norman J., and Shirley Elder Lyons. *Interest Groups, Lobbying, and Policymaking.* Washington, DC: Congressional Quarterly Press, 1978.

Oversight Hearing: US Refugee Admissions and Policy. Hearing before the Subcommittee on Immigration, Border Security, and Citizenship of the Committee on the Judiciary, US Senate, 109th Congress, Second Session, September 27, 2006. Washington, DC: Government Printing Office, 2007.

An Overview of Asylum Policy: Hearing before the Subcommittee on Immigration of the Committee on the Judiciary, US Senate, 107th Congress, First Session, May 3, 2001. Washington, DC: Government Printing Office, 2002.

Packer, George. "Iraqi Refugees: A Debt Defaulted." *New Yorker,* July 29, 2011. http://www.newyorker.com/online/blogs/georgepacker/2011/07/iraqi-refugees.html.

Parker, Alison, and Jamie Fellner. "Above the Law: Executive Power after September 11 in the United States." https://www.hrw.org/legacy/wr2k4/8.htm.

Patterns of Global Terrorism 2001. Washington, DC: US Department of State, May 2002. http://www.state.gov/documents/organization/10286.pdf.

Pešić, Vesna. *Serbian Nationalism and the Origins of the Yugoslav Crisis.* Washington, DC: US Institute of Peace, 1996.

Peterson, Linda S. *Central American Migration: Past and Present.* Washington, DC: Center for International Research, US Bureau of the Census, 1986.

Peterson, Scott. "Depleted Uranium Haunts Kosovo and Iraq." Middle East Research and Information Project. http://www.merip.org/mer/mer215/depleted-uranium-haunts-kosovo-iraq.

Pierce, Sara. "Unaccompanied Child Migrants in US Communities, Immigration Court, and Schools." *Migration Policy Institute.* October 2015. http://www.migrationpolicy.org/research/unaccompanied-child-migrants-us-communities-immigration-court-and-schools.

The Plight of Iraqi Refugees: Hearing before the Committee on the Judiciary, US Senate, 110th Congress, First Session, January 16, 2007. Washington, DC: Government Printing Office, 2007.

Power, Samantha. *A Problem from Hell: America and the Age of Genocide.* New York: Harper Perennial, 2007.

Prieto, Daniel B. "War about Terror: Civil Liberties and National Security after 9/11." Council on Foreign Relations. February 2009. http://www.cfr.org/terrorism-and-the-law/war-terror/p18373.

Processing of Soviet Refugees: Joint Hearing before the Subcommittee on Europe and the Middle East of the Committee on Foreign Affairs and the Subcommittee on Immigration, Refugees, and International Law of the Committee on the Judiciary, House of Representatives, 101st Congress, First Session, September 14, 1989. Washington, DC: Government Printing Office, 1990.

Prunier, Gérard. *Africa's World War: Congo, the Rwandan Genocide, and the Making of a Continental Catastrophe.* New York: Oxford University Press, 2009.

Prunier, Gérard. *The Rwanda Crisis: History of a Genocide.* Kampala: Fountain Publishers, 1999.

Public Broadcasting System. "Lost Boys of Sudan." http://www.pbs.org/pov/lost-boysofsudan/.

Public Broadcasting System. *Frontline.* "The Iraq War: How We Spent $800 Billion (and Counting)." March 18, 2013. http://www.pbs.org/wgbh/pages/frontline/iraq-war-on-terror/the-iraq-war-how-we-spent-800-billion-and-counting/.

Purcell, Susan Kaufmann. "Collapsing Cuba." *Foreign Affairs* 71.1 (1991): 131–145.

Quigley, John. "Most-Favored-Nation Status and Soviet Emigration: Does the Jackson-Vanik Amendment Apply?" *Loyola of Los Angeles International and Comparative Law Review* 543 (1989): 543–548. http://digitalcommons.lmu.edu/ilr/vol11/iss3/4.

Ramji-Nogales, Jaya., Andrew Ian Schoenholtz, and Philip G. Schrag. *Refugee Roulette: Disparities in Asylum Adjudication and Proposals for Reform.* New York: New York University Press, 2009.

Rawaf, Salman. "The 2003 Iraq War and Avoidable Death Toll." *Plos Medicine,* October 15, 2013. http://journals.plos.org/plosmedicine/article?id=10.1371/journal.pmed.1001532.

"Recommendation Regarding the Adjudication of Applications for Refugee Status." April 14, 2010. http://www.dhs.gov/ombudsman-recommendation-adjudication-applications-refugee-status.

"The Responsibility to Protect: A Report of the International Commission on Intervention and State Sovereignty." December 2001. http://responsibilitytoprotect.org/ICISS%20Report.pdf.

Riera, José and Andrew Harper. "Iraq: The Search for Solutions." *Forced Migration Review,* June 2007, 10–13.

Risse, Thomas, Steve C. Ropp, and Kathryn Sikkink, eds. *The Power of Human Rights: International Norms and Domestic Change.* Cambridge: Cambridge University Press, 1999.

Romanian Adoptions: Hearing before the Subcommittee on International Law, Immigration, and Refugees of the Committee on the Judiciary, House of Representatives, 102nd Congress, First Session, June 5, 1991. Washington, DC: Government Printing Office, 1991.

Rosenblum, Marc R. "Unaccompanied Child Migration to the United States: The Tension between Protection and Prevention." *Migration Policy Institute.* April 2015. http://www.migrationpolicy.org/research/unaccompanied-child-migration-united-states-tension-between-protection-and-prevention.

Rosenblum, Marc R. "US Immigration Policy since 9/11: Understanding the Stalemate over Comprehensive Immigration Reform." *Migration Policy Institute.* 2011. www.migrationpolicy.org.

Rotella, Sebastian, and Ana Arana. "Finding Oscar: Massacre, Memory and Justice in Guatemala." *ProPublica*. May 25, 2012. http://www.propublica.org/article/finding-oscar-massacre-memory-and-justice-in-guatemala.

Ruiz, Hiram A. "Afghanistan: Conflict and Displacement 1978 to 2001." *Forced Migration Review* 13 (June 2002): 8–10.

Rwanda: Genocide and the Continuing Cycle of Violence. Hearing before the Subcommittee on International Operations and Human Rights of the Committee on International Relations, House of Representatives, 105th Congress, Second Session, May 5, 1998. Washington, DC: Government Printing Office, 1999.

Salehyan, Idean. "The New Myth about Climate Change." *Foreign Policy*, August 14, 2007. http://www.foreignpolicy.com/articles/2007/08/13/the_new_myth_about_climate_change.

Sampaio, Anna. *Terrorizing Latina/o Immigrants: Race, Gender, and Immigration Politics in the Age of Security.* Philadelphia: Temple University Press, 2015.

Sánchez, Julian. "The Reauthorization of the Patriot Act." *Cato Institute.* March 9, 2011. http://www.cato.org/publications/congressional-testimony/reauthorization-patriot-act.

Sanford, Victoria, and Asale Angel-Ajani. *Engaged Observer: Anthropology, Advocacy, and Activism.* New Brunswick, NJ: Rutgers University Press, 2006.

Sarat, Austin, and Stuart A. Scheingold, eds. *Cause Lawyers and Social Movements.* Stanford, CA: Stanford Law and Politics, 2006.

Sassoon, Joseph. *The Iraqi Refugees: The New Crisis in the Middle East.* London: I.B. Tauris, 2009.

Schleussner, Carl-Friedrich, Jonathan F. Donges, Reik V. Donner, and Hans Joachim Schellnhuber. "Armed-Conflict Risks Enhanced by Climate-Related Disasters in Ethnically Fractionalized Countries." *Proceedings of the National Academy of Sciences* 113.33 (2016): 9216–9221.

Schoenholtz, Andrew Ian, Philip G. Schrag, and Jaya Ramji-Nogales. *Lives in the Balance: Asylum Adjudication by the Department of Homeland Security.* New York: New York University Press, 2014.

Schulman, Bruce J., ed. *Making the American Century: Essays on the Political Culture of Twentieth Century America.* Oxford: Oxford University Press, 2014.

Seelke, Clare Ribando. "Trafficking in Persons in Latin America and the Caribbean." Congressional Research Service, July 15, 2013. http://www.fas.org/sgp/crs/row/RL33200.pdf.

Sikkink, Kathryn. *The Justice Cascade: How Human Rights Prosecutions Are Changing World Politics.* New York: Norton, 2011.

Silk, James. *Despite a Generous Spirit: Denying Asylum in the United States.* Washington, DC: US Committee for Refugees, 1986.

Siskin, Alison, and Liana Sun Wyler. "Trafficking in Persons: US Policy and Issues for Congress." Congressional Research Service. February 27, 2013. http://www.fas.org/sgp/crs/row/RL34317.pdf.

Smith, Tony. *Foreign Attachments: The Power of Ethnic Groups in the Making of American Foreign Policy*. Cambridge, MA: Harvard University Press, 2000.

Snyder, Sarah B. *Human Rights Activism and the End of the Cold War: A Transnational History of the Helsinki Network*. New York: Cambridge University Press, 2011.

Spence, Jonathan D. *The Search for Modern China*. 3rd ed. New York: Norton, 2013.

Sridharan, Swetha. "The Difficulties of US Asylum Claims Based on Sexual Orientation." *Migration Information Source*. October 29, 2008. http://www.migrationpolicy.org/article/difficulties-us-asylum-claims-based-sexual-orientation/.

Staples, Amy L. S. *The Birth of Development: How the World Bank, Food and Agriculture Organization, and World Health Organization Changed the World, 1945–1965*. Kent, OH: Kent State University Press, 2006.

Stepick, Alex, and Dale Frederick Swartz. *Haitian Refugees in the US*. London: Minority Rights Group, 1982.

Stumpf, Juliet P. "The Crimmigration Crisis: Immigrants, Crime, and Sovereign Power." *American University Law Review* 56.2 (2006–2007): 367–420.

Stumpf, Juliet P. "Doing Time: Crimmigration Law and the Perils of Haste." *UCLA Law Review* 58.6 (2010–2011): 1705–1748.

"Summaries for the Refugee Protection Act of 2010." https://www.govtrack.us/congress/bills/111/s3113/summary.

"Summaries for the Refugee Protection Act of 2013." https://www.govtrack.us/congress/bills/113/s645/summary.

Swanwick, Daniel. "Foreign Policy and Humanitarianism in US Asylum Adjudication: Revisiting the Debate in the Wake of the War on Terror." *Georgetown Immigration Law Journal* 21 (2007): 129–149. http://scholarship.law.georgetown.edu/spps_papers/4.

Syria after Geneva: Next Steps for US Policy: Hearing before the Committee on Foreign Relations, United States Senate, 113th Congress, Second Session, March 26, 2014. Washington, DC: Government Publishing Office, 2015.

Takahashi, Saul, ed. *Human Rights, Human Security, and State Security: The Intersection*. Vols. 1–3. Santa Barbara, CA: Praeger, 2014.

Thomas, Dorothy Q. "We Are Not the World: US Activism and Human Rights in the Twenty-First Century." *Signs* 25.4 (2000): 1121–1124. http://www.jstor.org/stable/3175497.

The Tiananmen Papers. Compiled by Zhang Liang. Edited by Andrew J. Nathan and Perry Link. New York: Public Affairs, 2001.

Towell, Pat. "Senate Follows Clinton's Lead With $243.4 Billion Bill." *CQ Weekly*, August 13, 1994, 2361–2367. http://library.cqpress.com/cqweekly/WR103405346.

Transactional Records Access Clearinghouse (TRAC) Immigration Project. "Asylum Denial Rate Reaches All Time Low: FY 2010 Results, a Twenty-Five Year Perspective." http://trac.syr.edu/immigration/reports/240/.

"United Africans for Women and Children Rights." http://www.africanwomen-rights.org/.

United Nations. "Child Soldiers." http://www.un.org/cyberschoolbus/briefing/
    soldiers/soldiers.pdf.

United Nations. "Overview of Forced Displacement." http://www.un.org/en/global-
    issues/briefingpapers/refugees/overviewofforceddisplacement.html.

United Nations. The Universal Declaration of Human Rights. http://www.un.org/
    en/documents/udhr/index.shtml#a14.

United Nations High Commissioner for Refugees. "Afghan Solutions Strategy."
    http://www.unhcr.org/pages/4f9016576.html.

United Nations High Commissioner for Refugees. "Daily Press Briefing of Office
    of Spokesman for Secretary-General." April 1, 1999, http://www.un.org/News/
    briefings/docs/1999/19990401.db040199.html.

United Nations High Commissioner for Refugees. "Guidance Note on Refugee
    Claims Relating to Victims of Organized Gangs." March 2010. http://www.ref-
    world.org/docid/4bb21fa02.html.

United Nations High Commissioner for Refugees. "Protecting Refugees: Questions
    and Answers." February 2002. http://www.unhcr.org/3b779dfe2.html.

United Nations High Commissioner for Refugees. The State of the World's Refugees,
    1995: In Search of Solutions. London: Oxford University Press, 1995.

United Nations High Commissioner for Refugees. The State of the World's Refugees,
    1997–98: A Humanitarian Agenda. Oxford: Oxford University Press, 1997.

United Nations High Commissioner for Refugees. The State of the World's
    Refugees, 2000: Fifty Years of Humanitarian Action. Oxford: Oxford University
    Press, 2000.

United Nations High Commissioner for Refugees. "Text of the 1951 Convention and
    the 1967 Protocol." http://www.unhcr.org/pages/49da0e466.html.

United Nations High Commissioner for Refugees. "War Stokes Further Growth in
    Forced Displacement in the First Half of 2014." January 7, 2015. http://www.
    unhcr.org/54ac24226.html.

United Nations Convention Against Transnational Organized Crime and the Protocols
    Thereto. http://www.unodc.org/documents/treaties/UNTOC/Publications/TOC
    %20Convention/TOCebook-e.pdf.

United Nations Convention on the Prevention and Punishment of Genocide. http://
    www.hrweb.org/legal/genocide.html.

United Nations Office on Drugs and Crime. "'Put Yourself in My Shoes': A Human
    Trafficking Victim Speaks Out." http://www.unodc.org/unodc/en/frontpage/
    2012/November/put-yourself-in-my-in-my-shoes-a-human-trafficking-victim-
    speaks-out.html.

United Nations Office of Spokesman for the Secretary-General. "Daily Press Briefing,
    31 March 1999." http://www.un.org/News/briefings/docs/1999/19990331.
    db033199.html.

US Agency for International Development. "Syria." http://www.usaid.gov/crisis/
    syria.

US Citizenship and Immigration Services. "I-589, Application for Asylum and for Withholding of Removal." http://www.uscis.gov/sites/default/files/files/form/ i-589instr.pdf.

US Citizenship and Immigration Services. "Iraqi Refugee Processing Fact Sheet." June 6, 2013. http://www.uscis.gov/humanitarian/refugees-asylum/refugees/ iraqi-refugee-processing-fact-sheet.

US Citizenship and Immigration Services. "Obtaining Asylum in the United States." http://www.uscis.gov/humanitarian/refugees-asylum/asylum/ obtaining-asylum-united-states.

US Citizenship and Immigration Services. "Questions and Answers: Credible Fear Screening." http://www.uscis.gov/humanitarian/refugees-asylum/asylum/ questions-answers-credible-fear-screening.

US Citizenship and Immigration Services. "What Is TPS?" http://www.uscis. gov/humanitarian/temporary-protected-status-deferred-enforced-departure/ temporary-protected-status#What%20is%20TPS?

US Commission on Immigration Reform. *The National Interest: 1995 Executive Summary.* Washington, DC: US Commission on Immigration Reform, 1995.

US Commission on Immigration Reform. *US Immigration Policy: Restoring Credibility. A Report to Congress. 1994 Executive Summary.* Washington, DC: Commission on Immigration Reform, 1994.

US Commission on Immigration Reform. *US Refugee Policy: Taking Leadership.* Washington, DC: US Commission on Immigration Reform, 1997.

US Commission on International Religious Freedom. *Report on Asylum Seekers in Expedited Removal.* Washington, DC: United States Commission on International Religious Freedom, 2005.

US Congress. *Congress and Pressure Groups: Lobbying in a Modern Democracy. A Report.* Washington, DC: United States General Printing Office, 1986.

US Department of Homeland Security. "U Visa Law Enforcement Certification Resource Guide for Federal, State, Local, Tribal and Territorial Law Enforcement." PL 106-386, 114 Stat. 1464–1548 (2000). http://www.dhs.gov/xlibrary/assets/ dhs_u_visa_certification_guide.pdf.

US Department of Justice. "Asylum Reform: Five Years Later." February 1, 2000, http://www.uscis.gov.

US Department of Justice, Executive Office for Immigration Review. *FY 2012 Statistical Year Book.* http://www.justice.gov/eoir/statspub/fy12syb.pdf.

US Department of Justice, Executive Office for Immigration Review. "Operating Policies and Procedures Memorandum 07-01: Guidelines for Immigration Court Cases Involving Unaccompanied Alien Children." May 22, 2007. http://www.jus- tice.gov/sites/default/files/eoir/legacy/2007/05/22/07-01.pdf.

US Department of Justice, Office of International Affairs. "Guidelines for Children's Asylum Claims." http://www.nlada.org/Training/Train_Civil/Equal_Justice/ 2007_Materials/109_2007_Kerwin_handout7.

US Department of State. *Erasing History: Ethnic Cleansing in Kosovo.* Washington, DC: Department of State, 1999. http://1997-2001.state.gov/www/regions/eur/rpt_9905_ethnic_ksvo_exec.html.

US Department of State. "Fact Sheet: US Relations with Haiti." February 11, 2013. http://www.state.gov/r/pa/ei/bgn/1982.htm.

US Department of State. "The United States Humanitarian Assistance for Displaced Iraqis." October 5, 2007. http://www.state.gov/r/pa/prs/ps/2007/oct/93319.htm.

US Department of State, Bureau of Consular Affairs. "Special Immigrant Visas for Afghans Who Were Employed by/on Behalf of the US Government." http://travel.state.gov/content/visas/english/immigrate/afghans-work-for-us.html.

US Department of State, Bureau of Population, Refugees, and Migration, Office of Admissions-Refugee Processing Center. "Arrivals, Refugee and Special Immigrant Visas (SIV), Fiscal Year as of 31 May 2014." Published in "Admissions Reports." Refugee Processing Center. http://www.wrapsnet.org/Reports/AdmissionsArrivals/tabid/211/Default.aspx.

US General Accountability Office. *US Asylum System: Significant Variation Existed in Asylum Outcomes across Immigration Courts and Judges.* Washington, DC, September 2008.

US Institute of Peace. "Afghanistan: The Current Situation." http://www.usip.org/afghanistan-the-current-situation.

US Committee for Refugees. *Refugees at Our Border: The US Response to Asylum Seekers.* Washington, DC: American Council for Nationalities Service, 1989.

US Committee for Refugees. "Refugee Reports: 2004 Statistical Issue." 25, no. 9 (December 31, 2004).

US Committee for Refugees. *World Refugee Survey, 1995.* Washington, DC: US Committee for Refugees, 1995.

US Committee for Refugees and Immigrants. "Gang-Related Asylum Resources." http://www.refugees.org/resources/for-lawyers/asylum-research/gang-related-asylum-resources/.

US Refugee Programs for 1991: Hearing before the Committee on the Judiciary, US Senate, 101st Congress, Second Session, on the Proposed US Refugee Resettlement Admissions Program for Fiscal Year 1991, October 3, 1990. Washington, DC: Government Printing Office, 1991.

US Refugee Programs for 1992: Annual Refugee Consultations: Hearing before the Committee on the Judiciary, US Senate, 102nd Congress, First Session . . . September 24, 1991. Washington, DC: Government Printing Office, 1992.

US Refugee Programs for 1993: Annual Refugee Consultation: Hearing before the Committee on the Judiciary, US Senate, 102nd Congress, Second Session . . . July 23, 1992. Washington, DC: Government Printing Office, 1993.

US Refugee Programs for 1994: Annual Refugee Consultations: Hearing before the Committee on the Judiciary, US Senate, 102rd Congress, First Session, September 23, 1993. Washington, DC: Government Printing Office, 1994.

US Refugee Resettlement Program Watchdog Group. "What Was the Morrison-Lautenberg Amendment of 1989? Should It Be Renewed?" December 1, 2011. http://forefugees.com/2011/12/01/what-was-the-morrison-lautenberg-amendment-of-1989.

Van Hear, Nicholas. "Refugee Diasporas, Remittances, Development, and Conflict." *Migration Information Source.* June 2003. http://www.migrationinformation.org/Feature/display.cfm?ID=125.

Vaughan-Williams, Nick. *Europe's Border Crisis: Biopolitical Security and Beyond.* Oxford: Oxford University Press, 2015.

Vialet, Joyce. *Refugee Admissions and Resettlement Policy: Facts and Issues.* Washington, DC: Congressional Research Service, 1999. http://www.cnie.org/nle/crsreports/population/pop-6.cfm.

Wasem, Ruth Ellen. "Chinese Students and Other Chinese in the US: Immigrant Issues and Options." Congressional Research Service. June 23, 1989. HTTP://congressional.proquest.com/congressional/docview/t21.d22.crs-1989-epw-0066?accountid=10267.

Wasem, Ruth Ellen. "US Immigration Policy on Asylum Seekers." Congressional Research Service. May 5, 2005. http://www.fas.org/sgp/crs/misc/RL32621.pdf.

Washington Office on Latin America. "Elements of Successful Legal Arguments for Gang-related Asylum." *Central American Gang-Related Asylum: A Resource Guide.* May 2008. http://www.wola.org/sites/default/files/downloadable/Central%20America/past/CA%20Gang-Related%20Asylum.pdf.

Washington Office on Latin America. "Why a Resource Manual on Central American Gangs?" *Central American Gang-Related Asylum: A Resource Guide.* May 2008. http://www.wola.org/publications/central_american_gang_related_asylum_guide.

Waxman, Peter, and Val Colic-Peisker. *Homeland Wanted: Interdisciplinary Perspectives on Refugee Resettlement in the West.* New York: Nova Scotia Publishers, 2005.

Weimann, Gabriel. "Virtual Packs of Lone Wolves: How the Internet Made 'Lone Wolf' Terrorism a Misnomer." https://medium.com/p/17b12f8c455a.

Weiner, Myron. "The Clash of Norms: Dilemmas in Refugee Policies." *Journal of Refugee Studies* 11.4 (1998): 433–453.

Wiesel, Elie. *The Jews of Silence: A Personal Report on Soviet Jewry.* New York: Schocken Books, 1987.

Wilkinson, Ray. "Heart of Darkness." *Refugees Magazine,* December 1, 1997. http://www.unhcr.org/print/3b6925384.html.

Wilt, Harmen van der, Jeroen Vervliet, Goran Sluiter, and Johannes Houwink ten Cate, eds. *The Genocide Convention: The Legacy of 60 Years.* Leiden: M. Nijhoff Publishers, 2012.

Women's Commission for Refugee Women and Children. "The US Response to Human Trafficking: An Unbalanced Approach." May 2007. http://www.human-trafficking.org/uploads/publications/ustraff.pdf.

Wong, Carolyn. *Lobbying for Inclusion: Rights Politics and the Making of Immigration Policy.* Stanford, CA: Stanford University Press, 2006.

World Health Organization. "Female Genital Mutilation." Updated February 2014. http://www.who.int/mediacentre/factsheets/fs241/en/.

World Refugee Survey 1998—Bosnia and Herzegovina. January 1, 1998. http://www.refworld.org/docid/3ae6a8ab10.html.

Zake, Ieva. *Anti-communist Minorities in the US: Political Activism of Ethnic Refugees.* New York: Palgrave Macmillan, 2009.

Zimmerman, William. *Open Borders, Nonalignment, and the Political Evolution of Yugoslavia.* Princeton, NJ: Princeton University Press, 1987.

Zucker, Norman L., and Naomi Flink Zucker. *Desperate Crossings: Seeking Refuge in America.* Armonk, NY: M.E. Sharpe, 1996.

Index

Surnames starting with "al-" are alphabetized under the subsequent part of the name. Tables are indicated by "t" following page numbers.